SAINT THOMAS AQUINAS

SUMMA CONTRA GENTILES

BOOK FOUR: SALVATION

University
of
Notre Dame Press
Notre Dame
London

Translated,
with an Introduction
and Notes,
by
CHARLES J. O'NEIL

University of Notre Dame Press edition 1975

Copyright © 1957 by Doubleday & Company, Inc.

First published in 1957 by Hanover House as

On the Truth of the Catholic Faith

First paperback edition 1957 by Image Books

Published by arrangement with Doubleday & Company, Inc.

Printed in the United States of America

Library of Congress Cataloging in Publication Data

Thomas Aquinas, Saint, 1225?-1274.
   Summa contra gentiles.

   Reprint of the ed. published by Hanover House,
Garden City, N.Y., under title: On the truth of
the Catholic faith.
   Includes bibliographies.
   CONTENTS: book 1. God, translated, with an
introd. and notes, by A. C. Pegis. —book 2. Crea-
tion, translated, with an introd. and notes, by
J. F. Anderson. [etc.]
   1. Apologetics—Middle Ages, 600-1500. I. Ti-
tle.
[BX1749.T4 1975]   239   75-19883
ISBN 0-268-01675-5
ISBN 0-268-01676-3 pbk.

Contents

Introduction

As the General Introduction has already pointed out,[1] St. Thomas makes it very plain that his work in *Summa Contra Gentiles* is divided into two principal parts. He tells us that this work should "first seek to make known that truth which faith professes and reason investigates" (I, ch. 9, ¶3). It was to this part of his work that St. Thomas devoted *SCG, I-III.* He said that when this was accomplished one should "proceed to make known that truth which surpasses reason" (I, ch. 9, ¶3). We will find the same division in *SCG, IV.* Here (ch. 1, ¶9) we are told that the discussion which has gone before aimed at acquiring a knowledge of divine things so far as the natural reason can achieve this through creatures. But, he says, there remains to him the task of discoursing on the "things revealed for belief" which "surpass the human understanding."

The division of *SCG* into two chief parts, then, needs no further emphasis for the reader. Rather, to introduce him into the second of these two chief parts let us ask three questions. First, what is, in general, the content of this part which deals with things which "surpass the human understanding"? Second, if the content does, indeed, surpass human understanding, how can one "proceed to make known that truth which surpasses reason." This is to ask: What is the characteristic method of *SCG, IV*? Third, if there are two parts so distinct, what is the source of their unity? This is to ask: What is the relation of the unity of *SCG, IV* to the unity of the work as a whole?

To state wholly and in general the content of *SCG, IV,* is a less difficult task if one looks at the opening and the closing lines of the Book. Both are from Scripture. In the first, Job

---

1. See A. C. Pegis, General Introduction to St. Thomas Aquinas: *On The Truth of the Catholic Faith, Summa Contra Gentiles, Book One: God,* Hanover House, Garden City, New York, 1955.

speaks to us of the full thundering magnificence of mystery; in the second, Isaias speaks to us of a new creation in which joy and gladness will be everlasting. What, then, is contained in *SCG, IV*? It is, above all else, a discourse on the mysteries which can make men forever joyful and glad, a discourse on the mysteries of salvation.

Faith, of course, is the initial knowledge by which we enter into these mysteries. And this is clear in two ways. First, because it is precisely as mysterious that a mystery calls for faith. There is no way to accept the seemingly insoluble contradictions, the apparent impossibilities, if you will,[2] of what is most properly called mystery, other than the affirmation of faith.[3] This is clear, secondly, because St. Thomas expressly says that in this part of the work we are to know, because "the knowledge of faith descends from God to us" (ch. 1, ¶11). Thus, once again, the whole content of *SCG, IV*, is determined; determined by that knowledge by faith descending from God of the mysteries which beatify. Once again, this *is* the knowledge of salvation.

We should observe carefully, then, that there is no question here of making believers from unbelievers (ch. 1, ¶7);[4] rather, St. Thomas sets out to *enlighten* believers. Moreover, he does so as one who is himself a simple believer. Now, we simple believers have come to expect some order in the statement of these mysteries of our salvation. Some of these are so familiar that many will be surprised to hear them called "ordered statements of mysteries." Yet, the Sign of the Cross, the *Gloria*, the *Credo*, the most frequent Preface in the Mass, and—perhaps most familiar of all—the Apostles Creed are all of them just that: ordered statements of mysteries. Now, then, which of these orders does St. Thomas follow?

He shared with us every one of those just mentioned. But in *SCG, IV*, he does not, in fact, precisely follow the order of

2. See *SCG, IV*, ch. 50, ¶1, where St. Thomas says he has devoted eleven chapters to showing that what the faith teaches on the Incarnation "is not impossible."

3. See *Summa Theologiae*, II–II, 4, 1, and 1, 4–5; and É. Gilson, *Reason and Revelation in the Middle Ages* (New York, 1938), esp. pp. 69–84.

4. The mysteries revealed are such that "unbelievers cannot attack them."

any of these mentioned (although both the Apostles, and especially the Nicene, Creed would make excellent summaries of the Book). What, then, does he do? He follows the order which he considers the knowledge proper to this second chief part of his work, and which the structure of the whole work imposes upon him. In the earlier books, he tells us, he had proceeded from God and His perfections (I), through creation and the works of creation (II), to the providential disposal of things (III). And, now that he is preparing to deal with the things that are above reason, he thinks that the order should be the same: "First, to be specific, we must treat of the things about God Himself which surpass reason and are proposed for belief, such as the confession of the Trinity; second, of course, the things which surpass reason that have been done by God, such as the work of the Incarnation, and what follows thereon; third, however, the things surpassing reason which are looked for in the ultimate end of man, such as the resurrection and glorification of bodies, the everlasting beatitude of souls, and matters related to these" (ch. 1, ¶11).

The grandeur and profundity of each of the three parts thus neatly outlined hardly call for emphasis. We are to study (in ch. 2–26) the inner life of the triune God Himself, the generation of the Word in knowledge, the procession of the Holy Spirit in love. We are then to consider (in ch. 27–78) the man Christ Jesus who is incarnate God; we will consider Him as the man who suffered and died and as the God who raised the dead, who commanded the world's elements, who forgave sins, who rose from the dead and ascended into heaven. We will consider the duality of His nature in the unity of His person. We will consider the sacraments by which He extends His power, His grace, His presence, and His teaching "even to the consummation of the world" (Matt. 28:20). Our liberation from death at the consummation of the world as an effect of Christ's resurrection will be our third consideration (in ch. 79–97). With it we must consider the immortality of men, their glorification and damnation, the last judgment, and the new order of the new creation to come.

Many a reader of this translation may be unable to remember the time when he began to recognize these mysteries as the truths of salvation. What is needed, then, for the believing reader (especially if he is also a beginning reader), rather than emphasis on the grandeur of these truths, is this word of preparation: throughout each one of the large sections just described the reader will find what is familiar, and what is unfamiliar. What is familiar is always "the truth of the Catholic faith" itself. What may prove unfamiliar is the technique of St. Thomas' exposition.

But throughout SCG, IV the reader is well advised to stress for himself the familiar. More than any other thing, it will be the familiarity of that truth which will establish communication between himself and St. Thomas Aquinas. Thus, the reader will not expect to find that the Son is unequal in essence to the Father, nor will he—he will find it disproved. He does not expect to find that the Holy Spirit is a creature, nor will he—he will find it disproved. He does not expect to find that Christ is merely symbolically present in the Eucharist, nor will he—he will find it vigorously disproved. And in the last section he will not expect to find that there will be no difference after the resurrection between the bodies of the saved and the bodies of the damned, nor will he—he will find that it is necessarily so.

The point about stressing familiarity, then, is this. The assents to the teaching of the faith will always be familiar. The believing and beginning reader, therefore, who has chosen—how long since is unimportant—his salvation within "the truth of the Catholic faith" will always find himself at least as much at home here as he is in his own heart.

Another point should be made about what is familiar. The sources are familiar. From her Founder, and from the days of her Founder, the Church has been discovering this truth of faith eminently in sacred writings. Obviously, this is first and foremost the Scriptures. But the contemporary reader may need or welcome the reminder that St. Thomas Aquinas, who never overestimated the Bible as the "sole rule of faith," with equal ease introduces with his "witnesses of the sacred writing" not only the canonical Scripture, but conciliar teaching, the authority of the supreme Pontiff, the authorities of the Fathers, liturgical prayers, and even liturgical practices.[5]

5. For examples: ch. 24, ¶5–6 (conciliar and patristic); ch. 25, ¶5, ch. 38, ¶10, ch. 76, ¶9 (the "keys"); ch. 54, ¶6, ch. 81, ¶4

Of course, names like Cerinthus and Ebion may prove unfamiliar; what a quotation from Aristotle's *Metaphysics* is doing in a chapter (27, ¶1) which constitutes a Scriptural profession of faith in the Incarnation may prove unfamiliar; and what "fire seeking the upper place" has to do with the status of glorified bodies after the resurrection may be unfamiliar. These points, and others like them, have to do with the characteristic method of *SCG*, IV. All such points are related to the proper work of the theologian: the discussion of heretical opinions, the techniques of the metaphysician, the information supplied by his contemporary natural science; all these are things which the theologian-at-work "needs in his business"—as the phrase goes. But the point of the work will be missed—and we will do St. Thomas little honor—if we allow the theologian's theological technique, important as it is, to obscure the basic and sacred familiarity of the "truth of the Cathoic faith" itself.

The truly sacred may and does and must connote the remote, and even the unattainable; contrariwise, the familiar connotes that which is immediate and is one's very own. We have not thus juxtaposed the two for the sake of paradox, but as a reminder that in the act of faith there is an intimate and personal commitment by which a man has a right judgment in the things that are of faith, with no danger of "condemnation to them that walk in Christ Jesus" (Rom. 8:1).[6] On the other hand, he who cleaves to all "the articles of the Catholic faith" does so in one way, and this is through "the First Truth proposed to us in the Scriptures by the teaching of the Church understanding them."[7]

The familiarity of faith, therefore, is in the character of our persevering assent,[8] but its very sacred character is in that assent which involves the First Truth. But let us not deceive

---

(prayers); ch. 50, ¶9, ch. 60, ¶1-2, ch. 69, ¶4, ch. 75, ¶3, ch. 91, ¶7 (practices). On the "sole rule of faith," see ch. 25, ¶1-2.

6. See *Summa Theologiae*, II-II, 2, 3, ad 2m, which I am merely paraphrasing.

7. *Ibid.*, q. 5, 3, ad 2m.

8. This does not by reason of its personal lose its universal, that is, "catholic," character; see *ibid.*, q. 1, 9, ad 3m: "The confession of the faith is given in the Creed from the person, so to say, of the whole Church, and she is united by faith."

ourselves; the First Truth—and such is the very first point St. Thomas makes in SCG, IV (ch. 1, ¶1)—yields its character of mystery neither to "natural human reason" nor to faith. But it is central to the nobility of man's nature that "man's perfect good is that he somehow know God." Therefore, included in God's gifts to man is a threefold knowledge of God. The believer, therefore, who is also one who seeks God, knows that this threefold knowledge of God is related to faith; he knows that the whole of his knowledge is a kind of movement whose term is the hidden God; therefore he sees also that "The development of the whole SCG is thus within the faith."[9] But to locate the characteristic method of SCG, IV, let us now distinguish with St. Thomas that threefold knowledge of God: "The first is that in which man, by the natural light of reason, ascends to a knowledge of God through creatures. The second is that by which the divine truth—exceeding the human intellect—descends on us in the manner of revelation, not, however, as something made clear[10] to be seen, but as something spoken in words to be believed. The third is that by which the human mind will be elevated perfectly to gaze upon the things revealed" (ch. 1, ¶5).

Clearly, the third of these knowledges is never ours so long as "we are absent from the Lord," so long as "we walk by faith and not by sight" (II Cor. 5:6–7). Almost as clearly, the first of these knowledges describes the work of SCG already done.[11] It is, therefore, within the second that we shall find the work and the method proper to SCG, IV.

St. Thomas himself, as we shall presently see, distinguishes what we may call three moments in that work and that method. But before we follow him through each of those three moments we must come to grips with three notions of importance to the believer when he "proceeds to make known that truth which surpasses reason." These are: mystery, revelation, non-contradictory.

9. A. C. Pegis, General Introduction, p. 43.
10. "Made clear" is "pointed out"; on the "demonstrated," the "known," as concluded, and the "seen" and the "believed," see Summa Theologiae, II-II, 1, 5, esp. ad 1m, and the references cited above, n. 3.
11. See A. C. Pegis, General Introduction, pp. 41–43, and above, p. 13.

Each of these notions or terms enlightens the others. None is interchangeable with the others; the last appears most inclusive, but, not only is it not interchangeable with the others, it by no means exhausts the content of the others. Let us first observe that to say that *every* mystery is contained in the revelation granted by faith (ch. 1, ¶7) is to say much too much. God our God is a hidden God, and hidden He remains except to the Son and to them to whom the Son shall reveal Him. Even in the Son's revelation He is hidden, for the Son does not reveal all things. This is to say that faith is the "beginning of salvation," or, in St. Paul's words, "the substance of things to be hoped for, the evidence of things that appear not" (Heb. 11:1).[12] Let us note that the mysteries, the possession of the mysteries in beatitude, and the assent to the mysteries by faith in revelation are not the same thing. This is why St. Thomas distinguished the second from the third type of knowledge. Therefore, mystery and revealed are not interchangeable.

Neither is everything which is revealed mystery. The metaphysician who wills to can know demonstratively that God is one. Therefore, this is not a mystery which exceeds or surpasses human reason. Yet it is revealed.[13] It was, of course, precisely because not everything revealed is a mystery surpassing the reason that St. Thomas divided SCG into two principal parts. It remains true, of course, that, although everything which is revealed does not surpass the human reason, everything which is mystery, like everything which is revealed, *is* non-contradictory. We need never fear, in other words, that to repeat the revealed or to affirm the mystery involves us in propositions which make no sense.

We are now in a better position to describe the characteristic work and method of SCG, IV. As for the work, it is a meditation on the mysteries themselves. St. Thomas has no consistent word for it; he calls it now a "zealous pursuit," now

12. See Vatican Council, (Sess. III), *Constitutio de fide catholica,* cap. 3, in Denzinger-Bannwart-Umberg, *Enchiridion Symbolorum* (ed. 23, Rome, 1937), no. 1789; and *Summa Theologiae,* II-II, 4, 1.

13. For a series of texts on this twofold sense of "to reveal" from Rom. 1:19, including St. Thomas, see H. de Lubac, S.J., *Sur les chemins de Dieu* (Paris, 1956), pp. 261–262.

a "devout and earnest weighing" of these mysteries. But his method in this consideration has three clearly distinguishable moments: first, he shows that the mystery is, indeed, revealed. This serves as his point of departure. It also is his evidence. In the nature of the case it is the evidence "of things which appear not." Therefore, most commonly[14] he begins from sacred Scripture as read in the Church. Hence, the force of one of his own descriptions of this first moment: "We may take as point of departure what has been handed down in the sayings of sacred Scripture" (ch. 1, ¶10).[15]

In the second moment he shows us that the revealed mystery is non-contradictory. This moment appears in one of two ways; sometimes, in each of two ways. Against heretics he shows that the revealed mystery is non-contradictory by showing that Scripture passing the revelation on to us from the First Truth through the Church is not in contradiction with itself. Against straight unbelievers or the arguments they do or could adduce from human reason[16] he shows in the fashion of a metaphysician who is also a thorough Aristotelian that the revealed mystery is non-contradictory.

Let us observe in passing that it is most likely to be in this second moment that the believing and beginning reader will find the things we previously called unfamiliar: a familiar Scriptural text, for example, used by a heretic to prove that Christ is a "mere" or "pure" man, or an argument from an Aristotelian analysis of motion to prove that Christ cannot be present simultaneously on many altars. Let it also be observed that St. Thomas is in his "second moment" as theologian-at-work whenever he gives his—sometimes long—lists of argu-

14. But not always. If each of the sacraments is to be considered a distinct mystery, this is not the case for confirmation (ch. 60). Contrast the opening chapter (ch. 61) on the Eucharist with its pungent Scriptural climax from John 6:56: "My flesh is meat indeed: and My blood is drink indeed."

15. In ch. 2, ¶1, this same moment is approached thus: "what one must hold about it according to the testimonies of sacred Scripture."

16. The "audience" of this type which St. Thomas had in mind is explained by Dr. Pegis in the General Introduction, pp. 20–23, and in his "Creation and Beatitude in the *Summa Contra Gentiles* of St. Thomas Aquinas," *Proceedings of the American Catholic Philosophical Association*, 29 (1955), pp. 52–62.

ments against the truth of the Catholic faith; and very largely still in this moment when he gives his usually patient and courteous answers. This never means, of course, that he considers that by showing the non-contradictory character of the revealed mystery he has reduced mystery to the non-mysterious. Quite the contrary; he implies more than once that those who raise the difficulties have been failing to accept the mysteries as mysteries.[17] Finally, we should note regarding this second moment that to the theologian the source of the error that requires his attention is a matter of indifference: Whether it is Scripture, the philosophers, or something abstract called human reason, the mystery contained in the revelation is always non-contradictory, "since truth cannot be truth's contrary" (ch. 8, ¶1).

We must not, of course, allow the grave import of the work of the theologian in his second moment to obscure the distinction of the second moment from the third moment (ch. 2, ¶1). That Scripture should be ordered, intelligibly structured, and interpreted against heretics is of the utmost importance. But is the theologian-at-work doing no more than editing and making a doctrinal concordance of Scripture? And is the theologian doing no more in studying the mystery of the Trinity, let us say, than showing its non-contradictory character? The enormous importance of this task, its contribution to making our very act of faith "a reasonable service" (Rom. 12:1),[18] should not obscure for us the fact that he is doing something more. And the something more? Without ever ceasing to respect the mysteries as mysteries (ch. 1, ¶10), St. Thomas appears to be establishing within the mysteries themselves an intelligible structure. Paradoxical as it may

17. For examples: ch. 4, ¶1: "Now certain men, who perversely presumed to measure the truth of this doctrine by their *own comprehension* of it"; ch. 53, ¶1: "The faith of the Incarnation, of course, is counted foolishness by unbelievers"; ch. 55, ¶31: "Thus, then, from what has been set down *it is to some extent clear* that what the Catholic faith preaches about the Incarnation"; ch. 63, ¶1: "Although, of course, the divine power operates with a *greater sublimity* and *secrecy* in this sacrament *than a man's inquiry can search out*; nonetheless . . . *one must make the endeavor to exclude every impossibility*." Italics are added.
18. See *Constitutio* cited above, in n. 12, no. 1790.

sound, he is knowing mysteries through mysteries, he is knowing mysteries in mysteries, he is knowing and proving the relation of mysteries to one another;[19] he is also, as we shall see,
knowing and proving the relations of the mysteries to the end
of man.

St. Thomas does all this with such perfect ease, utter ra-
tionality, and complete impersonality that it is not hard to
miss his third moment and its distinction from the other two.
Let us, then, attempt to remove some obscurity by an example. "In divinity, therefore," he says, "one must not speak of
one person by reason of the unity of the subsisting essence,
but of many persons by reason of the relations" (ch. 14, ¶6).
What is he doing here? First, a conclusion is made ("therefore"), and a conclusion is made with demonstrative force
("one must . . . speak"). The conclusion is made with necessary and demonstrative force about a mystery, a mystery in
the face of which we are all simple believers, for we have
here a necessary and demonstrative conclusion about the
Trinity itself.

But let us also examine the elements that have gone into
this third moment of the theologian-at-work. That the Son
is eternal is a mystery. But the affirmation of the Son's eternity is not the theologian's work. The Son has revealed it:
"Before Abraham was made, I am" (John 8:58). That the
Father and Son are one is a mystery. But the affirmation of
the Son's unity with the Father is not the theologian's work.
The Son has revealed it: "Philip, he that seeth Me seeth the
Father also" (John 14:9) and "I and the Father are one"
(John 10:30). Note that Scripture reveals and faith affirms
these mysteries of the Son's eternity, the divine unity, and
the eternal relation of the Father and Son.

The theologian is taking a forward step when he says that
the subsistent divine essence cannot be understood apart from
the relation involved in the conception of the divine Word
(ch. 14, ¶6).[20] We should note here that the theologian is
not yielding the mystery of "Philip, he that seeth Me," nor

19. *Ibid.*, no. 1796.
20. On the subsisting essence, see also *SCG*, I, ch. 21, and esp. ch.
    22, ¶9–11.

is he yielding his previous conclusion that God is identified with His being.

The theologian is taking another step in saying that the Word spoken in the divine relation cannot be other than the divine essence and cannot be imperfect. In this step he is not yielding the mystery of "I and the Father are one," and at the same time yields nothing on the conclusion that there is no imperfection in God.[21] An imperfection in God's knowledge would be an imperfection in His being. At this point, then, the theologian is simply refusing to allow a contradiction within the mystery.

But his insistence that the revealed and the mystery are non-contradictory have led him to examine the mystery by analogies drawn from human knowing and human relations. By the acceptance of the mysteries as revealed on the one hand, and his scrutiny of them as non-contradictory on the other, he is now able to arrive at his properly theological conclusion: "There are *many* things subsisting if one looks to the relations; there is but *one* subsistent thing, of course, if one looks to the essence." He is now ready for the conclusion already quoted, a necessary and demonstrative conclusion, as we said, about the Trinity itself. Two words of caution: "necessary" in this moment is not a necessity that binds either God to reveal or man to accept; to be sure, man's moral obligation freely to accept remains unquestionable (Mark 16:16). Many a man has refused and still refuses to affirm by faith that Christ said *truly*: "I and the Father are one." Nor does "demonstrative" mean that anything has been demonstrated or "deduced" from some principles which are evident of themselves, or accessible in some kind of independence from the revealed. Instead, we must say that it is his very understanding of the mysteries by faith which has led him intelligibly to link the mysteries to one another. To elaborate his understanding of the mysteries would be to reproduce SCG, IV, not to introduce it. A final point should be noted to clarify the third moment of the theologian-at-work. In the example chosen, the mystery of God's subsisting and generative essence has been linked demonstratively to the mystery of God's plurality of persons; St. Thomas was able to do this because of his under-

21. SCG, I, ch. 38; for purposes of unity, note esp. ¶9–10.

standing within the mysteries of "subsisting" and "relation."

The reader will find that even when he is in his third moment of penetrating, defending, and linking the mysteries to one another in an intelligible order, St. Thomas is being helped by a very realistic rationalist. An odd but interesting bit of statistics may help to bring this out. After Scripture, the most common citation in this most theological unit of a theological work is Aristotle. This is not said to suggest that St. Thomas found either his theological evidences or his theological method in Aristotle. The first is entirely out of the question, for he finds his evidences—this is the "first moment" of the method—in the teaching of the Catholic faith, especially in "the Scriptures as the Church understands them." Nor can the method be found in Aristotle, because the method is within faith a knowledge which "descends from God upon us by revelation." Nevertheless, St. Thomas Aquinas looked upon Aristotle as a great authority in metaphysics. It is through metaphysics that there is a relation between Aristotle and the theologian-at-work in his "third moment." We can put this very simply: To know "subsisting" and "relation" is to know metaphysics; on the other hand, to know the mysteries in an intelligible order makes one capable of demonstratively linking one mystery to another without reducing the mystery to the non-mysterious. It must be, then, that in the three moments of his theological work St. Thomas is truly constructing an intelligible order within the mysteries, and *at the same stroke,* while he "studies to grasp in any way at all" those same mysteries, he must be constructing a metaphysics.

We may now recapitulate on the three moments of our theologian-at-work. We must always allow him those things which he "needs in his business." In his first moment he requires the "revealed mysteries" and faith's assent to these. In the second moment he requires some occasion to show their "non-contradictory" character. He requires some assault from "infidelity," as St. Thomas himself puts it, before the doctrine is defended and thus explored. Errors have the happy consequence, as he also himself puts it, of having "exercised the talents of the faithful toward a more diligent penetration and understanding of divine truth" (ch. 55, ¶9). This is the reason, by the way, that one sometimes finds so little development of a doctrine or so little exploration of it. Cases in point are papal infallibility and indulgences. They had not been attacked.[22] Finally, he must be allowed, in his third moment, the full use of his talent to explore the revealed mysteries as non-contradictory. It is true, of course, that the mysteries remain mysterious, but we must remember that the work of the theologian in both his second moment and his third moment is a rational construction of the human intellect. And upon a contradiction the human intellect is incapable of making any construction at all. The God of our Fathers was on Sinai (Exod. 3:14) a God of affirmation. True, from the same mountain He thundered negative precepts to lead us affirmatively to Himself. True, also, He is always a hidden God. But a God of contradiction He neither was, nor is, nor can be. Herein lies the reason why we must allow the theologian-at-work in his third moment to construct the metaphysics he needs while diligently, devoutly, and humbly and with "no presumption of perfect knowledge" he is constructing, as best he can, an intelligible order within the mysteries. And we must allow him to make use of every ordered and orderly human knowledge of which the order of the mysteries and the metaphysics (his most important knowledge-tool) may stand in need.

We may now return to the point previously made. To take what we there described[23] as unfamiliar away from the work and method of St. Thomas would be to deprive him of the very technique of theology itself. But it remains true that the basic familiarity of the faith is our best means of establishing communication between ourselves and St. Thomas Aquinas. On the side of the "unfamiliar" we must trust his learning, his patience, his well-known devotion to beginners[24] to establish communication with us. We should also note that in this two-way communication (our faith uniting us to his learn-

---

22. One does find the basis, for example, for the first in ch. 25, ¶4; for the second in ch. 76, ¶9. 23. See above, p. 15.
24. *Summa Theologiae*, I, Prologue. Note well that below, ch. 25, ¶5, after saying that a group of objections could be answered even by one little skilled in theology, he himself nevertheless answers them.

ing and faith; his learning and faith deepening and strengthening ours) something of still greater import can take place. Our personal commitment to these mysteries is deepened; our personal grip on these mysteries becomes more firm. And this is of the greatest import precisely because these are the mysteries of salvation.

And thus we return to the point from which we began, for within the faith itself there are two manners of knowing the hidden God.[25] But in one main part of SCG our measure of dealing with divine things has been this: one can arrive at a knowledge of God and creatures from knowing creatures. In the second main part of the work the measure is this: one can arrive at a knowledge of God by faith's knowledge of the mysteries which surpass the human reason, by knowing those mysteries because of the glimpses even creatures can give into their intelligibility, and by knowing them in whatever ordered and orderly relation to one another our "measure and power" can give.[26] One reason why St. Thomas Aquinas so carefully distinguishes these two manners of proceeding is utterly simple: to confuse the two is to destroy each of them. But this leaves us with the question previously asked: If there are two parts so distinct, what is the source of their unity?

We have already adverted to the fact that a unity for SCG, IV is indicated by the Scriptural texts which open and close it: it moves from the thundering magnificence of mystery not unfolded (Job 26:14) to the joy and gladness of a new creation (Isa. 65:17). We have also noted that it has a unity throughout, for the theologian-at-work can always be found in one of the three moments of the method proper to him. We have also noted—at least in passing—that there is this unity: we have that complete exposition of the "truth of the Catholic faith" which St. Thomas thought needful in his day —and in this: these are the mysteries of salvation. Is there, then, also a discoverable unity, and a principle of unity within

25. SCG, I, ch. 3, ¶2: "There is a twofold mode of truth in what we profess about God." This "profess" (confitemur) is exactly the same verb that St. Thomas uses to "profess" or "confess" the Incarnation or the Eucharist.

26. For example, on the Incarnation see below, ch. 41, ¶9–10; also, Scheeben, The Mysteries of Christianity (tr. C. Vollert, S.J., St. Louis, 1946), pp. 8–13.

the doctrine itself? There is. It is the very mystery of Jesus Christ Himself. This is the mystery on which St. Thomas Aquinas centers all the others. How does he do it? Remembering that we are only introducing the Book, not reproducing it, we will answer this question by pointing out the structural relation of the three large sections[27] of the work to one another.

After he has explained his method and entered into that method, the very first witness in the first of a number of "first moments" is none other than Jesus Christ: "No one knoweth the Son but the Father; neither doth any one know the Father but the Son" (Matt. 11:27). The first witness, then, to the first aspect of the Trinitarian mystery is Jesus Christ. For St. Thomas it is the revelation of Christ and the revelation which is Christ, that is, revealing "the truth that God is triune."[28]

But there is more. It is not only, for example, that the divinity of the Holy Spirit is established by a precept and a promise of Christ (ch. 15, ¶1), or the divine character of one of His "effects" by the sanctification of the members of Christ as the "temple of God" (ch. 21, ¶3), but Jesus Christ as Incarnate is said to be of all God's marvelous works the most marvelous, and it is said that toward faith in this most wonderful of wonders faith in all others is ordered (ch. 27, ¶1–2).[29] St. Thomas makes it stronger by introducing a causal principle from Aristotle, that the greatest in any class is the cause of all in that class. The introduction of Aristotle is, then, not so unfamiliar[30] after all. For St. Thomas is telling us that our faith in the Incarnation is the very beginning and principle of our faith in all the mysteries of salvation. In fact, the believer in Jesus Christ who reads this chapter (ch. 27), which we have called and call again a simple Scriptural confession of faith in the Incarnation, with a bit of reflection will

---

27. See above pp. 12–13.   28. *SCG*, IV, ch. 3, ¶2.
29. Anything approaching hyperbole is so rare in St. Thomas I add that I am here strictly paraphrasing, but this note of joy in mystery is repeated at the beginning ch. 54, ¶1, and ch. 73, ¶1. On the "enthusiasm" of the saint, see G. K. Chesterton, *St. Thomas Aquinas* (New York, Image Books, 1956), p. 157.
30. See above, p. 15.

find that it contains—germinally, perhaps, but contains—all the mysteries treated in this book.

The centrality of this mystery of the Incarnate God becomes even more clear when St. Thomas is passing from what we have been calling the "second moment" to the "third moment" in his treatment of the Incarnation. When he does so, he gives us one of the rare glimpses we get of the saint concealed by the theologian; he speaks of the Incarnation's "so great a depth of wisdom," and in what is—for him—a burst of enthusiasm refers to the "more and more wondrous" vistas which are opened to the mind which "devoutly considers" (ch. 54, ¶1) this mystery.

We will not anticipate the chapter which opens up these more and more wondrous vistas even by outlining it. But to our present discussion of unity three points are pertinent. First: "The Incarnation of God was the most efficacious assistance to man in his striving for beatitude" (ch. 54, ¶1). All is contained in this most effective help: salvation from despair, the remedy for man's frailty, the remedy for sin, the model for virtue, the assurance of God's friendship; in fact, whatever is needed in the order of knowledge or of love by one who tends toward the God of blessedness is contained—so St. Thomas tells us—in this ineffable mystery. We should note in particular (ch. 54, ¶4) that we have in the Incarnation the basic truth of faith which stands to all others as principle. Second: We should note that we have here not only the greatest assurance of the dignity of man's nature as a nature, but the greatest assurance of his dignity in the economy of creation: "man . . . the term of creatures, presupposing . . . all other creatures in the natural order of generation is suitably united to the First Principle of things to finish a kind of cycle in the perfection of things" (ch. 55, ¶7). Third: We should note that in these more and more wondrous vistas of the Incarnation everything else in SCG, IV is contained. For example, one passes readily to the sacraments (ch. 56, ¶7) because it is so utterly suitable and intelligible within the mystery for a visible Incarnate God to carry on His spiritual operations by visible signs. One passes readily, also, to the final resurrection by holding firmly to Christ's words: "The hour cometh, wherein all that are in the graves shall hear the voice of the Son of God" (John 5:28); or holding firmly with St. Paul: "Christ is risen from the dead, the firstfruits of them that sleep" (I Cor. 15:20); or holding firmly with Job (19:1, 25) troubled with woes and with words: "I know that my Redeemer liveth, and in the last day I shall rise out of the earth" (ch. 79, ¶2, 8–9).

In thus recalling Job and "the last day" we are, of course, only reminding ourselves once again that throughout SCG, IV we are dealing in a unified way with the mysteries of salvation. What we must now advert to is the fact that the central chapters of this Book contain also St. Thomas' statement of its central mystery: the mystery of Jesus Christ, Incarnate God. In this central mystery not only do all other mysteries find their center, but in this unity all the other unities of SCG are explained. There is a unity in the diversity of knowledges: Scripture, metaphysics, the sciences of nature —all these the Incarnation has reduced to one knowledge. There is a unity in diversity of the measures of knowledge: one measured by knowledge of creatures; the other measured by mysteries which surpass reason. Christ, God and man, has unified these knowledges. There is a unity in the diversity of grades of knowledge possessing the good: first, ascending to a knowledge of God through creatures; second, descending on us by faith in revelation; third, the knowledge by which the intellect will be elevated to see God as He is.[31] All these knowledges, too, the Incarnation unifies.[32] First of all, it unites the third—the beatifying knowledge—with the other two, because without the Incarnation there is no beatitude. Second, it unites the knowledge of the mysteries which surpass the reason, because the Incarnation is not only the central mystery, it is also the source of the grace by which a man cleaves to those mysteries. Finally, it unites the knowledge of

31. See above, pp. 11–13 and n. 10.
32. See A. C. Pegis, General Introduction, pp. 23–26, and his "Creation and Beatitude in the Summa Contra Gentiles," loc. cit., pp. 52–62, esp. pp. 59–60. I accept this interpretation of SCG and add only that the mystery of man's "conversion" to God is itself a mystery of the Incarnation. "God exalted Him . . . that every tongue should confess" (Eph. 2:9, 11). Man's offering himself is at once Christ's and man's. Again, the "natural" and supernatural is "theandric."

faith in the mysteries to the knowledge inspired by faith which seeks to investigate truth by natural reason. It does this because it is the culmination of two things: of the economy of creation ordered to God through the Incarnation and man's beatitude; of the striving of the "noblest of creatures" for a knowledge of God. Thus, "the Incarnation of God was the most efficacious assistance to man in his striving for beatitude." God knowable to reason, the economy of creation, man and his beatitude—all this diversity of knowledges, all these distinctions of method, are unified for St. Thomas Aquinas by one Lord Jesus Christ.

There remains now only the pleasant task of giving thanks: to Mr. John J. Delaney for much patience and courtesy through many delays; to Dr. A. C. Pegis for many stimulating suggestions; to my graduate assistant in Marquette University, Mr. Robert Perusse, a friend whose assistance was well "above and beyond the call of duty"; and finally to the priest, colleague, and friend to whom this translation is dedicated, because without his generous encouragement it would have neither beginning, middle, nor end. The doctrine is that of St. Thomas Aquinas; the inspiration and encouragement and help on many details are from friends; the errors I cheerfully claim as my own.

Marquette University   CHARLES J. O'NEIL
Milwaukee, Wisconsin

Bibliography

The translator especially recommends to the reader É. Gilson, *History of Christian Philosophy in the Middle Ages,* and M.-D. Chenu, O.P., *Introduction à l'étude de Saint Thomas d'Aquin.* The following is a bibliography of the sources, of some works cited in the introduction and notes, and of some which the reader may find helpful for modern presentations of Scriptural or theological problems.

I. SOURCES

1. Aristotle
Aristotelis Opera, 2 vols., Berlin Academy Edition based on I. Bekker, Berlin, G. Reimer, 1831.
The Works of Aristotle, English translation, edited by W. D. Ross, 11 vols., Oxford, Clarendon Press, 1928–1931.
The Basic Works of Aristotle, edited, with an introduction, by R. McKeon, New York, Random House, 1941.

2. St. Augustine
Basic Writings of St. Augustine, 2 vols., edited by M. Dodds, New York, Random House, 1948.

3. Avicenna
Avicennae perhypatetici philosophi ac medicorum facile primi opera . . . , Venetiis, 1508.

4. Peter Lombard
Petri Lombardi Libri IV Sententiarum, 2 vols., Ad Claras Aquas, Ex Typographia Collegii S. Bonaventurae, 1916.

5. Plato
The Dialogues of Plato, 2 vols., translated by B. Jowett, with an introduction by R. Demos, New York, Random House, 1937.

6. St. Thomas Aquinas

S. *Thomae Aquinatis Doctoris Angelici Opera Omnia, iussu impensaque Leonis XIII P.M. edita*, 16 vols., Ex Romae Typographia Polyglotta, 1882–1948.

S. *Thomae de Aquino Ordinis Praedicatorum Summa Theologiae*, 5 vols., Ottawa, Impensis Studii Generalis O. Pr., 1941–45. (Referred to in notes as "Ottawa edition".)

S. *Thomae de Aquino Doctoris Angelici Summa Contra Gentiles*, Editio Leonina Manualis, Romae, Apud Sedem Commissionis Leoninae, 1934.

S. *Thomae Aquinatis Scriptum Super Sententiis*, 4 vols. (incomplete), edited by P. Mandonnet (vols. 1–2) and M. F. Moos (vols. 3–4), Paris, P. Lethielleux, 1929–1947.

S. *Thomae Aquinatis Quaestiones Disputatae*, ed. R. Spiazzi, Taurini, Marietti, 1949, 2 vols.

S. *Thomae Aquinatis Quaestiones Quodlibetales*, ed. R. Spiazzi, Taurini, Marietti, 1949.

Basic Writings of St. Thomas Aquinas, 2 vols., edited and annotated by A. C. Pegis, New York, Random House, 1945.

St. Thomas Aquinas, *Compendium of Theology*, translated by C. Vollert, S.J., St. Louis, Herder, 1947.

7. Other

The Church Speaks to the Modern World, The Social Teachings of Leo XIII, edited and annotated by É. Gilson, New York, Image Books, 1954.

Denzinger, *Enchiridion Symbolorum, Definitionum et Declarationum de Rebus Fidei et Morum* (ed. Bannwart-Umberg), Friburgi Brisgoviae, Herder, 1937.

The Wisdom of Catholicism, edited by A. C. Pegis, New York, Random House, 1949.

Latin writers (St. Hilary, St. Augustine, Boethius, St. Gregory, and others) are quoted from J. P. Migne, *Patrologia Latina*, 221 vols., Paris, 1844–1864 (with later printings).

Greek writers (Pseudo-Dionysius, St. John Damascene, and others) are quoted from J. P. Migne, *Patrologia Graeca*, 162 vols., Paris, 1857–1866 (with later printings).

II. STUDIES

Adam, K., The Spirit of Catholicism, New York, Image Books, 1954.

Brunini, J. G., Whereon to Stand, New York, Harpers, 1946.

A Catholic Commentary on Holy Scripture, ed. Orchard, Sutcliffe, et al., New York, Nelson, 1953.

Chenu, M.-D., O.P., La théologie comme science au XIIIᵉ siècle, 2 éd., Paris, Vrin, 1943.

Chesterton, G. K., St. Thomas Aquinas, New York, Image Books, 1956.

Commentary on the New Testament, Archconfraternity of Christian Doctrine Edition, New York, Sadlier, 1942.

Garrigou-Lagrange, R., O.P., The Trinity and God the Creator, translated by F. Eckhoff, St. Louis, Herder, 1952.

Gilson, É., History of Christian Philosophy in the Middle Ages, New York, Random House, 1955.

Gilson, É., Philosophie et Incarnation selon Saint Augustin, Montréal, Institut D'études Médiévales, 1947.

Gilson, É., Reason and Revelation in the Middle Ages, New York, Scribner, 1928.

Gilson, É., The Spirit of Mediaeval Philosophy, translated by A. H. C. Downes, New York, Scribner, 1940.

Gilson, É., Le Thomisme, V éd., Paris, Vrin, 1947.

Hughes, P., A History of the Church, 3 vols., New York, Sheed & Ward, 1947.

Hughes, P., A Popular History of the Catholic Church, New York, Image Books, 1954.

La Grange, M. J., O.P., The Gospel of Jesus Christ (2 vols. in one), translated by the English Dominicans, London, Burns, Oates & Washbourne, 1950.

de Lubac, H., S.J., Catholicism, A Study of Dogma in Relation to the Corporate Destiny of Mankind, New York, Longmans, 1950.

de Lubac, H., S.J., Sur les chemins de Dieu, Paris, Aubier, 1956.

de Lubac, H., S.J., The Splendour of the Church, translated by M. Mason, New York, Sheed & Ward, 1956.

Pegis, A. C., "Creation and Beatitude in the *Summa Contra Gentiles* of St. Thomas," *Proceedings of the American Catholic Philosophical Association*, 29 (1955), pp. 52–62.

Penido, M. T.-L., *Le rôle de l'analogie en théologie dogmatique*, Paris, Vrin, 1931.

Prat, F., S.J., *Jesus Christ*, translated by J. Heenan, S.J., 2 vols., Milwaukee, Bruce, 1950.

Prat, F., S.J., *The Theology of Saint Paul*, 2 vols., translated by J. Stoddard, Westminster, Md., Newman, 1952.

Ricciotti, Guiseppe, *Paul, The Apostle*, translated by A. I. Zizzamia, Milwaukee, Bruce, 1952.

Scheeben, M., *The Mysteries of Christianity*, translated by Cyril Vollert, S.J., St. Louis, Herder, 1946.

Smith, G. D. (and others), *The Teaching of the Catholic Church*, 2 vols., New York, Macmillan, 1949.

Smith, G., S.J., *Natural Theology*, New York, Macmillan, 1951.

Van Ackeren, G. F., S.J., *Sacra Doctrina; The subject of the first question of the Summa Theologica of St. Thomas Aquinas*, Romae, Catholic Book Agency, 1952.

Van Dornik, (and others) *A Handbook of the Catholic Faith, A Tryptich of the Kingdom*, Garden City, Image Books, 1956.

Saint Thomas Aquinas

ON THE TRUTH OF THE CATHOLIC FAITH

BOOK FOUR: SALVATION

Chapter 1.

FOREWORD

"Lo, these things are said in part of His ways:
and seeing we have heard scarce a little drop of
His word, who shall be able to behold the
thunder of His greatness?"
(Job 26:14).

[1] The human intellect, to which it is connatural to derive its knowledge from sensible things, is not able through itself to reach the vision of the divine substance in itself, which is above all sensible things and, indeed, improportionately above all other things. Yet, because man's perfect good is that he somehow know God, lest such a noble creature might seem to be created to no purpose, as being unable to reach its own end, there is given to man a certain way through which he can rise to the knowledge of God: so that, since the perfections of things descend in a certain order from the highest summit of things—God—man may progress in the knowledge of God by beginning with lower things and gradually ascending. Now, even in bodily movements, the way of descending is the same as the way of ascending, distinguished by beginning and end.

[2] There is a twofold account of the descent of perfections from God just mentioned. One account looks to the first origin of things: for divine Wisdom, to put perfection in things, produced them in such order that the universe of creatures should embrace the highest of things and the lowest. The other account comes from the things themselves. For, since causes are more noble than their effects, the very first caused things are lower than the First Cause, which is God, and still stand out above their effects. And so it goes until one arrives at the lowest of things. And because in the highest summit of things, God, one finds the most perfect unity—and because everything, the more it is one, is the more powerful and more worthy—it follows that the farther one gets from the first prin-

ciple, the greater is the diversity and variation one finds in things. The process of emanation from God must, then, be unified in the principle itself, but multiplied in the lower things which are its terms. In this way, according to the diversity of things, there appears the diversity of the ways, as though these ways began in one principle and terminated in various ends.

[3] Through these ways our intellect can rise to the knowledge of God. But because of the weakness of the intellect we are not able to know perfectly even the ways themselves. For the sense, from which our knowledge begins, is occupied with external accidents, which are the proper sensibles—for example, color, odor, and the like. As a result, through such external accidents the intellect can scarcely reach the perfect knowledge of a lower nature, even in the case of those natures whose accidents it comprehends perfectly through the sense. Much less will the intellect arrive at comprehending the natures of those things of which we grasp few accidents by sense; and it will do so even less in the case of those things whose accidents cannot be grasped by the senses, though they may be perceived through certain deficient effects. But, even though the natures of things themselves were known to us, we can have only a little knowledge of their order, according as divine Providence disposes them in relation to one another and directs them to the end, since we do not come to know the plan of divine Providence. If, then, we imperfectly know the ways themselves, how shall we be able to arrive at a perfect knowledge of the source of these ways? And because that source transcends the above-mentioned ways beyond proportion, even if we knew the ways themselves perfectly we would yet not have within our grasp a perfect knowledge of the source.

[4] Therefore, since it was a feeble knowledge of God that man could reach in the ways mentioned—by a kind of intellectual glimpse, so to say—out of a superabundant goodness, therefore, so that man might have a firmer knowledge of Him, God revealed certain things about Himself that transcend the human intellect. In this revelation, in harmony with man, a certain order is preserved, so that little by little he comes

from the imperfect to the perfect—just as happens in the rest of changeable things. First, therefore, these things are so revealed to man as, for all that, not to be understood, but only to be believed as heard, for the human intellect in this state in which it is connected with things sensible cannot be elevated entirely to gaze upon things which exceed every proportion of sense. But, when it shall have been freed from the connection with sensibles, then it will be elevated to gaze upon the things which are revealed.

[5] There is, then, in man a threefold knowledge of things divine. Of these, the first is that in which man, by the natural light of reason, ascends to a knowledge of God through creatures. The second is that by which the divine truth—exceeding the human intellect—descends on us in the manner of revelation, not, however, as something made clear to be seen, but as something spoken in words to be believed. The third is that by which the human mind will be elevated to gaze perfectly upon the things revealed.

[6] It is this threefold cognition which Job suggests in the words set down. The words, "Lo, these things are said in part of His ways," refer to that knowledge by which our intellect ascends to a knowledge of God by the ways of creatures. And because we know these ways imperfectly, he rightly added: "in part." "For we know in part," as the Apostle says (I Cor. 13:9).

[7] What is added, however, "and seeing we have heard scarce a little drop of His word," refers to the second knowledge, in that the divine things we are to believe are revealed to us in speech; "faith then," as Romans (10:17) says, "cometh by hearing; and hearing by the word of God." Of this John (17:17) also says: "sanctify them in truth. Thy word is truth." Thus, then, since the revealed truth is proposed not about divine things to be seen, but to be believed, Job rightly says: "we have heard." But, since this imperfect knowledge flows down from that perfect knowledge wherein the divine Truth is seen in itself, while God reveals it to us through the ministry of angels who "see the face" of the Father (Matt. 18:10), Job rightly names it "a drop." Hence, Joel (3:18) also says: "In that day the mountains shall drop down sweet-

ness." Since not all the mysteries known in the vision of the
First Truth by the angels and the other blessed, but a certain
few are revealed to us, Job adds significantly: "a little." For
Ecclesiasticus (43:35–36) says: "Who shall magnify Him as
He is from the beginning? There are many things hidden from
us that are greater than these: for we have seen but a few of
His words." And our Lord says to the disciples in John
(16:12): "I have yet many things to say to you: but you cannot hear them now." The few things also which are revealed to
us are set forth in similitudes and the obscurities of words—as
a result, only the studious arrive at any sort of grasp of them
at all. Others, however, venerate them as things hidden, and
unbelievers cannot attack them; hence, the Apostle says: "We
see now through a glass in a dark manner" (I Cor. 13:12).
Significantly, then, does Job add "scarce" to bring out the
difficulty.[1]

[8]   But this addition, "Who shall be able to behold the
thunder of His greatness," refers to the third kind of knowledge, in which the First Truth will be known, not as believed, but as seen; "We shall see Him as He is," we read
(I John 3:2). So Job adds: "to behold." Nor will one perceive
some measure of the divine mysteries: the divine majesty itself will be seen and all the perfection of goods; hence, the
Lord said to Moses: "I will shew thee all good" (Exod. 33:19).
Rightly, then, does Job say "greatness." Nor will the truth be
set before man hidden under any veils, but will be entirely
manifest; hence, our Lord says to His disciples: "The hour
cometh when I will no more speak to you in proverbs; but
will shew you plainly of the Father" (John 16:25). Significantly, therefore, does Job speak of "the thunder" to suggest
the manifestation.

[9]   Now, the words set down fit our purpose. In what has

1. St. Thomas' text reads: vix parvam stillam. "Hardly" brings out the
difficulty better than the Douay "scarce." In SCG, IV, the need for
such minor deviations and adjustments of Douay is quite extensive.
Hereafter, when a slight adjustment of the Douay will make St.
Thomas' exposition more smooth, the adjustment will be made
without notation. Where a very minor addition will leave the
Douay in its familiarity without interpreting St. Thomas or
interfering with his exposition, the addition will be made without notation.

preceded we have dealt with divine things according as the natural reason can arrive at the knowledge of divine things through creatures. This way is imperfect, nevertheless, and in keeping with the reason's native capacity. That is why we can say with Job (26:14): "These things are said in part of His ways." We must now deal with those divine things that have been divinely revealed to us to be believed, since they transcend the human intellect.

[10] And the manner of proceeding in such matters the words set down do teach us. For, since we have hardly heard the truth of this kind in sacred Scripture as a little drop descending upon us, and since one cannot in the state of this life behold the thunder of the greatness, this will be the method to follow: What has been passed on to us in the words of sacred Scripture may be taken as principles, so to say; thus, the things in those writings passed on to us in a hidden fashion we may endeavor to grasp mentally in some way or other, defending them from the attacks of the infidels. Nonetheless, that no presumption of knowing perfectly may be present, points of this kind must be proved from sacred Scripture, but not from natural reason. For all that, one must show that such things are not opposed to natural reason, in order to defend them from infidel attack. This was also the method fixed upon in the beginning of this work.[2]

[11] But, since natural reason ascends to a knowledge of God through creatures and, conversely, the knowledge of faith descends from God to us by a divine revelation—since the way of ascent and descent is still the same—we must proceed in the same way in the things above reason which are believed as we proceeded in the foregoing with the investigation of God by reason.[3] First, to be specific, we must treat of the things about God Himself which surpass reason and are proposed for belief: such is the confession of the Trinity; second, of course, the things which surpass reason that have been done by God, such as the work of the Incarnation and what follows thereon; third, however, the things surpassing reason which are looked for in the ultimate end of man, such as the resurrec-

2. *SCG*, I, ch. 9; and see A. C. Pegis, "General Introduction," *Book One: God* (New York, Doubleday & Co., 1955), pp. 39–50.
3. *SCG*, I, ch. 9, ¶3–5.

tion and glorification of bodies, the everlasting beatitude of souls, and matters related to these.[4]

Chapter 2.

THAT THERE IS GENERATION, PATERNITY, AND SONSHIP IN THE DIVINITY

[1] Let us take the beginning of our study from the secret of the divine generation, and first set down what one must hold about it according to the testimonies of sacred Scripture. Then[1] we may set out the arguments against the truth of the faith which unbelief has invented; by achieving the solution of these[2] we will be pursuing the purpose of this study.

[2] Sacred Scripture, then, hands on to us the names of "paternity" and "sonship" in the divinity, insisting that Jesus Christ is the Son of God. One finds this most frequently in the books of the New Testament. Thus, Matthew (11:27): "No one knoweth the Son but the Father: neither doth any one know the Father but the Son." With this Mark begins his Gospel, saying: "The beginning of the gospel of Jesus Christ, the Son of God." John the Evangelist also frequently points to this, for he says: "The Father loveth the Son and He hath given all things into His hand" (3:35) and "As the Father raiseth up the dead, and giveth life: so the Son also giveth life to whom He will" (5:21). Paul the Apostle also frequently inserts these words, for he calls himself in Romans (1:1–3) "separated unto the gospel of God, which He had promised before by His prophets in the holy scriptures concerning His Son"; and says in Hebrews (1:1): "God, who, at sundry times and in divers manners, spoke in times past to the fathers by the prophets, last of all in these days hath spoken to us by His Son."

[3] This is also given us, although more rarely, in the books of the Old Testament. Thus, Proverbs (30:4) says: "What is His name, and what is the name of His Son, if thou knowest?" One reads it also in the Psalms (2:7; 88:27): "The Lord hath

4. The threefold discussion is covered in ch. 2–26, 27–78, 79–97.
1. See below, ch. 4–9 and especially ch. 10.
2. See below, especially ch. 11–14.

said to me: Thou art My Son"; and again: "He shall cry out to Me: Thou art My Father."

[4] To be sure, some would like to twist these last two sayings into another sense, so as to refer "The Lord hath said to Me: Thou art My Son" to David; and so as to ascribe "He shall cry out to Me: Thou art My Father" to Solomon. Nevertheless, the additions in each instance show that this cannot be quite the case. For David cannot be fitted into this addition: "This day have I begotten Thee" (Ps. 2:7); nor into this one: "I will give Thee the Gentiles for Thy inheritance, and the utmost parts of the earth for Thy possession" (2:8); since David's kingdom was not extended to the utmost parts of the earth, as the history of the Book of Kings shows. No more is the saying: "He shall cry out to Me: Thou art My Father" fitting to Solomon, since there follows: "I will make His rule to endure for evermore: and His throne as the days of heaven" (Ps. 88:30). Hence, one is given to understand that because some of the things joined to the texts mentioned are suitable to David and Solomon, some absolutely unsuitable, what is said of David and Solomon in these words is said, as customarily in Scripture, figuratively of that other in whom the whole is fulfilled.

[5] However, since the names of "Father" and "Son" follow on a generation, Scripture has not been silent about the very name of "divine generation." For in the Psalm (2:7), as was said, one reads: "This day have I begotten Thee." And Proverbs (8:24–25): "The depths were not as yet and I was already conceived: before the hills I was brought forth"; or, according to another reading: "Before all the hills did the Lord beget me." And Isaias (66:9, 8) also says: "Shall not I that make others to bring forth . . . Myself bring forth, saith the Lord? Shall I that give generation to others be barren, saith the Lord thy God?" We grant that one can say that this text must be related to the multiplication of the children of Israel returning from captivity into their own country, because earlier this is said: "Sion hath been in labour and hath brought forth her children." But this does not defeat our purpose. For, however the essence of it be adapted, the essence of it which is given from the voice of God remains fixed and stable thus: If He

Himself grants generation to others, He is not sterile. Nor would it become Him who makes others generate truly to generate Himself not truly but by a likeness. For a thing must be more nobly in its cause than in that which is caused, as was shown.[3] Again, it says in John (1:14): "We saw His glory, the glory as it were of the only-begotten of the Father"; and later: "The only-begotten Son who is in the bosom of the Father, He hath declared Him" (1:18). And Paul says: "And again when He bringeth in the first-begotten into the world He saith: 'And let all the angels of God adore Him'" (Heb. 1:6).[4]

Chapter 3.

THAT THE SON OF GOD IS GOD

[1]   Consideration must, of course, be given to the fact that the names mentioned are used by the divine Scripture in its exposition of the creation of things, for in Job (38:28–29) it says: "Who is the father of rain? Or who begot the drops of dew? Out of whose womb came the ice; and the frost from heaven who hath gendered it." Therefore, lest nothing more be understood by the words for "paternity," "sonship," and "generation" than the efficacy of creation, the authority of Scripture added something: When it was naming Him "Son" and "begotten", it was not silent about His being God, so that the generation mentioned might be understood as something more than creation. For John (1:1) says: "In the beginning was the Word, and the Word was with God, and the Word was God." That by the name "Word" one should understand Son is made plain in the sequel, for he adds: "The Word was made flesh and dwelt among us, and we saw His glory, the glory as it were of the only-begotten of the Father" (1:14). And Paul says: "The goodness and kindness of God our Savior appeared" (Titus 3:4).

[2]   Neither was the writing in the Old Testament silent about this; it named Christ God. For a Psalm (44:7–8) says: "Thy throne, O God, is for ever and ever: the sceptre of thy kingdom is a sceptre of uprightness. Thou hast loved justice,

3. See above, ch. 1, ¶2.   4. See Ps. 96:7.

and hated iniquity." That this is spoken to Christ is clear from what follows: "Therefore God, Thy God, hath anointed Thee with the oil of gladness above Thy fellows." And Isaias (9:6) says: "A Child is born to us, and a son is given to us, and the government is upon His shoulder: and His name shall be called, Wonderful, Counsellor, God the Mighty, the Father of the world to come, the Prince of peace."

[3] Thus, then, are we taught from sacred Scripture that the Son of God, begotten of God, is God. And Peter confessed that Jesus Christ is the Son of God. He said: "Thou art Christ, the Son of the living God" (Matt. 16:16). He Himself, therefore, is both the Only-begotten and God.

Chapter 4.

THE OPINION OF PHOTINUS ON THE SON
OF GOD, AND ITS REFUTATION

[1] Now, certain men, who perversely presumed to measure the truth of this doctrine by their own comprehension of it, conceived on the points just mentioned opinions both vain and various.

[2] Some among these took into consideration Scripture's custom of calling those who are justified by divine grace "sons of God," as in John (1:12): "He gave them power to be made the sons of God, to them that believe in His name." And Romans (8:16) says: "The Spirit Himself giveth testimony to our spirit, that we are the sons of God." And I John (3:1): "Behold what manner of charity the Father hath bestowed upon us, that we should be called, and should be the sons of God." And Scripture does not hesitate to call these "begotten of God," for it says in James (1:18): "For of His own will hath He begotten us by the word of truth"; and I John (3:9) says: "Whosoever is born of God committeth not sin: for His seed abideth in him." Also, to the same men, which is more marvelous, the name of "divinity" is applied. For the Lord said to Moses: "I have appointed thee the God of Pharao" (Exod. 7:1); and the Psalmist says: "I have said: You are gods and all of you the sons of the most High" (Ps. 81:6); and, as

our Lord says: "He called them gods, to whom the word of God was spoken" (John 10:35).

[3]   After this fashion, therefore, they formed the opinion that Jesus Christ was pure man, that He had had a beginning from the Virgin Mary, that by the merit of His blessed life He had received the honor of divinity above all others; and they thought that He was, like other men, a son of God by the spirit of adoption, begotten of God by grace, and by a kind of likeness to God called God in Scripture not by nature, but by partaking in the divine goodness, just as it says of the saints in II Peter (1:4): "That by these you may be made partakers of the divine nature: flying the corruption of that concupiscence which is in the world."

[4]   Such was the position they were trying to establish by the authority of sacred Scripture.

[5]   For our Lord says in Matthew (28:18): "All power is given to Me in heaven and in earth." But, if He were God before all times, He would not have received power in time.[1]

[6]   Again, Romans (1:34) says of the Son: "Who was made to Him," to God, namely, "of the seed of David according to the flesh"; and says that He was "predestinated the Son of God in power." But what was predestinated and was made seems not to be eternal.

[7]   The Apostle also says (Phil. 2:8): "He humbled Himself, becoming obedient unto death, even to the death of the cross. For which cause God also hath exalted Him, and hath given Him a name which is above all names." From this it appears clear that by the merit of His obedience and passion He was given divine honor and was exalted above all things.

[8]   Peter also says: "Therefore let all the house of Israel know most certainly, that God hath made both Lord and Christ, this same Jesus, whom you crucified" (Acts 2:36). Therefore, it seems that He was made God in time, not born before time.

[9]   They also bring in to shore up their opinion whatever Scripture says which seems to imply a defect in Christ: that He was carried in a woman's womb, that He progressed in age,

1. The arguments in ¶5–8 are answered below, ch. 9, ¶2–5.

that He suffered hunger, was wearied with fatigue, and was subject to death; that He advanced in wisdom, confessed He did not know the day of judgment; that He was stricken with the fear of death; and other things of this sort which could not be in agreement with a God existing by His nature. Hence their conclusion: that by merit Christ acquired divine honor through grace and that He was not by nature divine.

[10] Now, this position was first invented by certain ancient heretics, Cerinthus and Ebion;[2] later, Paul of Samosata renewed it;[3] and later it was strengthened by Photinus,[4] so that those who dogmatize thus are called Photinian.

[11] However, those who diligently examine the words of sacred Scripture do not find in them the meaning which these men have by their own opinion constructed. For, when Solomon says: "The depths were not as yet, and I was already conceived," (Prov. 8:24), he makes it clear enough that this generation existed before all bodily things. Hence, it follows that the Son begotten by God received no beginning of being from Mary. To be sure, they endeavored to debase these and other like testimonies by their perverse exposition. These, they said, should be understood after the manner of predestination: that before the foundation of the world it was arranged that a Son of God should be born of the Virgin Mary; *not* that the Son of God had been before the world. But they are refuted by this: Not only in predestination, but in reality as well, He had been before Mary. For after the words of Solomon just quoted this is added: "When He balanced the foundations of the earth: I was with Him forming all things" (Prov. 8:29–30); but, if He had been present in predestination only, He would have been able to do nothing. One gets this also from the words of John the Evangelist, for, when he had first set down: "In the beginning was the Word" (by which name the Son is understood as was shown[5]) to keep anyone from taking this as predestination, he adds: "All things were made by Him: and without Him was made nothing" (1:1, 3); and this could not be true if He had not really existed

---

2. St. Augustine, *De haeresibus*, 8, 10 (*PL*, 42, col. 27).
3. *Ibid.*, 44 (*PL*, 42, col. 34).   4. *Ibid.*, 45 (*PL*, 42, col. 34).
5. See above, ch. 3, ¶1.

before the world. Again, the Son of God says in John (3:13):
"No man hath ascended into heaven, but He that descended
from heaven, the Son of man who is in heaven"; and, again in
John (6:38): "I came down from heaven, not to do My own
will, but the will of Him that sent Me." Clearly, therefore,
He was before He descended from heaven.

[12] There is more. According to the position described
above, a man by the merit of his life advanced to being God.
The Apostle shows, on the contrary, that when He was God
He became man. For he says: "Who being in the form of
God, thought it not robbery to be equal with God: but emptied himself, taking the form of a servant, being made in the
likeness of men, and in habit found as a man" (Phil. 2:6).
Therefore, the position described is in conflict with apostolic
teaching.

[13] Furthermore, among all the rest of those who had the
grace of God, Moses had it in abundance; it says of him in
Exodus (33:11): "The Lord spoke to Moses face to face, as a
man is wont to speak to his friend." If, therefore, Jesus Christ
is not said to be a son of God except by the grace of adoption,
like other saints, on the same grounds Moses should be called
son and Christ, even though Christ was endowed with more
abundant grace: among the other saints, also, one is endowed
with greater grace than another, but all are called sons of
God on the same ground. But Moses is not called son on the
same ground that Christ is so called, for the Apostle distinguishes Christ from Moses as the Son from the servant. He
says in Hebrews (3:5–6): "Moses indeed was faithful in all
His house as a servant, for a testimony of those things which
were to be said: But Christ as the Son in His own house."
Manifestly, then, Christ is not called the Son of God by the
grace of adoption, as other saints are.

[14] One can gather a similar understanding from several
other places in Scripture, in which Christ is named in some
singular way and prior to others as the Son of God. Sometimes
singularly and without others He is named "Son": as the voice
of the Father thundered at the baptism: "This is my beloved
Son, in whom I am well pleased" (Matt. 3:17). Sometimes
He is named "Only-begotten" as in John: "We saw His glory,

the glory as it were of the only-begotten of the Father"; and again: "The only-begotten Son who is in the bosom of the Father, He hath declared Him" (1:14, 18). If He were to be called son in some common fashion like others, He could not be called the Only-begotten. Sometimes, also, He is named "First-begotten" to show an overflowing of sonship from Him to others: as in Romans (8:29): "Whom He foreknew, He also predestinated to be made conformable to the image of His Son; that He might be the first-born amongst many brethren"; and Galatians (4:4–5) says: "God sent His Son that we might receive the adoption of sons." On another ground, therefore, is He a Son, through likeness to whose sonship others are called sons.

[15] In sacred Scripture, moreover, certain works are properly attributed to God, and in such wise that they cannot be assigned to another: such are the sanctification of souls and the remission of sins; for it is said in Leviticus (20:8): "I am the Lord that sanctify you"; and in Isaias (43:25): "I am He that blot out thy iniquities for My own sake." Yet Scripture attributes each of these to Christ, for we read in Hebrews (2:11; 13:12): "Both he that sanctifieth, and they who are sanctified, are all of one"; and again: "Jesus also, that He might sanctify the people by His own blood, suffered without the gate." Our Lord Himself insisted that He had the "power to forgive sins," and confirmed this by a miracle as is told in Matthew (9:16). This is also what the angel foretold of Him when he said: "He shall save His people from their sins" (Matt. 1:21). Christ, therefore, who both sanctifies and forgives sins, is not called God as they are called gods who are sanctified, and whose sins are forgiven, but as one who has the power and the nature of divinity.

[16] The Scriptural testimonies by which they tried to show that Christ was not God by nature are useless for establishing their proposition. For it is our confession that in Christ the Son of God, after the mystery of the Incarnation, there were two natures; namely, human and divine. And so, things are said of Him which are proper to God by reason of the divine nature, and things are also said which seem to involve deficiency by reason of the human nature, as will be more

fully explained later.[6] But now, for the present consideration of the divine generation, let it suffice to have pointed out in accord with the Scriptures that Christ the Son of God is also called God, not only as a pure man is by the grace of adoption, but by reason of the nature of divinity.

Chapter 5.

THE OPINION OF SABELLIUS ON THE
SON OF GOD, AND ITS REFUTATION

[1] Since, of course, the fixed mental conception of all who think rightly about God is this: There can be but one God—certain men, conceiving from the Scriptures that Christ is truly and naturally God and the Son of God, have confessed that the one God is Christ the Son of God and God the Father; and that God, nevertheless, is not called Son in His nature or from eternity, but that He then received the name of sonship when He was born of the Virgin Mary in the mystery of the Incarnation. Thus, all the things which Christ bore in the flesh they used to attribute to God the Father: for example, that He was the son of the Virgin, conceived and born of her, that He suffered, died and rose again, and all else which the Scriptures say of Christ in the flesh.

[2] They attempted to strengthen their position by Scriptural authorities.[1] For it says in Exodus [i.e., Deut. 6:4]: "Hear, O Israel, the Lord our God is one Lord"; and in Deuteronomy (32:39): "I alone am and there is no other God besides Me"; and John (14:10, 9, 11): "The Father who abideth in Me, He doth the works"; and again: "He that seeth Me, seeth the Father also. . . . I am in the Father and the Father in Me."[2] From all these they used to conceive that God the Father was being called the very Son incarnate of the Virgin.

[3] This was, of course, the opinion of the Sabellians, who were also called Patripassionists, because they confess that the Father suffered, holding that the Father Himself was Christ.[3]

---

6. See below, especially ch. 9, 27, and 28.   1. See below, ch. 9, ¶6.
2. The Latin text shows that St. Thomas also had John 5:19 in mind.
3. St. Augustine, De haeresibus, 41 (PL, 42, col. 32).

[4] Now, the latter position differs from the one just described[4] with respect to Christ's divinity (for the latter confesses that Christ is true and natural God which the first denied); nevertheless, with respect to generation and sonship, each of the two opinions conforms with the other: for, as the first holds that there was no sonship and generation by which Christ is said to be Son before Mary, so the latter also maintains. Therefore, neither of these positions relates the generation and sonship to the divine nature, but to the human nature only. The second position has this special feature: that when one says "Son of God" one designates not a subsisting person but a kind of additional property of a pre-existing person, for the Father Himself, in that He assumed flesh from the Virgin, received the name of Son; it is not as though the Son is a subsisting Person distinct from the Person of the Father.

[5] The authority of Scripture makes the falsity of this position quite manifest. For Scripture does not call Christ merely the Virgin's son, but also the Son of God. We made this clear before.[5] But it cannot be that one be his own son, for, since a son is begotten by a father, and he who begets gives being to the begotten, it would follow that he who gives is identified with him who receives being—and this is entirely impossible. Therefore, God the Father is not Himself the Son, but the Son is other than He, and the Father is other than the Son.

[6] Then, too, our Lord says: "I came down from heaven, not to do My own will, but the will of Him that sent Me"; and: "Glorify Thou Me, O Father with Thyself" (John 6:38; 17:5). From all of these and similar sayings the Son is shown to be other than the Father.

[7] Of course, it can be said within this position that Christ is called the Son of God the Father in His human nature only; namely, because God the Father Himself created and sanctified the human nature which He assumed. Thus, then, the same one is in His divinity called His own Father in His humanity. Thus, there is also no objection to saying that the same one in His humanity is distinct from Himself in His

4. See above, ch. 4.   5. See above, ch. 2.

divinity. But in this fashion it will follow that Christ is called a son of God as are other men, whether by reason of creation, or by reason of sanctification. It has, however, already been shown[6] that Christ is called the Son of God for another reason than other holy men are. It cannot, therefore, be understood that the Father Himself is Christ and His very own son.

[8]   There is more. Where there is one subsisting supposit, it does not receive a plural predication. But Christ speaks of Himself and the Father in the plural; He says: "I and the Father are one" (John 10:30). The Son, therefore, is not the Father Himself.

[9]   Furthermore, if it is by the mystery of the Incarnation alone that the Son is distinguished from the Father, there was no distinction whatever before the Incarnation. In the sacred Scripture, however, the Son is found to have been distinct from the Father even before the Incarnation. For it says in John (1:1): "In the beginning was the Word, and the Word was with God, and the Word was God." So, the Word who was with God had some distinction from Him. This is our usual manner of speaking: one is said "to be with" another. In the same way in Proverbs (8:30) the Begotten says: "I was with Him forming all things." Here, again, an association and some distinction is designated. It says also in Osee (1:7): "I will have mercy on the house of Juda, and I will save them by the Lord their God," where God the Father is speaking of saving the people in God the Son, as of a person distinct from Himself, who is held worthy of the name of God. We read, also, in Genesis (1:26): "Let us make man to our image and likeness"; and in this the plurality and distinction of those who make man is expressly designated. Yet Scripture teaches that man was made by God alone. Thus, there was a plurality and distinction of God the Father and God the Son even before the Incarnation of Christ. Therefore, the Father Himself is not called the Son by reason of the mystery of the Incarnation.

[10]   Furthermore, true sonship relates to the supposit of the one called son, for it is not a man's hand or foot which receives the name of sonship properly speaking, but the man

6. See above, ch. 5.

himself whose parts they are. But the names of "paternity" and of "sonship" require a distinction in those to whom they are applied, just as "begetting" and "begotten" do. Necessarily, then, if one is truly called son he must be distinguished in supposit from his father. But Christ is truly the Son of God, for we read in I John (5:20): "That we may be in His true Son, Jesus Christ." Necessarily, then, Christ is distinct in supposit from the Father. Therefore, the Father Himself is not the Son. Furthermore, after the mystery of the Incarnation the Father proclaims of the Son: "This is My beloved Son" (Matt. 3:17). Such a designation is a reference to a supposit. Christ is, therefore, as a supposit other than the Father.

[11] The points by which Sabellius attempts to strengthen his position do not prove what he intends to prove. We will make this clear more fully later on.[7] For, by reason of the truth that "God is one," or that "the Father is in the Son and the Son in the Father," one does not hold that the Father and the Son are one in supposit; there can be a unity of two who are distinct in supposit.

Chapter 6.

THE OPINION OF ARIUS ABOUT THE SON OF GOD

[1] Now, sacred doctrine does not agree that the Son of God took His beginning from Mary, as Photinus used to say,[1] nor that He who was God from eternity and is the Father began to be the Son by taking flesh, as Sabellius had said.[2] And so, there were others who developed this opinion about the divine generation of which Scripture treats: that the Son of God existed before the mystery of the Incarnation and even before the foundation of the world; and, because that Son of God is other than God the Father, they judged He was not of the same nature with God the Father, for they could not understand and did not wish to believe that any two who are distinct as persons have one essence and nature. And because in the faith's teaching only the nature of God the Father is believed to be eternal, they believed that the nature of the Son

did not exist from eternity, although the Son was before other creatures. And since whatever is not eternal is made from nothing and created by God, they used to preach that the Son of God was made from nothing and was a creature. But, since the authority of Scripture forced them to name the Son God, also, as was brought out in the foregoing,[3] they used to say that He was one with God the Father—not, to be sure, by nature, but by a kind of union of consent, and by a participation in the divine likeness above all other creatures. Now, the highest creatures whom we call angels are named "gods" and "sons of God" in Scripture, as in Job (38:4, 7): "Where wast thou when the morning stars praised Me together, and all the sons of God made a joyful melody?" and in a Psalm (81:1): "God hath stood in the congregation of gods." Accordingly, this one should be called Son of God and God more than the others, to show that He is more noble than any other creature in that through Him God the Father established all the rest of creation.

[2]   They used to try to strengthen this position by the testimonies of sacred Scripture.[4]

[3]   For the Son says, speaking to the Father in John (17:3): "This is eternal life: that they may know Thee, the only true God." The Father alone, therefore, is true God. Since, therefore, the Son is not the Father, the Son cannot be true God.

[4]   The Apostle also says: "Keep the commandment without spot, blameless, unto the coming of our Lord Jesus Christ, which in His times He shall shew who is the Blessed and only Mighty, the King of kings, and Lord of lords; who only hath immortality, and inhabiteth light inaccessible" (I Tim. 6:14–16). These words make a distinction between the Father who shows and Christ who is shown. Therefore, only the Father who shows is the King of kings and Lord of lords; He alone is immortal and dwells in inaccessible light. Therefore, the Father alone is true God. Therefore, the Son is not.

[5]   Furthermore, our Lord says: "The Father is greater than I" (John 14:28); and the Apostle says: "When all things shall

---

3. See above, ch. 3.
4. For St. Thomas' own treatment of the texts in ¶3–13, see below, ch. 8, ¶2–17.

be subdued unto Him, then the Son also Himself shall be subject unto Him," namely, to the Father, "that put all things under Him" (I Cor. 15:28). But, if the nature of the Father and Son were one, their greatness and majesty would also be one. For then the Son would not be less than the Father, or subject to the Father. It follows, then, from Scripture that the Son is not of the same nature as the Father, so they believed.

[6] The nature of the Father, furthermore, suffers no need. But one finds need in the Son, for it is shown from Scripture that He receives from the Father—and he who receives is in need. For Matthew (11:27) says: "All things are delivered to Me by My Father"; and John (3:35): "The Father loveth the Son: and He hath given all things into His hand." The Son, therefore, seems not to be of the same nature with the Father.

[7] He is in need, moreover, who is taught and is helped. But the Son is taught and is helped by the Father. For John (5:19–20; 14:15) says: "The Son cannot do any thing of Himself, but what He seeth the Father doing"; and later: "The Father loveth the Son, and sheweth Him all things which Himself doth"; and the Son says to the disciples: "Whatsoever I have heard of My Father, I have made known to you." Therefore, the Son appears not to be of the same nature as the Father.

[8] There is more. To receive a command, to obey, to be sent seem proper to an inferior. But these we read about the Son. For the Son says in John (14:31): "As the Father hath given Me commandment, so do I"; and the Apostle: "Becoming obedient unto death" (Phil. 2:8). And John (14:16): "I shall ask the Father, and He will give you another paraclete." And the Apostle also says: "When the fulness of the time was come God sent His Son" (Gal. 4:4). Therefore, the Son is less than the Father and is subject to Him.

[9] Furthermore, the Son is glorified by the Father, as He Himself says in John (13:28): "Father, glorify thy name"; and thereafter: "A voice, therefore, came from heaven: I have both glorified it, and will glorify it again." The Apostle also says that God "raised up Jesus Christ from the dead" (Rom. 8:11). And Peter says that He "was exalted by the right hand of

God" (Acts 2:33). And from these it seems that the Son is inferior to the Father.

[10]   In the Father's nature, furthermore, there can be no failure. But one finds a failure in power in the Son, for He says in Matthew (20:23): "To sit on My right or left hand is not Mine to give to you, but to them for whom it is prepared by My Father." There is a failure also in knowledge; for He Himself says: "That day or hour no man knoweth, neither the angels in heaven, nor the Son, but the Father" (Mark 13:22). There is also a failure in stability of love, since Scripture asserts that there was sadness in the Son and anger and other changes of this sort. Therefore, the Son does not appear to be of the same nature as the Father.

[11]   It is, furthermore, found expressly in Scripture that the Son of God is a creature. For Ecclesiasticus (24:12, 14) says: "The creator of all things said to Me: and He that made Me rested in My tabernacle"; and again: "From the beginning, and before the world, was I created." Therefore, the Son is a creature.

[12]   What is more, the Son is numbered among creatures. For it says in the person of Wisdom: "I came out of the mouth of the most High, the firstborn before all creatures" (Eccli. 24:5). And the Apostle says of the Son that He is "the firstborn of every creature" (Col. 1:15). The Son, then, seems to belong to the order of creatures as one who holds the first rank therein.

[13]   The Son, moreover, says in John (17:22), praying for the disciples to the Father: "The glory which Thou hast given Me, I have given to them; that they may be one, as We also are one." Therefore, the Father and Son are one as He wished the disciples to be one. But He did not wish the disciples to be essentially one. Therefore, the Father and Son are not essentially one. Thus it follows that He is a creature and subject to the Father.

[14]   Now, this is the position of Arius and Eunomius.[5] And it seems to have arisen from the sayings of the Platonists, who used to hold that there was a supreme God, the Father and

5. St. Augustine, De haeresibus, 49 and 54 (PL, 49, col. 39–40).

Creator of all things, and from Him there emanated a certain "Mind" in which were the forms of all things, and it was superior to all things; and they named this the "paternal intellect"; after this they put the soul of the world, and then the other creatures. Therefore, what is said in sacred Scripture of the Son of God they used to understand of the mind just mentioned; and the more so because sacred Scripture names the Son of God "the Wisdom of God" and "the Word of God." And with this opinion the position of Avicenna[6] agrees; he holds that above the soul of the first heaven there is a first intelligence[7] moving the first heaven, and further beyond this he placed God at the summit.

[15] In this way, then, the Arians were inclined to think that the Son of God was a kind of creature, pre-eminent over all other creatures, the medium by which God had created all things; they were all the more so inclined by the fact that certain philosophers also held that things proceeded from their first source in an order, resulting in the creation of all things through one first creature.

Chapter 7.

REFUTATION OF THE OPINION OF ARIUS
ON THE SON OF GOD

[1] That this opinion is manifestly repugnant to divine Scripture anyone can see who considers diligently what sacred Scripture says.

[2] For, when divine Scripture names Christ the Son of God and angels the sons of God it does so for different reasons. Hence, the Apostle says: "To which of the angels hath He said at any time, '*Thou art My Son, today have I begotten Thee*'" (Heb. 1:5). And it was to Christ that this was said, he asserts. But, according to the aforesaid position, angels are called sons for the same reason as Christ, for the name of sonship is fitting to each according to a kind of sublimity of nature in which they were created by God.

6. Avicenna, *Metaphysics*, IX, IV, fol. 104v (Ven., 1508).
7. On this doctrine see É. Gilson, *The History of Christian Philosophy in the Middle Ages* (New York, 1955), pp. 187–216.

[3]   Neither is this objection met if Christ is of a nature more excellent than other angels. For, even among the angels diverse orders are discovered, which became clear above,[1] and for all that, to all of them the same notion of sonship is suitable. Therefore, Christ is not called the Son of God in the way the position described maintains.

[4]   Again, since by reason of creation the name of divine sonship is suitable to many—for it belongs to all the angels and saints—if Christ also were called Son on the same ground, He would not be "only-begotten," although by reason of the excellence of His nature over all others He could be called "firstborn." However, Scripture asserts that He is only-begotten: "We saw His glory, the glory as it were of the only-begotten of the Father" (John 1:14). It is not, therefore, by reason of creation that He is called the Son of God.

[5]   Moreover, the name of sonship properly and truly follows on the generation of living things in which the begotten proceeds from the substance of the one begetting; otherwise, the name of sonship is taken not in truth but in similitude, as when we call either students or others who are in our charge our sons. If, then, Christ were not called Son except by reason of creation, since that which is created by God is not derived from the substance of God, Christ could not be called Son truly. But He is called the true Son in I John (5:20): "that we may be," he says, "in His true Son, Jesus Christ." Therefore, He is not called the Son of God as created by God in an excellence of nature, however great, but as one begotten of God's substance.

[6]   What is more, if Christ is called Son by reason of creation, He will not be truly God. For nothing created can be called God unless by some similitude to God. But this same Jesus Christ is true God, for, when John had said: "that we may be in His true Son," he added: "This is the true God and life eternal." Therefore, Christ is not called the Son of God by reason of creation.

[7]   Furthermore, the Apostle says: "Of whom is Christ, according to the flesh, who is over all things, God blessed forever. Amen" (Rom. 9:5); and in Titus (2:13): "Looking for

1. SCG, III, ch. 80.

the blessed hope and coming of the glory of the great God and our Savior Jesus Christ." And Jeremias (23:5-6) says: "I will raise up to David a just branch"; and adds below: "and this is the name that they shall call Him: The Lord our just one." There in Hebrew the name is the *tetragrammaton*, which certainly is said of God alone. From these sayings it is clear that the Son of God is true God.

[8] Moreover, if Christ be the true Son, of necessity it follows that He is true God. For, that cannot truly be called son which is begotten of another, even if the thing be born of the substance of the one begetting unless it comes forth in species like the one begetting; the son of a man must be a man. If, therefore, Christ be the true Son of God, He must be true God. Therefore, He is not anything created.

[9] Again, no creature receives the complete fullness of divine goodness, because, as was made clear above,[2] perfections proceed from God to creatures in a kind of descent. But Christ has in Himself the complete fullness of the divine goodness, for the Apostle says: "In Him dwelleth all the fulness of the Godhead" (Col. 2:9). Therefore, Christ is not a creature.

[10] Grant, furthermore, that the intellect of an angel has a more perfect knowledge than the intellect of man; it is still in great want from the divine intellect. But the intellect of Christ is not in want of knowledge from the divine intellect, for the Apostle says that in Christ "are hid all the treasures of wisdom and knowledge" (Col. 2:3). Therefore, Christ the Son of God is not a creature.

[11] Furthermore, whatever God has in Himself is His essence, as was shown in Book I.[3] But, all things the Father has are the Son's. For the Son Himself says: "All things whatsoever the Father hath are Mine" (John 16:15); and in John (17:10), speaking to the Father, he says: "All My things are Thine, and Thine are Mine." The essence and nature, then, of the Father and Son is the very same. Therefore, the Son is not a creature.

[12] What is more, the Apostle says that the Son, before He emptied himself taking the form of a servant, was "in the form of God" (Phil. 2:6-7). By the form of God, however, nothing

is understood but the divine nature, just as by the form of the servant human nature is understood. The Son, then, is in the divine nature. Therefore, He is not a creature.

[13]   Furthermore, nothing created can be equal to God. The Son, however, is equal to the Father. For John (5:18) says: "The Jews sought the more to kill Him, because He did not only break the sabbath, but also said God was His Father, making Himself equal to God." And this is the narrative of the Evangelist whose "testimony is true" (John 19:13; 21:24): that Christ said He was the Son of God and the equal of God, and that for these things the Jews were persecuting Him. Nor is there doubt for any Christian that what Christ said of Himself is true, when the Apostle also says that He "thought it not robbery to be equal with God" (Phil. 2:6). The Son, therefore, is equal to the Father. He is not, then, a creature.

[14]   Moreover, in the Psalms (88:7; 82:1) we read that there is no likeness of anyone to God even among the angels who are called the sons of God. "Who," it says, "among the sons of God shall be like God?" And elsewhere: "O God, who shall be like to Thee?" This should be understood of perfect likeness; which is clear from the things treated in Book I.[4] But Christ showed his perfect likeness to the Father even in living, for John (5:26) says: "As the Father hath life in Himself, so He hath given to the Son also to have life in Himself." Therefore, Christ is not to be counted among the created sons of God.

[15]   Furthermore, no created substance represents God in His substance, for, whatever be the perfection of any creature whatever that appears, it is less than that which God is; hence, there is no creature through whom we can know *what-He-is* about God. But the Son does represent the Father, for of Him the Apostle says that He "is the image of the invisible God" (Col. 1:15). And lest He be judged a deficient image, one not representing the essence of God, one through which *what-He-is* could not be known of God (thus is man called the "image of God" in I Cor. 11:7); He is shown to be the perfect image, representing the very substance of God, when the Apostle says: "Who being the brightness of His glory, and the fig-

4. SCG, I, ch. 29.

ure of His substance" (Heb. 1:3). Therefore, the Son is not a creature.

[16] There is more. Nothing which is in a genus is the universal cause of those things which are in that genus. So, the universal cause of men is not a man for nothing is the cause of itself, but the sun which is outside the human genus is the universal cause of human generation, and beyond it God is. But, the Son is the universal cause of creatures, for John (1:3) says: "All things were made by Him"; and in Proverbs (8:30) the begotten Wisdom says: "I was with Him forming all things"; and the Apostle says: "In Him were all things created in heaven and on earth" (Col. 1:16). Therefore, He Himself is not in the genus of creatures.

[17] Similarly, it is clear from what was shown in Book II[5] that the incorporeal substances that we call angels cannot be made except by creation, and it was also shown that no substance can create but God alone.[6] But the Son of God, Jesus Christ, is the cause of the angels, bringing them into being, for the Apostle says: "whether thrones, or dominations, or principalities, or powers: all things were created by Him and in Him" (Col. 1:16). Therefore, the Son Himself, is not a creature.

[18] Furthermore, since the proper action of anything at all follows its very nature, a thing's proper action is fitting to nothing to which the nature of that thing is not fitting; thus, what does not have the human species does not have the human action. Now, the proper actions of God belong to the Son: to create (as already shown), to contain and conserve all things in being; and to wipe away sins. That these are proper to God is clear from the foregoing.[7] But of the Son it is said that "by Him all things consist" (Col. 1:17); and that He upholds "all things by the word of His power, making purgation of sins" (Heb. 1:3). The Son of God, then, is of the divine nature, and is not a creature.

[19] But because an Arian might say that the Son does these things not as a principal agent, but as an instrument of the principal agent which acts not by its own power but by the

5. *SCG*, II, ch. 98.   6. *SCG*, II, ch. 21.
7. *SCG*, III, ch. 65 and 167.

power of the principal agent, our Lord excluded this argument, saying in John (5:19): "what things soever the Father doth, these the Son also doth in like manner." Then, just as the Father operates of Himself and by His proper power, so also does the Son.

[20] A still further conclusion from this saying is that virtue and power are identified in the Son and the Father. For He says that the Son works not only like the Father but the same things "in like manner." But the same operation cannot be performed by two agents unless in dissimilarity: as the same thing done by a principal agent and its instrument; or, if in similarity, it must be that the agents come together in one power. Now, this power is sometimes collected from diverse powers in diverse agents, as when many men draw up a boat, for they all draw it up in the same way, and because the power of each is imperfect and insufficient for that effect, from the diverse powers is collected one power of them all which is sufficient for drawing up the boat. But, one cannot say this in the case of the Father and the Son, for the power of the Father is not imperfect but infinite, as was shown in Book I.[8] There must, then, be numerical identity in the power of the Father and the Son. And since power follows nature, there must be numerical identity in the nature and essence of the Father and the Son. This also can be concluded from the things that were said earlier. For, if in the Son there is the divine nature (as has been shown in many ways), and if the divine nature cannot be multiplied as was shown in Book I,[9] it follows necessarily that there is numerical identity of nature and essence in the Father and the Son.

[21] Again, our beatitude is ultimately in God alone, in whom alone also the hope of man must be placed, to whom alone also the honor of adoration must be given, as was shown in Book III.[10] But our beatitude is in the Son of God. For He says in John (17:3): "This is eternal life: that they may know Thee," namely, the Father, "and Jesus Christ whom Thou hast sent." And I John (5:20) says of the Son that He is "true God and life eternal." Now, it is certain that by the name

8. SCG, I, ch. 43.   9. SCG, I, ch. 42.
10. SCG, III, ch. 37, 52, and 120.

"life eternal" the sacred Scripture signifies ultimate beatitude. Isaias also says of the Son, as the Apostle brings out: "There shall be a root of Jesse, and He that shall rise up to rule the Gentiles, in Him the Gentiles shall hope" (Rom. 15:12; Isa. 11:10). It is said also in a Psalm (71:11): "And all the kings of the earth shall adore Him; all nations shall serve Him." And John (5:23): "That all men may honour the Son, as they honour the Father." And again a Psalm (96:7) says: "Adore Him, all you His angels." That this is said of the Son the Apostle sets forth in Hebrews (1:6). Manifestly, therefore, the Son of God is true God.

[22] The arguments are also valid for establishing this point which were previously[11] used against Photinus to show that Christ is not made God but true God.

[23] Taught, therefore, by those mentioned and very similar testimonies of sacred Scripture, the Catholic Church maintains that Christ is the true and natural Son of God, eternal, equal to the Father, true God, identical in essence and nature with the Father, begotten, not created, and not made.

[24] Wherefore it is clear that only in the Catholic Church does faith truly confess generation in God, when it relates the very generation of the Son to this: the Son has received the divine nature from the Father. But others who are heretics relate this generation to some extraneous nature: Photinus and Sabellius to human nature, indeed; Arius, however, to some created nature more worthy than all other creatures.

Arius also differs from Sabellius and Photinus in this: the former asserts that such generation was before the world was; the latter two deny that it was before the birth from the Virgin.

Sabellius nevertheless differs from Photinus in this: Sabellius confesses that Christ is true and natural God, but Photinus does not; neither does Arius. Photinus holds that He is pure man; Arius, that He is a kind of mixture of a certain very excellent creature both divine and human. The latter two, however, confess that the Person of the Father is other than the Person of the Son; this Sabellius denies.

[25] Therefore, the Catholic faith, keeping to the middle

11. See above, ch. 4.

road, holds with Arius and Photinus against Sabellius that the
Person of the Father is other than the Person of the Son, that
the Son is begotten, but the Father entirely unbegotten; but
with Sabellius against Photinus and Arius that Christ is true
and natural God, the same in nature as the Father, although
not the same in person. And from this, also, an indication of
the Catholic truth can be gathered. For, as the Philosopher
says,[12] even falsehoods give witness, for falsehoods stand apart
not only from the truth but from one another.

Chapter 8.

SOLUTION OF THE AUTHORITIES WHICH
ARIUS PROPOSED FOR HIMSELF

[1]   Since, however, truth cannot be truth's contrary, it is ob-
vious that the points of Scriptural truth introduced by the
Arians to confirm their error[1] cannot be helpful to their teaching. For, since it was shown[2] from divine Scripture that the
essence and divine nature of the Father and Son are numerically identical, and according to this each is called true God,
it must be that the Father and Son cannot be two gods, but
one God. For, if there were many gods, a necessary consequence would be the partition in each of the essence of divinity, just as in two men the humanity differs in number from
one to the other; and the more so because the divine nature
is not one thing and God Himself another. This was shown
above.[3] From this it follows necessarily that, since there exists
one divine nature in the Father and the Son, the Father and
the Son are one God. Therefore, although we confess that the
Father is God and the Son God, we are not withdrawing from
the teaching which sets down that there is one only God, which
we established both by reasonings and by authorities in Book
I.[4] Hence, although there is one only true God, we confess
that this is predicated of the Father and of the Son.

[2]   When our Lord, therefore, speaking to the Father, says
"that they may know Thee the only true God,"[5] it is not so to

12. Aristotle, *Prior Analytics*, II, 2 (53b 26).
1. See above, ch. 6, ¶2–13.   2. See above, ch. 7.
3. SCG, I, ch. 21.   4. SCG, I, ch. 42.   5. See above, ch. 6, ¶3.

be understood that the Father alone is true God, as though the Son is not true God (the contrary is proved clearly by Scriptural testimony); but it must be understood that the one sole true deity belongs to the Father, in such wise, nonetheless, that the Son is not excluded therefrom. Hence, it is significant that our Lord does not say: "that they may know the one only true God," as though He alone be God, but said: "that they may know Thee," and added "the only true God" to show that the Father, whose Son He insisted He was, is the God in whom one finds that only true divinity. And because a true son must be of the same nature as his father, it follows that the only true divinity belongs to the Son, rather than that the Son is excluded from it. Wherefore John, also, at the end of his first canonical Epistle (5:20)—expounding, as it were, these words of our Lord—attributes to the true Son each of the things which our Lord here says of the Father; namely, that He is true God and that in Him is eternal life. John says (5:20): "That we may know the true God, and may be in His true Son. He is the true God and life eternal."

If the Son had nevertheless confessed that the Father alone is true God, one would not for this reason need to understand that the Son is excluded from true divinity. For, since the Father and Son are one God, as was shown,[6] whatever is said of the Father by reason of divinity is the same as if it were said of the Son, and conversely. For, by reason of the fact that our Lord says: "No one knoweth the Son but the Father: neither does any one know the Father but the Son" (Matt. 11:27), it is not understood that the Father is excluded from knowledge of Himself, or that the Son is.

[3] It is also clear from this that the true divinity of the Son is not excluded by the words of the Apostle: "Which in His times He shall show who is the Blessed and only Mighty, the King of kings, and Lord of lords."[7] In these words the Father is not named, but that which is common to the Father and the Son. That the Son is the King of kings and Lord of lords is manifestly shown in the Apocalypse (19:13), which says: "He was clothed with a garment sprinkled with blood; and His name is called THE WORD OF GOD"; and adds below:

6. See above, ch. 7.   7. See above, ch. 6, ¶4.

"And He hath on His garment and on His thigh written: KING OF KINGS, AND LORD OF LORDS" (19:16). Nor is the Son excluded from that which is added: "Who only hath immortality," since He also bestows immortality on those who believe in Him. Thus, John (11:26) says: "Who believeth in Me shall not die for ever." But what is added,[8] "Whom no man hath seen, nor can see," certainly is also suitable to the Son, since our Lord says: "No one knoweth the Son but the Father" (Matt. 11:27). To this it is not an objection that He appeared visibly, for this was according to the flesh. However, He is invisible in His deity just as the Father is; wherefore the Apostle says in the same Epistle (I Tim. 3:16): "Evidently great is the mystery of godliness, which was manifested in the flesh." Nor are we forced to understand these sayings of the Father alone because it is said that there must be one who shows and another who is shown. The Son also shows Himself, for He says: "He that loveth Me shall be loved of My Father: and I will love him, and will manifest Myself to him" (John 14:21). Accordingly, we also say to Him: "Shew us thy face, and we shall be saved" (Ps. 79:4).

[4]   But, how the saying of our Lord, "The Father is greater than I,"[9] must be understood we are taught by the Apostle. Since "greater" is referred to "lesser," one must understand that this is said of the Son so far as He is *lessened*. Now, the Apostle shows that He is lessened by taking on the servile form —in such wise, however, that in the divine form He exists the equal of God the Father, for he says: "Who being in the form of God, thought it not robbery to be equal with God: but emptied Himself, taking the form of a servant" (Phil. 2:6–7). Nor is it wondrous if for this reason the Father be said to be greater than He; since He was even made lesser than the angels; the Apostle says: "We see Jesus, who was made a little lesser than the angels, for the suffering of death, crowned with glory and honour" (Heb. 2:9).

From this it is also clear that in the same way the Son is said to be "subject to the Father"; namely, in His human nature. This is to be gathered from the very context of the expression. For the Apostle had already said: "For by a man

8. The addition is I Tim. 6:16; it was not quoted in ch. 6, ¶4.
9. See above, ch. 6, ¶5, on John 14:28 and I Cor. 15:28.

came death, and by a man the resurrection of the dead"; and afterwards he had subjoined: "Everyone shall rise in his own order: the firstfruits Christ, then they that are of Christ"; and later he added: "Afterwards the end, when He shall have delivered up the kingdom to God and the Father"; and when he has shown what sort of kingdom this is, namely, that things must be subject to it, he consequently subjoins: "When all things shall be subdued unto Him, then the Son also Himself shall be subject unto Him that put all things under Him" (I Cor. 15:21–28). The very context of the expression, therefore, shows that this ought to be understood of Christ so far as He is man, for thus did He die and rise again. Now, in His divinity, since "whatever He does the Father does," as was shown,[10] He Himself also subjects all things to Himself; wherefore the Apostle says: "We look for the Savior, our Lord Jesus Christ, who will reform the body of our lowliness, made like to the body of His glory, according to the operation whereby also He is able to subdue all things unto Himself" (Phil. 3:20–21).

[5] From the fact that the Father is said in the Scriptures "to give" to the Son—from which it follows that He "receives" —one cannot show any indigence in Him.[11] But this is required by His being the Son, for He could not be called Son if He were not begotten by the Father. For everything which is generated receives from the generator the nature of the generator. Therefore, by this giving of the Father to the Son is understood nothing but the generation of the Son in which the Father gave the Son His nature. This very thing can be understood from that which is given. For our Lord says: "That which My Father hath given Me is greater than all" (John 10:29). But that which is greater than all is the divine nature, in which the Son is equal to the Father. And this our Lord's very words show, for He had said before that no man should pluck His sheep from His hand (John 10:28–30). For proof of this He introduces the word stated; namely, that which is given to Him by the Father is greater than all, and that "out of the hand of My Father"—as He adds—"nothing can be plucked." From this it follows that neither can it be plucked from the

10. A paraphrase of John 5:19; see above, ch. 7, ¶19–20.
11. See above, ch. 6, ¶6.

hand of the Son. But this would not follow unless through that which is given to Him by the Father He were equal to the Father. And so, to explain this more clearly, He adds: "I and the Father are one."

Similarly, the Apostle also says that God "has given Him a name which is above all names: that in the name of Jesus every knee should bow, of those that are in heaven, on earth, and under the earth" (Phil. 2:9–10). But the name higher than all names which every creature venerates is none other than the name of divinity. By this giving, therefore, the generation itself is understood in which the Father gave the Son true divinity. The same thing is shown by His saying that "all things are delivered to Me by My Father" (Matt. 11:27). But all things would not be given to Him unless "all the fullness of the Godhead" (Col. 2:9) which is in the Father were in the Son.

[6] Thus, by asserting that the Father has given to Him He therefore confesses that He is the true Son—against Sabellius.[12] Yet, from the greatness of that which is given He confesses that He is equal to the Father—so Arius is confounded. Clearly, therefore, such gift-giving does not indicate indigence in the Son. He was not the Son before He was given to Himself, since His generation is the very gift-giving. Nor does the fullness of the given allow that He can be in need to whom this gift was clearly made.

[7] Nor is this an obstacle to what has been said: that one reads in Scripture that the Father has given to the Son at a point in time; our Lord after the Resurrection, for example, says to the disciples: "All power has been given to Me in heaven and in earth" (Matt. 28:18); and the Apostle speaks of the cause for which God "exalted" Christ and "gave Him a name which is above all names" (Phil. 2:8–9), that is, He had become "obedient unto death," as though He has not had this name from eternity. For it is usual of Scripture to say that some things are or are made when they begin to be known. Now, the fact that the Son has from eternity received all power and the divine name was made known to the world after the Resurrection by the preaching of the disciples. And this, too,

12. See above, ch. 5 and 7, ¶23–25.

the words of our Lord reveal. For our Lord says: "Glorify Thou Me, O Father, with Thyself, with the glory which I had, before the world was" (John 17:5). For He asks that His glory which eternally He has received from the Father as God be declared to be in Him now made man.

[8] Now, from this it is manifest how the Son is taught, although He is not ignorant.[13] For it was shown in Book I[14] that in God to understand and to be are identical. Wherefore, communication of the divine nature is also the communication of understanding. Now, the communication of understanding can be called "showing" or "speech" or "teaching." By reason of the fact, then, that the Son received the divine nature in His birth from the Father, it is said that He has "heard something from the Father," or that the Father "has shown Him something,"[15] or one reads something else like this in the Scriptures; but not that first the Son was ignorant or did not know and afterward the Father taught Him. For the Apostle confesses: "Christ the power of God, and the wisdom of God" (I Cor. 1:24). Now, it is not possible that wisdom be ignorant, nor that power be feeble.

[9] The saying also, then, "the Son cannot do anything of Himself,"[16] does not point to any weakness of action in the Son. But, because for God to act is not other than to be, and His action is not other than His essence, as was proved above,[17] so one says that the Son cannot act from Himself but only from the Father, just as He is not able to be from Himself but only from the Father. For, if He were from Himself, He would no longer be the Son. Therefore, just as the Son cannot not be the Son, so neither can He act of Himself. However, because the Son receives the same nature as the Father and, consequently, the same power, although the Son neither is of Himself nor operates of Himself, He nevertheless is *through Himself* and *operates through Himself*,[18] since just as He is through His own nature received from the Father, so

---

13. See above, ch. 6, ¶7.   14. *SCG*, I, ch. 44–45.
15. For example, John 5:20.
16. See John 5:19 and, above, ch. 6, ¶7.   17. *SCG*, I, ch. 45.
18. The italics are in the Leonine text. The Son is begotten, *licet a se non sit*; but identity of nature is not a limit on being or operation, *tamen per se est et per se operatur.*

He operates through His own nature received from the Father. Hence, after our Lord had said: "the Son cannot do anything of Himself," to show that, although the Son does not operate of Himself, He does operate through Himself, He adds: "What things soever He doth"—namely, the Father—"these the Son also doth in like manner."

[10]   From the foregoing it also is clear how "the Father commands the Son" or "the Son obeys the Father" or "the Son prays to the Father" or "is sent by the Father."[19] For, all these things are suitable to the Son inasmuch as He is subject to the Father. And this is only according to the humanity He has assumed, as was shown.[20] The Father, therefore, commands the Son as subject to Him in His human nature. The very words of our Lord make this clear. For, when our Lord says "that the world may know that I love the Father: and as the Father hath given Me commandment, so do I," (John 14:31), what the commandment is is shown by what is added: "Arise, let us go hence." He said this approaching His passion. But the commandment to suffer clearly pertains to the Son only in His human nature. In the same way, where He says: "If you keep My commandments, you shall abide in My love; as I also have kept My Father's commandments, and do abide in His love," (John 15:10), these precepts clearly pertain to the Son as He is loved by the Father as man; just as He loved His disciples as men.

That the Father's commandments to the Son must be understood as pertaining to the human nature assumed by the Son is shown by the Apostle. He calls the Son obedient to the Father in the things which belong to His human nature, for he says: "He humbled himself, becoming obedient unto death, even to the death of the cross" (Phil. 2:8). The Apostle also shows that praying belongs to the Son in His human nature, for he says: "Who in the days of His flesh, with a strong cry and tears, offering up prayers and supplications to Him that was able to save Him from death, was heard for His reverence" (Heb. 5:7). The way in which He "was sent" by the Father is also shown by the Apostle. "God sent His Son,

19. For the objection and the Scriptural citations, see above, ch. 6, ¶8.
20. For example, see above, ¶4.

made of a woman" (Gal. 4:4). He is, therefore, said to be sent in that He was made of a woman, and certainly this belongs to Him in the flesh He has assumed. Clearly, then, in none of these can it be shown that the Son is subject to the Father except in His human nature. For all that, one should recognize that the Son is said to be sent by the Father invisibly and as divine, without prejudice to His equality to the Father, as will be shown below[21] when we deal with the sending of the Holy Spirit.

[11] It is clear, and in the same way, that from the fact that "the Son is glorified by the Father" or "raised up" or "exalted" one cannot show that the Son is less than the Father except in His human nature.[22] For, the Son needs no glory as one who receives new glory, since He professes that He had it "before the world was" (John 17:5). But His glory, hidden under the weakness of the flesh, necessarily had to be manifested by the glorification of the flesh, and the working of miracles, in the faith of peoples believing. Hence, of His glory being hidden, Isaias (53:3) says: "His look was as it were hidden and despised, whereupon we esteemed him not." And the way in which Christ was raised up is like the way He suffered and died, that is, in the flesh. For it says in I Peter (4:1): "Christ having suffered in the flesh, be you also armed with the same thought." To be exalted also became Him in the way in which He was humiliated, for the Apostle says: "He humbled Himself, becoming obedient unto death. . . . For which cause God also hath exalted Him" (Phil. 2:8–9).

[12] Thus, then, the fact that the Father glorifies, raises up, and exalts the Son does not show that the Son is less than the Father, except in His human nature. For, in the divine nature by which He is equal to the Father, the power of the Father and the Son is the same and their operation is the same. Hence, the Son Himself exalts Himself by His own power, as the Psalmist says: "Be Thou exalted, O Lord, in Thy own strength" (Ps. 20:14). He Himself raises Himself up, because He says of Himself: "I have power to lay down My life, and I have power to take it up again" (John 10:18). He also glorifies

---

21. See below, ch. 23.
22. For the objection and the Scriptural citations, see above, ch. 6, ¶9.

not Himself alone, but the Father as well, for in John (17:1)
He says: "Glorify Thy Son, that Thy Son may glorify Thee."
This is not because the Father is hidden by the veil of flesh
He has assumed, but by the invisibility of His nature. In this
way the Son also is hidden according to the divine nature, for
common to both Father and Son is the saying of Isaias
(45:15): "Verily Thou art a hidden God, the God of Israel,
the savior." The Son, of course, glorifies the Father, not by
giving Him glory, but by manifesting Him to the world; for
He Himself says in the same place: "I have manifested Thy
name to men" (John 17:6).

[13]   One must not, however, believe that in the Son of God
there is any failure of power,[23] since He Himself says: "All
power is given to Me in heaven and in earth" (Matt. 28:18).
Hence, His own saying, "To sit on My right or left hand is not
Mine to give to you, but to them for whom it is prepared by
My Father" (cf. Matt. 20:23), does not show that the Son
lacks the power of distribution over the seats of heaven, since
by seating of this kind one understands participation in eternal life, and that its bestowal belongs to Him He shows when
He says: "My sheep hear My voice: and I know them, and
they follow Me. And I give them life everlasting" (John 10:
27). One reads also: "The Father hath given all judgment to
the Son" (John 5:22); and it does belong to judgment that
some are to be established in heavenly glory according to their
merits. Hence, we read that the Son of Man "shall set the
sheep on His right hand, but the goats on His left" (Matt.
25:33). It does, then, belong to the Son's power to set someone on His right hand or His left. This is true if each of these
acts refers to differing participation in glory, or if the one
refers to glory and the other to punishment. Therefore, one
must take the meaning of the sentence proposed (Matt. 20:
23) from what went before it. Now, this is what went before
it (Matt. 20:20–21): The mother of the sons of Zebedee had
approached Jesus to ask Him that one of her sons should sit
at His right hand and the other at His left. She seems to have
been stimulated to this request by a certain confidence in her
close blood relationship to the man, Christ. Our Lord, then,

23. For the objection here and in ¶14–15, see above, ch. 6, ¶10.

in His answer did not say that it did not belong to His power to give what was asked, but that it did not belong to Him to give it to those for whom it was asked. For He did not say: "To sit on My right hand or My left is not Mine to give anyone." Indeed, He shows rather that it is His to give to "them for whom it is prepared" by His Father. For to give this was not proper to Him as the Son of the Virgin, but as the Son of God. Accordingly, this favor was not His to give to some just because they belonged to Him in so far as He was the Virgin's Son, that is, in close blood relationship. It was His to give to those who belonged to Him as the Son of God; namely, to those for whom it had been prepared by the Father through eternal predestination. But, that this very preparation is included in the power of the Son, our Lord Himself indicates, saying: "In My Father's house there are many mansions. If not, I would have told you: because I go to prepare a place for you" (John 14:2). The many mansions are the different grades of participation in beatitude, which in predestination God has eternally prepared. When, therefore, our Lord says: "If not,"[24] that is, if there were a deficiency of mansions prepared for the men who are to enter into beatitude, and adds: "I would have told you: because I go to prepare a place for you," He is showing that preparation of this sort belongs to His power.

[14] Nor, again, can it be understood that the Son is ignorant of the hour of His coming, since in Him "are hid all the treasures of wisdom and knowledge" (Col. 2:3), as the Apostle says, and since He knows perfectly that which is greater; namely, the Father (Matt. 11:27). But one must understand here that the Son, set as a man among men, considered Himself as ignoring something so long as He did not reveal it to His disciples. For it is usual in Scripture to say that God knows something if He makes someone know it; so we find in Genesis (22:12): "Now I know that thou fearest God," that is, "now I have made men begin to know it." Thus, conversely, the Son is said not to know that which He does not make us know.

24. St. Thomas' text reads: "*quod si in aliquo minus esset*" *idest si deficerent.* . . . This is more elaborate than the Douay "If not," but the sense is the same.

[15]   Sorrow, of course, and fear, and other things of this sort manifestly belong to Christ so far as He is man. Hence, one cannot apprehend in this fact any lessening of the divinity of the Son.

[16]   Consider, now, the saying that wisdom "is created."[25] First of all, one can understand it not of the Wisdom which is the Son of God, but of the wisdom which God bestowed on creatures. For one reads in Ecclesiasticus (1:9–10): "He created her," namely, wisdom, "in the Holy Spirit, . . . and He poured her out upon all His works." One can also refer this to the created nature assumed by the Son. Then the meaning is: "From the beginning, and before the world, was I created" (Ecclus. 24:14); that is, "I was foreseen in union with a creature." Or it may be that Wisdom *is* named (cf. Prov. 8:24–25), since both "created" and "begotten" suggest to us the mode of divine generation. For in generation the begotten receives the nature of him who begets, and this is a mark of perfection. But, in the generations which take place among us, he who begets is himself changed, and this is a mark of imperfection. In creation, on the other hand, the creator is not changed, but the created does not receive the nature of the creator. Therefore, the Son is called "created" and "begotten" at the very same time, that from creation one may gather the immutability of the Father, and from generation the unity of nature in the Father and the Son. It was thus that the Synod expounded the meaning of this sort of Scriptural expression. Hilary makes this clear.[26]

[17]   However, that the Son is called the "first-born of every creature"[27] is not because the Son is in the order of creatures, but because the Son both is from the Father and receives from the Father, from whom creatures both are and receive. But the Son receives from the Father the very same nature; creatures do not. Hence, the Son is not called merely "first-begotten," but "only-begotten" as well (John 1:18), by reason of His unique manner of receiving from the Father.

[18]   Now, our Lord says to the Father about the disciples:

---

25. See above, ch. 6, ¶11.
26. St. Hilary, De synodis, 17–18 (PL, 10, col. 493–495).
27. For the citations and the objections, see above, ch. 6, ¶12.

"that they may be one, as We also are one" (John 17:22).[28] This only shows that the Father and Son are one in the way in which the disciples should be one; namely, through love. Nevertheless, this mode of union does not exclude unity of essence; rather, it points to it, for John (3:35) says: "The Father loveth the Son: and He hath given all things into His hand." By this is the fullness of divinity shown to be in the Son, as was said.[29]

[19] Thus, then, it is clear that the testimonies of the Scriptures which the Arians were taking for themselves are not hostile to the truth which the Catholic faith maintains.

Chapter 9.

SOLUTION OF THE AUTHORITIES OF
PHOTINUS AND OF SABELLIUS

[1] From these considerations, of course, it appears that the points from Scripture which both Photinus and Sabellius[1] used to bring up in support of their opinions cannot confirm their errors.

[2] For what our Lord says after the resurrection,[2] "All power has been given to Me in heaven and in earth" (Matt. 28:18), is not said for this reason: that at that time He had newly received this power; but for this reason: that the power which the Son of God had eternally received had—because of the victory He had had over death by resurrection—began to appear in the same Son made man.

[3] Now, as to the Apostle's word concerning the Son, "Who was made to Him of the seed of David" (Rom. 1:3), one sees clearly how it should be understood from the addition: "according to the flesh." For he did not say that the Son of God had been made simply,[3] but that He had been made "of the seed of David, according to the flesh," by the assumption of human nature as John (1:14) puts it: "The Word was made flesh." Hence, also, the following phrase—"Who was

---

28. See above, ch. 6, ¶13.
1. See above, ch. 4–5.
3. See above, ch. 4, ¶6.

29. See above, ¶5–7.
2. See above, ch. 4, ¶5, and ch. 8, ¶13.

predestinated the Son of God in power"—clearly refers to the Son in His human nature. For, that a human nature be united to the Son of God, that thus a man could be called the Son of God, was not a matter of human merit. It was by the grace of God's predestination.

[4]   In a similar fashion, what the Apostle says in Philippians,[4] "God exalted Christ through the merit of His passion," must be referred to the human nature; the humility of the passion was in this human nature. Hence, also, what follows—"He hath given Him a name which is above all names" —must be referred to this: the name belonging to the Son in His eternal birth had to be manifested in the peoples' faith as belonging to the incarnate Son.

[5]   In this way it also is plain that what Peter says,[5] "God hath made both Lord and Christ, this same Jesus," (Acts 2:36), must be referred to the Son in His human nature; in which He began to have temporally what He had in the nature of divinity eternally.

[6]   The point which Sabellius[6] introduces on the unity of the Deity—"Hear, O Israel: the Lord our God is one Lord" and "See ye that I alone am, and there is no other God besides Me"—is not hostile to the teaching of the Catholic faith, which holds that the Father and the Son are not two gods, but one God, as we said before.[7]

[7]   In the same way, the sayings, "The Father who abideth in Me, He doth the works," and "I am in the Father and the Father in Me," do not show a unity of person, as Sabellius chose to understand, but that unity of essence which Arius denied.[8] For, if there were one person of the Father and the Son, one could not say suitably that the Father is in the Son and the Son in the Father, since properly the same supposit is not said to be in its very self; this is said only with reference to its parts. For, seeing that parts are in a whole, and that what is proper to parts can be attributed to a whole, sometimes a whole is said to be in itself. But this manner of speech

---

4. See above, ch. 4, ¶7, and Phil. 2:8–9. St. Thomas is paraphrasing.
5. See above, ch. 4, ¶8.
6. For the objection and the Scriptural citations, see above, ch. 5, ¶2.
7. See above, ch. 8, ¶1.   8. See above, ch. 5, ¶2, and ch. 6.

does not suit speech about divinity, in which there can be no parts, as was shown in Book I.[9] It remains true, then, that, when the Father is said to be in the Son and the Son in the Father, the Father and Son are not identical in supposit. One can see from this that the essence of the Father and the Son is one. For, once this is given, it is very clear in what way the Father is in the Son and the Son in the Father. For, since the Father is His essence, because in God essence is not other than what has essence, as we showed in Book I,[10] it follows that in anything in which the essence of the Father is the Father is; and by the same reasoning in anything in which the essence of the Son is the Son is. Hence, since the essence of the Father is in the Son and the essence of the Son in the Father, because the essence of each of the two is one essence (as the Catholic faith teaches), it clearly follows that the Father is in the Son and the Son in the Father. Thus, the selfsame saying (John 14:11) confutes the error of Sabellius as well as that of Arius.

Chapter 10.

ARGUMENTS AGAINST DIVINE GENERATION AND PROCESSION

[1] When all things are carefully considered, it is clear and manifest that sacred Scripture proposes this for belief about the divine generation: that the Father and Son, although distinguished as persons, are nevertheless one God and have one essence or nature. But one finds this far removed from the nature of creatures: that any two be distinguished in supposit, yet one in their essence; so, human reason, proceeding from the properties of things, experiences difficulties in a great variety of ways in this secret of divine generation.[1]

[2] Since the generation known to us is a certain mutation to which corruption is opposed, it seems hard to put generation in God, who is immutable, incorruptible, and eternal, as is clear from the foregoing.[2]

9. *SCG*, I, ch. 20.   10. *SCG*, I, ch. 21.
1. This series of objections is answered in ch. 14.
2. *SCG*, I, ch. 13–15.

[3] If generation, moreover, is a change, whatever is generated must be changeable. But what is changed goes from
potency to act, for "change is the act of the potential as such."[3]
If, therefore, the Son of God is begotten, He is not eternal,
it seems, as one going from potency to act; nor is He true God,
since He is not pure act, but something which has potential-
ity.[4]

[4] The begotten, furthermore, receives its nature from the
generator. If, then, the Son is begotten by the Father, it follows that He has received the nature which He has from the
Father. But it is not possible that He has received from the
Father a nature numerically other than the Father has, but
the same in species, as happens in univocal generations, when
man generates man, or fire, fire. For we showed above[5] the
impossibility of a numerical plurality of deities. It seems
equally impossible that He has received nature numerically
the same as the Father has. For, if He receives a part of it, it
follows that the divine nature is divisible; but, if the whole is
transfused into the Son, it ceases to be in the Father; and so,
in generation, the Father is corrupted. Nor, again, can it be
said that by a kind of exuberance the divine nature flows from
the Father to the Son, as the water of a spring flows into a
stream and the spring is not emptied, for the divine nature
cannot be divided, just as it cannot be increased. It seems,
therefore, to remain that the Son has received from the Father
a nature which is neither in number nor in species the same
as the Father's, but of another genus altogether. This is what
happens in equivocal generation when animals born of putrefaction are generated by the power of the sun, but do not
belong to its species. It follows, then, that the Son of God is
neither a true Son, since the Father's species is not His; nor
true God, since He does not receive the divine nature.

[5] If the Son, again, receives a nature from God the Father,
the recipient in Him must be other than the nature received,
for nothing receives itself. The Son, then, is not His own
essence or nature. Therefore, He is not true God.

[6] Moreover, let the Son be not other than the divine es-

3. Aristotle, *Physics*, III, 1 (201a 10).   4. *SCG*, I, ch. 16.
5. *SCG*, I, ch. 42.

sence; let the divine essence be something subsistent, as was proved in Book I;[6] clearly, the Father, also, is the divine essence. The conclusion appears to be that the Father and Son coincide in the very same subsisting thing. Now, "the subsistent thing in intellectual natures is called a person."[7] It follows, then, that if the Son is Himself the divine essence the Father and the Son coincide in person. But if the Son is not the very divine essence He is not true God. For we proved this about God in Book I.[8] It seems, therefore, either that the Son was not true God, as Arius used to say, or that personally He is not other than the Father, as Sabellius asserted.

[7] Furthermore, that in a thing which is the principle of its individuation cannot possibly be in a second thing distinguished as a supposit from the first. For what is in many is not a principle of individuation. But the essence of God is that by which God is individuated, for the essence of God is not a form in matter[9] so that God could be individuated by matter. There is, therefore, nothing in God the Father by which He might be individuated except His essence. Therefore, His essence cannot be in any other supposit. His essence, therefore, is not in the Son, and so the Son is not true God, following Arius; or the Son is not other in supposit than the Father, and so the Person of each is the same, following Sabellius.

[8] Again, if the Father and Son are two supposits or two Persons, yet are one in essence, there must be in them something other than the essence by which they are distinguished, for a common essence is ascribed to each and what is common cannot be a distinguishing principle. Therefore, that which distinguishes the Father from the Son must be other than the divine essence. The Person of the Son, then, is a composite of two, and so is the Person of the Father a composite of two: the common essence and the distinguishing principle. Therefore, each of the two is a composite and neither of the two is true God.

[9] But one may say that they are distinguished by a rela-

6. *SCG*, I, ch. 22.
7. Boethius, *De duabus naturis*, 3 (PL, 64, col. 1393).
8. *SCG*, I, ch. 21.   9. *SCG*, I, ch. 27.

tion only, inasmuch as one is the Father, the other the Son. What is predicated relatively, however, seems not to predicate *a something* in that of which it is said, but rather a *to something*. Thus, by such predication no composition is brought in. But this answer appears not adequate for avoiding the awkward results just mentioned.

[10] For there can be no relation without something absolute. In whatever is relative there must be understood that which is said of itself (*ad se*) and, additionally, that which is said referring to another (*ad aliud*). Thus is something said absolutely of "servant" and, additionally, something is said referring "to the master." Therefore, that relation by which the Father and the Son are distinguished must have something absolute on which it is founded. Now, then, either that absolute is one only, or there are two absolutes. If it is one only, a twofold relation cannot be founded upon it, unless, of course, it be a relation of identity which can produce no distinction—as when one says that the same is the same as the same. Therefore, if the relation be such that it calls for a distinction, there must be a prior understanding of a distinction of absolutes. Accordingly, it does not seem possible that the Persons of the Father and the Son are distinguished by relations only.

[11]   One ought, along the same line, to say that the relation which distinguishes the Son from the Father either is a thing or is in the intellect alone. Let it, then, be a thing, and it seems not to be that thing which is the divine essence, since the divine essence is common to the Father and the Son. Therefore, in the Son there will be something which is not His essence. Thus, He is not true God, for we showed in Book I[10] that there is nothing in God which is not His essence. But let that relation be in the intellect only, and it cannot, then, distinguish the Son from the Father personally, for things which are personally distinguished must be really distinguished.

[12]   Again, every relative depends on its correlative. But what depends on another is not true God. If, then, the persons

10. SCG, I, ch. 23.

of the Father and the Son are distinguished by relations, neither of them is true God.

[13] If the Father, moreover, is God and the Son is God, this name "God" ought to be predicated substantially of the Father and the Son, since divinity cannot be an accident.[11] But a substantial predicate is truly that of which it is predicated. For, when one says "Man is animal," what is truly man is animal; in the same way, when one says "Socrates is man," what is truly Socrates is man. And from this there seems to follow the impossibility of discovering a plurality on the part of the subjects when there is unity on the part of the substantial predicate: Socrates and Plato are not one man, although they are one in humanity. Nor are man and ass one animal, although they are one in *animal*. Therefore, if the Father and the Son are two Persons, it seems impossible that they are one God.

[14] Opposed predicates, furthermore, show a plurality in that of which they are predicated. But opposites are predicated of God the Father and of God the Son. The Father is God unbegotten and generating, but the Son is God begotten. Therefore, it does not seem possible that the Father and Son are one God.

[15] These, then, and others like these are the arguments by which some whose will it is to measure divine mysteries by their own reason strive to attack divine generation. But, because truth is strong in itself and is overcome by no attack, it must be our intention to show that the truth of faith cannot be overcome by reason.

Chapter 11.

HOW GENERATION IS TO BE UNDERSTOOD IN DIVINITY, AND WHAT IS SAID OF THE SON OF GOD IN SCRIPTURE

[1] As starting point for this intention,[1] one must take this: Following a diversity of natures, one finds a diverse manner

11. SCG, I, ch. 23.   1. See above, ch. 10, ¶15.

of emanation in things, and, the higher a nature is, the more intimate to the nature is that which flows from it.

[2] For, in all things, inanimate bodies have the lowest place. There can be no emanations in these except by the action of some one upon another one. For this is the way in which fire is generated by fire, when an extraneous body is changed by the fire and is brought to the quality and species of fire.

[3] Among animate bodies the next place is held by the plants, and in these the emanation does proceed somewhat from what is within: to the extent, namely, that the internal humor of the plant is converted into seed and that the seed committed to the soil grows into a plant. Here, then, one has already found the first grade of life, for living things are those which move themselves to action, but those which can move only things external to them are entirely devoid of life. And in plants this is the mark of life: that which is within them moves toward some form. The life of plants is nevertheless imperfect; this is because, although the emanation in plants proceeds from what is within, what comes forth little by little in the emanation is, at the end, found to be entirely external. For the humor first emerging from the tree becomes a blossom, and at length a fruit distinct from the tree's bark, yet still fastened to it. But, when the fruit is perfected, it is separated from the tree altogether; it falls to the ground and its seeding power produces another plant. If one also considers this carefully, he will see that originally this emanation comes from what is external, for the internal humor of the tree is taken through the roots from the soil from which the plant receives nourishment.

[4] Beyond the life of plants one finds a higher grade of life: that of the sensitive soul. Its emanation may have an external beginning, but has an internal termination, and, the more fully the emanation proceeds, the more it reaches what is within. For the exterior sensible impresses its form on the exterior senses; from these it proceeds to the imagination and, further, to the storehouse of the memory. Nevertheless, in each step of this emanation the principle and the term refer to different things; no sensitive power reflects upon itself. This

grade of life, then, is higher than the life of plants—higher to the extent that its operation takes place within the principles which are within; it is, nevertheless, not an entirely perfect life, since the emanation is always from some first to some second.

[5] That, then, is the supreme and perfect grade of life which is in the intellect, for the intellect reflects upon itself and the intellect can understand itself. But even in the intellectual life one finds diverse grades. For the human intellect, although it can know itself, does indeed take the first beginning of its knowledge from without, because it cannot understand without a phantasm, as is clear from the things said before.[2] There is, therefore, a more perfect intellectual life in the angels. In them the intellect does not proceed to self-knowledge from anything exterior, but knows itself through itself.[3] Nonetheless, it is not the ultimate perfection to which their life belongs. The reason is this: Although the intention understood is entirely intrinsic to them, the very intention understood is not their substance, for in them understanding is not identified with being (as is clear from the foregoing).[4] Therefore, the ultimate perfection of life belongs to God, in whom understanding is not other than being, as has been shown;[5] accordingly, the intention understood in God must be the divine essence itself.

[6] Now, I mean by the "intention understood" what the intellect conceives in itself of the thing understood. To be sure, in us this is neither the thing which is understood nor is it the very substance of the intellect. But it is a certain likeness of the thing understood conceived in the intellect, and which the exterior words signify. So, the intention itself is named the "interior word" which is signified by the exterior word. Indeed, that the intention aforesaid is not within us the thing understood is clear from this: It is one thing to understand a thing, and another to understand the intention itself, yet the intellect does so when it reflects on its own work; accordingly, some sciences are about things, and others

2. SCG, II, ch. 60.
4. SCG, II, ch. 52.

3. SCG, II, ch. 96.
5. SCG, I, ch. 45.

are about intentions understood. Now, that the intention understood is not the very intellect within us is clear from this: The act of being of the intention understood consists in its very being understood; the being of our intellect does not so consist; its being is not its act of understanding.

[7] Since in God, therefore, being and understanding are identical, the intention understood in Him is His very intellect. And because understanding in Him is the thing understood (for by understanding Himself He understands all other things, as was shown in Book I[6]), it follows that in God, because He understands Himself, the intellect, the thing understood, and the intention understood are all identical.

[8] From these considerations, then, we can somehow conceive how divine generation is to be taken. For, it is clearly impossible that divine generation is to be taken as one finds generation in inanimate things wherein the generating thing impresses its species on an exterior matter. For, as the faith sets down, the Son begotten by the Father must have true deity and be true God. But deity is not a form inhering in matter, nor is God a form existing out of matter, as was proved in Book I.[7] In the same way, divine generation cannot be taken in the mode of the generation one finds in plants, and even in animals which have nutritive and generative powers in common with plants. For something which was in the plant or the animal is separated from it for the generation of one like it in species, and this, at the term of generation, is entirely outside the generator. But, since God is indivisible, nothing can be separated from Him. The very Son begotten by the Father is not outside the Father, but in Him (which is clear from the authorities cited above[8]). Neither can one understand divine generation in the manner of emanation found in the sensitive soul. For, God does not receive from something exterior so as to able to influence some second thing; He would not then be the primary agent. Nor are the operations of the sensitive soul completed without bodily instruments. But, God is manifestly incorporeal. We are, therefore,

6. SCG, I, ch. 49.   7. SCG, I, ch. 17 and 27.
8. See above, ch. 9, ¶7.

left to understand the divine generation according to an intellectual emanation.

[9] This should be made clear in the following way. It is manifest, on the basis of Book I,[9] that God understands Himself. Now, whatever is understood should, as understood, be in him who understands, for the significance of the very act of understanding is this: the grasping of that which is understood by an intellect; hence, even our intellect understanding itself is within itself, not only as identified with itself by its essence, but also as grasped by itself in the act of understanding. God, therefore, must be in Himself as the thing understood in him who understands. But, the thing understood is in him who understands the intention understood and the word. There is, therefore, in God understanding Himself the Word of God, as it were, God understood; so the intellect's word of the stone is the stone understood. And to this point is the saying in John (1:1): "The Word was with God."

[10] The divine intellect, of course, since it does not pass from potency to act, but is always actually existent (which was proved in Book I[10]), must necessarily have always understood itself. And from its understanding of itself it follows that the Word of that intellect is in it; this has been shown.[11] Therefore, His Word necessarily always existed in God. His Word, then, is co-eternal with God, and is not acquired by Him in time, as our intellect acquires in time its interiorly conceived word which is the intention understood. Hence is the saying in John (1:1): "In the beginning was the Word."

[11] Now, since the divine intellect is not only always in act, but is itself pure act, as we proved in Book I,[12] the substance of the divine intellect must be its very act of understanding, and this is the act of the intellect. But the being of the Word interiorly conceived, or intention understood, is the very act of being understood. Therefore, the being of the divine Word is identical with that of the divine intellect and, consequently, with that of God, who is His own intellect. The being of God, of course, is His essence or nature, which is the same as God Himself, as was shown in Book I.[13] The

9. SCG, I, ch. 47.   10. SCG, I, ch. 55.   11. See above, ¶5–9.
12. SCG, I, ch. 16.   13. SCG, I, ch. 22.

Word of God, therefore, is the divine being and His essence, and is true God Himself. Of course, such is not the case with the word of the human intellect. For, when our intellect understands itself, the being of the intellect is one being, and that of its act of understanding another, for the substance of the intellect was in potency to understanding before it actually understood. Consequently, the being of the intention understood is one being and that of the intellect itself is another being, since the being of the intention understood is the very being understood. Necessarily, then, in a man understanding himself, the word interiorly conceived is not a true man having the natural being of man, but is only *man understood*, a kind of likeness, as it were, of the true man which the intellect grasps. But the Word of God, precisely because He is God understood, is true God, having the divine being naturally, because the natural being of God is not one being and that of His understanding another, as was said. This is why it says in John (1:1): "God was the Word." The fact that this is said absolutely shows that the Word of God must be understood to be true God. For the word of man could not be called "man" simply and absolutely, but relatively: to wit, "man understood"; hence, this would be false: "man is a word"; but this can be true: "man understood is a word." When, therefore, this is said: "God was the Word," this is shown: The divine Word is not merely an intention understood, as our word is, but it is also a thing existing and subsisting in nature. For God is a true subsistent thing, since His is substantial being in the highest degree.[14]

[12] But the nature of God is not in the Word of God thus: it is one in species and differs in number. The way in which the Word has the nature of God is the way in which God's act of understanding is His very being, as was said. Now, the act of understanding is the divine being itself. The Word, therefore, has the divine essence itself; has it with an identity not only of species but of number.

A nature, again, which is one in species, is not divided into a numerical many except by reason of matter. But the divine nature is entirely immaterial. It is, therefore, impossible that

14. *SCG*, I, ch. 13.

the divine nature be specifically one and numerically different. The Word of God, therefore, has a nature in common with God and has it with numerical identity. For this reason the Word of God and the God whose Word He is are not two gods, but one God. For the fact that among us two who have human nature are two men hinges on the fact that human nature is numerically divided in those two. But we showed in Book I[15] that things which are divided in creatures are in God simply one being; thus, in creatures the essence is one thing and the act of being another; and in some creatures even what subsists in the essence is one thing, and its essence or nature another; for *this man* is neither his humanity nor his act of being. But God *is* both His essence and His act of being.

[13] And although in God these are most truly one, there is still in God whatever belongs to the notion of a subsistent, or of essence, or of being itself: for it is suitable to Him that He should not be in something, in that He is subsistent; that He be *what* He is, in that He is essence; and that He be in act, by reason of His act of being. Therefore, since in God the one understanding, the act of understanding, and the intention understood are the same as His own Word, there must most truly be in God that which belongs to the notion of the one understanding, that which belongs to the notion of the act of understanding, and that which belongs to the notion of the intention understood, or word. But in the essence of interior word which is the intention understood there is this: that it proceeds from the one understanding in accord with his act of understanding, since it is, so to say, the intellectual term of the operation. For, in the act of understanding, the intellect conceives and forms the intention or the essence understood, and this is the interior word. From God, therefore, in His very act of understanding must His Word proceed. The Word of God is, therefore, compared to God understanding (whose Word He is) as to Him from whom He is, for this is essential to a word. Therefore, although in God the one understanding, the act of understanding, and the intention understood, or Word, are by essence one, and

although for this reason each is necessarily God, there remains the distinction of relation alone, in so far as the Word is related to the one who conceives as to Him from whom He is. This is why the Evangelist, seeing that he had said: "God was the Word," to keep one from understanding that all distinction between the Word and God speaking or conceiving the Word was taken away, added this: "This was in the beginning with God"; as though to say: "This Word, whom I have called God, is in a way distinct from God speaking, and so it can be said that He was with God."

[14] Of course, the word interiorly conceived is a kind of account and likeness of the thing understood. Now, a likeness of one thing existing in another is essentially an *exemplar* if it stands to the other as principle, or it is essentially an image if it is related to that whose likeness it is as to a principle. Now, in our intellect one sees an example of each of these situations. For, since the likeness of the artefact existing in the mind of the artist is the principle of the operation which constitutes the artefact, the likeness is related to the artefact as an exemplar to that exemplified; but the likeness of a natural thing conceived in our intellect is related to the thing whose likeness it is as to its *beginning*, for our act of understanding takes its *beginning* from the senses which are changed by natural things. Since, of course, God understands both Himself and other things, as was shown in Book I,[16] His act of understanding is the principle of things understood by Him, since they are caused by His intellect and will; but His act of understanding is referred to the intelligible which He Himself is as to a beginning, for this intelligible is identified with the intellect understanding, whose emanation, so to say, is the Word conceived. Therefore, the Word of God must be referred to the other things understood by God as *exemplar*, and must be referred to God Himself whose Word He is as *image*. Hence, one reads of the Word of God in Colossians (1:15) that He is "the image of the invisible God."

[15] Now, there is a difference between intellect and sense, for sense grasps a thing in its exterior accidents, which are color, taste, quantity and others of this kind, but intellect

16. SCG, I, ch. 47–59.

enters into what is interior to the thing. And, since every knowledge is perfected by the likeness between the knower and the known, there must be in the sense a likeness of the thing in its sensible accidents, but in the intellect there must be a likeness of the thing understood in its essence. Therefore, the word conceived in the intellect is the image or the exemplar of the substance of the thing understood. Since, then, the Word of God is the image of God (as we have shown), it is necessarily the image of God in His essence. Hence, we have what the Apostle says, that He is "the figure of the substance of God" (Heb. 1:3).

[16] However, things have images of two kinds. For there is an image which does not share the nature with that whose image it is: whether it be its image in respect to the exterior accidents (a bronze statue is the image of a man, yet is not, for all that, a man); or if it be an image in respect of the thing's substance, for the essence of man in the intellect is not a man. The reason, as the Philosopher says, is that "it is not the stone which is present in the soul, but the species of the stone."[17] But the image of a thing which has the same nature with that whose image it is is like the son of a king: in him the image of his father appears and he is the same in nature as his father. Now, it was shown that the Word of God is the image of the speaker in respect of His very essence and that the Word has the very nature in common with the speaker. The conclusion, therefore, is that the Word of God is not only the image, but also the Son. For so to be one's image as to be of the same nature with him is not discovered in one who cannot be called a son—so long as we are speaking of living things. For that which proceeds from a living thing in the likeness of species is called son. Hence, we read in a Psalm (2:7): "The Lord hath said to Me: Thou art My Son."

[17] Consideration must, furthermore, be given to this: Since in any nature the procession of the son from the father is natural, from the fact that the Word of God is called the Son of God He must proceed naturally from the Father. This is in agreement with the things said above, as one can perceive from what takes place in our intellect. For our intellect knows

17. Aristotle, *De anima*, III, 8 (431b 30).

some things naturally; thus the first principles of the intelligibles, whose intelligible conceptions—called interior words—naturally exist in the intellect and proceed from it. There are also certain intelligibles which our intellect does not know naturally; rather, it arrives at the knowledge of these by reasoning. The conceptions of these last do not exist in our intellect naturally, but are sought after by study. Manifestly, however, God understands Himself naturally just as He is naturally. For His act of understanding is His being (as was proved in Book I[18]). Therefore, the Word of God understanding Himself naturally proceeds from Him. And, since the Word of God is of the same nature as God speaking and His likeness, this follows: This natural proceeding is unto a likeness of Him from whom He does proceed with identity of nature. But, this is the essential of true generation in living things: that which is generated proceeds from him who generates as his likeness, and as identified with him in nature. Therefore, the Word of God is truly *begotten* by God speaking the Word; and His proceeding can be called "generation" or "birth." This is why the Psalmist says: "This day have I begotten Thee" (Ps. 2:7); that is, in eternity which always is present and in which essentially there is neither past nor future. In this way the falsity of what the Arians maintained is clear, that the Father generated the Son by His will. For things which are by will are not natural things.

[18]   One must also consider that what is generated, so long as it remains in the generator, is said to be "conceived." But the Word of God is begotten by God in such wise that it does not withdraw from Him, but abides in Him. (This is clear from the above.) Rightly, therefore, the Word of God can be called "conceived" by God. Hence, the Wisdom of God says in Proverbs (8:24): "The depths were not as yet, and I was already conceived." But there is a difference between the conception of the Word of God and the material conception discovered by us in animals. For the offspring, so long as it is conceived and is inclosed in the womb, does not have its final perfection so as to subsist of itself in a place distinct from the one generating; hence, in the corporeal generation

18. *SCG*, I, ch. 45.

of animals, the *conception* of the offspring begotten is necessarily one thing and the *delivery* another; in the latter the
offspring begotten is even spatially separated from the generator when it proceeds from the womb. Now, the Word of
God existing in God Himself speaking the Word is perfect,
subsists in Himself, and is distinct from God speaking: for
one does not look for a local distinction there, but they *are*
distinguished only by a relation as was said. Therefore, in the
generation of the Word of God conception and delivery are
identified. Therefore, after this saying from the mouth of
Wisdom, "I was already conceived," there is shortly added:
"Before the hills I was brought forth" (Prov. 8:24–25).

However, since in corporeal things conception and bearing
involve motion, in these things there must be a certain succession: the term of conception is the being of the conceived
in the one conceiving; the term of bearing is the being of the
one born apart from the parent. Thus, in corporeal things,
that which is conceived is necessarily not yet in being and
that which is brought forth is in the bearing not distinct from
the parent. Now, the conception and birth of an intelligible
word involves neither motion nor succession. Hence, at once
it is conceived and it is; at once it is born and is distinct; just
as that which is illuminated, at the moment of being illuminated, is illuminated because in illumination there is no succession. Since one discovers this situation in our intelligible
word, by so much the more is it proper to the Word of God—
not only because the intelligible conception is also birth, but
because each of the two exists in eternity in which there can
be neither before nor after. Accordingly, after the saying of
Wisdom: "Before the hills I was brought forth," to keep us
from thinking that while He was being brought forth He was
not, this is added: "While He was preparing the heavens I was
present" (Prov. 8:27). In this way—although in the fleshly generation of animals first a thing is conceived, then it is brought
forth, and finally it acquires a presence to the parent at once
associated with and distinct from the parent—we can understand that in divine generation all these are simultaneous.
For the Word of God is at once conceived, brought forth, and
present. And since what is born proceeds from a womb, just
as the generation of the Word of God to convey His perfect

distinction from the generator is called birth, it is called for a like reason "generation from the womb"; so we read in a Psalm (109:3): "From the womb before the day star I begot Thee." Nevertheless, since the distinction of the Word from the speaker is not the kind which prevents the Word from being in the speaker (as the things said make clear)—just as the distinctness of the Word is conveyed by calling Him "brought forth" or "begotten from the womb"—so, to show that this kind of distinction does not keep the Word from being in the speaker, John (1:8) says that He is "in the bosom of the Father."

[19]   One should, of course, note carefully that the fleshly generation of animals is perfected by an active power and by a passive power; and it is from the active power that one is named "father," and from the passive power that one is named "mother." Hence, in what is required for the generation of offspring, some things belong to the father, some things belong to the mother: to give the nature and species to the offspring belong to the father, and to conceive and bring forth belong to the mother as patient and recipient. Since, however, the procession of the Word has been said to be in this: that God understands Himself; and the divine act of understanding is not through a passive power, but, so to say, an active one; because the divine intellect is not in potency but is only actual; in the generation of the Word of God the notion of mother does not enter, but only that of father. Hence, the things which belong distinctly to the father or to the mother in fleshly generation, in the generation of the Word are all attributed to the Father by sacred Scripture; for the Father is said not only "to give life to the Son" (cf. John 5:26), but also "to conceive" and to "bring forth."

Chapter 12.

HOW THE SON OF GOD MAY BE CALLED
THE WISDOM OF GOD

[1]   However, since what is said of the divine Wisdom has been brought to bear on the generation of the Word,[1] one

1. See above, ch. 11, especially ¶18–19.

should in consequence show that by the divine Wisdom—from whose person the words adduced came forth—the Word of God can be understood.

[2] And in order to arrive at a knowledge of divine things from things human, this must be considered: One calls wisdom in a man a kind of habit by which our mind is perfected in knowledge of the highest matters,[2] and the divine are of this kind. But, when in accord with the habit of wisdom a conception of divinity is formed in our intellect, that same conception of the intellect which is its interior word usually receives the name of wisdom. This follows that manner of speaking in which acts and effects are named by the names of the habits from which they proceed, for what is done justly is sometimes called justice, and what is done courageously is called courage, and, generally speaking, what is done virtuously is called virtue. And in this manner, that which is wisely thought out is called someone's wisdom.

[3] Now, that there is wisdom in God must certainly be said by reason of the fact that God knows Himself; but, since He does not know Himself by any species except His own essence—in fact, His very act of understanding is His essence—the wisdom of God cannot be a habit, but is God's very essence. But from what has been said,[3] this is clear: The Son of God is the Word and conception of God understanding Himself. It follows, then, that the same Word of God, as wisely conceived by the divine mind, is properly said to be "conceived or begotten Wisdom"; and so the Apostle calls Christ: "the Wisdom of God" (I Cor. 1:24).

[4] But the very word of wisdom conceived in the mind is a kind of manifestation of the wisdom of the one who understands, just as in our case all habits are manifested by their acts. Since, then, the divine Wisdom is called light (for it consists in the pure act of cognition, and the manifestation of light is the brightness proceeding therefrom) the Word of divine Wisdom is named "the brightness of light." Thus the Apostle speaks of the Son of God: "Who being the brightness of His glory" (Heb. 1:3). Hence, also, the Son ascribes to

2. Aristotle, *Nicomachean Ethics*, VI, 7 (1141a 19–20).
3. See above, ch. 11.

Himself the manifestation of the Father. He says in John
(17:6): "Father, I have manifested Thy name to men."

[5]   But note: Although the Son who is the Word of God is
properly called "conceived Wisdom," the name of "wisdom"
must, nonetheless, when taken absolutely, be common to the
Father and the Son; since the wisdom resplendent by the
Word is the Father's essence, as was said; but the Father's
essence is common to Him and to the Son.[4]

Chapter 13.

THAT THERE IS BUT ONE SON IN THE DIVINITY

[1]   However, since God by understanding Himself understands all else, as Book I showed,[1] but understands Himself
by a single simple inward look, since His act of understanding
is His act of being,[2] necessarily the Word of God is unique.
Since, of course, in divinity the generation of the Son is not
other than the conception of the Word,[3] it follows that there
is one sole generation in divinity and that a unique Son is
alone begotten by the Father. Hence, John says: "We saw
Him, as it were the only-begotten of the Father"; and again:
"The only-begotten Son who is in the bosom of the Father, He
hath declared Him" (1:14, 18).

[2]   For all that, it seems to follow from the foregoing[4] both
that the divine Word has another word and the divine Son
another son. For it was shown that the Word of God is true
God. Whatever, therefore, belongs to God must belong also
to the Word of God. But God necessarily understands Himself. Therefore, the Word of God also understands Himself.
If, then, one says that because He understands Himself there
is in God a Word begotten by Him, it seems to follow that
in the Word so far as He understands Himself one must allow
another word. And thus there will be a word of the Word and
a son of the Son. And that word, if he be God, will again
understand himself and will have another word. In this way,
the divine generation will proceed to infinity.

4. See above, ch. 9, ¶7.   1. SCG, I, ch. 49.   2. SCG, I, ch. 45.
3. See above, ch. 11.   4. See above, ch. 11.

[3] Now, the solution of this difficulty can be gathered from the foregoing. For, when it was shown that the Word of God is God, it was nevertheless shown that He is not a god other than that God whose Word He is, but a God entirely one. In this alone is He distinct from Him: He is the Word proceeding from Him. But, just as the Word is not another god, so neither is He another intellect; consequently, not another act of understanding; hence, not another word. Neither does it follow from this that there is a word of the Word Himself because the Word understands Himself. For, in this alone is the Word distinguished from the speaker (as we said): that it is from Him. Everything else, therefore, must be attributed commonly to God speaking, who is the Father, and to the Word, who is the Son, precisely because the Word also is God. But this alone: that the Word is from Him must be ascribed properly to the Father; and this alone: being from God speaking must be attributed properly to the Son.

[4] From this it is also clear that the Son is not impotent, although He cannot generate a Son, whereas the Father does generate a Son. For the very same power is the Father's and the Son's as is the very same divinity. And, since generation in divinity is the intelligible Word's conception, namely, in that God understands Himself, it must be that the power to generate in God is like the power to understand Himself. And, since the act of understanding Himself is in God one and simple, the power of understanding Himself, which is not other than His act, must be only one power. Therefore, it is from the same power that the Word is conceived and that the speaker conceives the Word. Hence, it is from the same power that the Father generates and that the Son is generated. Therefore, the Father has no power which the Son does not have, but the Father has the generative power to beget, the Son has it to be begotten; that these are different only in relation is clear from what has been said.

[5] However, since the Apostle says that the Son of God has a word from which it seems to follow that there is a son of the Son and a word of the Word, one must weigh the fashion in which the words of the Apostle as he says this are to be understood. He says in Hebrews (1:2–3): "In these days

He hath spoken to us by His Son," and, later: "Who being the brightness of His glory and the figure of His substance, and upholding all things by the word of His power," etc. Now, our understanding of this must be taken from the things already said, for it was said[5] that the conception of wisdom, which is a word, deserves the name of wisdom for itself. Now, if one goes further, it is apparent that even the exterior effect which comes from the conception of wisdom can be called wisdom in the way in which an effect takes for itself the name of its cause. One's wisdom is not only that which he thinks out wisely, but also that which he does wisely. Thus it happens that even the unfolding of divine wisdom by His work in things created is called God's wisdom; for example, Ecclesiasticus (1:9–10): "He created her" (wisdom) "in the Holy Spirit"; and later: "And He poured her out upon all His works." Thus, also, then, what is effected by the Word gets the name of word. Even in our case the expression of the interior word by the voice is called a word, as though it were the "word's word," because it tends to manifest the interior word. Thus, then, not only is the conception of the divine intellect called a Word, which is the Son, but even the unfolding of the divinely conceived in exterior works is named the word of the Word. And thus must one understand that the Son upholds all things "by the word of His power," and thus what one reads in the Psalmist: "Fire, hail, snow, ice, stormy winds which fulfill His word" (Ps. 148:8); and that is this: by the powers of creatures the effects of the divine conception are unfolded in things.

[6]   However, since God by understanding Himself understands all other things—as was said—the Word conceived in God by His understanding of Himself must also be the Word of all things. Nevertheless, He is not in the very same way the Word of God and of other things. For He is God's Word as proceeding from Him; and He is the Word of other things, but not as proceeding from them. For God does not gather knowledge from things; rather, by His knowledge He produces things in being, as was shown above.[6] Therefore, the Word of God must for all the things which are made be the perfect

---

5. See above, ch. 12.   6. See above, ch. 11, ¶14.

existing intelligibility. But how He can be the intelligibility of things taken singly is manifest from the points treated in Book I. There it was shown that God has a proper knowledge of all things.[7]

[7] Whoever, of course, makes anything by understanding does his work through the account of the things made which he has in himself, for the house which is material is made by the builder according to the account of the house which he has in his mind. Now, it was shown above[8] that God produced things in being not by a natural necessity, but as an intellectual and voluntary agent. Therefore, God made all things by His Word, which is the intelligibility of things made by Him. Hence, we read in John (1:3): "All things were made by Him." In agreement with this, Moses, describing the origin of the universe, uses such a manner of speech for the single works: "God said: Be light made and light was made. . . . God said: Let there be a firmament made" (Gen. 1:1–3), and so of the rest. All of which the Psalmist includes, saying: "He spoke and they were made" (Ps. 148:5), for to speak is to produce a word. Thus, therefore, one must understand that God spoke and they were made because He produced the Word by which He produced things in being as by their perfect intelligibility.

[8] But, since there is identity between the cause of the conservation of things and of their production[9] as all things were made by the Word, so by the Word of God all things are conserved in being. Hence, the Psalmist says: "By the Word of the Lord the heavens were established," (Ps. 32:6), and the Apostle speaks of the Son "upholding all things by the word of His power" (Heb. 1:3). How this is to be taken was explained above.[10]

[9] One nevertheless ought to know that the Word of God differs from an account in the mind of an artist in this: The Word of God is subsistent God; the account of the artefact in the mind of the artist is not a subsistent thing, but only an intelligible form. But, if a form is not subsistent, it does not properly belong to it to act, for action belongs to a finished

7. SCG, I, ch. 50. 8. SCG, II, ch. 23.
9. SCG, III, ch. 65. 10. See above, ¶5.

and subsistent thing; but the latter acts by the form, for form is the principle by which an agent acts. Therefore, the plan of the house in the mind of the architect does not build the house; the architect builds it according to the plan. However, the Word of God, which is a plan of things made by God, does —since He is subsistent—act; there is not merely an action through Him. For this reason, the Wisdom of God says: "I was with Him forming all things" (Prov. 8:30); and in John (5:17) our Lord says: "My Father worketh, and I work."

[10] Consideration should also be given to this: A thing made by an understanding pre-exists in the plan understood even before it is in itself, for the house exists in the understanding of the architect before it is brought to actuality. Now, the Word of God is the knowledge of all those things which are made by God—as was shown. Necessarily, then, all those things which are made by God have pre-existed in the Word of God even before they are in their own proper nature. Now, what is in something is in it in the way proper to that in which it is; it is not in that thing in its own proper manner, for the building in the mind of the architect exists intelligibly and immaterially. Things must, therefore, be understood to have pre-existed in the Word of God in the manner of the Word Himself. The manner of the Word Himself is this: He is one, simple, immaterial, and not only living but even life, since He is His own being. Necessarily, then, the things made by God have pre-existed in the Word of God from eternity, immaterially, without any composition. Moreover, they can be nothing else in Him but the Word Himself who is life. For this reason, we read: "that which was made in Him," that is, in the Word, "was life" (John 1:3–4).

[11] Now, just as an intellectual agent, because of the account he has in himself, produces things in being, so also a teacher, because of the account he has in himself, causes science in another, since the science of the learner is drawn from the science of the teacher, as a kind of image of the latter. God is not only the cause by His intellect of all things which naturally subsist, but even every intellectual cognition is derived from the divine intellect, as is clear from the fore-

going.[11] Necessarily, then, it is by the Word of God, which is the knowledge of the divine intellect, that every intellectual cognition is caused. Accordingly, we read in John (1:4): "The life was the light of men," to wit, because the Word Himself who is life and in whom all things are life does, as a kind of light, make the truth manifest to the minds of men. Nor is it a failure of the Word that not all men arrive at a knowledge of the truth, but that some exist in darkness. This comes, rather, from a failure of men who are not converted to the Word and cannot fully grasp Him. Hence, there still remains darkness among men greater or less, as men are more or less converted to the Word and cleave to Him. Hence, John, to exclude every defect from the clarifying power of the Word when he had said that the "life was the light of men," adds that it "shineth in the darkness and the darkness did not comprehend it" (1:5). The darkness is not because the Word does not shine, but because some do not grasp the light of the Word, just as with the light of the bodily sun diffused through the world there is darkness for him whose eyes are closed or weak.

[12] Such, then, are the points on divine generation and the power of the only-begotten Son which—taught by holy Scripture—we can in some way comprehend.

Chapter 14.

SOLUTION OF THE ARGUMENTS AGAINST DIVINE GENERATION PREVIOUSLY INTRODUCED

[1] The truth, of course, excludes every falsehood and dissolves every doubt therefore it is now time to dispose of the arguments which appeared to offer difficulty about divine generation.[1]

[2] From what we have said[2] it is already clear that we assert an intelligible generation in God, and not such as that we find in material things wherein the generation is a kind of change which is the opposite of corruption. For not even in our intellect is the word conceived with some change, nor does

11. *SCG*, III, ch. 67 and 75.
1. For the arguments, see above, ch. 1   2. See above, ch. 11.

it have an opposing corruption. It is to this conception that the generation of the Son of God is similar, as is now clear.[3]

[3] In like manner, too, the word conceived by our intellect does not proceed from potency to act except in so far as the intellect proceeds from potency to act. For all that, the word does not arise in our intellect except as it exists in act; rather, simultaneously with its existence in act, there is a word conceived therein. But the divine intellect is never in potency, but is actual only, as was shown above.[4] Therefore, the generation of the Word Himself is not like the process from potency to act; rather, it is like the origin of act from act, as is brilliance from light and an understanding understood from an understanding in act. Hence, clearly also, generation does not prevent the Son of God from being true God, nor from being Himself eternal. Rather, He is indeed necessarily co-eternal with God whose Word He is, for an intellect in act is never without its word.[5]

[4] And since the Son of God's generation is not material, but intelligible, it is now stupid to doubt whether the Father gave His nature wholly or partially. For, manifestly, if God understands Himself, the whole fullness of Himself must be contained in His Word. Nevertheless, the substance given to the Son does not cease to be in the Father, for not even in our case does the proper nature cease to be in the thing which is understood. The word of our intellect owes it to the very thing understood that it contains intelligibly that very same nature.[6]

[5] Since, again, divine generation is not material, clearly there need not be in the Son of God something which receives and something else which is the nature received. For this necessarily happens in material generations in that the matter of the generated receives the form of the one generating. But, in an intelligible generation, such is not the case. For it is not thus that a word arises within an intellect: one part of it is previously understood as receiving, and one part as flowing from the intellect; but in its entirety the word has its origin from the intellect, as even in our case one word in its en-

---

3. See above, ch. 10, ¶2.   4. SCG, I, ch. 45.
5. See above, ch. 10, ¶3.   6. See above, ch. 10, ¶4.

tirety has its origin from others—a conclusion, for example, from principles. Where one thing in its entirety rises from another there is no marking off a receiver from the thing received, but the entire thing which arises is from him from whom it rises.[7]

[6] In this same way it is clear that the truth of divine generation is not ruled out by this: in God there can be no distinction of a plurality of subsistents. The divine essence, subsistent though it be, cannot for all that be separated from the relation which must be understood to be in God, because the conceived Word of the divine mind is from God Himself speaking. For the Word, too, is the divine essence, as was shown, and God speaking—from whom the Word is—is the divine essence; not a first and a second, but an essence numerically the same. But relations like this are not accidents in God; they are subsistent things; for nothing can happen to God, as was proved above.[8] There are, therefore, many things subsisting if one looks to the relations; there is but one subsistent thing, of course, if one looks to the essence. And on this account we speak of one subsisting God, because He is one subsisting essence; and we speak of a plurality of Persons, because of the distinction of subsisting relations. For the distinction of persons, even in things human, is not worked out in accordance with the specific essence, but in accordance with things adjoined to the specific nature. Now, in all the persons of men there is unity in the specific nature; there is, nevertheless, a plurality of persons simply because men are distinguished in these things which are adjoined to the nature. In divinity, therefore, one must not speak of one Person by reason of the unity of the subsisting essence, but of many Persons by reason of the relations.[9]

[7] From this, of course, it clearly does not follow that what serves as principle of individuation is in some other, because the divine essence is not in another god, nor is the paternity in the Son.[10]

[8] Although, of course, the two Persons—namely, that of the Father and that of the Son—are differentiated not by es-

7. See above, ch. 10, ¶5.
9. See above, ch. 10, ¶6.
8. *SCG*, I, ch. 22.
10. See above, ch. 10, ¶7.

sence, but by a relation, the relation is not, for all that, other than the essence in reality, since a relation in God cannot be an accident. Neither will this be looked on as impossible if one earnestly considers the points established in Book I. There it was shown[11] that in God are the perfections of all beings, not in any composition, but in the unity of a simple essence, for the diversity of perfections which a created thing acquires by many forms is God's in His one and simple essence. For a man lives by one form, is wise by another, and is just by another; and all of these belong to God by His essence. Therefore, just as wisdom and justice in a man are accidents indeed, but in God the same as the divine essence, so a relation (say, that of paternity or of sonship), although it be an accident in men, in God is the divine essence.[12]

[9] It is not, of course, said that the divine wisdom is His essence whereas in us wisdom adds something to the essence, because the divine wisdom is, as it were, something lesser than our wisdom; it is said because His essence exceeds our essence, so that a thing which exceeds our essence (namely, to know and to be just) is possessed by God in His essence perfectly. Therefore, whatever is fitting to us which is distinguished in accord with essence and with wisdom must be ascribed to God by reason of His essence at one and the same time. And a like proportion must be observed in other cases. Now, since the divine essence is the very relation of paternity or of sonship, whatever is the property of paternity must belong to God, although paternity be His very essence. However, this is the property of paternity: to be distinguished from sonship. For one is said to be a father to a son as to another. And this is essential to a father: to be the father of a son. Therefore, although God the Father is the divine essence, and in the same way God the Son is, from His being the Father He is distinguished from the Son, even though they be one in that each of the two is the divine essence.

[10]   From this it is also evident that a relation in divinity is not without an absolute. But a comparison to an absolute in God is other than a comparison to an absolute in created things. For in created things a relation is compared to an ab-

---

11. SCG, I, ch. 30.   12. See above, ch. 10, ¶8.

solute as an accident to a subject; not in God, of course—there the comparison is by way of identity, just as it is also in other things which are said about God. An identical subject, of course, cannot have opposed relations in itself: the same man, for example, being his father and his son. But the divine essence, by reason of its all round perfection, is identified with its wisdom and its justice and other things of this kind, which in our case are contained in differing genera. And in the same way nothing stops the one essence from being identified with paternity and sonship, and the Father and the Son from being one God, although the Father is not the Son; for it is by an identical essence that God has by nature being and His very own intelligible Word.[13]

[11] From what has been said it can be made clear that the relations in God are in reality, and not in understanding alone. For every relation which follows on the proper operation of any thing—whether potency, or quantity, or anything of this kind—really exists in that thing; otherwise, it would be in the thing by understanding alone, as is apparent in the instance of knowledge and the knowable. For the relation of knowledge to the knowable follows on the action of the knower; not, of course, on the action of the knowable. The knowable maintains itself as it is in itself, both when it is understood and when it is not understood. Accordingly, the relation is in the knower really, but it is in the knowable consequently upon understanding only, since one says that the knowable is understood relatively to the knowledge because the knowledge is related to the knowable. A like situation appears in the case of right and left. For there is in animals a distinction of the powers from which the relation of right and left arises, on which account such a relation truly and really exists in the animal. Hence, no matter how the animal is turned around, the relation always maintains itself in the same way, for the right part is never called the left. Inanimate things, to be sure, which lack the powers just mentioned, have no relation of this kind really existing in them, but one names them in the relation of right or of left from this: the animals in some way present themselves to the inanimate. Hence, the same column

is called now right, now left, inasmuch as the animal is compared to it in a different situation. Of course, the relation of
the Word to God who speaks and whose Word He is in the
divinity is based on the fact that God understands Himself.
This operation is, indeed, in God, or, rather, is God Himself,
as was shown above.[14] One concludes that the relations aforesaid are in God truly and really and not solely according to
our understanding.[15]

[12] Although, of course, one holds that there is a relation
in God, it does not, for all that, follow that there is in God
something which has a dependent being, for in us the relations
have a dependent being because their being is other than the
being of the substance. Hence, they have a proper mode of
being in their proper essence, just as happens in the case of the
other accidents. In view of the fact that all accidents are forms
of a sort superadded to the substance and caused by the principles of the substance, it must be that their being is superadded to the being of the substance and dependent on that
being. And by as much as the being of each and every one
of them is prior or posterior, by that much the accidental
form in its proper essence will be more like a substance or
more perfect. For this reason even a relation really accruing to
a substance has a being which is last in order and quite imperfect: last in order, that is, because not only is the being of
the substance prerequisite, but also the being of other accidents, out of which the relation is caused (thus to be one in
quantity causes equality, and one in quality similarity); quite
imperfect, in turn, because the proper essence of the relation
consists in its being toward-another—hence, its proper being,
which it adds to the substance, depends not only on the being
of the substance, but on the being of some exterior thing as
well. This situation, of course, has no place in divinity, since
there is in God no other being than that of substance, for
whatever is in God is substance. Just as the being of wisdom
in God, therefore, is not being by depending on substance
(since the being of wisdom is the being of substance), so the
being of relation is not being by depending either on substance or on another exterior thing (since the being of rela-

14. SCG, I, ch. 45.   15. See above, ch. 10, ¶11.

tion is also the being of substance). From the fact, then, that one puts a relation in God it does not follow that there is in Him some dependent being, but only that there is in Him some aspect in which aspect the essence of relation consists. Just so from the fact that one puts wisdom in God it does not follow that there is something accidental in Him, but only that there is a certain perfection in which the essence of wisdom consists.[16]

[13] Thus clearly, also, from the imperfection in created relations it does not follow that the divine persons—distinguished by relations—are imperfect, but it does follow that the distinction of the divine persons is minimal.[17]

[14] Clearly, also, from the points made, although God is substantially predicated of the Father and the Son, it does not for all that follow that, if the Father and the Son are a kind of plurality, they are a plurality of gods. For they are many by reason of the distinction of subsistent relations, yet one God, nevertheless, by reason of the unity of subsistent essence. This does not happen among men, of course—that is, that some plurality is one man—since the essence of humanity is not numerically one in each of the plurality, nor is the essence of humanity subsistent; that is, humanity is not a man.[18]

[15] From the fact that in God there is unity of essence and distinction of relations it becomes manifest that nothing stops one's finding opposites in the one God, at least those opposites which follow the distinction of relation: *begetting* and *begotten*, for instance, which are opposed relatively, and *begotten* and *unbegotten* which are opposed as affirmation and negation. For wherever there is a distinction one must find the opposition of negation and affirmation. Things which differ in no affirmation or negation are entirely undifferentiated, for the first would have to be in every respect one with the second, and thus they would be thoroughly identified, and in no way distinct.

[16] Let these points on the divine generation suffice, then.

16. See above, ch. 10, ¶12.   17. See above, ch. 10, ¶13.
18. See above, ch. 10, ¶14.

Chapter 15.

ON THE HOLY SPIRIT, THAT HE IS IN DIVINITY

[1] Now, divine Scriptures' authority not only tells us about
the Father and the Son in divinity, but together with these
two also numbers the Holy Spirit. For our Lord says: "Going,
therefore, teach ye all nations: baptizing them in the name of
the Father, and of the Son, and of the Holy Ghost" (Matt.
28:19). And I John (5:7) says: "there are three who give
testimony in heaven, the Father, the Word, and the Holy
Ghost." Sometimes, also, the procession of this Holy Spirit is
mentioned by Scripture. We read in John (15:26): "When
the Paraclete cometh, whom I will send you from the Father,
the Spirit of truth, who proceedeth from the Father, He shall
give testimony of Me."

Chapter 16.

ARGUMENTS WHICH MADE SOME THINK
THE HOLY SPIRIT A CREATURE

[1] Now, in the opinion of some, the Holy Spirit is a creature exalted over other creatures. They used the testimony of
sacred Scripture for this assertion.

[2] Amos (4:13) says, if we take the Septuagint literally:
"Behold He that formeth the mountains and createth the
spirit and declareth His word to man." And Zacharias (12:1):
"Thus saith the Lord who stretcheth forth the heavens, and
layeth the foundations of the earth, and createth the spirit of
man in it." It seems, then, that the Holy Spirit is a creature.

[3] Moreover, our Lord says, speaking of the Holy Spirit:
"He shall not speak of Himself, but what things soever He
shall hear, He shall speak" (John 16:13), and from this it appears that He speaks not with the authority of a further power,
but to one who commands He is in a service of obedience, for
to speak what one hears is proper to a servant. Therefore, the
Holy Spirit seems to be a creature subject to God.

[4] Again, "to be sent" appears proper to an inferior, since

there is in the sender an implication of authority. The Holy Spirit, of course, is sent by the Father and the Son, for our Lord says: "The Paraclete, the Holy Ghost, whom the Father will send in My name, He will teach you all things"; and: "When the Paraclete cometh, whom I will send you from the Father" (John 14:26; 15:26). The Holy Spirit, therefore, appears to be less than the Father and the Son.

[5] Moreover, divine Scripture, associating the Son with the Father in matters of divinity, makes no mention of the Holy Spirit. This is clear from Matthew (11:27), when our Lord says: "No one knoweth the Son but the Father: neither doth any one know the Father but the Son," making no mention of the Holy Spirit. And John (17:3) says: "This is eternal life: That they may know Thee, the only true God, and Jesus Christ, whom Thou hast sent." There, again, no mention is made of the Holy Spirit. The Apostle also says: "Grace to you and peace from God our Father, and from the Lord Jesus Christ" (Rom. 1:7); and: "To us there is but one God, the Father, of whom are all things, and we unto Him; and one Lord Jesus Christ by whom are all things and we by Him" (I Cor. 8:6); and in these places also there is nothing said about the Holy Spirit. It seems, therefore, that the Holy Spirit is not God.

[6] There is more. Whatever is moved is created, for it was shown in Book I[1] that God is immobile. But to the Holy Spirit motion *is* attributed by divine Scripture. One reads in Genesis (1:2): "And the Spirit of God was moved over the waters"; and in Joel (2:28): "I will pour out My spirit upon all flesh." It seems, therefore, that the Holy Spirit is a creature.

[7] Moreover, everything that can be increased or divided is mutable and created. These seem to be attributed to the Holy Spirit in sacred Scripture. For the Lord said to Moses: "Gather unto Me seventy men of the ancients of Israel; and I will take of thy spirit, and will give to them" (Num. 11:16–17). And IV Kings (2:9–10) says that Eliseus begged of Elias: "I beseech thee that in me may be thy double spirit"; and Elias answered: "If thou see me when I am taken from thee, thou

1. SCG, I, ch. 13.

shalt have what thou hast asked." The Holy Spirit, therefore, appears to be mutable and not to be God.

[8]   Again, no sorrow can come upon God, since sorrow is passion of a sort and God is not subject to passion.[2] But passion does come upon the Holy Spirit; as the Apostle reveals: "Grieve not the Holy Spirit of God" (Eph. 4:30); and Isaias (63:10) says: "They provoked to wrath and afflicted His Holy Spirit." The Holy Spirit, therefore, seems not to be God.

[9]   What is more, it is not suitable for God to entreat, but to be entreated. But to entreat is suitable to the Holy Spirit; we read in Romans (8:26): "The Spirit Himself asketh for us with unspeakable groanings." Therefore, the Holy Spirit appears not to be God.

[10]   Moreover, no one makes a thing a gift appropriately unless he has dominion over it. But God the Father gives the Holy Spirit, and so does God the Son. For our Lord says: "Your Father from heaven will give the good Spirit to them that ask Him" (Luke 11:13); and Peter speaks of "the Holy Ghost whom God hath given to all that obey Him" (Acts 5:32).

[11]   For these reasons it seems, then, that the Holy Spirit is not God.

[12]   Once again, if the Holy Spirit is truly God, He ought to have the divine nature. Thus, when the Holy Spirit "proceedeth from the Father" (as John 15:26 has it), necessarily He receives the divine nature from the Father. Of course, what receives its nature from a thing which produces it is generated by that thing. For it is proper to one begotten to be produced unto a similarity in species to its principle. Therefore, the Holy Spirit will be begotten and, consequently, the Son. And this is repugnant to sound faith.

[13]   If the Holy Spirit, furthermore, receives the divine nature from the Father and not as one begotten, the divine nature must be communicated in two ways: by way of generation in which the Son proceeds, and in that way in which the Holy Spirit proceeds. But one nature seems not to have two fitting modes of communication if one examines natures universally.

2. *SCG*, I, ch. 16 and 89.

It seems, therefore, that the Holy Spirit, since He does not receive the divine nature by generation, does not receive it in any way at all. He thus appears not to be true God.

[14] Now, this was the position of Arius,[3] who said that the Son and the Holy Spirit were creatures: the Son, to be sure, greater than the Holy Spirit, and the Holy Spirit the servant of the Son; just so, he said that the Son was lesser than the Father. Arius was followed in respect of the Holy Spirit by Macedonius, "who rightly held that the Father and the Son were of one and the same substance, but was unwilling to believe this of the Holy Spirit. He said that the Holy Spirit was a creature."[4] Hence, some[5] call the Macedonians Semi-Arians, because they are in partial agreement with the Arians, and in partial disagreement with the same group.

Chapter 17.

THAT THE HOLY SPIRIT IS TRUE GOD

[1] One shows, of course, by clear testimonies from Scripture that the Holy Spirit is true God. For to none but God is a temple consecrated, and so the Psalmist speaks of "God in His holy temple" (Ps. 10:5). Yet there is a temple assigned to the Holy Spirit, for the Apostle says: "Or know you not that your members are the temple of the Holy Ghost?" The Holy Spirit, therefore, is God. This is especially clear since our members, which the Apostle calls the temple of the Holy Spirit, are the members of Christ. For just above he had set down: "Know you not that your bodies are the members of Christ?" (I Cor. 6:19, 15). It obviously would be awkward (since Christ is true God, as is clear from the foregoing)[1] to have the members of Christ a temple of the Holy Spirit if the Holy Spirit were not God.

[2] Again, holy men do not give the cult of adoration except to the true God, for Deuteronomy (6:13) says: "Thou shalt fear the Lord thy God, and shalt serve Him only." But holy men serve the Holy Spirit, as the Apostle says: "We are the

---

3. St. Augustine, *De haeresibus*, 49 (PL, 42, col. 39).
4. *Ibid.*, 52 (PL, 42, col. 39).   5. *Ibid.*, 51 (PL, 42, col. 39).
1. See above, ch. 3.

circumcision who serve the Spirit of God" (Phil. 3:3). And although some books have "who serve in the spirit of the Lord," the Greek books and some of the more ancient Latin ones have: "who serve the Spirit of God." And from the Greek itself this clearly must be understood as the cult of adoration which is due to God alone.[2] Therefore, the Holy Spirit is true God to whom adoration is due.

[3]   Further, to sanctify men is the proper work of God, for Leviticus (22:32) says: "I am the Lord who sanctify you." It is, of course, the Holy Spirit who sanctifies, as the Apostle says: "You are washed, you are sanctified, you are justified in the name of our Lord Jesus Christ, and the Spirit of our God" (I Cor. 6:11). And in II Thessalonians (2:12) one reads: "God hath chosen you first fruits unto salvation, in sanctification of the Spirit and faith of the truth." Necessarily, therefore, the Holy Spirit is God.

[4]   And further, just as the life of corporeal nature is from the soul, so the life of justice of the soul itself is from God; and so our Lord says: "As the living Father hath sent Me, and I live by the Father; so He that eateth Me, the same also shall live by Me" (John 6:58). Of course, this kind of life is from the Holy Spirit, and so our Lord adds in the same place: "It is the Spirit that quickeneth" (John 6:54); and the Apostle says: "If by the Spirit you mortify the deeds of the flesh, you shall live" (Rom. 8:13). Therefore, the Holy Spirit is of the divine nature.

[5]   Our Lord, furthermore, when arguing His divinity against the Jews who could not bear the fact that He made Himself equal to God, asserts that there is in Him a power of raising to life. He says in John (5:21): "As the Father raiseth up the dead and giveth life, so the Son also giveth life to whom He will." The power of raising to life, of course, belongs to the Holy Spirit; as the Apostle says: "If the Spirit of Him that raised up Jesus from the dead dwell in you; He that raised up Jesus Christ from the dead shall quicken also your mortal bodies, because of His Spirit that dwelleth in you" (Rom. 8:11). Therefore, the Holy Spirit is of the divine nature.

2. Cf. St. Augustine, De Trinitate, I, 6, 13 (PL, 42, col. 828).

[6] Again, creation is the work of God alone, as was shown above.[3] But creation belongs to the Holy Spirit; as the Psalmist says: "Send forth Thy Spirit, and they shall be created" (Ps. 103:30); and Job (33:4) says: "The Spirit of God made me"; and Ecclesiasticus (1:9) says of God: "He created her," meaning wisdom, "in the Holy Ghost." Therefore, the Holy Spirit is of the divine nature.

[7] The Apostle says, further: "The Spirit searcheth all things, yea, the deep things of God. For what man knoweth the things of a man but the spirit of a man that is in him? So the things also that are of God no man knoweth, but the Spirit of God" (I Cor. 2:10–11). But to comprehend all the deep things of God is not the act of a creature. And this is clear from our Lord's words: "No one knoweth the Son but the Father, neither doth any one know the Father but the Son" (Matt. 11:27). And Isaias (24:16) says in the person of God: "My secret to Myself." Therefore, the Holy Spirit is not a creature.

[8] What is more, in the comparison by the Apostle just given, the Holy Spirit is to God as the spirit of man is to man. Now, the spirit of man is intrinsic to man and is not extraneous to him in nature, but is of his nature. Therefore, the Holy Spirit as well is not by nature extraneous to God.

[9] If one further compares the just quoted words of the Apostle with those of the Prophet Isaias, he will see clearly that the Holy Spirit is God. For Isaias (64:4) says: "The eye hath not seen, O God, besides Thee, what things Thou hast prepared for them that wait for Thee." And the Apostle, indeed, when he had introduced these words (I Cor. 2:9) adds the words just mentioned, to wit, that "the Spirit searcheth the deep things of God" (I Cor. 2:9–10). Manifestly, therefore, the Holy Spirit knows those deep things of God "which He has prepared for those that wait for Him." Therefore, if none sees these besides God, as Isaias says, clearly the Holy Spirit is God.

[10] Isaias, once again (6:8–9), says: "I heard the voice of God saying: Whom shall I send? And I said: Lo, here am I, send me. And He said: Go, and thou shalt say to His people:

3. *SCG*, II, ch. 21.

Hearing, hear, and understand not." Now, Paul ascribes these words to the Holy Spirit; and thus we are told that Paul said to the Jews: "Well, did the Holy Ghost speak . . . by Isaias the Prophet, saying: Go to this people and say to them: With the ear you shall hear and shall not understand" (Acts 28:25–26). Manifestly, therefore, the Holy Spirit is God.

[11] It is further apparent from sacred Scripture that it is God who speaks by the Prophets. For from the mouth of God, Numbers (12:6) says: "If there be among you a prophet of the Lord, I will appear to him in a vision, or I will speak to him in a dream." And a Psalm (84:9) says: "I will hear what the Lord God will speak in me." But it is plain to see that the Holy Spirit has spoken in the Prophets. One reads in Acts (1:16): "The Scripture must needs be fulfilled, which the Holy Ghost spoke before by the mouth of David." And in Matthew[4] our Lord says: "How do the scribes say that Christ is the son of David. For David himself sayeth by the Holy Ghost: The Lord said to my Lord: Sit thou at My right hand." And in II Peter (1:21) we read: "For prophecy came not by the will of man at any time, but the holy men of God spoke, inspired by the Holy Ghost." Therefore, one plainly gathers from the Scriptures that the Holy Spirit is God.

[12] Again, that the revelation of mysteries is a proper work of God is shown in Scripture, for in Daniel (2:28) it says: "There is a God in heaven that revealeth mysteries." But the revelation of mysteries is seen to be a work of the Holy Spirit, for we read in I Corinthians (2:10; 14:2): "To us God hath revealed them, by his Spirit"; and: "By the Spirit He speaketh mysteries." The Holy Spirit, therefore, is God.

[13] What is more, to teach within is a proper work of God, for the Psalmist says of God: "He that teacheth man knowledge" (93:10); and Daniel (2:21): "He giveth wisdom to the wise, and knowledge to them that have understanding." But that such is the proper work of the Holy Spirit is plain, for our Lord speaks in John (14:26): of "the Paraclete, the Holy Ghost whom the Father will send in My name: He will teach

---

4. This is Mark 12:35–36, and one of St. Thomas' very rare slips, but no great one; cf. Matt. 22:41–44.

you all things." The Holy Spirit, therefore, is of the divine nature.

[14] Furthermore, those who are identical in operation must be identical in nature. But the operation of the Son and the Holy Spirit is identical. For Christ speaks in the saints, as the Apostle shows in the words of II Corinthians (13:3): "Do you seek a proof of Christ that speaketh in me?" This also plainly appears to be a work of the Holy Spirit, for we read in Matthew (10:20): "It is not you that speak, but the Spirit of your Father who speaketh in you." There is, then, an identical nature in the Son and the Holy Spirit and, consequently, the Father, since it has been shown that the Father and Son are one nature.[5]

[15] Moreover, to dwell in the minds of the saints is the proper work of God, and so the Apostle says: "You are the temple of the living God; as God saith: I will dwell in them" (II Cor. 6:16). But the Apostle attributes the same thing to the Holy Spirit, for he says: "Know you not that you are the temple of God, and that the Spirit of God dwelleth in you?" (I Cor. 3:16). Therefore, the Holy Spirit is God.

[16] Once again, to be everywhere is proper to God, who says in Jeremias (23:24): "I fill heaven and earth." This belongs to the Holy Spirit, for we read in Wisdom (1:7): "The Spirit of the Lord hath filled the whole world," and the Psalmist says: "Whither shall I go from Thy Spirit? Or whither shall I flee from Thy face? If I ascend into heaven, Thou art there," and so forth (Ps. 138:7–8). Our Lord also says to the disciples: "You shall receive the power of the Holy Ghost coming upon you, and you shall be witnesses unto Me in Jerusalem, and in all Judea, and Samaria, and even to the uttermost parts of the earth" (Acts 1:8), from which it is clear that the Holy Spirit is everywhere; He dwells in those existing in every place. The Holy Spirit, therefore, is God.

[17] There is more. Scripture expressly names the Holy Spirit God, for Peter says: "Ananias, why hath Satan tempted thy heart, that thou shouldst lie to the Holy Ghost?" Later on, he adds: "Thou hast not lied to men, but to God" (Acts 5:3–4). The Holy Spirit, therefore, is God.

5. See above, ch. 11.

[18] We read again, in I Corinthians (14:2, 21): "He that speaketh in a tongue speaketh not unto men, but unto God; for no man heareth. Yet by the Spirit He speaketh mysteries," from which he gives one to understand that the Holy Spirit was speaking in those who spoke with different tongues. Later on, of course, he says: "In the Law it is written: In other tongues and other lips I will speak to this people; and neither so will they hear me, saith the Lord." Therefore, the Holy Spirit who speaks mysteries with diverse lips and tongues is God.

[19] Furthermore, after a bit, this is added: "If all prophesy, and there come in one that believeth not, or an unlearned person, he is convinced of all, he is judged of all. The secrets of his heart are made manifest; and so, falling down on his face, he will adore God, affirming that God is among you indeed" (I Cor. 14:24–25). Clearly, of course, from what he had previously set down, "the Spirit speaketh mysteries," the manifestation of the secrets of the heart is from the Holy Spirit. And this is a proper mark of divinity, for we read in Jeremias (17:9–10): "The heart of man is perverse . . . and inscrutable, who can know it? I am the Lord who search the heart and prove the reins." And so from this indication even an unbeliever (cf. I Cor. 14:24) is said to consider carefully that He who speaks these secrets of hearts is God. Therefore, the Holy Spirit is God.

[20] Again, a bit later, the Apostle says: "The spirits of the prophets are subject to the prophets. For God is not the God of dissension, but of peace" (I Cor. 14:32–33). Of course, the graces of the Prophets which he named "the spirits of the prophets" are from the Holy Spirit. Therefore, he shows that the Holy Spirit who distributes graces of this kind in such wise that from them follows not dissension but peace is God by these words: "God is not the God of dissension, but of peace."

[21] Furthermore, to adopt as sons can be the work of no other than God. For no spiritual creature is called son of God by nature, but by the grace of adoption. Hence, the Apostle attributes this work to the Son of God who is true God: "God sent His Son that we might receive the adoption of sons"

(Gal. 4:4–5). But the Holy Spirit is the cause of the adoption, as the Apostle says: "You have received the spirit of adoption of sons, whereby we cry: Abba (Father)" (Rom. 8:15). Therefore, the Holy Spirit is not a creature, but God.

[22] Again, if the Holy Spirit is not God, He must be a creature. Plainly enough, He is not a bodily creature. And neither is He a spiritual creature, for no creature is infused into a spiritual creature, since a creature is not participable, but rather participating. The Holy Spirit, of course, is infused into the minds of the saints, as it were participated by them, for we read that Christ was full of Him (Luke 4:1) and even the Apostles (Acts 2:4). The Holy Spirit, therefore, is not a creature but God.

[23] But, if one says that the aforesaid works which are God's are not attributed to the Holy Spirit in principalship as to God, but in ministry as it were to a creature, he says what is expressly false. And this is clear from the words of the Apostle: "There are diversities of operations, but the same God, who worketh all in all." Afterwards, when the Apostle had enumerated the different gifts of God, he adds: "All these things one and the same Spirit worketh, dividing to every one according as He will" (I Cor. 12:6, 11). Therein clearly he has set forth that the Holy Spirit is God: not only by saying that the Holy Spirit performs the works which he said before that God performs, but also by proclaiming that the Holy Spirit performs them according to a decision of His will. Manifestly, therefore, the Holy Spirit is God.

Chapter 18.

THAT THE HOLY SPIRIT IS A SUBSISTENT PERSON

[1] But, since some assert that the Holy Spirit is not a subsistent person, but, rather, the divinity of the Father and the Son (so some Macedonians are held to have said);[1] or even an accidental perfection of the mind bestowed on us by God—wisdom, for instance, or charity or something of this sort (and these are participated by us as certain created accidents); one

---

1. St. Augustine, *De haeresibus*, 52 (*PL*, 42, col. 39).

must on the contrary show that the Holy Spirit is nothing of this kind.

[2] For accidental forms have no proper operations; instead, one has *them* in accord with the decision of his will, for the wise man uses wisdom when he wills. But the Holy Spirit operates in accord with the decision of His will. This has been shown.[2] One must not, therefore, think of the Holy Spirit as an accidental perfection of the mind.

[3] The Holy Spirit, again, so we are taught by Scripture, is the cause of all the perfections of the human mind. For the Apostle says: "The charity of God is poured forth in our hearts, by the Holy Ghost, who is given to us" (Rom. 5:5); and: "To one indeed, by the Spirit, is given the word of wisdom, and to another, the word of knowledge, according to the same Spirit" (I Cor. 12:8), and so of the rest. The Holy Spirit, therefore, must not be thought of as an accidental perfection of the human mind, since He is, of all perfections of this kind, the existing cause.

[4] Of course, that in the name of the Holy Spirit the essence of the Father and Son is designated so as to be personally distinguished from *neither* of them conflicts with what divine Scripture hands on to us about the Holy Spirit. It says that the Holy Spirit "proceedeth from the Father" and that He receives from the Son (John 15:26; 16:14). And this cannot be understood of the divine essence, since the divine essence neither proceeds from the Father nor receives from the Son. One must, then, say that the Holy Spirit is a subsisting Person.

[5] Again, sacred Scripture manifestly speaks of the Holy Spirit as of a subsisting divine person, for it says: "As they were ministering to the Lord, and fasting, the Holy Ghost said to them: "Separate Me Saul and Barnabas, for the work whereunto I have taken them"; and later: "So they, being sent by the Holy Ghost, went" (Acts 13:2). And in Acts (15:28) the Apostles say: "It hath seemed good to the Holy Ghost and to us, to lay no further burden upon you," and so forth; and these things would not be said of the Holy Spirit if He

2. See above, ch. 17, ¶23.

were not a subsistent person. The Holy Spirit is, therefore, a subsistent person.

[6] Furthermore, since the Father and Son are subsisting persons and of the divine nature, the Holy Spirit would not be numbered along with them unless He also were a person subsisting in the divine nature. He is numbered with them, of course. This is clear from Matthew (28:19), where our Lord says to the disciples: "Going, therefore, teach ye all nations; baptizing them in the name of the Father, and of the Son, and of the Holy Spirit"; and from II Corinthians (13:13): "The grace of our Lord Jesus Christ, and the charity of God, and the communication of the Holy Ghost be with you all"; and from I John (5:7): "There are three who give testimony in heaven, the Father, the Word, and the Holy Ghost." From this it shows clearly that He is not only a subsistent person like the Father and the Son, but has unity of essence with Them.

[7] One could, of course, calumniate against the foregoing, saying that the "Spirit of God" is one thing and the "Holy Spirit" another. To be sure, in certain of the authorities set down, the "Spirit of God" is named, and in certain others "the Holy Spirit," but the identity of the "Spirit of God" and "the Holy Spirit" is clearly shown from the words of the Apostle, when he had premised: "God hath revealed them, by His Spirit," by way of confirmation he says: "the Spirit searcheth all things, yea, the deep things of God"; and finally he concludes: "so the things also that are of God no man knoweth, but the Spirit of God" (I Cor. 2:10–11). From this there is manifestly apparent the identity of the Holy Spirit and the Spirit of God.

[8] The same point is apparent from this: our Lord says in Matthew (10:20): "It is not you that speak but the Spirit of your Father that speaketh in you." But in place of these words Mark says (13:11): "It is not you that speak, but the Holy Spirit." Manifestly, the Holy Spirit is the same as the Spirit of God.

[9] Since from the authorities set down it is clear in so many ways that the Holy Spirit is not a creature, but true God, it is accordingly manifest that we are not compelled to say that

one must understand the Holy Spirit filling and dwelling in the minds of the saints in the same way that one understands the devil to be filling and dwelling in some minds. One finds in John (13:27): "After the morsel, Satan entered into him"; and in Acts (5:3) Peter says—so some books have it: "Ananias, why hath Satan tempted thy heart?" For, since the devil is a creature, as was manifested in the foregoing,[3] he fills no one by a participation in himself, and he cannot dwell in a mind through his substance; rather, he is said to fill some men by the effect of his wickedness. Hence, Paul says to a certain one: "O full of all guile and of all deceit" (Acts 13:10). The Holy Spirit, of course, since He is God, dwells in a mind by His substance and makes men good by participation in Himself. For He is His own goodness, since He is God. And this can be true of no creature. Neither does this, for all that, change the fact that by the effect of His power He fills the minds of the holy.

Chapter 19.

HOW ONE MUST UNDERSTAND WHAT
IS SAID ABOUT THE HOLY SPIRIT

[1] Taught by holy Scripture, therefore, we maintain this firmly about the Holy Spirit: that He is true God, subsistent, personally distinct from the Father and the Son. But one ought to consider how a truth of this kind must be grasped somehow, in order to defend it from the attacks of unbelievers.

[2] To get at the evidence one must first premise that in every intellectual nature a will must be discovered. For an intellect is made to be in act by an intelligible form so far as it is understanding, as a natural thing is made to be in act in its natural being by its proper form. But a natural thing, through the form by which it is perfected in its species, has an inclination to its proper operations and to its proper end, which it achieves by operations, "for as everything is so does it operate,"[1] and it tends to what is fitting for itself. Hence, also, from an intelligible form there must follow in one who

3. SCG, II, ch. 15.
1. Aristotle, Nicomachean Ethics, III, 5, (1114a32–b1).

understands an inclination to his proper operations and his proper end. Of course, this inclination in an intellectual nature is the will, which is the principle of operations in us, those by which he who understands operates for an end. For end and the good are the will's object. One must, therefore, discover a will in everyone who understands.

[3] Although several acts seem to belong to the will, to desire, to delight in, to hate, and others of this kind, nevertheless for all of these love is found to be the one principle and the common root. This can be gathered from the following points. The will, as was said, is related to intellectual things as natural inclination to natural things (this is also called natural appetite). But natural inclination arises thus: The natural thing has an affinity and correspondence from its form (which we have called the principle of the inclination) with that to which it is moved. The heavy has such a relation with the lower place. Hence, also, every inclination of the will arises from this: by an intelligible form a thing is apprehended as suitable or affective. To be affected toward something—so far as it is of this kind—is to love that thing. Therefore, every inclination of will and even of sensible appetite has its origin from love. For from the fact that we love something we desire that thing if it be absent; we rejoice, of course, if it be present; and we are sad when we are kept from it; and we hate those things which keep us from the beloved, and grow angry against them.

[4] Thus, then, what is loved is not only in the intellect of the lover, but in his will as well; but in one way and another. It is in the intellect by reason of the likeness of its species; it is in the will of the lover, however, as the term of a movement is in its proportioned motive principle by reason of the suitability and proportion which the term has for that principle. Just so, in a certain way, there is in fire the upper place by reason of that lightness which gives it proportion and suitability to such a place, but the fire which is generated is in the fire which generates by reason of the likeness of its form.

[5] Since, then, it has now been shown that in every intellectual nature there is will, and that God, of course, is intelligent was shown in Book I[2], there must, then, be will

2. *SCG*, I, ch. 44.

in Him; the will of God, to be sure, is not something which
accrues to His essence, just as His intellect is not, as was
shown above[3], but the will of God is His very substance. And
since the intellect of God, as well, is His very substance, it
follows that the one thing in God is intellect and will. However, the manner in which what in other things are many things
in God are one thing can be manifest from the points made
in Book I.[4]

[6]   And because it was shown in Book I[5] that the operation
of God is His very essence, and that the essence of God is
His will[6], it follows that will is not in God by way of potency,
or of habit, but by way of act. It was shown, of course, that
every act of will is rooted in love. Hence, in God there must
be love.

[7]   And because, as was shown in Book I[7], the proper object
of the divine will is His goodness, necessarily it is first and
principally His goodness and Himself that God loves. But,
since it has been shown that the beloved must somehow be
in the will of the lover, and that God Himself loves Himself,
it needs must be that God Himself is in His will as the beloved in the lover. But the beloved is in the lover so far as it
is loved—an act of love, of course, is a kind of act of will—
but the act of will of God is His being, just as His will is
His being. Therefore, the being of God in His will by way of
love is not an accidental one—as it is in us—but is essential
being. And so it must be that God, when He is considered
existing in His own will, is truly and substantially God.

[8]   But a thing's being in the will as a beloved in a lover
bears a certain order to the conception by which the intellect
conceives the thing, and to the thing itself whose intellectual
conception is called a word. For it would not be loved unless
it were somehow known; neither is the beloved's knowledge
alone loved, but the beloved as good in itself. Necessarily,
therefore, does the love by which God is in the divine will
as a beloved in a lover proceed both from the Word of God
and from the God whose Word He is.

[9]   Now, since it has been shown that the beloved is not

---

3. SCG, I, ch. 45 and 73.   4. SCG, I, ch. 31.   5. SCG, I, ch. 45.
6. SCG, I, ch. 73.   7. SCG, I, ch. 74.

in the lover by a likeness of species, as the thing understood is present in the one understanding, whereas whatever proceeds from another as one generated does proceed by a likeness of species from the generator, this follows: A thing's proceeding in order to be in the will as the beloved is in the lover is *not* a proceeding by way of generation, just as a thing's proceeding in order to be in the intellect does have the essentials of generation, as was shown above.[8] Therefore, God proceeding by way of love does not proceed as begotten. And He, therefore, cannot be called Son.

[10] But, because the beloved in the will exists as inclining, and somehow inwardly impelling the lover toward the very thing beloved, and an impulse of a living thing from within belongs to a spirit, this is suitable: that God proceeding by way of love be called His "spirit," as it were a kind of existing spiration.

[11] Hence it is that the Apostle attributes to the Spirit and to Love a kind of impulse; for he says in Romans (8:14): "Whosoever are led by the Spirit of God, they are the sons of God," and: "The charity of Christ presseth us" (II Cor. 5:14).

[12] However, since every intellectual motion is named from its term, and the love aforesaid is that by which God Himself is loved, quite fittingly is God proceeding by way of love called "Holy Spirit"; for the things assigned to God have customarily been called "holy."

Chapter 20.

ON THE EFFECTS ATTRIBUTED TO THE HOLY SPIRIT
IN SCRIPTURE REGARDING THE WHOLE CREATION

[1] One must, of course, in harmony with what has been said, give thought to the effects which sacred Scripture attributes to the Holy Spirit.

[2] For it was shown in the foregoing[1] that the goodness of God is His reason for willing that other things be, and that by His will He produces things in being. The love, then, by which He loves His own goodness is the cause of the creation

8. See above, ch. 11.　　　　　1. *SCG*, I, ch. 75.

of things: whence, even certain ancient philosophers held that "the love of the gods" is the cause of all things as is plain in *Metaphysics* I;[2] and Dionysius says that "the divine love did not allow itself to be without seed."[3] But it was held in the preceding[4] that the Holy Spirit proceeds by way of the love by which God loves Himself. Therefore, the Holy Spirit is the principle of the creation of things. And this is signified in the word of the Psalmist: "Send forth Thy Spirit, and they shall be created" (Ps. 103:30).

[3] It is also from the fact that the Holy Spirit proceeds by way of love—and love has a kind of driving and moving force—that the movement which is from God in things seems properly to be attributed to the Holy Spirit. Of course, the first existing mutation in things from God is understood to be this: He produced the different species out of formless created matter. Hence, this work is what sacred Scripture attributes to the Holy Spirit. For we read in Genesis (1:2): "The Spirit of God moved over the waters." For by "waters" Augustine wants one to understand prime matter[5] over which the Spirit of the Lord is said to be borne, not as though He Himself is moved, but because He is the principle of the movement.

[4] Again, the government of things by God is understood to be according to a kind of motion, in that God directs and moves all things to their proper ends. If, then, drive and motion belong to the Holy Spirit by reason of love, the government and propagation of things is fittingly attributed to the Holy Spirit. Hence Job (33:4) says: "The Spirit of God made me"; and the Psalmist: "Thy good spirit shall lead me into the right land" (Ps. 142:10).

[5] And because a master's proper act is to govern subjects, dominion is fittingly attributed to the Holy Spirit, for the Apostle says: "Now the Lord is a Spirit" (II Cor. 3:17); and the Creed of our faith says: "I believe in the Holy Spirit, the Lord."

2. Aristotle, *Metaphysics*, I, 4 (984b 23–29).
3. Pseudo-Dionysius, *De divinis nominibus*, 4 (*PG*, 3, col. 708b).
4. See above, ch. 19.
5. St. Augustine, *De genesi ad litteram*, I, 15 (*PL*, 34, col. 240).

[6] Life also is especially manifested in motion, for we say that self-moving things *live* and in general we say this of everything which puts itself into operation. If, then, by reason of love, drive and motion are suited to the Holy Spirit, life is also suitably attributed to Him. For John (6:64) says: "It is the Spirit that quickeneth"; and Ezechiel (37:5): "I will send Spirit into you, and you shall live"; and in the Creed of our faith we profess to believe in the Holy Spirit, "the giver of life."[6] This also harmonizes with the name "Spirit," for even the bodily life of animals is due to a vital spirit diffused from the principle of life into the rest of the members.

Chapter 21.

ON THE EFFECTS ATTRIBUTED TO THE HOLY SPIRIT
IN SCRIPTURE REGARDING THE RATIONAL CREATURE,
SO FAR AS GOD'S GIFTS TO US ARE CONCERNED

[1] Looking to the effects which He properly produces in the rational nature, we must also give consideration to this fact: When we are somehow made like a divine perfection, perfection of this kind is said to be given us by God; so wisdom is said to be a gift from God to us when we are somehow made like the divine wisdom. Since, then, the Holy Spirit proceeds by way of the love by which God loves Himself, as was shown,[1] from the fact that in loving God we are made like to this love, the Holy Spirit is said to be given to us by God. Hence the Apostle says: "The charity of God is poured forth in our hearts, by the Holy Ghost, who is given to us" (Rom. 5:5).

[2] One should realize, for all that, that what is in us from God is related to God as to an efficient and as to an exemplar cause. We say as to an efficient cause inasmuch as something is accomplished in us by the divine operative power. We say as to an exemplar cause so far as we are, thanks to that in us which is from God, imitating God. Since, then, the power

6. The Nicene Creed, 'Credo in Spiritum sanctum, Dominum et vivificantem,' from the Ordinary of the Mass.
1. See above, ch. 19.

of the Father, and of the Son, and of the Holy Spirit is identical just as the essence is, necessarily whatever God effects in us must be, as from an efficient cause, simultaneously from the Father and the Son and the Holy Spirit. Nevertheless, the "word of wisdom" (cf. Dan. 1:20) by which we know God, and which God sends into us, is properly representative of the Son. And in like fashion the love by which we love God is properly representative of the Holy Spirit. And thus the charity which is in us, although it is an effect of the Father, the Son, and the Holy Spirit, is nonetheless for a special sort of reason said to be in us through the Holy Spirit.

[3] However the divine effects not only begin to be by the divine operation, by it they are also maintained in being (as is clear from the foregoing).[2] And nothing operates where it is not, for the agent and that acted upon must be simultaneously in act, just as the mover and the moved.[3] Necessarily, then, wherever there is an effect of God, there God Himself is efficient. Hence, since the charity by which we love God is in us by the Holy Spirit, the Holy Spirit Himself must also be in us, so long as the charity is in us. And so the Apostle says: "Know you not that you are the temple of God, and that the Spirit of God dwelleth in you?" (I Cor. 3:16). Therefore, since we are made lovers of God by the Holy Spirit, and every beloved is in the lover as such, by the Holy Spirit necessarily the Father and the Son dwell in us also. And so our Lord says: "We will come to him"—He means to one who loves God—"and will make our abode with him" (John 14:23). And in I John (3:24) we read: "In this we know that He abideth in us, by the Spirit which He hath given us."

[4] Moreover, God manifestly loves in the greatest degree those whom He has made lovers of Himself through the Holy Spirit, for He would not confer so great a good save by loving us. Hence, we read in Proverbs (8:17) from the Person of God: "I love them that love Me"; "not as though we had loved God, but because He hath first loved us" as we read in I John (4:10). Of course, every beloved is in a lover. Therefore, by the Holy Spirit not only is God in us, but we also are in God. Hence, we read in I John (4:16, 13): "He that abideth in

charity abideth in God, and God in him;" and: "In this we know that we abide in Him and He in us: because He hath given us of His Spirit."

[5] Of course, this is the proper mark of friendship: that one reveal his secrets to his friend. For, since charity unites affections and makes, as it were, one heart of two, one seems not to have dismissed from his heart that which he reveals to a friend; and so our Lord says to His disciples: "I will not now call you servants but friends: because all things whatsoever I have heard of My Father I have made known to you" (John 15:15). Therefore, since by the Holy Spirit we are established as friends of God, fittingly enough it is by the Holy Spirit that men are said to receive the revelation of the divine mysteries. Hence, the Apostle says: "It is written that eye hath not seen, nor ear heard, neither hath it entered into the heart of man, what things God hath prepared for them that love Him. But to us God hath revealed them, by His Spirit" (I Cor. 2:9–10).

[6] It is from the things a man knows that his speech is formed; fittingly, therefore, a man speaks the mysteries through the Holy Spirit. Hence, the words of I Corinthians (14:2): "By the Spirit He speaketh mysteries"; and Matthew (10:20): "It is not you that speak, but the Spirit of your Father that speaketh in you." And of prophets, II Peter (1:21) says that "the holy men of God spoke, inspired by the Holy Ghost." Hence, also, in the Creed of our faith we say of the Holy Spirit: "Who spoke through the prophets."

[7] Now, it is not only proper to love that one reveal his secrets to a friend by reason of their unity in affection, but the same unity requires that what he has he have in common with the friend. For, "since a man has a friend as another self,"[4] he must help the friend as he does himself, making his own possessions common with the friend, and so one takes this as the property of friendship "to will and to do the good for a friend."[5] This agrees with I John (3:17): "He that hath the substance of this world, and shall see his brother in need, and shall shut up his bowels from him: how doth the charity

4. Aristotle, *Nicomachean Ethics*, IX, 4 (1166a 32).
5. *Ibid.* (1166a 3).

of God abide in him?" But such is especially the case with God whose will is efficacious on its effect. Therefore, it is fitting that all the gifts of God are said to be gifts from the Holy Spirit; thus, in I Corinthians (12:8, 11): "To one, indeed, by the Spirit is given the word of wisdom, and to another, the word of knowledge, according to the same Spirit"; and later on, having mentioned many, it says: "One and the same Spirit worketh, dividing to every one according as He will."

[8]   This, too, is manifest: Just as, to get a body to the place of fire, it must be likened to fire by acquiring that lightness according to which fire is moved by its own motion; so also, to get a man to the beatitude of divine enjoyment which is proper to God in His own nature, these are necessary: first, that by spiritual perfections he be likened to God; then, that he operate with these perfections; and thus, lastly, achieve that beatitude we mentioned. Of course, the spiritual gifts are given to us by the Holy Spirit, as was shown. And thus by the Holy Spirit we are configured to God and through Him we are made ready for good operation. And by the same Spirit the road to beatitude is opened to us. The Apostle implies all three of these when he says: "He that confirmeth us . . . is God who also hath sealed us, and given the pledge of the Spirit in our hearts" (II Cor. 1:21, 22). And in Ephesians (1:13, 14): "You were signed with the Holy Spirit of promise, who is the pledge of our inheritance." For the "signing" seems to belong to the likeness of configuration; the "confirming" to man's readiness for perfect operation; the "pledge," of course, to the hope by which we are ordered to the heavenly inheritance, and this is perfect beatitude.

[9]   Further, since out of the good will which one has to another it comes about that he adopt that other as his son—and so the inheritance belongs to that other as adopted—it is fitting that the adoption of the sons of God is attributed to the Holy Spirit; in the words of Romans (8:15): "You have received the Spirit of adoption of sons, whereby we cry: Abba (Father)."

[10]   Of course, by the fact that one is established as the friend of another, every offense is removed, because friendship and offense are contraries. Thus, we read in Proverbs

(10:12): "Charity covereth all sins." Therefore, since we are established as friends of God by the Holy Spirit, it is by Him that God remits our sins, and so our Lord says to His disciples (John 20:22–23): "Receive ye the Holy Ghost. Whose sins you shall forgive, they are forgiven." Therefore, also, in Matthew (12:31) blasphemers against the Holy Spirit are denied the remission of sins, as though they do not have that by which a man achieves the remission of his sins.

[11] Hence, also, it is by the Holy Spirit that we are said to be renewed, and cleansed or washed; as the Psalmist has it: "Send forth Thy Spirit, and they shall be created, and Thou shalt renew the face of the earth" (Ps. 103:30); and Ephesians (4:23): "Be renewed in the Spirit of your mind"; and Isaias (4:4): "If the Lord shall wash away the filth of the sons of Sion and cleanse away the blood of her daughters in the midst by the Spirit of judgment and the Spirit of burning."

Chapter 22.

ON THE EFFECTS ATTRIBUTED TO THE HOLY SPIRIT IN THAT HE MOVES THE CREATURE TO GOD

[1] Now that we have considered the things which are said to be done in us by God through the Holy Spirit, we ought to consider how through the Holy Spirit we are moved to God.

[2] First, indeed, this appears to be especially proper to friendship: really to converse with the friend. Now, the conversation of man with God is by contemplation of Him, just as the Apostle used to say: "Our conversation is in heaven" (Phil. 3:20). Since, therefore, the Holy Spirit makes us lovers of God, we are in consequence established by the Holy Spirit as contemplators of God. Hence, the Apostle says: "But we all beholding the glory of the Lord with open face, are transformed into the same image from glory to glory, as by the Spirit of the Lord" (II Cor. 3:18).

[3] It is also a property of friendship that one take delight in a friend's presence, rejoice in his words and deeds, and find in him security against all anxieties; and so it is especially in our sorrows that we hasten to our friends for consolation.

Since, then, the Holy Spirit constitutes us God's friends, and makes Him dwell in us, and us dwell in Him (as was shown[1]), it follows that through the Holy Spirit we have joy in God and security against all the world's adversities and assaults. And so we read in the Psalmist: "Restore unto me the joy of Thy salvation and strengthen me with Thy lordly Spirit" (Ps. 50:14); and in Romans (14:17): "The kingdom of God is not meat and drink; but justice, and peace, and joy in the Holy Ghost"; and in Acts (9:31): "The church had peace and was edified, walking in the fear of the Lord, and was filled with the consolation of the Holy Ghost." For this reason, too, our Lord calls the Holy Spirit the *Paraclete*, that is, *Comforter*, in John (14:26): "But the Paraclete, the Holy Ghost," and so forth.

[4]   Similarly, too, it is proper to friendship to consent to a friend in what he wills. Of course, the will of God is set forth for us by His precepts. Therefore, it belongs to the love by which we love God that we fulfill His commandments, as the Word in John (14:15) says: "If you love Me, keep My commandments." Hence, since we are established as God's lovers by the Holy Spirit, by Him, too, we are in a way driven to fulfill the precepts of God, as the Apostle's word goes: "Whosoever are led by the Spirit of God, they are the sons of God" (Rom. 8:14).

[5]   For all that, one must bear in mind that the sons of God are driven not as slaves, but as free men. For, since he is free who is for his own sake,[2] we do that freely which we do of our very selves. But this is what we do of our will, but what we do against our will we do not freely but as slaves: be the violence absolute, as when "the whole principle is extrinsic, with the sufferer contributing nothing"[3]—for instance, a man is pushed into motion; or be the violence mixed with the voluntary—for instance, when one wishes to do or to suffer what is less contrary to his will to avoid what is more contrary to it. But the Holy Spirit so inclines us to act that He makes us act voluntarily, in that He makes us lovers of God. There-

1. See above, ch. 21, ¶¶3–4.
2. Aristotle, *Metaphysics*, I, 2 (982b 25).
3. Aristotle, *Nicomachean Ethics*, III, 1 (1110b 1–3).

fore, the sons of God are impelled by the Holy Spirit freely out of love, not slavishly out of fear. Hence, the Apostle says: "You have not received the spirit of bondage again in fear; but the Spirit of adoption of sons" (Rom. 8:15).

[6] The will, of course, is ordered to that which is truly good. But if, by reason of passion or of bad habit or disposition, a man be turned away from that which is truly good, he acts slavishly, in that he is diverted by some extraneous thing, if consideration be given the will's natural order itself. But if one considers the act of the will as inclined to an apparent good, one acts freely when he follows passion or a corrupt habit; he acts slavishly, of course, if while his will remains such he—for fear of a law to the contrary—refrains from that which he wills. Therefore, since the Holy Spirit inclines the will by love toward the true good, to which the will is naturally ordered, He removes both that servitude in which the slave of passion infected by sin acts against the *order* of the will, and that servitude in which, against the movement of his will, a man acts according to the law; its slave, so to say, not its friend. This is why the Apostle says: "Where the Spirit of the Lord is, there is liberty" (II Cor. 3:17); and: "If you are led by the Spirit, you are not under the law" (Gal. 5:18).

[7] Hence it is that the Holy Spirit is said to mortify the deeds of the flesh, inasmuch as a passion of the flesh does not turn us away from the true good, and to this the Holy Spirit orders us by love; hence, we read in Romans (8:13): "If by the Spirit you mortify the deeds of the flesh, you shall live."

Chapter 23.

AN ANSWER TO THE ARGUMENTS GIVEN ABOVE
AGAINST THE DIVINITY OF THE HOLY SPIRIT

[1] One must now answer the arguments previously given,[1] those in which the conclusion seemed to be that the Holy Spirit is a creature, and not God.

[2] In this matter our first consideration must be that the name "spirit" seems to be taken from the respiration of ani-

1. St. Thomas here answers the arguments of ch. 16.

mals, in which with some change air is taken in and expelled. And so the name "spirit" is extended to every impulse and movement of every single airy body; thus, the wind is called a "spirit" in the words of the Psalmist: "Fire, hail, snow, ice, stormy winds which fulfill His word" (Ps. 148:8). Thus, also, the fine vapor diffused through the members for their movements is called "spirit." Again, because air is invisible, the name "spirit" was carried further to all invisible and motive powers and substances. And on this account the sensible soul, the rational soul, the angels, and God are called "spirits"— and properly God proceeding by way of love, because love implies a kind of moving force. Accordingly, one understands the saying of Amos, "creating a spirit," as referring to the wind; so our translation[2] more expressly says, and this is also harmonious with what goes before: "forming mountains." But what Zacharias says about God "creating" or "forming the spirit of man in him" one understands of the human soul. Hence, the conclusion cannot be that the Holy Spirit is a creature.[3]

[3]   In the same way, of course, one cannot from our Lord's saying about the Holy Ghost, "He shall not speak of Himself; but what things soever He shall hear, He shall speak," conclude that the Holy Spirit is a creature.[4] For it was shown that the Holy Spirit is God.[5] Hence, He must have His essence from another, just as we said about the Son of God above.[6] And thus, since in God the knowledge and the power and the operation of God are His essence, in the Son and in the Holy Spirit all the knowledge and power and operation are from another. But the Son's is from the Father only; that of the Holy Spirit is from the Father and from the Son. Therefore, since one of the operations of the Holy Spirit is His speaking in saintly men, as was shown,[7] it is on this score said that "He shall not speak of Himself," since He does not operate of Himself. "To hear," of course, in His case is to receive knowledge, as He does essence, from the Father and the Son; and this because we receive knowledge by hearing, for it is customary in Scripture to deal with things divine in the fashion of things

2. He means of the Septuagint, of course.   3. See above, ch. 16, ¶2.
4. See above, ch. 16, ¶3.   5. See above, ch. 17.
6. See above, ch. 11.   7. See above, ch. 21, ¶6.

human. Nor need one be disturbed by His saying: "He shall hear," speaking of future time, so to say. For the Holy Spirit receives eternally, and the verbs of any tense can be applied to the eternal, because eternity embraces the whole of time.

[4] Following the same points, it is also clear that the sending of the Holy Spirit by the Father and the Son does not justify concluding that He is a creature. For it was said above[8] that in this the Son of God is said to have been sent: that He appeared to men in visible flesh. Thus, He was in a new kind of fashion in the world, a fashion in which previously He had not been—namely, visibly; and for all that He had always been in it invisibly as God. The Son's doing so, of course, was His from the Father, and so in this He is said to have been sent by the Father. Thus, of course, the Holy Spirit visibly appeared: "as a dove" (Matt. 3:16) above Christ at His baptism, or "in tongues of fire" (Acts 2:3) above the Apostles. And, granted He did not become a dove or a fire as the Son became man, He nevertheless did appear in certain signs of His own in visible appearances of this kind; thus, He also in a new kind of fashion—namely, visibly—was in the world. And this presence was His from the Father and the Son; wherefore, He, too, is called sent by the Father and the Son. Yet this indicates not His being the lesser, but His proceeding.

[5] Nevertheless, there is another way in which both the Son and the Holy Spirit are said to be invisibly sent. For from what has been said it is plain that the Son proceeds from the Father by way of the knowledge by which God knows Himself,[9] and that the Holy Spirit proceeds from the Father and the Son by way of the love by which God loves Himself.[10] Hence, as was said,[11] when by the Holy Spirit one is made a lover of God, the Holy Spirit is dwelling within that one, and thus in a new kind of way He is in a man: to wit, dwelling in the man according to a new proper effect. And that the Holy Spirit produce this effect in man is His from the Father and the Son; and on this account He is said to be sent invisibly by the Father and the Son. And reasoning equally, in a human

8. See above, ch. 8.

9. See above, ch. 11.

10. See above, ch. 19.

11. See above, ch. 21.

mind the Son is said to be invisibly sent when a man is in such wise established in the divine knowledge that the love of God comes forth in the man. Hence, clearly, neither does that fashion of being sent indicate in the Son or in the Holy Spirit His being the lesser, but His proceeding from another.[12]

[6]   Similarly, also, the Holy Spirit is not excluded from the Divinity by the occasional connumeration of the Father and the Son without mention of the Holy Spirit, just as the Son is not excluded from the Divinity by occasional mention of the Father without the Son. In this way Scripture tacitly suggests that whatever relating to Divinity is said of one of the Three must be understood of all, because they are one God. Nor is it possible to understand God the Father without a Word and a Love, nor is the converse possible. For this reason, in one of the Three all Three are understood. Hence, mention occasionally is made of the Son on a point common to the Three; such is the case in Matthew (11:27): "Neither doth any one know the Father, but the Son," although both the Father and the Holy Spirit know the Father. In the same way, we read about the Holy Spirit in I Corinthians (2:11): "The things . . . of God no man knoweth, but the Spirit of God," whereas it is certain that from this cognition of Divinity neither the Father nor the Son is excluded.[13]

[7]   Clearly, also, one cannot show that the Holy Spirit is a creature because one finds sacred Scripture saying things about Him which pertain to motion. They must be taken metaphorically. For sometimes, also, sacred Scripture attributes motion to God; for example, Genesis (3:8; 18:21): "When they heard the voice of the Lord God walking in paradise"; and later: "I will go down and see whether they have done according to the cry that is come to Me." Therefore, the saying, "the Spirit of God was borne over the waters," must be understood to be said as the will is said to be borne on the willed, or the love on the beloved. This, also, by the way, some choose not to understand of the Holy Spirit, but of the air which has its natural place above the water, and so it was to indicate its manifold mutation that Scripture said it "was moved over the waters."

12. See above, ch. 16, ¶4.   13. See above, ch. 16, ¶5.

This further saying, "I will pour out My Spirit upon all flesh," must be understood as said of the way in which the Holy Spirit is sent to men by the Father and the Son. This was mentioned.[14] Of course, in the word, "poured out," the abundance of the effect of the Holy Spirit is grasped: He will not be stopped at one but will move on to many, and from these also somehow to others; this is clear when things are "poured out" corporeally.[15]

[8] In like manner, the saying, "I will take of thy Spirit, and will give to them," must not be referred to the essence or person of the Holy Spirit, since He is indivisible. The reference is to His effects, by which He dwells in us, and these can be increased or diminished in a man: not with the result, for all that, that what is subtracted from one is bestowed on another remaining numerically identical (this happens in bodily things), but so that a like thing may increase in one which decreases in another. Nor does this demand that to increase the effect in one it must be subtracted from another, for a spiritual thing can be possessed by many simultaneously without any loss. Hence, concerned with spiritual gifts, one must not understand that something was withdrawn from Moses to be conferred on others; the reference is rather to his act or office, for what the Holy Spirit had previously done through Moses alone He later effected through many.

Thus, also, Eliseus did not beg that the essence or person of the Holy Spirit be increased by duplication, but that the twofold effect of the Holy Spirit which had been in Elias— namely, prophecy and the working of miracles—be also in himself. To be sure, there is no awkwardness in one's participating in the Holy Spirit more abundantly than another, be it by the double or by any other ratio whatever, for the measure in each participant is finite. For all that, Eliseus would not have had the presumption to ask that in a spiritual effect he should be greater than his master.[16]

[9] Again, it is plainly the custom of sacred Scripture to pass over into God a likeness to the passions of the human spirit; we read in the Psalms (105:40–41): "And the Lord was ex-

ceedingly angry with His people." God is said to be angered
by similarity in the effect, for He punishes, which is what the
angered do; so this is added below: "And He delivered them
into the hands of the nations." Thus, the Holy Spirit is said
to be "made sorrowful," for He leaves sinners as those who are
made sorrowful leave those who make them sorrowful.[17]

[10]   It is also the usual manner of speech in sacred Scripture to attribute to God what He does in man; hence, Genesis
(22:12): "Now I know that thou fearest God"—that is, "now
I have made you know." And in this way the Holy Spirit is
said to petition, for He makes others petition; He makes the
love of God be in our hearts; out of this we desire to enjoy
Him, and in our desiring we petition.[18]

[11]   Of course, since the Holy Spirit proceeds by way of the
love by which God loves Himself, and by that same love and
for His own goodness God loves Himself and other things,
manifestly that love pertains to the Holy Spirit, the love by
which God loves us. So, also, does the love by which we love
God, for He makes us lovers of God. This has been explained.[19] It is in regard to each of these loves that "to be
bestowed" is fitting to the Holy Spirit. It is fitting by reason
of the love by which God loves us in that manner of speech
wherein each is said "to give his love" to someone when he
begins to love him. Although there is no one whom God begins to love in time, if one considers the divine will by which
He loves us, there is, nevertheless, an effect of His love caused
in time in the one whom He draws to Himself. It is fitting
to the Holy Spirit by reason of the love by which we love
God, for the Holy Spirit makes this love in us. Hence, in accord with this love, He dwells in us—clearly from what has
been said[20]—and so we possess Him as one whose resources
we enjoy. Now, this is in the Holy Spirit from the Father and
the Son: that by the love which He causes in us He be in
us and be possessed by us. Fittingly, therefore, He is said "to
be bestowed" upon us by the Father and the Son. Nor does
this show Him to be one lesser than the Father and the Son,
but to be one who has His origin from them. He is said also

to be given us even by Himself in that He causes in us the love by which He dwells in us together with the Father and the Son.[21]

[12] Although the Holy Spirit is, of course, true God and has the true divine nature from the Father and the Son, He need not, for all that, be a son. For son is said of one because he is begotten. Hence, if a thing should receive its nature from another not by begetting, but in any other way whatever, it would lack the essential of sonship. If, for example, a man had the power divinely conceded to him to make a man out of some part of his own body, in some exterior fashion as one makes artefacts, the man produced would not be called the son of the producing, for he would not proceed from him by birth. But the procession of the Holy Spirit does not have the essentials of birth (as was shown above[22]). Hence, the Holy Spirit, although He has the divine nature from the Father and the Son, cannot, for all that, be called Their son.[23]

[13] But that in the divine nature alone nature be communicated in several ways is reasonable. For in God alone is His operation His being. Hence, since in Him, as in any intellectual nature, there is an act of understanding and an act of will, that which proceeds in Him by way of understanding as Word, or by way of love and will as Love, must have the divine being and be God. And thus, not only the Son but the Holy Spirit is true God.[24]

[14] Let these, then, be our points about the divinity of the Holy Spirit. But other difficulties about His procession ought to be considered in the light of what has been said about the nativity of the Son.[25]

Chapter 24.

THAT THE HOLY SPIRIT PROCEEDS FROM THE SON

[1] We find some who make this mistake about the procession of the Holy Spirit: they say the Holy Spirit does not pro-

21. See above, ch. 16, ¶10.
23. See above, ch. 16, ¶12.
25. See above, ch. 13–14.
22. See above, ch. 19.
24. See above, ch. 16, ¶13.

ceed from the Son. For this reason we must show that the
Holy Spirit does proceed from the Son.

[2]   It is manifest in sacred Scripture that the Holy Spirit is
the Spirit of the Son, for Romans (8:9) says: "If any man
have not the Spirit of Christ, he is none of His." But that
one might not be able to say that the Spirit that proceeds
from the Father is one, and the Son's Spirit another, it is
shown from the words of the same Apostle that the Holy
Spirit of the Father and of the Son is identified. For the words
just cited, "If any man have not the Spirit of Christ, he is
none of His," the Apostle added after he had said: "If so be
that the Spirit of God dwell in us," and so forth. But one
cannot say that the Holy Spirit is the Spirit of Christ merely
because He had Him as man, according to the words of Luke
(4:1): "Jesus being full of the Holy Ghost, returned from the
Jordan." For one reads in Galatians (4:6): "Because you are
sons, God hath sent the Spirit of His Son into your hearts,
crying: Abba (Father)." The Holy Spirit, therefore, makes us
the sons of God precisely because He is the Spirit of the Son
of God. But we are made the adoptive sons of God by assimila-
tion to the natural Son of God, as Romans (8:29) has it:
"Whom He foreknew, He also predestined to be made conformable to the image of His Son, that He might be the first-
born amongst many brethren." Thus, then, is the Holy Spirit
the Spirit of Christ: so far as He is God's natural Son. But
there is no relation in accord with which the Holy Spirit can
be called the Spirit of the Son of God except a relation of
origin, for this is the only distinction we find in divinity.
Therefore, one must say that the Holy Spirit is the Son's
Spirit by proceeding from Him.

[3]   The Holy Spirit, again, is sent by the Son; consider John
(15:26): "When the Paraclete cometh, whom I will send you
from the Father." But whoever sends has an authority over
the one sent. One must, then, say that the Son has an authority in regard to the Holy Spirit: not, of course, that of being
master or being greater, but in accord with origin only. In this
wise, then, the Holy Spirit is from the Son. Now, let one say
that the Son is sent by the Holy Spirit as well, because we
read in Luke (4:18–21) that our Lord said Isaias' words

(61:1) were fulfilled in Him: "The Spirit of the Lord is upon Me, He hath sent Me to preach the gospel to the poor." But consideration must be given this: the Son is sent by the Holy Spirit in accord with the assumed nature. But the Holy Spirit has not assumed a created nature, so that in accord with it He can be called sent by the Son, or so as to give the Son authority in His regard. Therefore, this remains: it is considered as an eternal person that the Son has authority over the Holy Spirit.

[4] There is more. In John (16:14–15), the Son says of the Holy Spirit: "He shall glorify Me because He shall receive of Mine." Of course, this cannot be said: He receives what is the Son's, but does not receive from the Son; by saying, for instance, that He receives the Son's divine essence *from* the Father. Hence, our Lord adds: "All things whatsoever the Father hath are mine. Therefore, I said that He shall receive of Mine." For, if all things which are the Father's are the Son's as well, the Father's authority as principle of the Holy Spirit must be the Son's as well. Therefore, just as the Holy Spirit receives what is the Father's from the Father, so He receives what is the Son's from the Son.

[5] Here one can also introduce the testimonies of the Doctors of the Church, the Greeks included. Athanasius says: "The Holy Spirit is from the Father and the Son—not made, not created, not begotten, but proceeding."[1] Cyril, too, in his epistle received by the Council of Chalcedon,[2] says: "The Spirit of the truth is named and is the Spirit of the Truth and flows from Him just as, indeed, from God the Father"[3] Didymus also says in his book *On the Holy Spirit:* "The Son is nothing else than what is given to Him by the Father, and the substance of the Holy Spirit is no other than that given Him by the Son."[4] Of course, it is ridiculous that some concede that the Holy Spirit "is from the Son" or "flows from the Son," but does not "proceed from Him." For the verb "to proceed," among all those which refer to origin, turns up most

1. This is cited from the liturgical Athanasian Creed.
2. Cf. Philip Hughes, *A Popular History of the Catholic Church* (New York, Image Books, 1954), pp. 31–40.
3. St. Cyril, *Epistola XVII ad Nestorium* (PG, 77, col. 117).
4. St. Jerome's translation, n. 37 (PL, 23, col. 141).

commonly; for, if anything is in any way at all from something, we say it proceeds from that thing. And since divinity is better designated by what is common than by what is special, in the origin of the divine persons the verb *proceeding* is the most suitable. And so, if one concedes that the Holy Spirit "is from the Son" or "flows from the Son," it follows that "He proceeds from the Son."

[6]   There is this, too, in the determination of the Fifth Council: "In all matters we follow the holy Fathers and Doctors of the Church: Athanasius, Hilary, Basil, Gregory the theologian, and Gregory of Nyssa, Ambrose, Augustine, Theophilus, John of Constantinople, Cyril, Leo, Proclus; and we accept what they have set down on the correct belief and the condemnation of heretics."[5] But it is manifest from many testimonies of Augustine, especially his *On the Trinity* and his *Exposition of John*, that the Holy Spirit is from the Son. It must, then, be conceded that the Holy Spirit is from the Son just as He is from the Father.

[7]   This is also clarified by straight reasoning. For among things, with the material distinction gone (and in the divine Persons such can have no place), one discovers no differentiation except by some opposition. For things which have no opposition to one another can be simultaneously in something identical; thus, no distinction can be caused by them. Take white and triangular. Although they are diverse, they can, because they are not opposed, be in an identical thing. But one must set down, according to the documents of the Catholic faith, that the Holy Spirit is distinct from the Son; otherwise, there would not be a Trinity, but a duality of Persons. Therefore, a distinction of this kind must take place through some opposition. But it is not the opposition of affirmation and negation,[6] for such is the distinction of being from non-being. Nor is it the opposition of privation and habit, for such is the distinction of the perfect from the imperfect. Neither is it the opposition of contrariety, for such is the distinction of diversity of form. For contrariety as philosophers[7] teach, is a "difference following on form." And this difference is not suited

5. For the text see Mansi, *Amplissima Collectio*, tom. IX, col. 183.
6. Aristotle, *Categories*, 10 (13b 1).
7. Aristotle, *Metaphysics*, X, 10 (1058b 26).

to the divine Persons, since their form is one, just as their essence is. Hence, the Apostle says, speaking of the Son, "being in the form of God" (Phil. 2:6), the form, namely, of the Father.

Therefore, the conclusion remains that one divine Person is not distinguished from another except by the opposition of relation: thus, the Son is distinguished from the Father consequently to the relative opposition of father and son. It is because in the divine Persons there can be no relative opposition except, consequently, on origin. For a relative opposition is founded on quantity—say the double or the half; or on action and passion—say master and servant, mover and moved, father and son. Further, among the relative oppositions founded on quantity, some are founded on diversity of quantity—say the double and the half, the greater and the lesser; some on unity itself—say identity, which means one in substance, and equality, which means one in quantity, and similarity, which means one in quality. The divine Persons, therefore, cannot be distinguished by relations founded on diversity of quantity, because this would take away the equality of the three Persons. Nor, again, by the relations which are founded on unity, because relations of this kind cause no distinction; rather, in them one finds more of what pertains to agreement, although some of them may presuppose a distinction. In all relations founded on action and passion, however, there is always one of the two which is a subject and unequal in power to the other; here, exception is made only for the relations of origin, and in such there is no lesser indicated, because one finds there something producing that which is similar and equal to itself in nature and power. The conclusion, therefore, must be that the divine Persons cannot be distinguished except by relative opposition in origin. Therefore, if the Holy Spirit is distinguished from the Son, He is necessarily *from* the Son, for we do not say that the Son is from the Holy Spirit, since the Holy Spirit is, rather, said to be *of* the Son and given *by* the Son.

[8] Again, the Son is from the Father and so is the Holy Spirit. Therefore, the Father must be related both to the Son and the Holy Spirit as a principle to that which is from the principle. He is related to the Son by reason of paternity, but

not to the Holy Spirit; for then the Holy Spirit would be the Son, because paternity is not said except of a son. There must, then, be another relation in the Father by which He is related to the Holy Spirit; and *spiration* is its name. In the same way, since there is in the Son a relation by which He is related to the Father, the name of which is sonship, there must also be in the Holy Spirit another relation by which He is related to the Father, and this is called *procession.* And thus, in accord with the origin of the Son from the Father, there are two relations, one in the originator, the other in the originated: to wit, paternity and sonship; and there are two others in reference to the Holy Spirit: to wit, spiration and procession. Therefore, paternity and spiration do not constitute two Persons, but pertain to the one Person of the Father, for they have no opposition to one another. Therefore, neither would sonship and procession constitute two persons, but would pertain to one, unless they had an opposition to one another. But there is no opposition to assign save that by way of origin. Hence, there must be an opposition of origin between the Son and the Holy Spirit so that the one is from the other.

[9]   What is more, when things come together by something common to them, they must, if they are to be distinguished, be distinguished by differences which belong *per se* and not accidentally to that common thing. Thus, man and horse meet in *animal,* and are distinguished from one another not by black and white, which are related accidentally to animal, but by rational and irrational, which are *per se* pertinent to animal. This is because animal is what has soul [*animam*], and this must be distinguished by having this or that kind of soul—say, rational or irrational. Now, manifestly, the Son and the Holy Spirit agree in their *being from another,* since each is from the Father. And in this the Father suitably differs from each, in that He can have no birth-origin [*innascibilis*]. Therefore, if the Holy Spirit be distinguished from the Son, this must take place by differences which *per se* divide this *being from another.* And such, indeed, can only be differences of the same genus—namely, pertaining to origin—so that one of them is from the other. One concludes, then, that the distinction of the Holy Spirit from the Son requires that He be from the Son.

[10]   Let one say, further, that the Holy Spirit is distin-

guished from the Son not because He is from the Son, but by reason of their differing origin from the Father. The difficulty really returns to the same point, for, if the Holy Spirit is other than the Son, the origin or procession of each must be other. But two origins cannot be distinguished except by term, or by principle, or by subject. Thus, the origin of a horse differs from the origin of a cow by way of term, in that these two origins have their terms in natures diverse in species. There is difference by way of principle if we suppose that some animals in the same species are generated by the active power of the sun alone, and some others along with this power by the active power of the seed. There is difference by way of subject when the generation of this horse differs from that as the nature of the species is received in diverse matters. But this distinction on the part of subject can have no place in the divine Persons, since they are entirely immaterial. In the same way, also, on the part of the term, granting one may speak so, there can be no distinction of processions. For the divine nature, one and the same, which the Son receives by His birth, the Holy Spirit receives by His proceeding. It remains, therefore, that the distinction of each origin can be only on the part of the principle. Manifestly, of course, the principle of the origin of the Son is the Father alone. If, therefore, the principle of the procession of the Holy Spirit is the Father alone, the procession of the Holy Spirit will not be other than the generation of the Son; thus, neither will the Holy Spirit be distinct from the Son. Therefore, that there may be otherness in processions and otherness in those proceeding, one of necessity says that the Holy Spirit is not from the Father alone, but from the Father and the Son.

[11] But, again, if one says that the processions differ in principle, in that the Father produces the Son by way of intellect as Word, and the Holy Spirit by way of will as Love, it will be necessary to say that in accord with a difference of intellect and will in God the Father the two processions and the two proceeding are to be distinguished. Will and intellect in God the Father are not distinguished really, but only rationally, as was shown in Book I.[8] It follows, then, that the two

8. *SCG*, I, ch. 45 and 73.

processions and the two proceeding differ only rationally. Now, things which differ only rationally are predicated of each other: it will be truly said that the divine intellect is the divine will, and conversely. Therefore, it will be true to say that the Holy Spirit is the Son, and conversely. This is the Sabellian impiety.[9] Therefore, it does not suffice for the distinction of the Holy Spirit and the Son to say that the Son proceeds by way of intellect and the Holy Spirit by way of will, unless along with this one says the Holy Spirit is from the Son.

[12] There is more. From the very fact of saying that the Holy Spirit proceeds by way of will and the Son by way of intellect it follows that the Holy Spirit is from the Son. For love proceeds from a word: we are able to love nothing but that which a word of the heart conceives.

[13] Again, if one considers the diverse species of things, a certain order appears in them: the living are above the non-living; animals are above plants; and man is above the other animals. And in each of these, different grades are discovered according to different species; hence, even Plato said that the species of things are numbers,[10] which are varied in species by the addition and subtraction of unity. Hence, in immaterial substances there can be no distinction except that of order. But in the divine Persons who are entirely immaterial there can be no other order than that of origin. Therefore, there are not two Persons proceeding from one, unless one of those proceeds from a second. And thus, necessarily, the Holy Spirit proceeds from the Son.

[14] Moreover, the Father and the Son, unity of essence considered, do not differ save in this: He is the Father and He is the Son. So, anything other than this is common to the Father and the Son. But to be the principle of the Holy Spirit is not included in the notion of paternity and of sonship, for it is one relation by which the Father is Father, and another by which He is the principle of the Holy Spirit, as was said above.[11] Therefore, to be the principle of the Holy Spirit is common to the Father and the Son.

9. See above ch. 5, and ch. 9, ¶7.
10. For the suggestion see Aristotle, *Physics*, VII, 4 (249b 20); for Plato, see *Republic*, VI (511).   11. See above, ¶8.

[15] Furthermore, whenever one thing is not opposed to the essential intelligibility of another, there is no impossibility—unless, perhaps, accidentally—about their coming together. But to be the principle of the Holy Spirit is not contrary to the intelligibility of the Son: not in so far as He is God, because the Father is the principle of the Holy Spirit; nor in so far as He is Son, because the procession of the Holy Spirit is other than that of the Son. It is, of course, not repugnant to have what is from a principle according to one procession be the principle of another procession. It follows, then, that it is not impossible for the Son to be the principle of the Holy Spirit. But that which is not impossible can be. "In divinity being and possibility do not differ."[12] Therefore, the Son is the principle of the Holy Spirit.

Chapter 25.

ARGUMENTS OF THOSE WHO WANT TO SHOW THAT THE HOLY SPIRIT DOES NOT PROCEED FROM THE SON AND THE ANSWERS

[1] There are some, pertinacious in their willful resistance to the truth, who make some points to the contrary which are hardly worth an answer. They say that our Lord, speaking of the procession of the Holy Spirit, says that He proceeds from the Father, without mentioning the Son. So one reads in John (15:26): "When the Paraclete cometh, whom I will send you from the Father, the Spirit of truth, who proceedeth from the Father." Hence, since nothing must be held about God which is not given in Scripture, it must not be said that the Holy Spirit proceeds from the Son.

[2] But this is entirely frivolous. For, by reason of unity of essence, what is said in the Scriptures about one Person ought to be understood of another, unless it is repugnant to His propriety as a Person, and this even if some exclusive phrase is added. For, although it says in Matthew (11:27): "No one knoweth the Son, but the Father," neither the Son nor the Holy Spirit is, for all that, excluded from knowledge of the

12. See Aristotle, *Physics*, III, 4 (203b 30).

Son. Hence, even if it is said in the Gospel that the Holy
Spirit does not proceed from any but the Father, this would
not exclude His proceeding from the Son. For this is not repugnant to the propriety of the Son, as was shown.[1] Neither
is there cause to marvel if our Lord said that the Holy Spirit
proceeds from the Father, saying nothing about Himself; His
custom is to refer everything to His Father from whom He
has whatever He has. Thus, He says in John (7:16): "My
doctrine is not Mine, but His that sent Me." Many things of
this kind are discovered in the words of our Lord which establish in the Father the authority of the principle. And, for all
that, in the passage just mentioned our Lord was not altogether silent about His being the principle of the Holy Spirit.
He called Him "the Spirit of Truth," and He had previously
called Himself "the Truth" (John 14:6).

[3]   They further object that in certain councils one finds it
prohibited under penalty of anathema to add anything to the
Creed ordered by the council. In this, they say, there is no
mention of the procession of the Holy Spirit from the Son.
And so they hold the Latins guilty of anathema because they
have added this to the Creed.

[4]   But such arguments are inefficacious. For the declaration
of the Synod of Chalcedon says that the Fathers gathered at
Constantinople corroborated the doctrine of the Synod of
Nicea.[2] This they did, "not as though to imply that the
doctrine was something less, but to declare by Scriptural testimonies the understanding of the Holy Spirit of their predeces-
sors against those who attempted to reject that understanding." One must say, similarly, that the procession of the Holy
Spirit from the Son is implicitly contained in the Creed of
Constantinople, for the latter says that "He proceeds from the
Father,"[3] and what is understood of the Father must be understood of the Son, as was said.[4] And the authority of the
Roman Pontiff sufficed for this addition; by this authority,
too, all the ancient councils were confirmed.

[5]   They maintain, also, that the Holy Spirit, since He is

---

1. See above, ch. 24, ¶15.
2. See Mansi, *Amplissima Collectio*, tom. VII, col. 114.
3. *Ibid.*, col. 566.   4. See above, ch. 24, ¶14, and ch. 8.

simple, cannot be from two; and that the Holy Spirit, if He proceeds perfectly from the Father, does not proceed from the Son; and other arguments of this sort. These are easy to solve, even if one is but little skilled in theological matters. For the Father and the Son are a single principle of the Holy Spirit by reason of the unity of divine power, and by one production they produce the Holy Spirit; thus, also, the three Persons are one principle of creatures and by one action they produce creatures.

Chapter 26.

THAT THERE ARE BUT THREE PERSONS IN DIVINITY: THE FATHER, THE SON, AND THE HOLY SPIRIT

[1] From what has been said, then, one must hold that in the divine nature three Persons subsist: the Father, the Son, and the Holy Spirit; and that these three are one God, distinguished from one another by relations only. For the Father is distinguished from the Son by the relations of paternity and innascibility; the Son from the Father by the relation of sonship; the Father and the Son from the Holy Spirit by spiration, so to say; and the Holy Spirit from the Father and the Son by the procession of love; by this He proceeds from each of Them.

[2] Beside these three Persons, no fourth in the divine nature can be asserted. For the divine Persons, since they agree in essence, cannot be distinguished except by relation of origin, as is clear.[1] These relations of origin one must understand not as a procession which inclines to what is without— for what proceeds thus is not co-essential with its principle —one must understand them as proceeding within. Of course, a thing which proceeds and remains its own principle is found only in the operation of the intellect and will, as was made clear.[2] Hence, the divine Persons cannot be multiplied save by the requirements of the procession of the intellect and will in God. It is, of course, not possible that there be in God more than one proceeding within His understanding, because

1. See above, ch. 24.   2. See above, ch. 11, 19, and 24.

His act of understanding is one, simple, and perfect, for in understanding Himself He understands all things else. And thus, there can be in God but one proceeding of the Word. In like manner, too, must the proceeding of Love be one only, for the divine will act is one and simple—by loving Himself He loves all things else. Therefore, it is not possible that in God there be more than two Persons proceeding: one by way of intellect, as Word—namely the Son; the other by way of Love, as the Holy Spirit. There is also one Person who does not proceed—namely, the Father. Therefore, in the Trinity there can be only three Persons.

[3]   Again, let the divine Persons be distinguished by proceeding. But the mode of a person in proceeding can be but threefold: namely, to be altogether not proceeding, which is the Father's mode; to be proceeding from one who does not proceed, which is the Son's; to be proceeding from one who proceeds, which is the Holy Spirit's. Therefore, it is impossible to assert more than three Persons.[3]

[4]   We grant, of course, that in other living things relations of origin can be multiplied—for example, in human nature there can be many fathers and many sons—but in the divine nature this is altogether impossible. For sonship, since in one nature it is of one species, cannot be multiplied except by matter or by subject; this is also the case with other forms. Hence, since in God there is neither matter nor subject, and since the relations are themselves subsistent (which is clear from what was said above[4]) it is impossible that there be a plurality of sonships of God. The same reasoning holds for the other Persons. Thus, in God there are only three Persons.

[5]   Of course, an objector may say that in the Son who is perfect God there is infinite intellective power, and thus He can produce a word; in like fashion, since there is in the Holy Spirit infinite goodness which is the principle of communication, He will be able to communicate the divine nature to another person. But such a one ought to consider that the Son is God, as begotten not as begetting; and so the intellective power is in Him as proceeding in the way of the Word, and

3. For the bases see above, ch. 24, especially ¶7 and 10.
4. See above, ch. 14.

not in Him as producing the Word. Similarly, since the Holy Spirit is God as proceeding, there is infinite goodness in Him as the Person receiving, and not in Him as communicating the infinite goodness to another. For the Persons are not distinguished from one another except by relations, as is clear from the things said above.[5] Therefore, all the fullness of divinity is the Son, numerically identical with that in the Father, but with the relation of birth, as it is in the Father with the relation of active generation. Hence, if the relation of the Father be attributed to the Son, all distinction is removed. And the same reasoning holds for the Holy Spirit.

[6]   Now, this divine Trinity has a likeness in the human mind which we can consider. For the mind itself, because it understands itself, conceives within itself a word. And this is nothing but the intelligible intention of the mind, which is called *the mind understood* and exists within the mind. When this mind further loves itself, it produces its very self in the will as beloved. Of course, it does not proceed further within itself, but the cycle is concluded when by love it returns to the very substance from which the proceeding began by the intention understood. The proceeding extends to external effects when from love of itself it proceeds to make something. Thus, three things are discovered in the mind: the mind itself, the source of the proceeding, existing in its nature; and mind conceived in the intellect; and mind beloved in the will. For all that, these three are not one nature, for the mind's act of understanding is not its being; and its will act is neither its being, nor its act of understanding. For this reason, also, the mind understood and the mind beloved are not persons, since they are not subsisting. Even the mind itself existing in its nature is not a person, for it is not the whole which subsists, but a part of the subsistent; namely, of the man.[6]

[7]   Therefore, in our mind one finds a likeness of the divine Trinity in regard to proceeding, "and this multiplies the

5. See above, ch. 14 and 24.
6. This is related to an Augustinian theme, almost an Augustinian commonplace; see *On the Trinity* IX, 3–5. The absence of St. Augustine's name may be because of this very "commonplace" character; see, however, *Summa Theologiae*, II–II, I, 5, and *ad* 2m.

Trinity."[7] For from the exposition this is clear: there is in the divine nature God unbegotten, who is the source of the whole divine proceeding, namely the Father; there is God begotten by way of a word conceived in the intellect, namely the Son; there is God by way of love proceeding, namely the Holy Spirit. Of course, no further proceeding is discovered within the divine nature, but only a proceeding to exterior effects. In this, of course, the mind fails in representing the divine Trinity: the Father and the Son and the Holy Spirit are one in nature, and in each of these the person is perfect, simply because the act of understanding and the act of will are the divine being itself, as was shown.[8] For this reason one considers the divine likeness in man just as one considers the likeness of Hercules in stone: with regard to the representation of form, not with regard to the agreement of nature. And so one says that in the mind of man there is the "image of God"[9] according to the Word: "Let us make man to our image and likeness" (Gen. 1:26).

[8]   One also finds in other things a likeness of the divine Trinity, so far as anything in its substance is one, formed in a kind of species, ordered in some fashion. Just as is clear from the things said,[10] the conception of the intellect in intelligible being is like the species formation in natural being; love, of course, is like the inclination or order in a thing of nature. And so the species of things in nature from afar represent the Son; their order, of course, the Holy Spirit. Accordingly, by reason of the remote and obscure representation in irrational things, one speaks of the "vestige" of the Trinity in them, not of the "image"; so we read in Job (11:7): "Thou wilt comprehend the steps of God," and so forth.

[9]   And this is enough to say about the divine Trinity for the present.

7. Boethius, De Trinitate, 6 (PL, 64, col. 1255A).
8. SCG, I, ch. 45 and 73.
9. See above, ch. 11, especially ¶12, 14, 16, and 18. For other texts in St. Thomas on this doctrine see the translator's "St. Thomas and the Nature of Man," Proceedings of the American Catholic Philosophical Association, 25 (1951), pp. 41–66.
10. See above, ch. 11 and 19.

Chapter 27.

ON THE INCARNATION OF THE WORD ACCORDING TO THE TRADITION OF SCRIPTURE

[1] Since, of course, when divine generation was dealt with above,[1] it was said of the Son of God, our Lord Jesus Christ, that some things belong to Him in His divine nature, and some in that human nature by the assumption of which in time the eternal Son chose to be incarnate, it now remains to speak of the mystery of the Incarnation itself.[2] Indeed, among divine works, this most especially exceeds the reason: for nothing can be thought of which is more marvelous than this divine accomplishment: that the true God, the Son of God, should become true man. And because among them all it is most marvelous, it follows that toward faith in this particular marvel all other miracles are ordered, since "that which is greatest in any genus seems to be the cause of the others."[3]

[2] This marvelous incarnation of God, of course, which divine authority hands down, we confess. For it says in John (1:14): "The Word was made flesh, and dwelt among us." And the Apostle Paul says: "Who being in the form of God, thought it not robbery to be equal with God: But emptied Himself, taking the form of a servant being made in the likeness of men, and in habit found as a man" (Phil. 2:6–7).[4]

[3] This is also shown clearly by the words of our Lord Jesus Christ Himself, since at times He says lowly and human things of Himself, such as: "The Father is greater than I" (John 14:28) and "My soul is sorrowful even unto death" (Matt. 26:38), which become Him in His assumed humanity; but at times He says sublime and divine things, such as: "I and the Father are one" (John 10:30) and "all things whatsoever the Father hath are Mine" (John 16:15), which certainly belong to Him in His divine nature.

1. See especially ch. 4 and 8.
2. See above, ch. 1, and Introduction, pp. 23–28.
3. Aristotle, *Metaphysics*, II, 1 (993b 25).
4. For earlier and later explanations of this important text see F. Prat, S.J., *The Theology of St. Paul*, tr. J. Stoddard (Westminster, Md., 1952), I, 310–325, 456–466.

[4]   Even the things which we read about what our Lord did show this. That He feared, that He was grieved, that He thirsted, that He died: these belong to the human nature. That by His own power He healed the sick, that He raised the dead, that He effectively commanded the elements of the world, that He drove out devils, that He forgave sins, that when He chose He rose from the dead: these reveal the divine power in Him.

Chapter 28.

ON THE ERROR OF PHOTINUS ABOUT THE INCARNATION

[1]   There are, of course, those who have debased Scripture and have conceived a perverse understanding of the divinity and humanity of our Lord Jesus Christ.

[2]   For there have been some, like Ebion and Cerinthus, and, later, Paul of Samosata and Photinus, who confess in Christ a human nature only. But divinity was in Him, not by nature, but by a kind of outstanding participation of divine glory which He had merited by His deeds. Hence, they fabricate, as was said above.[1]

[3]   But—to pass over the other things said against this position above—this position destroys the Incarnation's mystery.[2]

[4]   For, according to this position, God would not have assumed flesh to become man; rather, an earthly man would have become God. Thus, the saying of John (1:14) would not be true: "The Word was made flesh"; on the contrary, flesh would have been made the Word.

[5]   In the same way, also, emptying Himself and descent would not fit the Son of God; rather, glorification and ascent would fit the man. Thus, there would be no truth in the Apostle's saying: "Who being in the form of God emptied Himself, taking the form of a servant" (Phil. 2:6–7, 9), but only in the exaltation of the man to divine glory about which he adds later: "For which cause God also hath exalted Him."

[6]   Neither would there be truth in our Lord's word: "I came down from heaven," but only in His saying: "I ascend

1. See above, ch. 4.   2. Ibid.

to My Father," in spite of the Scripture which joins these two, for our Lord says: "No man hath ascended into heaven, but He that descended from heaven, the Son of man who is in heaven" (John 6:38; 20:17; 3:13); and, again: "He that descended is the same also that ascended above all the heavens" (Eph. 4:10).

[7] Thus, also, it would not become the Son to have been sent by the Father, nor to have gone out from the Father to come into the world, but only to go to the Father, although He Himself, for all that, unites the two, saying: "I go to Him that sent Me" and "I came forth from the Father, and am come into the world: again I leave the world, and I go to the Father" (John 16:5, 28). In each of these cases both the humanity and the divinity is established.

Chapter 29.

ON THE ERROR OF THE MANICHEANS
ABOUT THE INCARNATION

[1] There also have been others who denied the truth of the Incarnation and introduced a kind of fictional incarnation. The Manicheans said that God's Son assumed not a real, but a phantasy, body;[1] thus, He could not be a true man, but only an apparent one. Consequently, the things He did as man —such as being born, eating, drinking, walking, suffering, and being buried—were done not in truth but in a kind of false appearance. Thus, clearly, they reduce the whole mystery of the Incarnation to a fiction.

[2] First, of course, this position wipes out the authority of Scripture. Since the likeness of flesh is not flesh, the likeness of walking not walking, and so of the rest, Scripture lies in saying: "The Word was made flesh" (John 1:14)—if it was but phantasy flesh. It also lies when it says that Jesus Christ walked, ate, died, and was buried—if these things took place only in an apparent phantasy. But, if even in a moderate way the authority of Scripture be decried, there will no longer be

1. St. Augustine, *De haeresibus*, 46 (PL, 42, col. 37–38).

anything fixed in our faith which depends on sacred Scripture, as in John's words (20:31): "These are written, that you may believe."

[3] Someone can say, of course, that the truth is certainly not lacking to sacred Scripture when it deals with an appearance as though it were a fact, because the likenesses of things are equivocally and figuratively called by the names of the things themselves; a man in a picture, for example, is called a man equivocally. Sacred Scripture itself is accustomed to this manner of speech; thus the Apostle: "And the rock was Christ" (I Cor. 10:4). Of course, many bodily things are found to be said of God in Scripture by reason of mere metaphor: so He is named lamb, or lion, or something of the sort.

[4] However, although the likenesses of things may at times take the names of things by equivocation, it is nonetheless unsuitable to sacred Scripture to set down the whole story of one event under such an equivocation, and so to do it that from other Scriptural passages the plain truth cannot be had. For from this would follow not men's instruction, but their deception instead, whereas the Apostle says: "For what things soever were written, were written for our learning" (Rom. 15:4); and in II Timothy (3:16): "All scripture, inspired of God, is profitable to teach and to instruct." Moreover, the entire Gospel story would be but poetry and fable if it narrated the apparent similarities of things as the things themselves; whereas II Peter (1:16) says: "For we have not by following artificial fables made known to you the power of the Lord, Jesus Christ."

[5] But, when the Scriptural narrative is of things which had appearance, but not existence, the very manner of the narration makes us understand this. For Genesis (18:2, 27, 25) says: "And when he" (Abraham) "had lifted up his eyes, there appeared to him three men." This gives us to understand that they were men by appearance. And so in them he adored God and acknowledged Divinity, and he said: "I will speak to my Lord whereas I am but dust and ashes"; and again: "This is not beseeming Thee, Thou who judgest all the earth." However, the fact that Isaias and Ezechiel and other Prophets have described some things which were seen in imagination pro-

duces no error, for they do not set these things down in the narration of history, but in the description of prophecy. And they nonetheless add something which designates apparition: thus, Isaias (6:1): "I saw the Lord sitting," and so forth; Ezechiel (1:3–4; 8:3): "The hand of the Lord was there upon him. And I saw," and so forth; "The likeness of a hand was put forth and took me and brought me in the vision of God into Jerusalem."

[6] Even the fact that Scripture sometimes speaks of things divine through a comparison cannot produce error, and this both for this reason—the likenesses are taken from things so lowly it is manifest that the passage deals with similitude and not with the existence of things; and for this reason—some things are found said properly in Scripture through which the truth is expressly clarified, and this truth in other places is hidden under similitudes. This, indeed, does not take place in this case, for there is no Scriptural authority touching what is read of Christ's humanity which precludes the truth of what is said.

[7] Perhaps one may say that we are given so to understand by the words of the Apostle: "God sending His own Son, in the likeness of sinful flesh" (Rom. 8:3). Or by this in Philippians (2:7): "Made in the likeness of men, and in habit found as a man." But here the meaning is excluded by what is added, for it does not merely say "in the likeness of flesh," but adds "sinful," because Christ had, indeed, true flesh, but not "sinful flesh"—for there was no sin in Him. But His was similar to "sinful flesh," for His was the captive of suffering, and such did the flesh of man become through sin. In the same way, a fictional understanding is excluded from the saying, "Made in the likeness of men," by the addition: "taking the form of a servant." It is clear that "form" is put here in place of nature rather than of likeness because he had said: "Who being in the form of God" (Phil. 2:6). There, for nature, "form" is put, for the words do not assert that Christ was God by some mere similarity. Further exclusion of fictional understanding is in the addition: "Becoming obedient even unto death" (Phil. 2:8). Likeness is not, therefore, taken for the likeness of an appearance, but for natural likeness of the species; as all men are said to be alike in species.

[8]   But sacred Scripture more expressly excludes the suspicion of apparition. For we read in Matthew (14:26–27) that the disciples, seeing Jesus "walking upon the sea, were troubled, saying: It is an apparition. And they cried out for fear." This very suspicion of theirs our Lord consequently took away; and so the addition: "And immediately Jesus spoke to them saying: Be of good heart; it is I, fear ye not." However one takes it, this appears irrational: that it should escape the disciples' notice that He had assumed but a phantasy body, since He had chosen them to give testimony of the truth about Him from what they "had seen and heard" (Acts 4:20); or, if it did not escape their notice, then the thought of an apparition should not have stricken them with fear.

[9]   But again, more expressly, the suspicion of a phantasy body was removed from the minds of the disciples by our Lord after the resurrection. For we read in Luke (24:37–39) that the disciples, "being troubled and frighted, supposed that they saw a spirit," namely, when they saw Jesus. "And He said to them: Why are you troubled and why do thoughts arise in your hearts? See My hands and feet, that it is I Myself. Handle and see: for a spirit hath not flesh and bones, as you see Me to have." For in vain did He offer Himself to be touched, if he had had none but a phantasy body.

[10]   Again, the Apostles show themselves suitable witnesses of Christ, for Peter says: "Him," namely, Jesus, "God raised up the third day, and gave Him to be made manifest. Not to all the people, but to witnesses preordained by God, even to us, who did eat and drink with Him after He arose again from the dead" (Acts 10:40–41). And John the Apostle, at the beginning of his Epistle, says: "That which we have heard, which we have seen with our eyes, which we have looked upon, and our hands have handled of the word of life: we witness" (I John 1:1–2). But there can be no efficacy in witness to the truth based on things done, not in real existence, but in appearance only. If, therefore, the body of Christ was a phantasy and He did not truly eat and drink, and if He was not truly seen and handled, but in phantasy only, no fitness is found in the testimony of the Apostles about Christ. And thus, "vain is their preaching, and our faith is vain," as Paul says (I Cor. 15:14).

[11] But, again, if Christ had no true body, He did not truly die. Therefore, neither is He truly risen. Therefore, the Apostles are false witnesses of Christ when they preach to the world that He has risen. Hence, the Apostle says in the same place: "We are found false witnesses of God: because we have given testimony against God, that He hath raised up Christ; whom He hath not raised up" (I Cor. 15:15).

[12] What is more, falsity is not a suitable way to the truth. As Ecclesiasticus (34:4) has it: "What truth can come from that which is false?" But Christ's coming into the world was for the manifestation of truth. He Himself says: "For this was I born, and for this came I into the world; that I should give testimony to the truth" (John 18:37). There was not, then, any falsity in Christ. But there would have been if what He says of Himself had been about mere appearance, for the "false is that which is not as it seems."[2] Therefore, everything said of Christ was in accord with real existence.

[13] Moreover, we read in Romans (5:9) that "we are justified by His blood" and in the Apocalypse (5:9): "Thou hast redeemed us, O Lord, in Thy blood." Therefore, if Christ did not have true blood, He did not truly shed it for us. Therefore, we are neither truly justified nor truly redeemed. Therefore, there is no usefulness to being in Christ.

[14] Again, if there is nothing but apparition to be understood of Christ's coming into the world, nothing new took place in Christ's coming. For, in the Old Testament, God appeared to Moses and the Prophets under multiple figures, as even the writings of the New Testament witness.[3] Yet this position wipes out the whole teaching of the New Testament. Therefore, it was not a phantasy body, but a true one, which the Son of God assumed.

2. Aristotle, *Metaphysics*, IV, 29 (1024b 26).
3. For example, Mark 12:26 and Hebrews 1:1.

Chapter 30.

ON THE ERROR OF VALENTINE ABOUT
THE INCARNATION

[1] The opinions of Valentine, of course, were close to these in regard to the mystery of the Incarnation. For he said that Christ did not have an earthly body, but brought one from heaven; that He received nothing from the Virgin Mother, but passed through her as through an aqueduct.[1] The occasion of his error he seems to have found in some words of sacred Scripture. For we read in John (3:13, 31): "No man hath ascended into heaven, but He that descended from heaven, the Son of man who is in heaven . . . He that cometh from above, is above all"; and in John (6:38) our Lord says: "I came down from heaven not to do My own will but the will of Him that sent Me." And I Corinthians (15:47) has: "The first man was of the earth, earthly; the second man, from heaven, heavenly." All of these they want to have so understood that one believes that Christ came down from heaven even in the body.

[2] But this position of Valentine and that of the Manicheans just mentioned[2] proceed from one false root: they believed that all these earthly things were created by the devil. And so, since "the Son of God appeared that He might destroy the works of the devil," as I John (3:8) says, it was unsuitable for Him to assume a body from a creature of the devil, since Paul also says: "What fellowship hath light with darkness? What concord hath Christ with Belial?" (II Cor. 6:14–15).

[3] And since things which come from the same root produce similar fruits, this position lapses into the same discordant falsity as the previous one. For in every single species there are determined essential principles (matter, I mean, and form) from which comes the essential constitution of the species in things composed of matter and form. But just as human flesh and bone and the like are the proper matter of man, so fire, air, earth, and water and the like, such as we sense, are

---

1. St. Augustine, De haeresibus, 11 (PL, 42, col. 28).
2. See above, ch. 29.

the matter of flesh and bone and parts of this kind. Therefore, if the body of Christ was not earthly, it was not true flesh and true bone, but in appearance only. And thus, also, He was not a true, but an apparent, man, whereas, as was noted,[3] He Himself nonetheless says: "A spirit hath not flesh and bones, as you see Me to have" (Luke 24:39).

[4] A heavenly body, moreover, is in its nature incorruptible and inalterable, and cannot be moved outside of its own place.[4] Of course, it was not seemly that the Son of God should diminish the dignity of the nature He assumed, but that He exalt it. Therefore, He did not carry a celestial or incorruptible body below; rather, He assumed an earthly body, capable of suffering, and rendered it incorruptible and heavenly.

[5] Again, the Apostle says about the Son of God that He "was made of the seed of David according to the flesh" (Rom. 1:3). But the body of David was earthly. Therefore, too, was the body of Christ.

[6] The Apostle further says that "God sent His Son, made of a woman" (Gal. 4:4). And Matthew (1:16) says: "Jacob begot Joseph the husband of Mary, of whom was born Jesus, who is called Christ." But He would not be called made of her, or born of her, if He had only passed through her as a channel, assuming nothing from her. Therefore, He assumed His body from her.

[7] Furthermore, Mary could not be called the Mother of Jesus, which the Evangelist (Matt. 1:18) witnesses, unless He had received something from her.

[8] Again, the Apostle says: "Both He that sanctifies," namely, Christ, "and they who are sanctified," namely, Christ's faithful, "are all of one. For which cause He is not ashamed to call them brethren saying: I will declare Thy name to My brethren"; and farther on: "Therefore, because the children are partakers of the flesh and blood, He also Himself in like manner hath been partaker of the same" (Heb. 2:11–12, 14). But, if Christ had a heavenly body only, clearly, since we have an earthly body, we are not one with Him, and, consequently, we cannot be called His brothers. Neither did

3. See above, ch. 29, ¶9.   4. Aristotle, *De caelo*, I, 3 (270a 10–35).

He Himself partake of flesh and blood, for we know that flesh and blood are composed of the lower elements, and are not of the celestial nature. Plainly, therefore, the position aforesaid is contrary to the Apostolic teaching.

[9] The points on which they rely are clearly frivolous. For Christ did not descend from heaven according to soul or to body, but inasmuch as He was God. And this can be gathered from the very words of our Lord. For, when He was saying: "No man hath ascended into heaven, but He that descended from heaven," he added: "the Son of Man who is in heaven" (John 3:13); in which He is pointing out that He has so descended from heaven that He has not, for all that, ceased to be in heaven. But this is proper to deity: so to be on earth as to fill the heaven also, as Jeremias (23:24) has it: "I fill heaven and earth." Therefore, the Son of God does not have to descend from heaven by a local motion, for what is moved locally so approaches one place as to withdraw from another. Therefore, the Son of God is said to have descended in that He joined an earthly substance to Himself: just as the Apostle calls Him "emptied" in that He took the form of a servant, in such wise, nonetheless, that He did not lose the nature of divinity.

[10]   However, that which they assume for the root of this position the foregoing shows to be false, for it was made plain in Book II[5] that bodily things are not from the devil, but are made by God.

Chapter 31.

ON THE ERROR OF APOLLINARIS ABOUT
THE BODY OF CHRIST

[1]   Even more irrational than these were the errors of Apollinaris about the mystery of the Incarnation.[1] Nonetheless, he agrees with those mentioned in one thing: Christ's body was not assumed from the Virgin, but (and this is a greater impiety) he says that something of the Word was changed into

5. SCG, II, ch. 15 and 21.
1. St. Augustine, De haeresibus, 55 (PL, 42, col. 40).

the flesh of Christ. The occasion of his error he finds in John (1:14): "The Word was made flesh." He thought this must be understood as though the Word Himself were changed into flesh, as the other text in John (2:9) is understood: "When the steward tasted the water made wine." For this latter is said because the water was changed into wine.

[2] The impossibility in this error is easy to grasp from the things shown above. For it was shown[2] that God is entirely immutable, but whatever is changed into another is manifestly mutable. Since, then, the Word of God is true God, as was shown,[3] it is impossible that the Word of God be changed into flesh.

[3] The Word of God, again, since He is God, is simple; for it was shown above[4] that there is no composition in God. Therefore, if something of the Word of God is changed into flesh, the whole Word must be changed. But what is changed into another ceases to be what it was before; just as the water changed into wine is no longer water, but wine. Therefore, after the Incarnation, according to the position described the Word will simply not be. And this is evidently impossible: both because the Word is eternal, as in John (1:1): "In the beginning was the Word"; as well as because after the Incarnation Christ is said to be the Word of God, as in the Apocalypse (19:13): "He was clothed with a garment sprinkled with blood; and His name is called THE WORD OF GOD."

[4] There is more. Things which do not share matter and are not in one genus cannot possibly undergo conversion into one another. For from a line whiteness is not made: they are of different genera; nor can an elementary body be converted into one of the celestial bodies, or into some incorporeal substance, nor conversely, since they have no matter in common. But the Word of God, since He is God, has neither genus nor matter in common with anything else whatsoever, for God is not in a genus and has no matter.[5] It is, therefore, impossible that the Word was converted into flesh or into anything else whatever.

2. *SCG,* I, ch. 13.   3. *SCG,* I, ch. 3.
4. *SCG,* I, ch. 18.   5. *SCG,* I, ch. 17 and 25.

[5]   Furthermore, it is essential to flesh, to bone, to other parts of this sort that they be of determined matter. Therefore, if the Word of God be converted into flesh, as the position described holds, it will follow that there was not in Christ true flesh or anything else of the sort. And thus, also, He will not be true man, but an apparent one only; and so for the other points which we made against Valentine previously.[6]

[6]   Plainly, then, the saying of John, "The Word was made flesh," must not be understood as though the Word had been changed into flesh, but that He assumed flesh so as to dwell with men and appear visible to them. Hence there is added: "And dwelt among us, and we saw His glory," and so forth; just as Baruch (3:38) also says of God: "He was seen upon earth, and conversed with men."

Chapter 32.

ON THE ERROR OF ARIUS AND APOLLINARIS
ABOUT THE SOUL OF CHRIST

[1]   It is, however, not only about the body of Christ but also about His soul that one finds some bad opinions.

[2]   For Arius held that in Christ there was no soul,[1] but that He assumed only flesh, and that divinity stood to this as soul. And he seems to have been led to this position by a certain necessity. For he wanted to maintain that the Son of God was a creature and less than the Father, and so for his proof he picked up those Scriptural passages which show human infirmity in Christ. And to keep anyone from refuting him by saying that the passages he picked referred to Christ not in His divine, but in His human, nature, he evilly removed the soul from Christ to this purpose: since some things are not harmonious with a human body, that He wondered, for example, that He feared, that He prayed—all such must necessarily imply the inferiority of the Son of God Himself. Of course, he picked up for the assertion of his position the words of John just mentioned, "The Word was made flesh," and from

6. See above, ch. 30.
1. St. Augustine, *De haeresibus*, 49 (*PL*, 42, col. 39).

this he wanted to gather that the Word only assumed flesh, not a soul. And in this position even Apollinaris followed him.[2]

[3] But it is clear from what has been said that this position is impossible. For it was shown above[3] that God cannot be the form of a body. Since, therefore, the Word of God is God, as was shown,[4] it is impossible that the Word of God be the form of a body, so as to be able to stand as a soul to flesh.

[4] This argument, of course, is useful against Apollinaris, who confessed the Word of God to be true God; and granted Arius would deny this last, the argument just given goes against him, also. For it is not God alone who cannot be the form of a body; neither can any of the supercelestial spirits among whom Arius held the Son of God supreme. Exception might be made for the position of Origen, who held that human souls were of the very same species and nature as the supercelestial spirits. The falsity of this opinion was explained above.[5]

[5] Take away, moreover, what is of the essence of man, and no true man can be. Clearly, of course, the soul is chiefly of the essence of man, since it is his form. Therefore, if Christ had no soul He was not true man, whereas the Apostle does call Him man: "There is one mediator of God and men, the man Christ Jesus" (I Tim. 2:5).

[6] It is on the soul, furthermore, that not only man's essence, but that of his single parts, depends; and so, with the soul gone, the eye, the flesh, and the bone of a dead man are equivocally named, "like a painted or a stone eye."[6] Therefore, if in Christ there was no soul, of necessity there was neither true flesh in Him nor any of the other parts of man, whereas our Lord says that He has these in Himself: "A spirit hath not flesh and bones, as you see Me to have" (Luke 24:39).

[7] Further, what is generated from another cannot be

2. Ibid., 55 (PL, 42, col. 40).
4. See above, ch. 3.
6. Aristotle, *De anima*, II, 1 (412b 21).

3. SCG, I, ch. 23.
5. SCG, II, ch. 94–95.

called his son unless he comes forth in the same species; the maggot is not called the son of the animal from which it is generated. But, if Christ had no soul, He was not of the same species as other men, for things which differ in form cannot be identical in species. Therefore, one will not be able to say that Christ is the Son of the Virgin Mary or that she is His Mother. Nonetheless, Scripture asserts this in the Gospels (Matt. 1:18; Luke 2:7).

[8] There is more. The Gospel expressly says that Christ had a soul; Matthew (26:38) for instance: "My soul is sorrowful even unto death"; and John (12:27): "Now is My soul troubled."

[9] And lest they say perhaps that the very Son of God is called soul because in their position He stands to the flesh as soul, one must take our Lord's own saying: "I have power to lay My soul down: and I have power to take it up again" (John 10:18). From this one understands that there is another than the soul in Christ, which had the power of laying the soul down and taking it up again. It was, of course, not in the power of the body to be united to the Son of God or be separated from Him, since this, too, exceeds the power of nature. One must, then, understand that in Christ the soul was one thing and the divinity of the Son of God another, to whom such power justly is attributed.

[10] Another reason: Sorrow, anger and the like are passions of the sensitive soul; the Philosopher makes this plain.[7]

[11] But, since one can say that the human things in the Gospels are said of Christ metaphorically, just as the sacred Scriptures speak of God in many places, one must take something which is understood properly of necessity. For, just as other bodily things which the Evangelists relate of Christ are understood properly and not metaphorically, so it must not be understood of Christ metaphorically that He ate and that He hungered. Only he who has a sensitive soul hungers, since hunger is the appetite for food. Necessarily, then, Christ had a sensitive soul.

7. Aristotle, *Physics*, VII, 3 (247a 15–16).

Chapter 33.

ON THE ERROR OF APOLLINARIS, WHO SAYS THERE WAS
NO RATIONAL SOUL IN CHRIST; AND THE ERROR
OF ORIGEN, WHO SAYS THE SOUL OF CHRIST
WAS CREATED BEFORE THE WORLD

[1] Won over, however, by this Gospel testimony, Apollinaris confessed that there was a sensitive soul in Christ; nonetheless, it was without mind and intellect, so that the Word of God was in that soul in place of intellect and mind.[1]

[2] But even this is not sufficient to avoid the awkward consequences described, for man gets his human species from his having a human mind and reason. Therefore, if Christ did not have these, He was not true man, nor was He of the same species with us. For a soul which lacks reason belongs to a species other than that of the soul which has reason. For, according to the Philosopher,[2] in definitions and species any essential difference which is added or subtracted varies the species, just as unity does in numbers. But *rational* is the specific difference. Therefore, if in Christ there was a sensitive soul without reason, it was not of the same species with our soul, which does have reason. Neither, then, was Christ Himself of the same species with us.

[3] Again, among the sensible souls themselves which lack reason there exists diversity by reason of species. This appears from consideration of the irrational animals which differ from one another in species; nonetheless, each of them has its species according to its proper soul. Thus, then, the sensitive soul lacking reason is, so to say, one genus including within itself many species. But nothing is in a genus which is not in one of its species. If, then, the soul of Christ was in the genus of sensitive soul lacking reason, it must have been included in one of its species; for example, it was in the species of lion soul, or some other beast. And this is entirely absurd.

[4] The body, moreover, is compared to the soul as matter

1. Cf. St. Augustine, *De haeresibus*, 55 (*PL*, 42, col. 40).
2. Aristotle, *Metaphysics*, VIII, 3 (1043b 34–1044a 2).

to form, and as instrument to principal agent. But the matter must be proportionate to the form, and the instrument to the principal agent. Therefore, consequent on the diversity of souls, there must be a diversity of bodies. And this is sensibly evident, for in diverse animals one finds diverse dispositions of the members, in which they concord with the diverse dispositions of the souls. Therefore, if in Christ there was not a soul such as our soul is, neither would He have had members like the human members.

[5] There is more. Since, according to Apollinaris, the Word of God is true God,[3] wonder cannot be seemly in Him, for we wonder at those things whose cause we ignore.[4] But, in the same way, wonder cannot be fitting for the sensitive soul, since solicitude for the knowledge of causes does not belong to the sensitive soul. But there was wonder in Christ; so one proves from the Gospels. It says in Matthew (8:10) that Jesus heard the words of the centurion and "marveled." One must, then, in addition to the divinity of the Word and His sensitive soul put in Christ that which can make wonder seemly in Him; namely, a human mind.

[6] Manifestly, therefore, from the aforesaid there was in Christ a human body and a true human soul. Thus, therefore, John's saying (1:14), "The Word was made flesh," is not thus to be understood, as though the Word has been converted into flesh; or as though the Word has assumed the flesh only; or with a sensitive soul without a mind; but after Scripture's usual manner the part is put for the whole, so that one says: "The Word was made man." "Soul" is sometimes used in place of man in Scripture; Exodus (1:5) says: "And all the souls that came out of Jacob's thigh were seventy"; in the same way, also, "flesh" is used for the whole man; Isaias (40:5) says: "All flesh together shall see that the mouth of the Lord hath spoken." Thus, then, "flesh" is here used for the whole man, also, to express the weakness of the human nature which the Word of God assumed.

[7] But, if Christ had human flesh and a human soul, as was shown, it is plain that there was no soul of Christ before His body's conception. For it was shown that human souls do

3. See above, ch. 31.   4. Aristotle, *Metaphysics*, I, 2 (982b 14–19).

not pre-exist their proper bodies.[5] Hence is clear the falsity of that tenet of Origen, who said that in the beginning, before all bodily creatures, the soul of Christ was created with all other spiritual creatures and assumed by the Word of God, and that finally, toward the end of the ages, for men's salvation it was endowed with flesh.[6]

Chapter 34.

ON THE ERROR OF THEODORE OF MOPSUESTE AND NESTORIUS ON THE UNION OF THE WORD TO MAN

[1] From the things set down,[1] therefore, it appears that Christ was not without divine nature, as Ebion, Cerinthus, and Photinus said; nor without a true human body, as in the error of Mani and Valentine; nor without a human soul, as Arius and Apollinaris held. Since, then, these three substances met in Christ—namely, divinity, the human soul, and the true human body—what one should think about their union following the Scriptural teachings remains for inquiry.[2]

[2] Now, then, Theodore of Mopsueste and Nestorius, his follower, offered one sort of opinion on the aforesaid union. They said that the human soul and the true human body came together in Christ by a natural union to constitute one man of the same species and nature with other men, and that in this man God dwelt as in His temple, namely, by grace, just as in other holy men. Hence, it says in John (2:19, 21), that He said to the Jews: "Destroy this temple and in three days I will raise it up"; and later the Evangelist by way of exposition adds: "But he spoke of the temple of His body"; and the Apostle says: "In Him it hath well pleased the Father, that all fullness should dwell" (Col. 1:19). And out of these arose further a certain affective union between that man and God, when that man cleaved to God with his own good will, and God lifted up that man with His will, in the words of John (8:29): "He that sent me is with me, and He hath not

5. *SCG*, II, ch. 83.
6. Origen, *Peri Archon*, II, 8 (PG, 11, col. 224–225); cf. St. Augustine, *De haeresibus*, 43 (PL, 42, col. 33).
1. See above, ch. 28–33.   2. In ch. 34–38.

left me alone: for I do always the things that please Him."
Let one thus understand that the union of that man to God
is such as was the union of which the Apostle said: "He who
is joined to God is one spirit" (I Cor. 6:17). And just as,
from the latter union, names which properly befit God are
transferred to men so that they are called "gods," and "sons
of God," and "lords," and "holy ones," and "christs"—as is
clear from a diversity of places in Scripture; so also the divine
names befit that man so that, by reason of God's indwelling
and the affective union, he is called God, and the Son of God,
and Holy, and Christ. Nonetheless, because there was in that
man a greater fullness of grace than in other holy men, he was
before all the rest the temple of God, he was united to God
more closely in affection, and it was by a singular kind of
privilege that he shared the divine names. And because of this
outstanding grace he was established in a share of the divine
dignity and honor—namely, that he be co-adored with God.
So, then, consequently on the things just said there must be
one Person of the Word of God, and another person of that
man who is co-adored with the Word of God. And if one
Person of each of the two be mentioned, this will be by reason
of the affective union aforesaid; so that man and the Word of
God may be called one Person, as is said of man and woman
that "now they are not two, but one flesh" (Matt. 19:6).

Now, such a union does not bring it about that what is said
of the first can be said of the second (for not everything which
becomes the man is true of the woman, or conversely); therefore in the union of the Word and that man they think this
must be observed: The things proper to that man and pertinent to the human nature cannot be said becomingly of God's
Word, or of God. Just so it becomes that man that he was
born of a virgin, that he suffered, died, was buried, and this
kind of thing; and all of these, they assert, ought not be said
of God, or of the Word of God. But, since there are certain
names which, although they are chiefly befitting to God, are
nonetheless communicated to men in a fashion—"christ," for
instance, "lord," "holy," and even "son of God"—nothing according to them keeps one from the use of such names in
predication of the things just mentioned. For, according to
them, we say fittingly that Christ, or the "Lord of glory," or

the "Saint of saints," or "God's son" was born of a virgin, suffered, died and was buried. Hence, too, the Blessed Virgin must not be named the mother of God, or of the Word of God, but the mother of Christ, they say.

[3] But let one earnestly consider the matter and he will see that the position described excludes the truth of the Incarnation. For, in that position, the Word of God was united to that man only through an indwelling by grace, on which a union of wills follows. But the indwelling of God's Word in a man is not for God's Word to be made flesh. For the Word of God and God Himself have been dwelling in all the holy men since the world was founded; as the Apostle says: "You are the temple of the living God; as God saith: I will dwell in them" (II Cor. 6:16). And this indwelling, for all that, cannot be called incarnation; otherwise, God would have repeatedly been made flesh since the beginning of the world. Nor does it suffice for the notion of incarnation if the Word of God or God dwelt in that man with a fuller grace, for "greater and less do not diversify the species of union." Since the Christian religion is based on faith in the Incarnation, it is now quite evident that the position described removes the basis of the Christian religion.

[4] In addition is the very manner of speech of Scripture, which makes the falsity of the position described plain. For the indwelling of the Word of God in holy men is usually designated by Scripture in these ways: "The Lord spoke to Moses"; "The word of the Lord came to Jeremias" (or to some other Prophet); "The word of the Lord came to the hand of Aggaeus the Prophet." But one never reads the "Word of the Lord was made" Moses, or Jeremias, or one of the others. Yet thus uniquely was the union of God's Word to the flesh of Christ marked by the Evangelist: "The Word was made flesh," as was explained before.[3] Clearly, then, it was not by indwelling alone that God's Word was in the man, Christ, if we follow Scripture.

[5] Again, whatever was made is what it was made; thus, what was made man is man, and what was made white is white. But God's Word was made man, as is gathered from

3. See above, ch. 33.

the foregoing. So God's Word is man. It is, of course, impossible when two things differ in person, or hypostasis, or supposit that one be predicated of the other; for, when we say "Man is animal," that which is animal man is. And when we say "Man is white," the signification is that man himself is white, although whiteness is other than the essence of humanity. Accordingly, there is no way to say Socrates is Plato or anyone of the singulars of his own or another species. So, if "the Word was made flesh," that is, "man," as the Evangelist witnesses (John 1:14), it is impossible that there be two persons, or hypostases, or supposits of the Word of God and of that man.

[6] Demonstrative pronouns, moreover, refer to the person, or hypostasis, or supposit. For no one says "I run" when another is running, except figuratively, perhaps, when another is running in his place. But the man called Jesus says about Himself: "Before Abraham was made, I am" and "I and the Father are one" (John 8:58; 10:30), and several other things which clearly pertain to the divinity of the Word. Therefore, the person and hypostasis of the man speaking is plainly the very person of the Word of God.

[7] There is more. From our exposition one sees that the body of Christ did not descend from heaven as in Valentine's error,[4] nor did His soul according to Origen's.[5] What is left is this: one can say pertinently of the Word of God that He descended, not by some local motion, but by reason of the union to a lower nature. This was said above.[6] But that man, speaking in His own person, says that He descended from heaven in John (6:51): "I am the living bread which came down from heaven." Necessarily, then, the person and hypostasis of that man must be the person of the Word of God.

[8] Again, to ascend into heaven plainly belongs to Christ the man who "was raised up while the disciples looked on," as Acts (1:9) says. But to descend from heaven is proper to the Word of God. But the Apostle says: "He that descended is the same also that ascended above all the heavens" (Eph. 4:10). The very person and hypostasis of that man is, accordingly, the person and hypostasis of the Word of God.

4. See above, ch. 30.   5. See above, ch. 33.   6. See above, ch. 30.

[9] Moreover, that whose origin is in the world, which had no being before the world, does not properly "come into the world." But the man Christ in the flesh had His origin in the world, since He had a true, human, earthly body, as was shown.[7] In His soul, as well, He had no being before He was in the world, for He had a true human soul in whose nature there is no being before it is united to the body.[8] So, then, it does not belong to that man's humanity to "come into the world." He Himself says, of course, that He came into the world: "I came forth from the Father," He says, "and I came into the world" (John 16:28). Plainly, then, what belongs to the Word of God is truly said of that man. For, that it belongs to the Word of God to come into the world John the Evangelist clearly shows (1:10–11): "He was in the world, and the world was made by Him, and the world knew Him not; He came unto His own." So, the person and hypostasis of the man speaking is the person and hypostasis of the Word of God.

[10] Again, the Apostle says: "When He cometh into the world He saith: Sacrifice and oblation Thou wouldest not: but a body Thou hast fitted to Me" (Heb. 10:5). But He who enters the world is the Word of God, as was shown. It is, then, to God's very Word that a body is fitted; namely, so as to be His own body. And one could not say this if the hypostasis of God's Word were not identified with that of the man. Therefore, the hypostasis of the Word of God and of that man are the very same.

[11] Every change or passion, furthermore, proper to one's body can be ascribed to him whose body it is. So, if the body of Peter is wounded, scourged, or dies, it can be said that Peter is wounded, scourged, or dies. But the body of that man is the body of the Word of God, as was just proved.[9] Therefore, every suffering that took place in the body of that man can be ascribed to the Word of God. So it is right to say that the Word of God—and God—suffered, was crucified, died, and was buried. And this they[10] used to deny.

[12] The Apostle also says: "It became Him, for whom are all things, and by whom are all things, who, had brought many

---

7. See above, ch. 29–31.   8. SCG, II, ch. 83 and 87.
9. See above, ¶10.   10. See above, ¶2.

children into glory, to perfect the author of their salvation, by His passion" (Heb. 2:10). Thus one holds: He for whom all things are, through whom all things are, He who leads men to glory, and who is the Author of human salvation suffered and died. But these four are God's in a singular way; they are attributed to no other. For we read in Proverbs (16:4): "The Lord hath made all things for Himself"; in John (1:3) of the Word of God: "All things were made by Him"; in the Psalmist: "The Lord will give grace and glory"; and elsewhere: "The salvation of the just is from the Lord" (Ps. 83:12; 36:39). It is, then, plainly right to say that "God, God's Word, suffered and died."

[13] There is more. Granted someone may be called a lord by sharing in lordship: no man at all, no creature in fact, can be called "Lord of glory," for God alone by His nature possesses the glory of the future beatitude. But others do so by the gift of grace, and so the Psalmist says: "The Lord of hosts, He is the King of glory" (Ps. 23:8–10). But the Apostle says the Lord of glory was crucified (I Cor. 2:8). Then truly it can be said: God was crucified.

[14] The Word of God, furthermore, is called God's Son by nature; this was made plain above.[11] But a man through the indwelling is called God's son by the grace of adoption. But in the position now opposed, one must accept in our Lord Jesus Christ each of these modes of sonship; for the indwelling Word is the Son of God by nature; the man in whom He dwells is a son of God by the grace of adoption. Hence, that man cannot be called "the very own" or "only-begotten Son of God"; the Word of God alone in His own proper birth is uniquely begotten of the Father. But Scripture attributes the passion and death to God's very own and only-begotten Son, for the Apostle says: "He hath spared not even His own Son, but delivered Him up for us all" (Rom. 8:32); and John (3:16) says: "God so loved the world as to give His only-begotten Son, that whosoever believeth in Him may not perish, but may have life everlasting." And that He spoke of "giving" Him over to death is clear from this: John had previously used the very same words about the crucified Son of

11. See above, ch. 11.

Man when he said: "As Moses lifted up the serpent in the desert, so must the Son of man be lifted up, that whosoever believeth in Him" (John 3:14), and the rest. And the Apostle makes the death of Christ an indication of the divine love for the world by saying: "God commendeth His charity towards us; because when as yet we were sinners, according to the time, Christ died for us" (Rom. 5:8–9). Rightly, then, does one say that the Word of God, that God, suffered and died.

[15] Again, one is said to be the son of a mother because his body is taken from her, although his soul is not taken from her, but has an exterior source. But the body of that man was taken from the Virgin Mother. Now, it was proved that the body of that man is the body of the natural Son of God, that is, of the Word of God.[12] So it becomes us to say that the Blessed Virgin is "the Mother of the Word of God," and even "of God." Of course, the divinity of the Word is not taken from His Mother, for a son need not take the whole of his substance from his mother, but his body only.

[16] The Apostle says further that "God sent His Son, made of a woman" (Gal. 4:4). These words show us how to understand the sending of the Son of God: He is called sent thither, where He was made of a woman. This could not, of course, be true if the Son of God had not been before He was made of a woman, for that which is sent into another is understood to be previously to its being in that other to which it is sent. But that man, the Nestorian adoptive son, had no being before he was born of the woman. The Apostle's word, "God sent His Son," cannot, therefore, be understood of the adoptive son, but must be understood of the natural Son, that is, of God the Word of God. But if one is made of a woman, he is called the woman's son. Therefore, God the Word of God is the Son of a woman.

[17] Perhaps we will be told not to understand the word of the Apostle thus: that the Son of God was sent to be made of a woman; but to understand it thus: that God's Son, made of a woman and under the Law, was sent "that He might redeem them who were under the Law" (Gal. 4:5). And in this

12. See above, ch. 34, ¶10.

reading "his son" need not be understood of the natural Son, but of that man who was the son by adoption. But the very words of the Apostle exclude this meaning. For no one can release from the Law save him who exists above the Law, the author of the Law. But the Law was established by God. Only God, then, can take away servitude to the Law. But the Apostle attributes this to the Son of God of whom he speaks. So, the Son of God of whom he speaks is the natural Son. Therefore, it is true to say: The natural Son of God, that is, God the Word of God, is made of a woman.

[18]   The very same point is clarified by Scripture's attribution of the redemption of the human race to God Himself; thus the Psalmist: "Thou hast redeemed me, O Lord, the God of truth" (Ps. 30:6).

[19]   Furthermore, the adoption of God's sons is made by the Holy Spirit, according to Romans (8:15): "You have received the spirit of adoption of sons." But the Holy Spirit is a gift, not of man, but of God. And so, the adoption of sons is not caused by man, but by God. But it is caused by the Son of God sent by God and made of a woman. This is clear from the Apostle's addition: "That we might receive the adoption of sons" (Gal. 4:5). One ought, then, to understand the Apostle's expression of God's natural Son. It is, accordingly, God the Word of God who "was made of a woman"; that is, of the Virgin Mother.

[20]   And, again, John says: "The Word was made flesh." But He has no flesh, except from a woman. The Word, then, is made of a woman; that is, of the Virgin Mother. Therefore, the Virgin is the Mother of God the Word.

[21]   The Apostle further says that Christ is from the fathers[13] "according to the flesh, Who is over all things, God blessed for ever" (Rom. 9:5). But he is not from the fathers save through the Virgin. God, then, who is above all things, is from the Virgin in the flesh. The Virgin, then, is the Mother of God in the flesh.

---

13. St. Thomas abbreviates. St. Paul speaks (v. 3) "of my kinsmen" (v. 4), "who are Israelites" (v. 5), "Whose are the fathers, and of whom is Christ," etc. as in the body. On this text see Prat, S.J., *The Theology of Saint Paul*, II, 125–128.

[22] The Apostle, once more, says of Christ Jesus that, "being in the form of God, emptied Himself, taking the form of a servant, being made in the likeness of men" (Phil. 2:6–7). Now, clearly, if, following Nestorius, we divide Christ into two—into that man who is the adoptive son, and into God's natural Son who is the Word of God—this text cannot be understood of that man. For that man, if he be pure man, was not first in the form of God, so as to be made later in the likeness of man; rather conversely: the existing man was made to share in divinity; in this he was not emptied, but exalted. The text must, then, be understood of the Word of God who first was eternally in the form of God, that is, in the nature of God, and later emptied Himself, made in the likeness of man.

But that emptying cannot be understood solely by the indwelling of the Word of God in the man Jesus Christ. For, since the beginning of the world, the Word of God has dwelt in all the saints by grace. It is not, for all that, emptied, since God communicates His goodness to creatures so that nothing is subtracted from Him. Rather, He is somehow exalted, in that the goodness of the creatures manifests His sublimity, and so much the more so as the creatures have been better. Hence, if the Word of God has dwelt more fully in the man Christ than in the other saints, then even less in this case than in others is the emptying harmonious with the Word.

Plainly, then, the union of the Word with the human nature must not be understood in accordance merely with the indwelling of the Word of God in that man (as Nestorius held), but in accordance with this fact: The Word of God truly was made man. In this wise only, then, will there be place for "emptying": namely, let the Word of God be called "emptied," that is, made small, not by the loss of His own greatness, but by the assumption of human smallness; just so would it be if the soul were to pre-exist the body, and were said to be made the corporeal substance which man is: not by a change of its own nature, but by the assumption of corporeal nature.

[23] There is more. Manifestly, the Holy Spirit dwelt in the man Christ, for Luke (4:11) says: "Jesus, being full of the Holy Ghost, returned from the Jordan." If, then, our under-

standing of the Incarnation of the Word is this alone—the Word of God dwelt most fully in that man—we will have to say that the Holy Spirit was incarnate also. And this is altogether foreign to the teaching of the faith.

[24] This is also clear: The Word of God dwells in the holy angels, and by sharing the Word they are filled with understanding. But the Apostle says: "Nowhere doth He take hold of the angels: but of the seed of Abraham he taketh hold" (Heb. 2:16). Clearly, then, the assumption of human nature by the Word is not merely to be taken as indwelling.

[25] If, furthermore, as in the Nestorian position, Christ be separated into two differing in hypostasis—that is, into the Word of God and that man—the Word of God cannot possibly be called "Christ." This is clear, for one thing, from Scripture's manner of speaking: Scripture before the Incarnation never names God, or the Word of God, Christ. It is clear, as well, from the very account of the name. For one says "Christ" only as though to say "anointed." But one understands anointed with the "oil of gladness" (Heb. 1:9; Ps. 44:8), that is, "with the Holy Ghost" (Acts 10:38), as Peter explains. Yet, one cannot say that the Word of God is anointed with the Holy Spirit, for the Holy Spirit would thus be greater than the Son, as the sanctifier is greater than the sanctified. It will be necessary, then, to understand the name "Christ" only of that man. Therefore, this word of the Apostle, "Let this mind be in you, which was also in Christ Jesus" (Phil. 2:5–6), must be referred to that man. Yet he adds: "Who being in the form of God, thought it not robbery to be equal with God." Truly, then, one speaks of that man in the form, that is, the nature of God, and equal to God. Yet, granted men are called "gods" or "sons of God" by God's indwelling, one never calls them "equal to God." Clearly, then, the man Christ is not called God merely by reason of the indwelling.

[26] Granted, again, that the name of God is used for holy men by reason of the indwelling of grace, nonetheless works which are God's alone—the creation of heaven and earth, for example, or something of the sort—are never ascribed to any saint by reason of the indwelling of grace. But to Christ the man the creation of all things is attributed. We read in

Hebrews (3:1-4): "Consider the apostle and high priest of our confession Jesus Christ who is faithful to Him that made Him, as also was Moses in all His house." This must be understood of that man and not of God's Word; both because it was shown that in the Nestorian position God's Word cannot be called Christ, as well as because God's Word is not made, but begotten. The Apostle, of course, adds: "This man was counted worthy of greater glory than Moses, by so much as He that built the house hath greater honor than the house." Now, the man Christ built the house. This the Apostle proves subsequently when he adds: "For every house is built by some man: but He that created all things is God." Thus, then, the Apostle proves that the man Christ built the house of God from the fact that God created all things. But this would be no proof at all if Christ were not the God who creates all things. And so to that man the creation of the worlds is ascribed, a thing which is God's very own work. The man Christ, then, is God Himself by hypostasis and not merely by reason of indwelling.

[27] Further, it is clear that the man Christ, speaking of Himself, says many divine and supernatural things: so this in John (6:40): "I will raise him up in the last day"; and again: "I give them life everlasting" (10:28). This would be the height of pride if that man speaking were not by hypostasis God Himself, but merely had God indwelling. But pride is not suited to the man Christ, who says of Himself: "Learn of me, because I am meek, and humble of heart" (Matt. 11:29). There is, then, identity in person between that man and God.

[28] There is more. Just as we read in Scripture that the man is "exalted"—as in Acts (2:33): "Exalted therefore by the right hand of God," and the rest, so also we read that God is "emptied" in Philippians (2:7): "He emptied himself," and the rest. Thus, just as sublime things can be said of that man by reason of the union—that He is God, that He raises the dead, and others of this sort—so of God can lowly things be said: that He was born of the Virgin, suffered, died, and was buried.

[29] Then, too, both relative verbs and pronouns bring out identity of supposit. The Apostle says, speaking of the Son of

God: "In Him were all things created in heaven and on earth, visible and invisible"; then, later, he adds: "And He is the head of the body, the Church, who is the beginning, the first-born from the dead" (Col. 1:16, 18). Now, clearly, the text, "In Him were all things created," refers to the Word of God; whereas the text, "first-born from the dead," belongs to the man Christ. Therefore, God's Word and the man Christ are one supposit and, consequently, one Person; and whatever is said of that man must be said of the Word of God, and conversely.

[30]   Again, the Apostle says: "There is one Lord Jesus Christ, by whom are all things" (I Cor. 8:6). But Jesus, the name of that man through whom all things are, clearly befits the Word of God. Thus, then, the Word of God and that man are one Lord; and these are not two lords, or two sons, as Nestorius held. From this it follows further that there is one person of the Word of God and the man.

[31]   Let one consider the matter earnestly and he sees that this Nestorian opinion on the Incarnation differs very little from that of Photinus.[14] For each held that the man was called God only by reason of the indwelling grace. Photinus, of course, said that the man merited the name and glory of divinity by suffering and good works; and Nestorius confessed that from the beginning of his conception he had this name and glory by reason of the fullness of God's dwelling within him. Of course, on the eternal generation of the Word they differed greatly: Nestorius confessed it, but Photinus denied it completely.

Chapter 35.

AGAINST THE ERROR OF EUTYCHES

[1]   Since the mystery of the Incarnation—as has been shown[1] in many ways—must be understood thus: there is one and the same person of the Word of God and the man, a certain difficulty remains in the consideration of this truth. For necessarily its personality follows the divine nature. The case seems to

14. See above, ch. 4 and 28.   1. See above, ch. 34.

be the same for human nature, for everything which subsists in an intellectual or a rational nature fulfills the account of person. Hence, it does not seem possible that there be one Person and two natures, divine and human.

[2] Now, for the solution of this difficulty various men have proposed various positions. Eutyches, for instance, to preserve the unity of person in Christ against Nestorius, says there is one nature, also. He says that, although before the union there were two distinct natures, the divine and human, they came together, nevertheless, in the union into one nature. And so he said that the person of Christ "is from two natures," but does not "subsist in two natures." For this he was condemned by the Council of Chalcedon.[2]

[3] The falsity of this position, of course, appears in many ways. For we showed above[3] that there was in Christ Jesus a body, a rational soul, and divinity. And, clearly, the body of Christ even after the union was not the very divinity of the Word; for the body of Christ even after the union could be touched, could be seen with bodily eyes, and had distinctly outlined members. All of these are foreign to the divinity of the Word, as the foregoing[4] make clear. And in like fashion the soul of Christ after the union was other than the divinity of the Word, because after the union the soul of Christ was affected by the passions of sadness, of sorrow, and of anger. These, too, are entirely disproportionate to the divinity of the Word, as the foregoing shows.[5] But a human soul and a human body constitute a human nature. Thus, then, even after the union, the human nature in Christ was other than the divinity of the Word which is the divine nature. Therefore, in Christ, even after the union, there are two natures.

[4] Again. It is by its nature that something is called a natural thing. One calls it a natural thing because it has a form, as one does with an artificial thing; one does not call a house a house before it has the form of its architecture, nor a horse a horse before it has the form of its nature. The form of a natural thing is, then, its nature. But one must say that in Christ

---

2. Mansi, *Amplissima Collectio*, col. 115; on Eutyches see Hughes, *A Popular History*, pp. 35–40.   3. See above, ch. 28–30 and 34.
4. *SCG*, I, ch. 17, 18, and 20.   5. *SCG*, I, ch. 89.

there are two forms, even after the union. For the Apostle says of Christ Jesus, when he was "in the form of God, He took the form of a servant" (Phil. 2:6–7). Of course, one cannot say that the form of God is the same as the form of the servant. For nothing receives what it already has, and so, if the form of God and of the servant are the same, He would not —since He already had the form of God—have received the form of servant. Neither, again, can one say that the form of God in Christ is corrupted by the union, because thus after the union Christ would not be God. Nor, again, can one say that the form of the servant was corrupted in the union, because thus He would not have received the form of the servant. But neither can one say that the form of the servant is mixed thoroughly with the form of God, for things mixed thoroughly do not retain their integrity; rather, each is in part corrupted; and so the Apostle would not say that He had received the form of the servant, but something of the servant. Hence, one ought to say respecting the words of the Apostle that in Christ even after the union there were two forms; therefore, two natures.

[5]   The name "nature," moreover, in its first imposition had as meaning the very generation of things being born. Thence it was carried over to meaning the principle of this kind of generation, and then to signifying the principle of motion intrinsic to the moveable thing. And because this kind of principle is matter or form, nature is further called the form or matter of a thing which has in itself a principle of motion. And since form and matter constitute the essence of the natural thing, the name was extended to meaning the essence of everything whatsoever which exists in nature. As a result of this, the nature of a thing is called "the essence signified by the definition."[6] In this last fashion nature is in question here, for thus we say that there is in Christ human nature and divine.

[6]   Now, then, if, as Eutyches held, the human nature and the divine were two before the union, but from those in the union one nature was breathed together, this should take place

6. Aristotle, *Physics*, II, 1 (193a 30).

in one of the ways in which it is natural that one comes to be from many.

[7] Now, one way in which one comes from many is the way of *order* alone; so from many homes a city comes to be, or from many soldiers an army. Another way is that of *order and composition*; so a house comes to be when they join together its parts and its walls. But neither of these two ways fits the constitution of one nature from a plurality. For things whose form is order or juxtaposition are not natural things. The result is that their unity cannot be called a unity of nature.

[8] In a third way, one comes from many by *mixture*, as from the four elements one gets a mixed body. And this way, too, does not fit the present consideration. The *first* reason is this: Mixture is only of things which have matter in common and by nature act and react reciprocally. Such cannot, indeed, be the case here, for it was shown in Book I[7] that God is entirely immaterial and subject to no action. The *second* reason is this: When one thing greatly exceeds another there can be no mixture, for, if a man puts a drop of wine into a thousand measures of water, he is not mixing, but spoiling, the wine.[8] For the same reason we do not say that wood thrown into a furnace is mixed with the fire, but—by reason of the superior power of the fire—consumed by the fire. The divine nature, of course, exceeds the human by infinity, since the divine power is infinite, as was shown in Book I.[9] There cannot, then, be any mixture at all of each nature. The *third* reason is this: If a mixture were to come into being, neither nature would be preserved. For things subject to mixture are not preserved in the mixed product, if it be a true mixture. Given, then, a thorough mixture of each of the two natures— the divine, namely, and the human—neither of the two natures would remain, but some third. What Eutyches said, then, cannot be understood thus: There were two natures before the union, but after the union one nature in our Lord Jesus Christ, as though from two natures one nature has been established. Therefore, the understanding of it which remains is this: Ei-

7. *SCG*, I, ch. 18–23.
8. Aristotle, *De generatione et corruptione*, I, 10 (328a 25–30).
9. *SCG*, I, ch. 43.

ther the one or the other remained after the union. Either,
then, there was in Christ the divine nature only and what appeared human in Him was but phantasy as Mani said; or the
divine nature was converted into the human as Apollinaris
said. But against these we have previously disputed.[10] The
conclusion, then, is that it is impossible that before the union
there were two natures in Christ; after the union, but one.

[9] There is more. One never finds one coming to be from
two abiding natures, because any nature is a kind of whole,
but its constituents are accounted for as parts. Hence, when
one comes to be from a soul and a body, neither the soul nor
the body can be called a nature (as we are now speaking of
nature), because neither has the complete species, but each is
a part of the one nature. Since human nature, then, is a kind
of complete nature, and the divine nature is similarly, it is
impossible that they concur in one nature without the corruption either of each of the two, or of one of the two. Now,
this cannot be, since from our previous points[11] the one
Christ clearly is both true God and true man. It is impossible,
then, that in Christ there is only one nature.

[10] Again, from two abiding one nature is constituted:
from bodily parts, if you like, as an animal is constituted of
its members—which cannot be said in this case, since the divine nature is not something bodily; if you like, something
one is constituted from matter and form, as an animal is constituted of its soul and body. Neither can this be said in the
present discussion, for it was shown in Book I[12] that God can
neither be matter nor the form of anything. Then, if Christ
is true God and true man, as was seen,[13] it is impossible that
in Him there be one nature only.

[11] The subtraction or addition of an essential principle,
furthermore, varies the species of a thing; consequently, it
changes the nature which is not other than "the essence which
the definition signifies."[14] For this reason we see that a specific difference added to a definition or subtracted from it
makes a difference in species; so the rational animal and the

10. See above, ch. 29 and 31.
12. SCG, I, ch. 17 and 27.
14. See above, ¶5–6.

11. See above, ch. 34.
13. See above, ch. 34.

one lacking reason differ in species, just as in numbers the addition or subtraction of unity makes another species of number.[15] But form is an essential principle. So, every addition of form makes another species and another nature (as we are now speaking of nature). If, then, the divinity of the Word be added to the human nature as a form, it will make another nature. And thus Christ will not be of the human nature but of some other; just as an animated body is of another nature than that which is body only.

[12] Then, again, things which do not agree in nature are not similar in species; man and horse, for example. But, if Christ's nature be a composite of the divine and human, clearly Christ's nature will not be in other men. Therefore, He will not be similar to us in species. And this is contrary to the Apostle's word: "It behooved Him in all things to be made like unto His brethren" (Heb. 2:17).

[13] There is more. One species is always constituted of form and matter which is actually or potentially predicable of many according to the essentials of the species. If, then, the divine nature accrues to the human nature as a form, some common species must spring from the mixture of the two, and in this many should be able to share. And this is plainly false. For there is but one Jesus Christ (I Cor. 8:6), God and man. Therefore, the divine and human natures have not established one nature in Christ.

[14] Moreover, even this saying of Eutyches seems foreign to the faith, that before the union there were two natures in Christ. For, since a human nature is constituted of a soul and a body, it would follow that the soul, or the body, or both were in being before Christ's incarnation. And this the points made above[16] show to be false. This, then, is contrary to the faith: to say that before the union there were two natures in Christ and, after the union, one.

15. Aristotle, *Metaphysics*, VIII, 3, (1043b 34–1044a 2).
16. See above, ch. 30 and 34.

Chapter 36.

ON THE ERROR OF MACARIUS OF ANTIOCH, WHO HOLDS THERE IS BUT ONE WILL IN CHRIST

[1]   Now, the position of Macarius of Antioch seems to come to just about the same thing. He says that in Christ there is only one operation and will.[1]

[2]   Every nature, of course, has a proper operation of its own, for the form is the principle of operation, and in accord with its form every nature has the species proper to it. Hence, as of diverse natures there are diverse forms, there must be also diverse actions. If, then, in Christ there be one action, it follows that there is in him but one nature. This last belongs to the Eutychean heresy.[2] We then conclude that it is false to say there is but one operation in Christ.

[3]   Again. In Christ there is the perfect divine nature by which He is consubstantial with the Father, and a perfect human nature by which He is one in species with us. But the perfection of the divine nature includes having will (this was shown in Book I[3]); similarly, also, the perfection of human nature includes having a will by which a man has free choice. There must, then, be in Christ two wills.

[4]   The will, further, is one potential part of the human soul, as the intellect is. If, then, in Christ there was no other will than the will of the Word, by an equal account there was no other intellect than the intellect of the Word. Thus we return to the position of Apollinaris.[4]

[5]   If, moreover, there was in Christ but one will, surely it was only the divine will. For the divine will which the Word had from eternity He could not lose. But the divine will is unrelated to merit because he merits who is tending toward perfection. Thus, then, Christ by His passion would have merited nothing—whether for Himself, or for us. The contrary of this is taught by the Apostle: "He was made obedient to the

---

1. See Mansi, *Amplissima Collectio*, col. 350; and on Monothelism see Hughes, *A Popular History of the Catholic Church*, pp. 46–49.
2. See above, ch. 35.   3. SCG, I, ch. 72.   4. See above, ch. 33.

Father even unto death, for which cause God also hath exalted Him" (Phil. 2:8–9).

[6] What is more, if there was no human will in Christ, it follows that by His assumed nature He had no free choice. So, then, Christ used to act not after the fashion of man, but after the manner of the other animals who lack free choice. Then, nothing in His acts was virtuous or laudable, nothing a model for imitation by us. In vain, then, he says in Matthew (11:29): "Learn of Me because I am meek, and humble of heart"; and in John (13:15): "I have given you an example, that as I have done to you, so do you also."

[7] Again, in one who is pure man, although he is one in supposit, there are many appetites and operations according to the diversity of natural principles. For in his rational part there is will; in his sensitive, the irascible and concupiscible appetites; and, further, the natural appetite following on natural powers. In the same way he sees with the eye, hears with the ear, steps with the foot, speaks with the tongue, and understands with the mind; and these are diverse operations. The case is such because the operations are not multiplied according to diverse subjects operating only, but as well according to diverse principles by which one and the same subject operates, and from which the operations take their species. But the divine nature is much more removed from human nature than the principles of human nature are from one another. Therefore, the will and operation of the divine and the human nature in Christ are distinguished from one another, although Christ Himself is one in each of the natures.

[8] Furthermore, Scriptural authority clearly shows that in Christ there were two wills. He Himself says: "I came down from heaven, not to do My own will, but the will of Him that sent Me" (John 6:38); and again: "Not My will, but Thine be done" (Luke 22:42). From these words it is clear that there was in Christ another will apart from the will of the Father. But, clearly, there was in Him a will common to Him and the Father. For, just as the Father's and the Son's nature is one, so also is their will. Therefore, there are two wills in Christ.

[9] But this is as clear of their operations. For in Christ

there was an operation common to Him and the Father, for He says: "What things soever the Father doth these the Son also doth in like manner" (John 5:19). But there is another operation in Him which is not proper to the Father: to sleep, for example, to be thirsty, to eat, and others of this sort which Christ made man did or suffered; so the Evangelists tell us. Therefore, there was not one operation.

[10] Now, the present position seems to have had its rise in this: its authors did not know how to distinguish between what is simply one, and what is one by order. For they saw the human will in Christ *ordered* entirely beneath the divine will, so that Christ willed nothing with His human will except that which the divine will disposed Him to will. In like manner, also, Christ did nothing in His human nature, whether by acting or by suffering, except as the divine will disposed; hence we read: "I do always the things that please Him" (John 8:29). The human operation of Christ, also, achieved a kind of divine efficacy by union with the divinity, just as the action of a secondary agent achieves a kind of efficacy from the principal agent; and this resulted: every action or suffering of His was salutary. For this reason Dionysius calls the human operation of Christ "theandric," that is, "God-mannish"; and also because it is of God and a man. So, those men, seeing the human operation and will of Christ ordered beneath the divine in an infallible order, decided that there was in Christ only one will and operation, although there is no identity (as was said) between *one by order* and *one simply*.

Chapter 37.

AGAINST THOSE WHO SAID THAT THE SOUL AND BODY DO NOT CONSTITUTE A UNITY IN CHRIST

[1] From the foregoing[1] it is clear that there is only one Person in Christ as the faith maintains; and that there are two natures, contrarily to what Nestorius and Eutyches held. Yet this appears foreign to what natural reason experiences,

1. See above, ch. 35–36.

and therefore there were some later on[2] who took a position on this union such as the following. The soul and body union constitutes *a man*, but the union of this soul and this body constitutes *this man*. And this is the designation of person or hypostasis. Wishing, then, to avoid being pushed into asserting in Christ some hypostasis or person other than the hypostasis or Person of the Word, these men said that the soul and body were not united in Christ, nor was a substance made from them. In saying this they were trying to avoid the Nestorian heresy. This also seemed impossible: that one thing be substantial to another, yet not be of the nature which that other previously had, without any mutation taking place; and the Word, of course, is entirely immutable. Therefore, lest they be forced to make the assumed soul and body belong to the nature which the Word had eternally, they laid it down that the Word assumed the human soul and body in an accidental fashion, just as a man puts on his clothes. By this they wished to exclude the error of Eutyches.

[2] But this position is entirely repugnant to the teaching of the faith. For a soul and body by their union constitute a man, since a form which accrues to matter constitutes a species. If, then, soul and body were not united in Christ, Christ was not a man. This goes against the Apostle's words: "The mediator of God and men, the man Christ Jesus" (I Tim. 2:5).

[3] Again, every one of us is said to be a man on this account that he is constituted of a rational soul and a body. But, if Christ is not called man on that account, but only because He had a soul and a body, although not united, He will be called man equivocally and will not be in the same species with us. This is against the Apostle's words: "It behooved Him in all things to be made like unto His brethren" (Heb. 2:17).

[4] Furthermore, not every body belongs to human nature, but the human body alone. Of course, it is not a human body except for the fact that it has been vivified by union with the rational soul. For one says neither eye, nor hand, nor foot, nor flesh, nor bone—with the soul gone—except by equivoca-

---

2. See Peter Lombard, *Libri IV Sententiarum*, l. III, d. vi, cap. 4 (ed. Quaracchi, II, p. 579).

tion.[3] Therefore, one will not be able to say that the Word assumed human nature if He did not assume a body united to a soul.

[5]   What is more, the human soul by its nature has a capacity for union with the body. Therefore, a soul which is never united to a body to constitute something is not a human soul, for "what is apart from nature can never be."[4] If then, the soul of Christ is not united to His body to constitute something, we conclude that it is not a human soul. And, thus, in Christ there was no human nature.

[6]   There is more. If the Word was united to the soul and body accidentally, as one is to clothing, the human nature was not the nature of the Word. Then the Word, after the union, was not subsisting in two natures; just as a man in his clothing is not said to subsist in two natures. It was for saying this that Eutyches was condemned at the Council of Chalcedon.[5]

[7]   Again, what the clothes suffer is not referred to the wearer. One does not say a man is born when he is dressed, nor wounded if his clothes are torn. If the Word, then, took on a soul and a body, as a man does his clothes, no one will be able to say that God was born, or that He suffered by reason of the body He assumed.

[8]   If the Word, moreover, assumed human nature only as a garment in which to be apparent to the eyes of men, He would have assumed the soul in vain. This by its nature is invisible.

[9]   Furthermore, in this fashion the Son's assumption of the flesh would not have differed from the Holy Spirit's assumption of the form of a dove in which He appeared (Matt. 3:16). And this is plainly false. For one does not say the Holy Spirit has "become dove" or is "less than the Father," as one says that the Son "has become man" and is less than the Father in the nature assumed (John 14:28).

[10]   Again, when it is earnestly weighed, the awkwardness of a diversity of heresies follows on this position. For in saying that the Son of God is united to the soul and the flesh in an

3. Aristotle, De anima, II, 1 (412b 22).
4. Aristotle, De coelo, II, 3 (286a 18).
5. See Mansi, Amplissima Collectio, tom. VII, col. 115.

accidental mode as a man is to his garments, it agrees with the opinion of Nestorius, who claimed the union took place by the indwelling of God's Word in a man.[6] God's being clothed, of course, cannot be understood through bodily touch but only through indwelling grace. And in saying that the union of the Word to the soul and human flesh was accidental, one must be saying that the Word after the union was not subsistent in two natures. And this Eutyches said.[7] For nothing subsists in that to which it is accidentally united. But, when this position says that the soul and body are not united to constitute something, it partially agrees with Arius and Apollinaris: they held that the body of Christ was not animated by the rational soul;[8] and it partially agrees with Mani: he held that Christ was not true man, but a phantasy only.[9] For, if the soul is not united to the flesh for the constitution of something, it was but phantasy when Christ appeared similar to other men constituted by the union of soul and body.

[11] This position, of course, had as its occasion the words of the Apostle: "In habit found as a man" (Phil. 2:70). They did not understand that this was said metaphorically. But things said metaphorically need not be similar in every respect. So, the human nature assumed by the Word has a kind of likeness to clothing, in that the Word was seen in His visible flesh just as a man is seen in his clothing; but the likeness is not in this, that the union of the Word to human nature in Christ was in an accidental mode.

Chapter 38.

AGAINST THOSE WHO PUT TWO SUPPOSITS OR HYPOSTASES IN THE ONE PERSON OF CHRIST

[1] Others, indeed, have avoided this position by reason of the awkwardness described above. They have held that soul and flesh in our Lord Jesus Christ constitutes one substance, namely, a certain man of the same species as other men. They call this man united to the Word of God, not in nature, indeed, but in person, so that there is one person of the Word

6. See above, ch. 34.
8. See above, ch. 32.

7. See above, ch. 35.
9. See above, ch. 29.

of God and of that man. But, since that man is a kind of individual substance—and this is to be an hypostasis and supposit—some say[1] that in Christ the hypostasis and supposit of that man is one and that of the Word of God another; but that there is one person of each of the two. On account of this unity, the Word of God, as they say, is predicated of that man and that man of the Word of God. This sense results: "The Word of God is man," and that is: "The person of the Word of God is the person of the man," and conversely. And in this account whatever is predicated of the Word of God is, they say, able to be predicated of that man; and, conversely, although with a kind of reduplication, so that, when it is said "God has suffered," the sense is "A man who is God by unity of person has suffered," and "A man created the stars" means "He who is man."

[2] But, of necessity, this position lapses into the error of Nestorius. For, if the difference of person and hypostasis be marked, one finds that person is not foreign to hypostasis, but a kind of part of hypostasis. For a person is nothing else than a hypostasis of a certain nature; namely, rational. This is clear from Boethius' definition: "person is the individual substance of a rational nature."[2] Clearly, then, although not every hypostasis is a person, every hypostasis of human nature is, nonetheless, a person. If, therefore, from the mere union of soul and body in Christ there is constituted a certain particular substance which is the hypostasis—namely, that man—it follows that from the same union a person is constituted. There will be, then, in Christ two persons: one, and newly constituted, of that man; the other, eternal, of the Word of God. And this belongs to the Nestorian impiety.

[3] Again, even if the hypostasis of that man could not be called a person, the hypostasis of the Word of God is nonetheless the same as His Person. If, therefore, the hypostasis of the Word of God is not that of the man, neither will the Person of the Word of God be the person of the man. This

---

1. On this position see Peter Lombard, *Libri IV Sententiarum*, l. III d. vi, cap. 2 (ed. Quaracchi, II, p. 574).
2. Note that part here means part as a species is part of a genus. For the definition see Boethius, *De duabus naturis*, III (*PL*, 64, col. 1343).

will falsify their own assertion that the person of that man is the Person of the Word of God.

[4] If one were to grant, further, that person is other than the hypostasis of God's Word or of the man, one could find no difference save one: person adds some property to hypostasis. Nothing, of course, pertaining to the genus of substance can be added, since hypostasis is the most complete thing in the genus of substance, and it is called "first substance."[3] If, then, the union is made in person and not in hypostasis, it follows that the union takes place only according to some accidental property. This, too, comes again back to the error of Nestorius.

[5] Cyril, moreover, in his letter to Nestorius approved by the Council of Ephesus, has this to say: "If anyone does not confess that the Word from the Father is united to the flesh in subsistence, that Christ is one with his flesh, that is to say, that the same one is God and man at the same time, let him be anathema."[4] And almost everywhere in the synodal writings this is assigned as the error of Nestorius, who put two hypostases in Christ.

[6] Damascene, moreover, in Book III, says: "It was from two perfect natures, we say, that the union took place, and not in a prosopic," that is, personal way, "as God's enemy Nestorius says, but according to the hypostasis."[5] Thus, clearly and expressly, this was the position of Nestorius: to confess one person and two hypostases.

[7] Again, hypostasis and supposit must be identified. Everything else is predicated of the first substance, which is the hypostasis: namely, the universals in the genus of substance as well as accidents, as the Philosopher says in his *Categories*.[6] If, therefore, there are not two hypostases in Christ, neither are there two supposits.

[8] If the Word and that man, furthermore, differ in sup-

3. See Aristotle, *Categories*, 5 (2a 15).
4. For the text see Mansi, *Amplissima Collectio*, IV, cols. 1068, 1082, 1086; and IX, col. 221.
5. *De fide orthodoxa*, III, 4 (PG, 94, col. 994); on John Damascene, see Gilson, *History of Christian Philosophy*, pp. 91, 600.
6. Aristotle, *Categories*, 3 (2a 15-33).

posit, it must be that when that man is supposed[7] the Word of God is not supposed, nor is the converse true. But, if the supposits are distinct, what is said of them must be distinguished, for the divine predicates mentioned are disproportionate to the man's supposit except by reason of the Word; and the converse is true. Therefore, one must take separately the things said of Christ in Scripture; namely, the divine and the human. And this is contrary to the opinion of Cyril confirmed by the Synod: "If one divides between two persons or subsistences the words said in the evangelical and apostolic Scriptures—whether they be said about Christ by the saints, or by Him about Himself; and marks off some of them, indeed, as for a man especially understood alongside that Word from God; and marks off others as capable of being said by God, for that Word from God the Father alone: let him be anathema."[8]

[9] Moreover, in the position described, things proportioned to the Word of God by nature would not be said of that man except by a certain association in one person; this is what the interposed reduplication means when they expound thus: "That man created the stars," that is, "the Son of God, who is that man," and similarly with others of that sort. Hence, when one says: "That man is God," one understands it thus: "That man exists by the Word of God." But it is this kind of expression that Cyril condemns when he says: "If anyone dares to say that the man assumed ought to be co-adored with God's Word, co-glorified, and co-named God, a second of two with the first, so to speak (for that is what "co" forces us to understand as often as it is added), and does not honor Emmanuel with one adoration and offer Him one glorification, inasmuch as the Word was made flesh; let him be anathema."[9]

[10]   There is more. If that man is other than the Word in

7. The force of supposed here is this: made the subject of predication. The condemned heretical position is this one: in "I thirst" the supposit, or supposed, or subject of predication is "that man"; in "I will raise him up on the last day" the supposit, or supposed, or subject of predication is the Word. In non-technical English, "supposed" rarely has this signification.
8. See Mansi, Amplissima Collectio, tom. IV, col. 1082–1083.
9. Ibid., col. 1083.

supposit, he cannot belong to the person of the Word except by the assumption by which He was assumed by the Word. But this is foreign to a correct understanding of the faith, for the Council of Ephesus says in the words of Felix, Pope and martyr: "We believe in God our Jesus, born of the Virgin Mary: that He is God's everlasting Son and Word, and not a man assumed by God so that there is another beside Him. Nor did God's Son assume a man that there be another beside Him; but the perfect existing God was made at the same time perfect man, made flesh of the Virgin."[10]

[11] Again, things which are many in supposit are many simply, and they are but incidentally one. If, then, in Christ there are two supposits, it follows that He is two simply and not incidentally. And this is "to dissolve Jesus" (I John 4:3), for everything, in so far as it is, is one.[11]

Chapter 39.

WHAT THE CATHOLIC FAITH HOLDS
ABOUT THE INCARNATION OF CHRIST

[1] From what has been set down above[1] it is clear that according to the tradition of the Catholic faith we must say that in Christ there is a perfect divine nature and a perfect human nature, constituted by a rational soul and human flesh; and that these two natures are united in Christ not by indwelling only, nor in an accidental mode, as a man is united to his garments, nor in a personal relation and property only, but in one hypostasis and one supposit. Only in this way can we save what the Scriptures hand on about the Incarnation. Since, then, sacred Scripture without distinction attributes the things of God to that man, and the things of that man to God (as is plain from the foregoing), He of whom each class is said must be one and the same.

[2] But opposites cannot be said truly of the same thing in the same way: the divine and human things said of Christ are, of course, in opposition, *suffering* and *incapable of suffering*, for example, or *dead* and *immortal*, and the remainder of this

10. *Ibid.*, col. 1187.   11. Aristotle, *Metaphysics*, IV, 2, (1003b 24).
1. In ch. 28–38.

kind; therefore, it is necessarily in different ways that the divine and the human are predicated of Christ. So, then, with respect to the "about which" each class is predicated no distinction must be made, but unity is discovered. But with respect to "what" is predicated, a distinction must be made. Natural properties, of course, are predicated of everything according to its nature; thus to be borne downward is predicated of this stone consequently on its nature as heavy. Since, then, there are different ways of predicating things human and divine of Christ, one must say there are in Christ two natures neither confused nor mixed. But that about which one predicates natural properties consequently on the proper nature pertaining to the genus of substance is the hypostasis and supposit of that nature. Since, then, that is not distinct and is one about which one predicates things divine and human concerning Christ, one must say that Christ is one hypostasis and one supposit of a human and a divine nature. For thus truly and properly will things divine be predicated of that man in accord with the fact that the man bears the supposit not only of the human but of the divine nature; conversely, one predicates things human of God's Word in that He is the supposit of the human nature.

[3] It is clear also from this that, although the Son is incarnate, neither the Father nor the Holy Spirit, for all that, need be incarnate, since the Incarnation did not take place by a union in the nature in which the three divine Persons are together, but in hypostasis or supposit, wherein the three Persons are distinguished. And thus, as in the Trinity there is a plurality of Persons subsisting in one nature, so in the mystery of the Incarnation there is one Person subsisting in a plurality of natures.

Chapter 40.

OBJECTIONS AGAINST FAITH IN THE INCARNATION

[1] But against this statement of the Catholic faith many difficulties come together, and by reason of these the adversaries of the faith attack the Incarnation.[1]

1. See below, ch. 49, for the solutions.

[2] We showed in Book I[2] that God is neither a body nor a power in a body. But, if He assumed flesh, it follows either that He was changed into a body or that He was a power in a body after the Incarnation. It seems, then, impossible that God was incarnate.

[3] Again, whatever acquires a new nature is subject to substantial change; for in this is a thing generated, that it acquires a nature. Then, if the hypostasis of the Son of God becomes a subsistent anew in human nature, it appears that it was substantially changed.

[4] Furthermore, no hypostasis of a nature extends outside that nature; rather, indeed, the nature is found outside the hypostasis, since there are many hypostases under the nature. If, then, the hypostasis of the Son of God becomes by the Incarnation the hypostasis of a human nature, the Son of God —one must conclude—is not everywhere after the Incarnation, since the human nature is not everywhere.

[5] Once again; one and the same thing has only one *what-it-is*, for by this one means a thing's substance and of one there is but one. But the nature of any thing at all is its *what-it-is*, "for the nature of a thing is what the definition signifies."[3] It seems impossible, then, that one hypostasis subsist in two natures.

[6] Furthermore, in things which are without matter, the quiddity of a thing is not other than the thing, as was shown above.[4] And this is especially the case in God, who is not only His own quiddity, but also His own act of being.[5] But human nature cannot be identified with a divine hypostasis. Therefore, it seems impossible that a divine hypostasis subsist in human nature.

[7] Once again; a nature is more simple and more formal than the hypostasis which subsists therein, for it is by the addition of something material that the common nature is individuated to this hypostasis. If, then, a divine hypostasis subsists in human nature, it seems to follow that human nature is more simple and more formal than a divine hypostasis. And this is altogether impossible.

---

2. *SCG*, I, ch. 20.
4. *SCG*, I, ch. 21; II, ch. 54.
3. Aristotle, *Physics*, II, 1 (193a 30).
5. *SCG*, I, ch. 22.

[8]   It is, furthermore, only in matter and form composites that one finds a difference between the singular thing and its quiddity. This is because the singular is individuated by designated matter, and in the quiddity and nature of the species the latter is not included. For, in marking off Socrates, one includes this matter, but one does not in his account of human nature. Therefore, every hypostasis subsisting in human nature is constituted by signate matter. This cannot be said of the divine hypostasis. So, it does not seem possible that the hypostasis of God's Word subsist in human nature.

[9]   Furthermore, the soul and body in Christ were not less in power than in other men. But in other men their union constitutes a supposit, an hypostasis, and a person. Therefore, in Christ the union of soul and body constitutes a supposit, hypostasis, and person of the Word of God; this is eternal. Therefore in Christ there is another supposit, hypostasis, and person beside the supposit, hypostasis, and person of the Word of God. Or so it seems.

[10]   There is more. Just as soul and body constitute human nature in common, so this soul and this body constitute *this man*, and this is the hypostasis of a man. But this soul and this body were in Christ. Therefore, their union constitutes an hypostasis, it seems. And we conclude exactly as before.

[11]   Again, this man who is Christ, considered as consisting of soul alone and body, is a certain substance; not, of course, a universal one; therefore, a particular one. Therefore, it is an hypostasis.

[12]   Moreover, if the supposit of the human and the divine nature in Christ is identified, then in one's understanding of the man who is Christ there ought to be a divine hypostasis. Of course, this is not in one's understanding of other men. Therefore, *man* will be said equivocally of Christ and others. Hence, He will not belong to the same species with us.

[13]   In Christ, what is more, one finds three things, as is clear from what was said:[6] a body, a soul, and divinity. The soul, of course, since it is nobler than the body, is not the supposit of the body, but its form. Neither, then, is what is

6. See above, ch. 39.

divine the supposit of the human nature; it is, rather, formally related to that nature.

[14] Furthermore, whatever accrues to something after its being is complete accrues to it accidentally. But, since the Word is from eternity, plainly the flesh assumed accrues to Him after His being is complete. Therefore, it accrues to Him accidentally.

Chapter 41.

HOW ONE SHOULD UNDERSTAND THE INCARNATION OF THE SON OF GOD

[1] Now, to get at the solution of these objections, one must begin somewhat more fundamentally. Since Eutyches set it down that the union of God and man took place in nature;[1] Nestorius, that it was neither in nature nor in person;[2] but the Catholic faith holds this: that the union takes place in Person, not in nature—it seems necessary to know first what it is "to be made one in nature," and what it is "to be made one in person."

[2] Grant, then, that *nature* is a word used in many ways: the generation of living things, and the principle of generation and of motion, and the matter and the form are all called nature. Sometimes, also, nature[3] is said of the *what-it-is* of a thing, which includes the things that bear on the integrity of the species; in this way we say that human nature is common to all men, and say the same in all other cases. Those things, therefore, are made one in nature from which the integrity of a species is established; just as the soul and human body are made one to establish the species of the animal, so, universally, whatever the parts of a species are.

[3] Of course, it is impossible that to a species already established in its integrity something extrinsic be united for the unity of its nature without losing the species. For, since species are like numbers, and in these any unity added or substracted makes the species vary, if to a species already perfected some-

1. See above, ch. 35.   2. See above, ch. 34.
3. See above, ch. 35, ¶5.

thing be added, necessarily it is now another species; thus, if to animate substance one adds only *sensible*, one will have another species, for animal and plant are different species. It does happen, nonetheless, that one finds something which is not integral to the species; in an individual included under that species—white and dressed, for instance, in Socrates or in Plato, or a sixth finger, or something of the sort. Hence, nothing prevents some things being made one in the individual which are not united in one integrity of species; thus, human nature and whiteness and music in Socrates; and things of this kind are united and are called "one by subject." Now, the individual in the genus of substance is called *hypostasis*, and even in rational substances is called *person*; therefore, all things such as those mentioned are suitably said to be united "in the hypostasis" or even "in the person." Clearly, then, nothing prevents some things not united in nature from being united in hypostasis or person.

[4]   But, when the heretics heard that in Christ a union of God and man took place, they approached the exposition of this point in contrary ways, but neglected the way of the truth. For some thought of this union after the mode of things united into one nature: so Arius and Apollinaris, holding that the Word stood to the body of Christ as soul or as mind;[4] and so Eutyches, who held that before the Incarnation there were two natures of God and man, but after the Incarnation only one.

[5]   But others, seeing the impossibility of this position, went off on a contrary road. Now, the things which accrue to one having a nature, but do not belong to the integrity of that nature, seem either to be accidents—say, whiteness and music; or to stand in an accidental relation—say, a ring, a garment, a house, and the like. Of course, they weighed this: Since the human nature accrues to the Word of God without belonging to the integrity of His nature, it is necessary (so they thought) that the human nature have an accidental union with the Word. To be sure, it clearly cannot be in the Word as an accident: both because God is not susceptible to an accident (as was previously proved);[5] and because human nature, being

4. See above, ch. 32.   5. SCG, I, ch. 23.

in the genus of substance, cannot be the accident of anything. Hence there appeared to be this remaining: Human nature accrues to the Word, not as an accident, but as a thing accidentally related to the Word. Nestorius, then, held that the human nature of Christ stood to the Word as a kind of temple, so that only by indwelling was the union of the Word to the human nature to be understood. And because a temple possesses its individuation apart from him who dwells in the temple, and the individuation suitable to human nature is personality, this was left: that the personality of the human nature was one, and that of the Word another. Thus, the Word and that man were two persons.

[6]   To be sure, others wished to avoid this awkwardness.[6] So, regarding the human nature they introduced a disposition such that personality could not be properly suitable to it. They said that the soul and the body, in which the integrity of human nature consists, were so assumed by the Word that the soul was not united to the body to establish any substance, lest they be forced to say that the substance so established fulfilled the account of person. But they held the union of the Word to soul and body to be like a union to things in an accidental relation, for instance, of the clothed to his clothes. In this they were somehow imitating Nestorius.

[7]   Now, with these accounts set aside by the foregoing,[7] it must be laid down that the union of the Word and the man was such that one nature was not breathed together out of two; and that the union of the Word to the human nature was not like that of a substance—a man, say—to those externals which are accidentally related to him, like a house and a garment. But let the Word be set down as subsisting in a human nature as in one made His very own by the Incarnation; and in consequence that body is truly the body of the Word of God, and the soul in like manner, and the Word of God is truly man.

[8]   And although to explain this union perfectly is beyond man's strength, nonetheless, in accord with our measure and power, we will try to say something "for the upbuilding of the

6. See above, ch. 37.   7. See above, ch. 34–38.

faith" (cf. Eph. 4:29), so that concerning this mystery the Catholic faith may be defended from the infidels.

[9]   Now, in all created things nothing is found so like this union as the union of soul to body. And the likeness would be greater, as Augustine also says, in *Against Felician*,[8] if there were one intellect in all men. So some have held, and according to them one ought to say that the pre-existing intellect is in such wise united anew to a man's conception that from each of these two a new person is made; just as we hold that the pre-existing Word is united to the human nature in a unity of person. Accordingly, and by reason of the likeness of these two unions, Athanasius says in the Creed: "as the rational soul and flesh are one man, so God and man are one Christ."

[10]   However, since the rational soul is united to the body both as to matter and as to an instrument, there cannot be a likeness so far as the first mode of union is concerned, for thus from God and man one nature would be made, since the matter and the form properly establish the nature of a species. Therefore, what is left is to look upon the likeness so far as the soul is united to the body as an instrument. With this, also, there is the concordance of the ancient Doctors, who held that the human nature in Christ was "a kind of organ of the divinity," just as the body is held to be an organ of the soul.

[11]   Now, the body and its parts are the organ of the soul in one fashion; external instruments in quite another. For this axe is not the soul's very own instrument, as this hand is, for by an axe many can operate, but this hand is deputy to this soul in its very own operation. For this reason the hand is an instrument of the soul united to it and its very own, but the axe is an instrument both external and common. This is the way, then, in which even the union of God and man can be considered. For all men are related to God as instruments of a sort, and by these He works: "for it is God who worketh in you both to will and to accomplish according to His good will" (Phil. 2:3), as the Apostle says. But other men are related to God as extrinsic and separated instruments, so to say; for God does not move them only to operations which are His very own, but to the operations common to every rational nature,

8. St. Augustine, *Contra Felicianum*, 12 (*PL*, 42, col. 1166).

to understand the truth, for example, to love the good, to do what is just. But the human nature in Christ is assumed with the result that instrumentally He performs the things which are the proper operation of God alone: to wash away sins, for example, to enlighten minds by grace, to lead into the perfection of eternal life. The human nature of Christ, then, is compared to God as a proper and conjoined instrument is compared, as the hand is compared to the soul.

[12] Nor is there departure from the course of natural things because one thing is by nature the proper instrument of another, and this other is not its form. For the tongue, so far as it is the instrument of speech, is the intellect's very own organ; and the intellect is nevertheless, as the Philosopher proves,[9] not the act of any part of the body. In like manner, too, one finds an instrument which does not pertain to the nature of the species, which is, nevertheless, on the material side fitted to this individual; a sixth finger, for example, or something of the sort. Therefore, nothing prevents our putting the union of the human nature to the Word in this way: that the human nature be, so to speak, an instrument of the Word—not a separated, but a conjoined, instrument; and the human nature, nonetheless, does not belong to the nature of the Word, and the Word is not its form; nevertheless the human nature belongs to His person.

[13] But the examples mentioned have not been set down so that one should look in them for an all-round likeness; for one should understand that the Word of God was able to be much more sublimely and more intimately united to human nature than the soul to its very own instrument of whatever sort, especially since He is said to be united to the entire human nature with the intellect as medium. And although the Word of God by His power penetrates all things, conserving all, that is, and supporting all, it is to the intellectual creatures, who can properly enjoy the Word and share with Him, that from a kind of kinship of likeness He can be both more eminently and more ineffably united.

9. Aristotle, *De anima*, III, 4, (429a 25).

Chapter 42.

THAT THE ASSUMPTION OF HUMAN NATURE
WAS MOST SUITED TO THE WORD OF GOD

[1] From this it is also clear that the assumption of human nature was outstanding in suitability to the person of the Word. For, if the assumption of human nature is ordered to the salvation of men, if the ultimate salvation of man is to be perfected in his intellective part by the contemplation of the First Truth, it should have been by the Word who proceeds from the Father by an intellectual emanation that human nature was assumed.

[2] There especially seems to be, furthermore, a kind of kinship of the Word for human nature. For man gets his proper species from being rational. But the Word is kin to the reason. Hence, among the Greeks "word" and "reason" are called *logos*. Most appropriately, then, was the Word united to the reasonable nature, for by reason of the kinship mentioned the divine Scripture attributes the name "image" to the Word and to man; the Apostle says of the Word that He is "the image of the invisible God" (Col. 1:15); and the same writer says of man that "the man is the image of God" (I Cor. 11:7).

[3] The Word also has a kind of essential kinship not only with the rational nature, but also universally with the whole of creation, since the Word contains the essences of all things created by God, just as man the artist in the conception of his intellect comprehends the essences of all the products of art. Thus, then, all creatures are nothing but a kind of real expression and representation of those things which are comprehended in the conception of the divine Word; wherefore all things are said (John 1:3) to be made by the Word. Therefore, suitably was the Word united to the creature, namely, to human nature.

Chapter 43.

THAT THE HUMAN NATURE ASSUMED BY THE WORD DID NOT PRE-EXIST ITS ASSUMPTION, BUT WAS ASSUMED IN THE CONCEPTION ITSELF

[1] However, since the Word assumed the human nature into a unity of person (this is clear from the things already said[1]), necessarily the human nature did not pre-exist before its union to the Word.

[2] Now, if it were pre-existing, since a nature cannot pre-exist except in an individual, there would have had to be some individual of that human nature pre-existing before the union. But the individual of human nature is an hypostasis and person. Then one will be saying that the human nature to be assumed by the Word had pre-existed in some hypostasis or person. If, then, that nature had been assumed with the previous hypostasis or person remaining, two hypostases or persons would have remained after the union: one of the Word, the other of a man. And thus the union would not have taken place in the hypostasis or person. This is contrary to the teaching of the faith. But if that hypostasis or person in which the nature to be assumed by the Word had pre-existed were not remaining, this could not have happened without corruption, for no singular ceases to be what it is except through corruption. Thus, then, would that man have had to be corrupted who pre-existed the union and, in consequence, the human nature, as well, which was existing in him. It was impossible, then, that the Word assume into a unity of person some pre-existing man.

[3] But at the same time it would detract from the perfection of the incarnation of God's Word, if something natural to man were lacking to it. But it is natural to man to be born in a human birth. But God's Word would not have this if He had assumed a pre-existing man, for that man in his birth would have existed as pure man, and so his birth could not be attributed to the Word, nor could the Blessed Virgin be called

1. See above, ch. 39.

the Mother of the Word. But what the Catholic faith confesses regarding natural things is that He is "in all things like
as we are, without sin" (Heb. 4:15); and it says that the Son
of God was "made of a woman," following the Apostle (Gal.
4:4), that He was born and that the Virgin is the Mother of
God. This, then, was not seemly, that He assume a pre-existing man.

[4]   Hence, also, it is clear that from the first moment of
conception He united human nature to Himself. Just as God's
Word's being human demands that the Word of God be born
by a human birth, in order to be a true and natural man in
complete conformity with us in respect to nature, so, too, it
requires that God's Word be conceived by a human conception, for, in the order of nature, no man is born unless first he
be conceived. But, if the human nature to be assumed had
been conceived in any state whatever before it was united to
the Word, that conception could not be so attributed to the
Word of God that one might call Him conceived by a human
conception. Necessarily, then, from the first moment of conception the human nature was united to the Word of God.

[5]   Again, the active power in human generation acts toward
the completion of human nature in a determined individual.
But, if the Word of God had not assumed human nature from
the first moment of His conception, the active power in the
generation would, before the union, have ordered its action to
an individual in human nature, and this is a human hypostasis
or person. But after the union the entire generation would
have had to be ordered to another hypostasis or person,
namely, to God's Word who was being born in the human
nature. And such a generation would not have been numerically one, if thus ordered to two persons. Neither would it—in
its entirety—have been one in form; this seems foreign to the
order of nature. Therefore, it was not suitable that the Word
of God assume human nature after the conception, but in the
conception itself.

[6]   Once again, this seems to be required by the order of
human generation: the one who is born must be the same as
the one conceived, not another, for conception is ordered to
birth. Hence, if the Son of God was born by a human birth,

it must be that it was the Son of God who was conceived in a human conception, and not a pure man.

Chapter 44.

THAT THE HUMAN NATURE ASSUMED BY
THE WORD IN THE CONCEPTION ITSELF
WAS PERFECT IN SOUL AND BODY

[1] Now, this further point is also clear: In the very beginning of conception the rational soul was united to the body.

[2] The Word of God, of course, assumed the body through the soul's mediation,[1] for the body of a man is not more subject to assumption by God than other bodies except because of the rational soul. The Word of God, then, did not assume the body without the rational soul. Therefore, since the Word of God assumed the body in the very beginning of conception, necessarily the rational soul was united to the body in the very beginning of conception.

[3] Moreover, one who grants what is posterior in a generation must grant also that which is prior in the order of generation. But the posterior in a generation is that which is most perfect. But the most perfect is the generated individual, and this in human generation is an hypostasis or person, and it is toward constituting this that the body and soul are ordered. Granted, then, a personality of the man generated, there must needs exist a body and a rational soul. But the personality of the man Christ is not different from the personality of God's Word. But the Word of God united a human body to Himself in the very conception. Therefore, the personality of that man was there. Therefore, the rational soul must also have been there.

[4] It would also have been awkward if the Word, the fount and origin of all perfections and forms, were united to a thing not formed, which still was lacking the perfection of nature. Now, anything corporeal that comes into being is, before its animation, formless and still lacking the perfection of nature. It was, therefore, not fitting for the Word of God to be united

1. See above, ch. 41.

to a body not yet animated. Thus, from the moment of conception that soul had to be united to the body.

[5] Hence, this point, too, is clear: The body assumed in the moment of conception was a formed body, if the assumption of something not formed was improper for the Word. But the soul demands its proper matter, just as any other natural form does. But the proper matter of the soul is the organized body, for a soul is "the entelechy of a natural organic body having life potentially."[2] If, then, the soul from the beginning of the conception was united to the body (this has been shown[3]), the body from the beginning of the conception was of necessity organized and formed. And even the organization of the body precedes in the order of generation the introduction of the rational soul. Here, again, if one grants what is posterior, he must grant what is prior.

[6] But there is no reason why a quantitative increase up to the due measure should not follow on the body's being animated. And so, regarding the conception of the man assumed, one should hold that in the very beginning of conception the body was organized and formed, but had not yet its due quantity.

Chapter 45.

THAT IT BECAME CHRIST TO BE BORN OF A VIRGIN

[1] It is, of course, now plain that of necessity that man was born from a Virgin Mother without natural seed.

[2] For the seed of the man is required in human generation as an active principle by reason of the active power in it. But the active power in the generation of the body of Christ could not be a natural power, in the light of the points we have seen. For the natural power does not of a sudden bring about the entire formation of the body; it requires time for this, but the body of Christ was in the first moment of conception formed and organized as was shown.[1] Therefore, one concludes that the generation of Christ was without natural seed.

---

2. Aristotle, *De anima*, II, 1 (412a 21).   3. See above, ¶3.
1. See above, ch. 44.

[3] Again, the male seed, in the generation of any animal at all, attracts to itself the matter supplied by the mother, as though the power which is in the male seed intends its own fulfillment as the end of the entire generation; hence, also, when the generation is completed, the seed itself, unchanged and fulfilled, is the offspring which is born. But the human generation of Christ had as ultimate term union with the divine Person, and not the establishment of a human person or hypostasis, as is clear from the foregoing.[2] In this generation, therefore, the active principle could not be the seed of the man; it could only be the divine power. Just as the seed of the man in the common generation of men attracts to its subsistence the matter supplied by the mother, so this same matter in the generation the Word of God has assumed into union with Himself.

[4] In like manner, of course, it was manifestly suitable that, even in the human generation of the Word of God, some spiritual property of the generation of a word should shine out. Now, a word as it proceeds from a speaker—whether conceived within or expressed without—brings no corruption to the speaker; rather, the word marks the plenitude of perfection in the speaker. It was in harmony with this that in His human generation the Word of God should be so conceived and born that the wholeness of His Mother was not impaired. And this, too, is clear: It became the Word of God, by whom all things are established and by whom all things are preserved in His wholeness, to be born so as to preserve His Mother's wholeness in every way. Therefore, suitably this generation was from a virgin.

[5] And for all that, this mode of generation detracts in nothing from the true and natural humanity of Christ, even though He was generated differently from other men. For clearly, since the divine power is infinite, as has been proved,[3] and since through it all causes are granted the power to produce an effect,[4] every effect whatever produced by every cause whatever can be produced by God without the assistance of that cause of the same species and nature. Then, just as the natural power which is in the human seed produces a true man

2. *Ibid.*   3. SCG, I, 43; II, 22.   4. SCG, III, ch. 66–67.

who has the human species and nature, so the divine power, which gave such power to the seed, can without its power produce that effect by constituting a true man who has the human species and nature.

[6]   But let someone object: a naturally generated man has a body naturally constituted from the seed of the male and what the female supplies—be that what it may; therefore, the body of Christ was not the same in nature as ours if it was not generated from the seed of a male. To this an answer may be made in accordance with a position of Aristotle;[5] he says that the seed of the male does not enter materially into the constitution of what is conceived; it is an active principle only, whereas the entire matter of the body is supplied by the mother. Taken thus, in respect of matter the body of Christ does not differ from ours; for our bodies also are constituted materially of that which is taken from the mother.

[7]   But, if one rejects the position of Aristotle just described, then the objection just described has no efficacy. For the likeness or unlikeness of things in matter is not marked off by the state of the matter in the principle of generation, but by the state of the matter already prepared as it is in the term of the generation. There is no difference in matter between air generated from earth and that from water, because, although water and earth are different in the principle of generation, they are nonetheless reduced by the generating action to one disposition. Thus, then, by the divine power the matter taken from the woman alone can be reduced at the end of the generation to a disposition identical with that which matter has if taken simultaneously from the male and female. Hence, there will be no unlikeness by reason of diversity of matter between the body of Christ which was formed by the divine power out of matter taken from the mother alone, and our bodies which are formed by the natural power from matter, even though they are taken from both parents. Surely this is clear; the matter taken simultaneously from a man and a woman and that "slime of the earth" (Gen. 2:7) of which God formed the first man (very certainly a true man and like us in everything) differ more from one another than

5. Aristotle, De generatione animalium, I, 20 (729a 20).

from the matter taken solely from the female from which the body of Christ was formed. Hence, the birth of Christ from the Virgin does not at all diminish either the truth of His humanity or His likeness to us. For, although a natural power requires a determined matter for the production of a determined effect therefrom, the divine power, the power able to produce all things from nothing, is not in its activity circumscribed within determinate matter.

[8] In the same way, that she as a virgin conceived and gave birth diminishes not at all the dignity of the Mother of Christ —so that she be not the true and natural mother of the Son of God. For, while the divine power worked, she supplied the natural matter for the generation of the body of Christ—and this alone is required on the part of the mother; but the things which in other mothers contribute to the loss of virginity belong not to the process of being a mother, but to that of being a father, in order to have the male seed arrive at the place of generation.

Chapter 46.

THAT CHRIST WAS BORN OF THE HOLY SPIRIT

[1] Although, of course, every divine operation by which something is accomplished in creatures is common to the entire Trinity (as has been shown in the points made above[1]), the formation of Christ's body, which was perfected by the divine power, is suitably ascribed to the Holy Spirit although it is common to the entire Trinity.

[2] Now, this seems to be in harmony with the Incarnation of the Word. For, just as our word mentally conceived is invisible, but is made sensible in an external vocal expression, so the Word of God in the eternal generation exists invisibly in the heart of the Father, but by the Incarnation is made sensible to us. Thus, the Incarnation of God's Word is like the vocal expression of our word. But the vocal expression of our word is made by our spirit, through which the vocal formation of our word takes place. Suitably, then, it is through the

---

1. See above, ch. 21.

Spirit of the Son of God that the formation of His flesh is said to have taken place.

[3] This is also in harmony with human generation. The active power which is in the human seed, drawing to itself the matter which flows from the mother, operates by the spirit, for this kind of power is founded on the spirit, and by reason of its control the seed must be cloudy and white.[2] Therefore, the Word of God taking flesh to Himself from the Virgin is suitably said to do this by His Spirit—to form flesh by assuming it.

[4] This also helps to suggest a cause moving to the Incarnation of the Word. And this could, indeed, be no other than the unmeasured love of God for man whose nature He wished to couple with Himself in unity of person. But in the divinity it is the Holy Spirit who proceeds as love, as was said.[3] Suitably, then, was the task of Incarnation attributed to the Holy Spirit.

[5] Sacred Scripture, too, is accustomed to attributing every grace to the Holy Spirit, for what is graciously given seems bestowed by the love of the giver. But no greater gift has been bestowed on man than union with God in person. Therefore, suitably is this work marked as the Holy Spirit's own.

Chapter 47.

THAT CHRIST WAS NOT THE SON OF
THE HOLY SPIRIT IN THE FLESH

[1] Now, although Christ is said to be conceived of the Holy Spirit and of the Virgin, one cannot for all that say that the Holy Spirit is the father of Christ in the human generation as the Virgin is His mother.

[2] For the Holy Spirit did not produce the human nature of Christ out of His substance, but by His power alone operated for its production. It cannot, therefore, be said that the Holy Spirit is the father of Christ in His human generation.

[3] It would, furthermore, be productive of error to say that

2. Aristotle, De generatione animalium, II, 2 (736a 8–9).
3. See above, ch. 19.

Christ is the son of the Holy Spirit. Plainly, God's Word has a distinct Person in that He is the Son of God the Father. If, then, He were in His human nature called the son of the Holy Spirit, one would have to understand Christ as being two sons, since the Word of God cannot be the son of the Holy Spirit. And thus, since the name of *sonship* belongs to a person and not to a nature, it would follow that in Christ there are two Persons. But this is foreign to the Catholic faith.[1]

[4] It would be unsuitable, also, to transfer the name and the authority of the Father to another. Yet this happens if the Holy Spirit is called the father of Christ.

Chapter 48.

THAT CHRIST MUST NOT BE CALLED A CREATURE

[1] It is clear, moreover, that, although the human nature assumed by the Word is a creature, it cannot, for all that, be said without qualification that Christ is a creature.

[2] For to be created is to become something. Now, since becoming is terminated in being simply, a becoming is of that which has subsistent being, and it is a thing of this kind which is a complete individual in the genus of substance, which, indeed in an intellectual nature is called a person or even an hypostasis. But one does not speak of forms and accidents and even parts becoming, unless relatively, since they have no subsistent being in themselves, but subsist in another; hence, when one becomes white, this is not called becoming simply, but relatively. But in Christ there is no other hypostasis or person save that of God's Word, and this person is uncreated, as is clear from the foregoing.[1] Therefore, one cannot say without qualification: "Christ is a creature," although one may say it with an addition, so as to say a creature "so far as man" or "in His human nature."

[3] Granted, however, that one does not, in the case of a subject which is an individual in the genus of substance, refer to that as becoming simply which belongs to it by reason of accidents or parts, but that one calls it becoming only rela-

1. See above, ch. 34. 1. See above, ch. 38.

tively, one does predicate simply of the subject whatever follows naturally on the accidents or parts in their own intelligibility; for one calls a man "seeing" simply: this follows the eye; or "curly" because of his hair; or "visible" because of his color. Thus, then, the things which follow properly on human nature can be asserted of Christ simply: that He is "man"; that He is "visible"; that He "walked," and that sort of thing. But what is the person's very own is not asserted of Christ by reason of His human nature, unless with some addition whether expressed or implied.

Chapter 49.

SOLUTION OF THE ARGUMENTS AGAINST
THE INCARNATION GIVEN ABOVE

[1] With what has now been said the points made previously[1] against faith in the Incarnation are easily disposed of.

[2] For it has been shown that one must not understand the Incarnation of the Word thus: that the Word was converted into flesh[2] or that He is united to the body as a form.[3] Hence, it is not a consequence of the Word's Incarnation that He who is truly God is a body or a power in a body as the first argument[4] was trying to proceed.

[3] Neither does it follow[5] that the Word was substantially changed by the fact that He assumed human nature. For no change was made in the Word of God Himself, but only in the human nature which was assumed by the Word, in accord with which it is proper that the Word was both temporally generated and born, but to the Word Himself this was not fitting.

[4] What is proposed in the third argument[6] is also without necessity. For an hypostasis is not extended beyond the limits of that nature from which it has subsistence. The Word of God, of course, has no subsistence from the human nature; rather, He draws the human nature to His subsistence or per-

---

1. See above, ch. 40.   2. See above, ch. 31.   3. See above, ch. 32.
4. See above, ch. 40, ¶2.   5. See above, ch. 40, ¶3.
6. See above, ch. 40, ¶4.

sonality. It is not through, but in, human nature that He subsists. Hence, nothing prevents the Word of God from being everywhere, although the human nature assumed by the Word of God is not everywhere.

[5] Thus, also, the fourth[7] is answered. For in any subsistent thing there must be only one nature by which it has being simply. And so, the Word of God has being simply by the divine nature alone, not, however, by the human nature; by human nature He has being *this*—namely, being a man.

[6] The fifth[8] also is disposed of in the very same way. For it is impossible that the nature by which the Word subsists be other than the very person of the Word. Of course, He subsists by the divine nature and not by the human nature, but He draws the latter to His own subsistence that He may subsist in it, as was said. Hence, it is not necessary that the human nature be identical with the person of the Word.

[7] From this also follows the exclusion of the sixth objection.[9] For an hypostasis is less simple—whether in things or in the understanding—than the nature through which it is established in being: in the thing, indeed, when the hypostasis is not its nature; or in the understanding alone in the cases in which the hypostasis and the nature are identified. The hypostasis of the Word is not established simply by the human nature so as to have being through the human nature, but through it the Word has this alone: that He be man. It is, then, not necessary that the human nature be more simple than the Word so far as He is the Word, but only so far as the Word is this man.

[8] From this also the way is open to solving the seventh objection.[10] For it is not necessary that the hypostasis of the Word of God be constituted simply by signate matter, but only so far as He is this man. For only as this man is He constituted by the human nature, as was said.

[9] Of course, that the soul and body in Christ are drawn to the personality of the Word without constituting a person other than the person of the Word does not point to a less-

7. See above, ch. 40, ¶5.
9. See above, ch. 40, ¶7.

8. See above, ch. 40, ¶6.
10. See above, ch. 40, ¶8.

ened power, as the eighth argument[11] would have it, but to a greater worthiness. For everything whatever has, when united to what is worthier, a better being than it has when it exists through itself; just so, the sensible soul has a nobler being in man than it has in the other animals in which it is the principal form, for all that it is not such in man.

[10] Hence, also, comes the solution to the ninth objection.[12] In Christ there was, indeed, this soul and this body, for all that there was not constituted from them another person than the person of God's Word, because they were assumed unto the personality of God's Word; just as a body, too, when it is without the soul, does have its own species, but it is from the soul, when united to it, that it receives its species.

[11] Thus, also, one answers what the tenth argument proposed. It is clear that this man who is Christ is a certain substance which is not universal, but particular. And He is an hypostasis; nevertheless, not another hypostasis than the hypostasis of the Word, for human nature has been assumed by the hypostasis of the Word that the Word may subsist in human as well as in divine nature. But that which subsists in human nature is this man. Hence, the Word itself is supposed[13] when one says "this man."

[12] But, let one move the very same objection over to human nature and say it is a certain substance, not universal but particular and consequently an hypostasis—he is obviously deceived. For human nature even in Socrates or Plato is not an hypostasis, but that which subsists in the nature is an hypostasis.

[13] But to call a human nature a substance and particular is not to use the meaning in which one calls an hypostasis a particular substance. "Substance" we speak of with the Philosopher[14] in two ways: for the supposit, namely, in the genus of substance which is called hypostasis; and for the *what-it-is* which is "the nature of a thing." But the parts of a substance are not thus called particular substances—subsisting, so to say, in themselves; they subsist in the whole. Hence, neither can

---

11. See above, ch. 40, ¶9.   12. See above, ch. 40, ¶10.
13. On this use of "supposed" see above, ch. 38, n. 7.
14. Aristotle, *Categories*, 5, (2a 11–25).

one call them hypostases, for none of them is a complete substance. Otherwise, it would follow that in one man there are as many hypostases as there are parts.[15]

[14] Now, to the eleventh argument[16] in opposition. The solution is that equivocation is introduced by a diversity of the form signified by a name, but not by diversity of supposition. For this name "man" is not taken as equivocal because sometimes it supposes Plato, sometimes Socrates. Therefore, this name "man" said of Christ and of other men always signifies the same form; namely, human nature. This is why it is predicated of them univocally; but it is only the supposition which is changed, and, to be sure, in this: when it is taken for Christ it supposes an uncreated hypostasis, but when it is taken for others it supposes a created hypostasis.

[15] Nor, again, is the hypostasis of the Word said to be the supposit of the human nature, as though subjected to the latter as to a more formal principle, as the twelfth argument[17] proposed. This would, of course, be necessary if it were the human nature which establishes the hypostasis of the Word in being simply. This is obviously false: for the hypostasis of the Word is the subject of the human nature so far as He draws this latter unto His own subsistence, just as something drawn to a second and nobler thing to which it is united.

[16] For all that, it does not follow that the human nature accrues to the Word accidentally, because the Word pre-exists from eternity, as the final argument[18] was trying to conclude. For the Word assumed human nature so as to be truly man. But to be man is to be in the genus of a substance. Therefore, since by union with human nature the hypostasis of the Word has the being of man, this does not accrue to the Word accidentally. For accidents do not bestow substantial being.

15. See above, ch. 40, ¶11.
17. See above, ch. 40, ¶13.

16. See above, ch. 40, ¶12.
18. See above, ch. 40, ¶14.

Chapter 50.

THAT ORIGINAL SIN IS TRANSMITTED FROM
THE FIRST PARENT TO HIS DESCENDANTS

[1]   It has been shown, then, in the points set down[1] that what the Catholic faith preaches about the Incarnation of the Son of God is not impossible. And the next thing is to make plain the suitability of the Son of God's assumption of human nature.

[2]   Now, the reason for this suitability the Apostle seems to situate in original sin, which is passed on to all men; he says: "As by the disobedience of one man many were made sinners: so also by the obedience of one many shall be made just" (Rom. 5:19). However, since the Pelagian heretics[2] denied original sin, we must now show that men are born with original sin.

[3]   First, indeed, one must take up what Genesis (2:15–17) says: "The Lord God took man and put him into the paradise of pleasure, saying: Of every tree of paradise thou shalt eat but of the tree of knowledge of good and evil thou shalt not eat. For in what day soever you shall eat of it, thou shalt die the death." But, since it was not on the very day that he ate that Adam actually died, one has to understand the words "thou shalt die the death" as "you will be handed over to the necessity of death." And this would be said pointlessly if man from the institution of his nature had the necessity of dying. One must, then, say that death and the necessity of dying is a penalty inflicted on man for sin. But a penalty is not justly inflicted except for a fault. Therefore, in every single one of those in whom one finds this penalty one must of necessity find a fault. But this penalty is found in all men, even from the very moment of birth, for since that day man is born handed over to the necessity of death. Hence, too, some die immediately after birth, "carried from the womb

---

1. See above, ch. 28–49.
2. St. Augustine, De haeresibus, 88, (PL, 42, col. 48); on Pelagius, see Gilson, History of Christian Philosophy, pp. 78, 595.

to the grave" (Job 10:19). In them, therefore, there is some sin. But it is not actual sin, for children do not have the use of free will, and without this nothing is imputed to man as sin (which is clear from the things said in Book III[3]). One must, therefore, say that sin is in them, passed on to them in their origin.

[4] This is also made clear and explicit by the Apostle's words: "As by one man sin entered into this world and by sin death, and so death passed upon all men, in whom all sinned" (Rom. 5:12).[4]

[5] Of course, one cannot say that by one man sin entered the world by way of imitation. For, thus, sin would have reached only those who in sinning imitate the first man; and, since death entered the world by sin, death would reach only those who sin in the likeness of the first man sinning. It is to exclude this that the Apostle adds that "death reigned from Adam unto Moses even over them also who have not sinned after the similitude of the transgression of Adam" (Rom. 5:14). Therefore, the understanding of the Apostle is not that sin entered the world through one man by way of imitation, but by way of origin.

[6] There is more. If the Apostle were speaking of the entry of sin into the world by way of imitation, he should rather have said that sin entered the world by the devil than by one man; as is said also expressly in Wisdom (2:24–25): "By the envy of the devil death came into the world: they follow him that are of his side."

[7] David says furthermore, in a Psalm (50:7): "Behold I was conceived in iniquities and in sins did my mother conceive me." But this cannot be understood of actual sin, since David is said to be conceived and born of a legitimate marriage. Therefore, this must be referred to original sin.

[8] Moreover, Job says (14:4): "Who can make him clean that is conceived of unclean seed? Is it not Thou who only art?" One gathers clearly from this that from the uncleanness

---

3. SCG, III, ch. 10, 90, and 140.
4. On the exegesis and history of this and the previous text with ample reference to the teaching of St. Thomas, see Prat, *Theology of St. Paul*, I, 210–237, 429–455.

of human seed there extends an uncleanness to the man conceived of the seed. One must understand this of the uncleanness of sin, the only one for which a man is brought into judgment, for Job (14:3) had already said: "And dost Thou think it meet to open Thy eyes upon such a one, and to bring him into judgment with Thee." Thus, then, there is a sin contracted by man in his very origin which is called "original."

[9]   Once again; baptism and the other sacraments of the Church are remedies of a sort against sin, as will be clarified later.[5] But baptism, according to the common custom of the Church, is given to children recently born. It would be given quite in vain unless there were sin in them. But there is no actual sin in them, for they lack the exercise of free will, without which no act is imputed to a man as a fault. Therefore, one must say that there is in them a sin passed on by their origin, since in the works of God and the Church there is nothing futile or in vain.[6]

[10]   But one may say: Baptism is given to infants not to cleanse them from sin, but to admit them to the kingdom of God, to which there is no admission without baptism, since our Lord says: "Unless a man be born again of water and the Holy Ghost he cannot enter into the kingdom of God" (John 3:5). This objection is in vain. For no one is excluded from the kingdom of God except for some fault. The end of every rational creature is to arrive at beatitude, and this cannot be save in the kingdom of God. And this, in turn, is nothing but the *ordered society of those who enjoy the divine vision*, in which true beatitude consists, which is clear from the points made in Book III.[7] But nothing fails its end except through a sin. Therefore, if children not yet baptized cannot reach the kingdom of God, one must say there is some sin in them.

[11]   Thus, then, according to the tradition of the Catholic faith one must hold that men are born with original sin.

5. See below, ch. 56, 59, 61, and 72.
6. Cf. Aristotle, *De anima*, III, 9, (432b 21), and 12 (434a 30).
7. SCG, III, ch. 48–63.

Chapter 51.

OBJECTIONS AGAINST ORIGINAL SIN

[1] There are, of course, certain things which appear to be adversaries of this truth.[1]

[2] For the sin of one man is not imputed as fault to others. So Ezechiel (18:20) says: "the son shall not bear the iniquity of the father." And the reason for this is that we are neither praised nor blamed except for the things which are in ourselves. But these are the things to which we are committed by will. Therefore, the sin of the first man is not imputed to the entire human race.

[3] But let one answer that when one sinned, "all sinned in him," as the Apostle seems to say[2] and so the sin of one is not imputed to another, but the sin is his own. Yet even this, it seems, cannot stand. For those born of Adam were, when Adam sinned, not yet in him actually, but only in his power, as in their first origin. But to sin, since it is to act, is proportionate only to one who actually exists. Therefore, we did not all sin in Adam.

[4] But let it be said that we sinned in Adam as though originally the sin comes from him to us along with the nature. Even this seems impossible. For an accident, since it does not pass from one subject to another, cannot be passed on unless the subject is passed on. But the subject of sin is the rational soul, which is not passed on to us from our first parent, but is created by God in each and one by one, as was shown in Book II.[3] Therefore, it is not by origin that the sin of Adam flowed on to us.

[5] Further, if the sin of our first parent flows into others because they take their origin from him, then, since Christ took His origin from our first parent, He, also, it seems, was subject to original sin. And this is foreign to the faith.

[6] Moreover, what follows on a thing from its natural origin

---

1. These objections are answered in ch. 52, ¶7, and following.
2. See Rom. 5:12 and, above, ch. 50, ¶2 and n. 4.
3. *SCG*, II, ch. 86–89.

is natural to that thing. But what is natural to a thing is not a sin in it; thus, the lack of vision is not a sin in a mole. Therefore, sin could not flow into others by reason of their origin from the first man.

[7] But let it now be said that the sin flows from the first parent into his descendants by way of origin, not inasmuch as the origin is natural, but inasmuch as the origin is vitiated; this also, it seems, cannot stand. For a failure in nature's work takes place only through the failure of some natural principle; due to some corruption in the seed, for example, monstrous births in animals are caused. But one cannot grant the corruption of a natural principle in human seed. It seems, then, that a sin does not flow from the first parent into his descendants by a vitiated origin.

[8] Once again; the sins of nature, appearing among its works by the corruption of a principle, take place neither always nor frequently except in a few cases. Therefore, if by a vitiated origin sin flows from the first parent into his descendants, it will not flow into all, but into some few.

[9] And if, furthermore, due to a vitiated origin, a failure appears in the offspring, that failure ought to be of the same genus as the vice which is in the origin, for effects are conformed to their causes. The origin, of course, of human generation, since it is a perfection of the generative power, which shares reason not at all, can have no vice in it which belongs to the genus of fault. For only in those acts can there be virtue or vice, which are subject to reason in some fashion. And so one does not call it a man's fault if, due to a vitiated origin, he is born a leper or blind. Therefore, there is no way for a blameworthy failure to come down from the first parent to his descendant by origin.

[10] Yet again; nature's good is not taken away by sin. Wherefore, even in the demons natural goods remain, as Dionysius says.[4] But generation is an act of nature. Therefore, the sin of the first man could not vitiate the origin of human generation so that the sin of the first man should flow into his descendants.

---

4. Pseudo-Dionysius, *De divinis nominibus*, IV (PG 3, col. 724).

[11] Man, moreover, generates one like himself in species. In things, then, which have no bearing on the generation of the species, the son need not be made like his parents. But sin cannot bear on the essentials of the species, for sin is not among the things of nature; rather, it is a corruption of the natural order. There is, then, no necessity that from a first man sinning other sinners be born.

[12] There is more. Sons are more likened to their proximate than to their remote parents. But at times it happens that the proximate parents are without sin and even in the act of generation no sin takes place. It is not, therefore, by the sin of the first parent that all are born sinners.

[13] And again, if the sin of the first man flowed into others, and—on the other hand—the good is more powerful in acting than the evil (as was shown above[5]), then by so much the more was the satisfaction of Adam, and his justice, transferred through him to others.

[14] If the sin of the first man, moreover, was by origin propagated to his descendants, by an equal reason the sins of other parents pass down to their descendants. And in this way the later would always be more burdened with sins than the earlier generations. Especially must this follow if, in fact, the sin passes on from the parent to the offspring, and satisfaction cannot pass on.

Chapter 52.

SOLUTION OF THE OBJECTIONS PROPOSED

[1] Now, for the solution of these points one should first set down that certain signs of the original sin appear with probability in the human race. For, since God takes care of human acts so as to give reward for good works and set a penalty for bad works, as was previously shown,[1] it is from the very penalty that we can assure ourselves of the fault. Now, the human race commonly suffers various penalties, both bodily and spiritual. Greatest among the bodily ones is death, and to this all the others are ordered: namely, hunger, thirst, and

---

5. *SCG*, III, ch. 12.   1. *SCG*, III, ch. 140.

others of this sort. Greatest, of course, among the spiritual penalties is the frailty of reason: from this it happens that man with difficulty arrives at knowledge of the truth; that with ease he falls into error; and that he cannot entirely overcome his beastly appetites, but is over and over again beclouded by them.

[2]   For all that, one could say that defects of this kind, both bodily and spiritual, are not penalties, but natural defects necessarily consequent upon matter. For, necessarily, the human body, composed of contraries, must be corruptible; and the sensible appetite must be moved to sense pleasures, and these are occasionally contrary to reason. And, since the possible intellect is in potency to all intelligibles, possessing none of them actually, but by nature acquiring them from the senses, one must arrive at knowledge of the truth with difficulty, and due to the phantasms one with ease deviates from the truth. But, for all that, let one weigh matters rightly, and he will be able to judge with probability enough—granted a divine providence which for every perfection has contrived a proportionate perfectible—that God united a superior to an inferior nature for this purpose: that the superior rule the inferior, and that, if some obstacle to this dominion should happen from a failure of nature, it would be removed by His special and supernatural benefaction. And the result would be, since the rational soul is of a higher nature than the body, belief that the rational soul was united to the body under such a condition that in the body there can be nothing contrary to the soul by which the body lives; and, in like fashion, if reason in man is united to the sensual appetite and other sensitive powers, that the reason be not impeded by the sensible powers, but be master over them.

[3]   Thus, then, according to the teaching of the faith, we set it down that man from the beginning was thus established by God: As long as man's reason was subject to God, not only did the inferior powers serve reason without obstacle, but the body also could not be impeded in subjection to reason by any bodily obstacle—God and His grace supplying, because nature had too little for perfecting this establishment. But, when reason turned away from God, not only did the inferior

powers rebel from reason, but the body also sustained passions contrary to that life which is from the soul.

[4] Of course, although defects of this kind may seem natural to man in an absolute consideration of human nature on its inferior side, nonetheless, taking into consideration divine providence and the dignity of human nature on its superior side, it can be proved with enough probability that defects of this kind are penalties. And one can gather thus that the human race was originally infected with sin.

[5] These things now seen, one must answer to the points made as contrary objections.

[6] Now, there is no awkwardness in saying that when one sins the sin is propagated to all in their origin, even though each is praised or blamed according to his own act; as the first argument[2] attempted to proceed. For things go one way in matters of a single individual, and another way in matters of the entire nature of a species, since "by participation in the species many men are as one man," as Porphyry says.[3] A sin, then, which refers to an individual man or his person is not imputed to another as fault unless he be the sinner, since personally one is divided off from another. But, if there is a sin which looks to the nature of the species itself, there is nothing awkward about its propagation from one to another, just as the nature of the species is communicated through one to others. But, since sin is a kind of evil of rational nature, and evil a privation of good, one judges on the basis of the missing good whether a sin is related to a nature commonly or to a person properly. Of course, actual sins which are committed by all men commonly deprive the person of the sinner of a good: grace, for instance, and the due order of the parts of the soul. This is why they are personal, and why, when one sins, the sin is not imputed to another. But the first sin of the first man not only deprived him of his proper and personal good— namely, grace, and the due order of the parts of the soul; he was deprived as well of a good related to the common nature. For—as we said above—human nature was established in its first beginning so that the inferior powers were perfectly sub-

---

2. See above, ch. 51, ¶2.
3. Porphyry, *Isagoga*, III, tx. 10 (*PL*, 64, col. 111c).

ject to reason, the reason to God, the body to the soul, and God was by His grace supplying what nature lacked for this arrangement. Now, this kind of benefit which some call "original justice"[4] was conferred on the first man in such wise that he was to propagate it to his descendants along with human nature. But in the sin of the first man reason withdrew itself from the divine subjection. And it has followed thereon that the lower powers are not perfectly subject to the reason nor is the body to the soul; and this is not only the case for the first sinner, but the same consequent defect follows into his posterity and to the posterity in whom the original justice mentioned was going to follow. Thus, then, the sin of the first man from whom all other men are derived according to the teaching of faith was not only personal in that it deprived the first man of his own good, but natural, also, in that it deprived him and consequently his descendants of the benefit bestowed on the entire human nature. Thus, too, this kind of defect which is in others as a consequence from the first parent still has in others the essentials of fault so far as all men are counted as one man by participation in the common nature. For one discovers the voluntary character in a sin of this kind in the will of the first parent much as the action of the hand has the essentials of fault from the will of the first mover, which is the power of reason; as a result, in a sin of nature judgments are made about the diverse men as though parts of a common nature, much as they are made in a personal sin about diverse parts of one man.

[7]   In this way, then, it is true to say that when one sinned, "all sinned in him," as the Apostle says, and on this basis the second argument[5] made its proposal. Other men were present in Adam, however, not in act, but only in his power as in an original principle. Nor are they said to have sinned in him as exercising any act, but so far as they belong to Adam's nature which was corrupted by sin.

[8]   Let the sin be propagated from the first parent to his descendants. Nevertheless, it does not follow, although the subject of sin is the rational soul, that the rational soul is

4. St. Anselm, *De conceptu virginali*, 1 (*PL*, 158, col. 434).
5. See above, ch. 51, ¶3.

propagated along with the seed; as the progress of the third argument[6] had it. For the manner of propagating this sin of nature which is called original is like that of the very nature of the species, and this nature, although it is perfected by the rational soul, is for all that not propagated with the seed; such propagation is only of the body fitted by nature to receive such a soul. It was in Book II[7] that we showed this.

[9] We grant that Christ was a descendant of the first parent in the flesh. For all that, He did not incur the contamination of original sin as the fourth argument[8] concluded. For it was only the matter of His human body which He received from the first parent; the power to form His body was not derived from the first parent, but was the power of the Holy Spirit, as was shown.[9] Accordingly, He did not receive human nature from Adam as an agent, although He did receive it from Adam as from a material principle.

[10] One should consider this, also: The nature's origin passes along the defects mentioned because the nature has been stripped of that help of grace which had been bestowed on it in the first parent to pass on to his descendants along with the nature. Now, since this stripping came from a voluntary sin, the consequent defect has the character of fault. Hence, defects of this kind are faulty when referred to their first principle, which is the sin of Adam; and they are natural when referred to the nature already stripped. Accordingly, the Apostle says: "We were by nature children of wrath" (Eph. 2:3). In this way one answers the fifth objection.[10]

[11] Clearly, then, from what has been said, the vice of origin in which the original sin is caused comes from the failure of a principle, namely, the gratuitous gift which human nature at its institution had had bestowed upon it. To be sure, this gift was in a sense natural: not natural as caused by the principles of the nature, but natural because it was given to man to be propagated along with his nature. But the sixth objection[11] was dealing with the natural which is caused by the principles of the nature.

6. See above, ch. 51, ¶4.
8. See above, ch. 51, ¶5.
10. See above, ch. 51, ¶6.

7. *SCG*, II, ch. 86.
9. See above, ch. 46.
11. See above, ch. 51, ¶7.

[12] The seventh objection[12] proceeds in the same way, from a defect of a natural principle belonging to the nature of the species. Of course, what comes from a defect of a natural principle of this kind happens in but few cases. But the defect of original sin comes from the defect of a principle added over and above the principles of the species, as we said.

[13] Be it observed, also, that in the act of the generative powers there can be no vice in the genus of actual sin which depends on the will of a single person, because the act of the generative power is not obedient to reason or to will, as the eighth objection[13] went. But nothing prevents our finding the vice of original sin—this refers to nature—in an act of the generative power, since acts of the generative powers are called natural.

[14] The ninth objection,[14] of course, can readily be answered from the points already made. For sin does not take away that good of nature which belongs to the nature's species. But that good of nature which grace added over and above nature could be removed by the sin of our first parent. This was said before.

[15] From the same points one easily answers the tenth objection.[15] For, since privation and defect correspond to one another mutually, in that characteristic in original sin are the children made like to the parents in which the gift also, granted the nature in the beginning, would have been propagated to their descendants; for, although the gift did not belong to the essentials of the species, it was given by divine grace to the first man to flow from him into the entire species.

[16] This, too, must be considered: Let one by the sacraments of grace be cleansed from original sin so that it is not imputed a fault in him (and for him personally this is to be freed from original sin); for all that, the nature is not entirely healed; therefore, in an act of the nature the original sin is transmitted to his descendants. Thus, then, in a man who generates there is no original sin in so far as he is a given person; and it also happens that in the act of generation there

---

12. See above, ch. 51, ¶8.   13. See above, ch. 51, ¶9.
14. See above, ch. 51, ¶10.   15. See above, ch. 51, ¶11.

is no actual sin, which the eleventh argument[16] was proposing. But so far as the man who generates is the natural principle of generation, the infection of the original sin which bears on nature remains in him and in his act of generation.

[17] Be it observed, also, that the actual sin of the first man passed over into nature because the nature in him had been further perfected by the benefit bestowed on the nature. But, when by his sin the nature was stripped of the benefit, his act was simply personal. Hence, he could not satisfy for the entire nature, nor could he make the good of nature whole once more by his act. But the only satisfaction of which he was somewhat capable was that which had a bearing on his own person. Therein the answer to the twelfth argument[17] appears.

[18] In like manner, of course, one answers the thirteenth,[18] for the sins of later parents find a nature stripped of the benefit which was at the outset granted to the nature itself. Hence, from those sins no defect follows which is propagated to the descendants, but only a defect which infects the person of the one sinning.

[19] Thus, then, it is neither unsuitable nor irrational to affirm the presence of original sin in men, and thus the heresy of the Pelagians, which was a denial of original sin, is confounded.

Chapter 53.

ARGUMENTS WHICH SEEM TO PROVE THAT GOD'S INCARNATION WAS NOT SUITABLE

[1] Faith in the Incarnation, of course, is counted foolishness by unbelievers, as the Apostle has it: "It pleased God by the foolishness of our preaching to save them that believe" (I Cor. 1:21); and it seems foolish to preach a thing which is not just impossible, but also unbecoming; therefore, the unbelievers press on their fight against the Incarnation, and they try not only to show that what the Catholic faith preaches

16. See above, ch. 51, ¶12.　　　17. See above, ch. 51, ¶13.
18. See above, ch. 51, ¶14.

is impossible, but also that it is inharmonious, and that it ill befits the divine goodness.[1]

[2]   For it does befit the divine goodness that all things stand fast in order. Now, the order of things is this: that God be exalted above all things, but man hemmed in among the lowest creatures. Therefore, it ill befits the divine majesty to be united to human nature.

[3]   Once more; if it was suitable for God to become man, this had to be for some usefulness coming therefrom. But whatever be the usefulness granted, since God is omnipotent He could produce this usefulness merely by His will. Therefore, since it becomes everything whatever to be done as quickly as possible, it was unnecessary for a utility of this sort that God unite human nature to Himself.

[4]   Since God is, moreover, the universal cause of all things, He should especially attend the usefulness of things in their universal entirety. But the assumption of human nature looks only to the usefulness of man. It was, therefore, not seemly for God, if He was to take on a foreign nature, to assume only human nature.

[5]   Moreover, the more one thing is like another, the more suitably it is united to the other. But the angelic nature is more like God and closer to Him than human nature. Therefore, it was not suitable to assume human nature and pass over the angelic.

[6]   There is more. The chief thing in man is his understanding of the truth. And in this man seems to be impeded if God assumed human nature, for man is thus given an occasion of error; its result is agreement with those who held that God is not exalted above all bodies. Therefore, it contributed nothing useful to human nature for God to assume human nature.

[7]   Again, we can learn from experience that many an error concerning the Incarnation of God has arisen. It seems, then, that it was not becoming human salvation that God should be incarnate.

[8]   Furthermore, among all the things that God has done,

1. These objections are answered below, in ch. 55.

that appears the greatest: His own assumption of flesh. But from the greatest work one should look for the greatest usefulness. If, then, the Incarnation of God is ordered to the salvation of men, it appears that it was becoming that He should have saved the entire human race, since even all men's salvation scarcely seems to be useful enough that so great a work should have been done for it.

[9] What is more, if God assumed human nature for the salvation of men, apparently it was suitable that there be enough indications for men of His divinity. But it seems this did not happen, for some other men simply assisted by the divine power and without God's union to their nature are discovered doing miracles like or even greater than those which Christ did (cf. John 14:12). It seems, then, that God's Incarnation did not take place with enough care for human salvation.

[10] There is more. If it was necessary for human salvation that God take on flesh, since there were men from the beginning of the world, it appears that from the beginning of the world He ought to have assumed human nature, and not, so to say, in the last days, for it seems that the salvation of all the preceding men was passed over.

[11] For the same reason, also, He should have dwelt among men to the very end of the world, in order to instruct men by His presence and govern them.

[12] Then, too, this is, above all, useful to men: to solidify in them the hope of future beatitude. But this hope would have been better conceived from an incarnate God if He had assumed an immortal, impassible, and glorious flesh and had displayed this to all men. Therefore, it seems not suitable to have assumed a mortal and frail flesh.

[13] Apparently it was suitable, furthermore, to show that whatever is in the world is from God, He should have put to use the abundance of earthly things, living in riches and the greatest honors. It is the contrary we read of Him: that He led a poor and abject life, that He suffered a shameful death. Therefore, what the faith preaches about the incarnate God is not suitable.

[14] The fact, moreover, that He suffered abjectly did most to obscure His divinity. Nonetheless, the most necessary thing

for men all the while was this: that they know His divinity—
if He was God incarnate. It seems, then, that what the faith
preaches is not in harmony with human salvation.

[15]   Let a man say that the Son of God underwent death
by reason of His obedience to the Father—this also appears unreasonable. For obedience consists in one's conforming himself to the will of him who commands. But the will of God
the Father cannot be unreasonable. If, then, it was unbecoming for God made man to suffer death because death seems
contrary to divinity which is life, the reason for this thing
cannot suitably be found in obedience to the Father.

[16]   God's will, moreover, is not for the death of men, even
sinners, but for life, as Ezechiel (18:23, 32) says: "I will
not the death of the sinner, but rather that he be converted
and live." By so much the less, then, could it have been the
will of God that the most perfect man be subject to death.

[17]   It seems, furthermore, impious and cruel to command
an innocent to be led to death, especially on behalf of the
impious who are worthy of death. But the man Christ Jesus
was innocent. Therefore, it would have been impious if at the
command of God the Father He had undergone death.

[18]   But let a man say that this was necessary as a demonstration of humility, as the Apostle appears to say, that Christ
"humbled Himself, becoming obedient unto death" (Phil.
2:8)—this reason is not suitable either, because, in the first
place, one must commend humility in him who has a superior
to whom he can be subject. This cannot be said of God. Therefore, it was not suitable for God's Word to be humbled unto
death.

[19]   Again, men were able to be informed sufficiently about
humility by the divine words—to which faith must wholly
cling—and by human examples. Therefore, to set an example
of humility it was not necessary for the Word of God either
to assume flesh or to undergo death.

[20]   But, again, let one say that it was necessary for the
cleansing of our sins that Christ undergo death and the other
seemingly abject things; as the Apostle says: "He was delivered
up for our sins" (Rom. 4:25); and again: "He was offered
once to exhaust the sins of many" (Heb. 9:28). This, too,

seems awkward, because, in the first place, only by God's grace are men cleansed of sins.

[21] In the next place, because, if satisfaction was required, it was suitable that he should give satisfaction who had sinned. For in the just judgment of God "every one shall bear his own burden" (Gal. 6:5).

[22] Again, if it was becoming for someone greater than pure man to satisfy for man, it seems it would have been sufficient for an angel to take flesh and fulfill this sort of satisfaction, since an angel is by nature superior to a man.

[23] What is more, sin is not expiated by sin, but increased. Then, if Christ had to satisfy by death, His death should have been such that no man sinned therein; that is to say, He should have died not a violent, but a natural, death.

[24] If Christ, moreover, had to die for the sins of men, since men sin frequently He should have had to undergo death frequently.

[25] Now, let one say that it was especially because of original sin that Christ had to be born and to suffer, and that sin had infected the whole human race when the first man sinned. But this seems impossible. For, if other men are not equal to satisfying for original sin, neither does the death of Christ seem to have been satisfactory for the sins of the human race, since He Himself died in His human, not in His divine, nature.

[26] Furthermore, if Christ made satisfaction enough for the sins of the human race, it seems unjust that men still suffer the penalties which were brought in, Scripture says, by sin.[2]

[27] There is more. If Christ made satisfaction enough for the sins of the human race, no further remedies for the absolution of sins need be sought. But they are constantly sought by all who have care for their salvation. Therefore, it seems that Christ did not sufficiently take away the sins of men.

[28] These and similar points, then, can make it appear to a man that what the Catholic faith preaches about the Incarnation has not been harmonious with the divine majesty and wisdom.

2. See above, ch. 50.

Chapter 54.

THAT IT WAS SUITABLE FOR GOD TO BE MADE FLESH

[1]   However, if one earnestly and devoutly weighs the mysteries of the Incarnation, he will find so great a depth of wisdom that it exceeds human knowledge. In the Apostle's words: "The foolishness of God is wiser than men" (I Cor. 1:25). Hence it happens that to him who devoutly considers it, more and more wondrous aspects of this mystery are made manifest.

[2]   First, then, let this be taken into consideration: The Incarnation of God was the most efficacious assistance to man in his striving for beatitude. For we have shown in Book III[1] that the perfect beatitude of man consists in the immediate vision of God. It might, of course, appear to some that man would never have the ability to achieve this state: that the human intellect be united immediately to the divine essence itself as an intellect is to its intelligible; for there is an unmeasured distance between the natures, and thus, in the search for beatitude, a man would grow cold, held back by very desperation. But the fact that God was willing to unite human nature to Himself personally points out to men with greatest clarity that man can be united to God by intellect, and see Him immediately. It was, then, most suitable for God to assume human nature to stir up man's hope for beatitude. Hence, after the Incarnation of Christ, men began the more to aspire after heavenly beatitude; as He Himself says: "I am come that they may have life and may have it more abundantly" (John 10:10).

[3]   At the same time, too, some obstacles to acquiring beatitude are removed from man. For, since the perfect beatitude of man consists in the enjoyment of God alone, as shown above,[2] necessarily every man is kept from participation in the true beatitude who cleaves as to an end to these things which are less than God. But man was able to be misled into this clinging as to an end to things less than God in existence

1. SCG, III, ch. 48-63.   2. SCG, III, ch. 48-62.

by his ignorance of the worthiness of his nature. Thus it happens with some. They look on themselves in their bodily and sentient nature—which they have in common with other animals—and in bodily things and fleshly pleasures they seek out a kind of animal beatitude. But there have been others who considered the excellence of certain creatures superior to man in some respects. And to the cult of these they bound themselves. They worshiped the universe and its parts because of the greatness of its size and its long temporal duration; or spiritual substances, angels and demons, because they found these greater than man both in immortality and in sharpness of understanding. They judged that in these, as existing above themselves, the beatitude of man should be sought. Now, although it is true, some conditions considered, that man stands inferior to some creatures, and even that in certain matters he is rendered like to the lowest creatures, nothing stands higher in the order of end than man except God alone, in whom alone man's perfect beatitude is to be found. Therefore, this dignity of man—namely, that in the immediate vision of God his beatitude is to be found—was most suitably manifested by God by His own immediate assumption of human nature. And we look upon this consequence of God's Incarnation: a large part of mankind passing by the cult of angels, of demons, and all creatures whatsoever, spurning, indeed, the pleasures of the flesh and all things bodily, have dedicated themselves to the worship of God alone, and in Him only they look for the fulfillment of this beatitude; and so the Apostle exhorts: "Seek the things that are above where Christ is sitting at the right hand of God. Mind the things that are above, not the things that are upon the earth" (Col. 3:1–2).

[4] Since man's perfect beatitude, furthermore, consists in the sort of knowledge of God which exceeds the capacity of every created intellect (as was shown in Book III), there had to be a certain foretaste of this sort of knowledge in man which might direct him to that fullness of blessed knowledge; and this is done through faith, as we showed in Book III.[3] But the knowledge by which man is directed to his ultimate

3. SCG, III, ch. 147 and 152.

end has to be most certain knowledge, because it is the principle of everything ordered to the ultimate end; so, also, the principles naturally known are most certain. But there cannot be a most certain knowledge of something unless the thing be known of itself, as the first principles of demonstration are known to us; or the thing be resolved into what is known of itself, in the way in which the conclusion of a demonstration is most certain for us. Of course, what is set forth for us to hold about God by faith cannot be known of itself to man, since it exceeds the capacity of the human intellect. Therefore, this had to be made known to man by Him to whom it is known of itself. And, although to all who see the divine essence this truth is somehow known of itself, nevertheless, in order to have a most certain knowledge there had to be a reduction to the first principle of this knowledge—namely, to God. To Him this truth is naturally known of itself, and from Him it becomes known to all. And just so the certitude of a science is had only by resolution into the first indemonstrable principles. Therefore, man, to achieve perfect certitude about the truth of faith, had to be instructed by God Himself made man, that man might in the human fashion grasp the divine instruction. And this is what John (1:18) says: "No man hath seen God at any time: the only-begotten Son who is in the bosom of the Father, He hath declared Him." And our Lord Himself says: "For this was I born and for this came I into the world, that I should give testimony to the truth" (John 18:37). And for this reason we see that after Christ's Incarnation men were the more evidently and the more surely instructed in the divine knowledge; as Isaias (11:9) has it: "The earth is filled with the knowledge of the Lord."

[5]   Again, since man's perfect beatitude consists in the enjoyment of divinity, man's love had to be disposed toward a desire for the enjoyment of divinity, as we see that there is naturally in man a desire of beatitude. But the desire to enjoy anything is caused by love of that thing. Therefore, man, tending to perfect beatitude, needed inducement to the divine love. Nothing, of course, so induces us to love one as the experience of his love for us. But God's love for men could be demonstrated to man in no way more effective than this: He willed to be united to man in person, for it is proper to love

to unite the lover with the beloved so far as possible.[4] Therefore, it was necessary for man tending to perfect beatitude that
God become man.

[6] Furthermore, since friendship consists in a certain equality, things greatly unequal seem unable to be coupled in
friendship.[5] Therefore, to get greater familiarity in friendship
between man and God it was helpful for man that God became man, since even by nature man is man's friend;[6] and so
in this way, "while we know God visibly, we may [through
Him] be borne to love of things invisible."[7]

[7] In like fashion, too, it is clear that beatitude is the reward of virtue.[8] Therefore, they who tend to beatitude must
be virtuously disposed. But we are stimulated to virtue both
by words and by examples. Of course, his examples and words
of whose goodness we have the more solid opinion induce us
the more effectively to virtue. But an infallible opinion of
goodness about any pure man was never tenable; even the
holiest of men, one finds, have failed in some things. Hence,
it was necessary for man to be solidly grounded in virtue to
receive from God made human both the teaching and the
examples of virtue. For this reason our Lord Himself says:
"I have given you an example that as I have done to you so
you do also" (John 13:15).

[8] By virtues, again, man is disposed to beatitude, and so
by sin he is blocked therefrom. Sin, of course, the contrary
of virtue, constitutes an obstacle to beatitude; it not only induces a kind of disorder in the soul by seducing it from its
due end, but it also offends God to whom we look for the
reward of beatitude, in that God has the custody of human
acts. And sin is the contrary of divine charity, as we showed
more fully in Book III. What is more, man, being aware of
this offense, loses by sin that confidence in approaching God
which is necessary to achieve beatitude. Therefore, the human

4. See Pseudo-Dionysius, *De divinis nominibus*, IV (PG, 3, col. 713).
5. Aristotle, *Nicomachean Ethics*, VIII, 5, (1157b 35–40).
6. Aristotle, *Nicomachean Ethics*, VIII, 1 (1155a 15–25).
7. Preface, Mass of the Nativity of our Lord and of Corpus Christi;
   St. Thomas has omitted *per hunc*.
8. See Aristotle, *Nicomachean Ethics*, I, 9 (1099b 10–20).

race, which abounds in sins, needed to have some remedy against sin applied to it. But this remedy can be applied only by God, who can move the will of man to good and bring it back to the order due; who can, as well, remit the offense committed against Him—for an offense is not remitted except by him against whom the offense is committed. But, if man is to be freed from awareness of past offense, he must know clearly that God has remitted his offense. But man cannot be clear on this with certainty unless God gives him certainty of it. Therefore, it was suitable and helpful to the human race for achieving beatitude that God should become man; as a result, man not only receives the remission of sins through God, but also the certitude of this remission through the man-God. Hence, our Lord Himself says: "But that you may know that the Son of Man hath power to forgive sins" (Matt. 9:6), and the rest; and the Apostle says that "the blood of Christ will cleanse our conscience from dead works to serve the living God" (Heb. 9:14).

[9] The tradition of the Church, moreover, teaches us that the whole human race was infected by sin. But the order of divine justice—as is clear from the foregoing[9]—requires that God should not remit sin without satisfaction. But to satisfy for the sin of the whole human race was beyond the power of any pure man, because any pure man is something less than the whole human race in its entirety. Therefore, in order to free the human race from its common sin, someone had to satisfy who was both man and so proportioned to the satisfaction, and something above man that the merit might be enough to satisfy for the sin of the whole human race. But there is no greater than man in the order of beatitude, except God, for angels, although superior to man in the condition of nature, are not superior in the order of end, because the same end beatifies them.[10] Therefore, it was necessary for man's achievement of beatitude that God should become man to take away the sin of the human race. And this is what John the Baptist said of Christ: "Behold the Lamb of God, behold Him who taketh away the sin of the world" (John 1:29). And the Apostle says: "As by the offense of one, unto all men to

9. SCG, III, ch. 158.   10. SCG, III, ch. 57.

condemnation; so also by the justice of one, unto all men to justification" (Rom. 5:16).

[10] These points, then, and similar ones make us able to conceive that it was not out of harmony with the divine goodness for God to become man, but extremely helpful for human salvation.

Chapter 55.

ANSWER TO THE ARGUMENTS PREVIOUSLY SET DOWN AGAINST THE SUITABILITY OF THE INCARNATION

[1] Now, then, the points opposed to this doctrine above are disposed of easily.

[2] It is not contrary to the order of things for God to become man, as the first argument[1] proceeded. This is the case because, although the divine nature exceeds the human nature to infinity, man in the order of his nature has God Himself for end and has been born to be united to God by his intellect. And this union had as example and testimony of a sort the union of God to man in person; nonetheless, what was proper to each nature was preserved, so that nothing of the excellence of the divine nature was lost, nor was there an exaltation which drew the human nature beyond the bounds of its species.

[3] There is the following to be considered, also. By reason of the perfection and immobility of the divine goodness, God loses no dignity no matter how closely a creature draws near to Him, although this makes the creature grow in dignity. For He communicates His goodness to creatures in such wise that He Himself suffers no loss.

[4] In like fashion, too, one grants that God's will suffices for doing all things; nevertheless, the divine wisdom requires that provision be made for the various classes of things in harmony with themselves, for He has suitably established the proper causes of various things. Be it granted, accordingly, that God was able by His will alone to effect in the human race every useful good which we are saying came from God's In-

1. See above, ch. 53, ¶2.

carnation, as the second argument[2] was proposing; nevertheless, it was in harmony with human nature to bring about these useful goods through God made man, just as the arguments given[3] make apparent to some extent.

[5]   The answer to the third argument[4] is also plain. For, since man is constituted of a spiritual and of a bodily nature, and stands, so to say, on the *boundary*[5] of each nature, that appears to belong to the whole of creaturehood which is done for the salvation of man. For the lesser bodily creatures seem to yield to man's use and are in some way subject to him. But the superior spiritual, namely the angelic, creature has the achievement of the ultimate end in common with man (this is plain from the foregoing[6]). Thus, it seems suitable that the universal cause of all things assume that creature into unity of person in which the cause shares more with other creatures.

[6]   This fact should be considered, also: To act of itself belongs only to the rational creature, for irrational creatures are more acted upon by a rational force than they are acting of themselves. Hence, they are rather in the order of instrumental causes than bearing themselves as principal agents. But the assumption of a creature by God had to be of the kind which could act of itself as a principal agent. For whatever acts as an instrument acts as moved into action, but a principal agent acts of itself. If, then, something was to be done divinely by an irrational creature, it sufficed, the creature's condition considered, that it merely be moved by God. But it would not be assumed in person for the person to act; since its natural condition was not susceptible of this, it was only the condition of the rational nature which was so susceptible. Therefore, for God to assume an irrational creature was not suitable; whereas to assume a rational one, whether human or angelic, was.

[7]   And, although one finds in the angelic nature natural properties making it more excellent than the human nature, as the fourth argument was proposing,[7] the human nature

2. See above, ch. 53, ¶3.
4. See above, ch. 53, ¶4.
6. SCG, III, ch. 25.

3. See above, ch. 54.
5. SCG, II, ch. 68.
7. See above, ch. 53, ¶5.

was nevertheless assumed with greater fitness. First, indeed, this is because in man sin is subject to expiation; and this is so because his choice is not unchangeably fixed on something, but can be perverted from good to evil, and from evil restored to good. In man's reason, also, this happens: Since it gathers the truth from sensible things and certain signs, the way lies open to contradictory positions. But an angel, just as he has an unchangeable grasp of truth because he knows by simple understanding, so also he has an unchangeable choice. Accordingly, he is either not fixed upon evil at all, or, if he is fixed on evil, is fixed so immutably. Hence, his sin is not subject to expiation. Since, then, the chief cause of the divine incarnation appears to be the expiation of sin, as divine Scripture teaches us,[8] it was more fitting that God assume a human than an angelic nature. Second, the assumption of the creature by God is in person, not in nature—as the foregoing makes clear.[9] It was, therefore, more suitable to assume the human than the angelic nature because in man the nature is other than the person, for man is composite of matter and form; but this is not so in the angel, who is immaterial. Third, the angel, in what is proper to his nature, is closer to the knowledge of God than man is whose knowledge arises from the senses. Therefore, it was sufficient for the angel to be intelligibly instructed by God regarding divine truth. But the condition of man required that God instruct man sensibly about Himself as Man. This was done by the Incarnation. Then, again, the very distance of man from God seemed more repugnant to the divine enjoyment. Therefore, man needed to be assumed by God more than an angel did, that man's hope for beatitude be stimulated. Lastly, man, since he is the term of creatures, presupposing, so to say, all other creatures in the natural order of generation, is suitably united to the first principle of things to finish a kind of cycle in the perfection of things.

[8] But the fact that God assumed human nature gives no occasion of error, as the fifth argument[10] was trying to show. For the assumption of humanity, as already said, took place

---

8. See Matt. 1:21; I Tim. 1:15; and see above, ch. 50.
9. See above, ch. 39 and 41.   10. See above, ch. 53, ¶6.

in a unity of person, not in a unity of nature, which might result in our agreement with those who held that God is not exalted above all things, and said that God was the soul of the universe, or something of the sort.

[9] We grant, of course, that respecting God's Incarnation certain errors have arisen, as the sixth argument[11] objected; nevertheless, it is manifest that after the Incarnation many more errors were removed. For, just as in the creation of things which proceeded from the divine goodness some evils followed, and this was proportionate to the condition of creatures which are able to fail, so also in the manifestation of divine truth it is not astonishing that some errors have arisen from the failure of human minds. And these errors, for all that, exercised the talents of the faithful toward a more diligent penetration and understanding of divine truth, just as the evils which occur in creatures are ordered by God to some good.

[10] Although, of course, every created good turns out to be negligible in comparison to the divine good, nevertheless, because in things created nothing can be greater than the salvation of the rational creature (which consists in the enjoyment of the divine goodness itself)—since human salvation has followed upon the divine Incarnation—it was no small usefulness which the Incarnation mentioned brought to the universe (so the seventh argument[12] was proceeding). And it need not follow on this that all men should be saved, but only those who adhere to the Incarnation mentioned by faith and the sacraments of the faith. To be sure, the power of the divine Incarnation is equal to the salvation of all men, but the fact that some are not saved thereby comes from their indisposition: they are unwilling to take unto themselves the fruit of the Incarnation; they do not cleave to the incarnate God by faith and love. For men were not intended to lose that freedom of choice by which they are able to cleave or not to cleave to the incarnate God, lest the good of man be produced by coercion—a good without merit and without praise.

[11] There have also been sufficient indications to make this Incarnation of God manifest to men. For there is no more

suitable way to manifest divinity than by things which are God's very own. But this is God's very own: the power to change the laws of nature by doing something above that nature whose very author He is. Most suitably, then, is something proved divine by doing works above the laws of nature, to enlighten the blind, for instance, or to cleanse lepers, or to raise the dead. Works of this kind are what Christ did. Accordingly, when He was asked: "Art thou He that art to come or look we for another?" by these works He Himself indicated His divinity in His reply: "The blind see, the lame walk, the deaf hear" (Matt. 11:15, 5), and so forth. But to create another world was not necessary; and this was not consonant either with the divine wisdom or with the nature of things. One may, of course, say—as the eighth argument[13] was proposing—that we read of others also performing miracles of this kind; but it must be borne in mind that Christ performed them very differently and more divinely. For we read of others doing these things by praying; Christ did them by commanding, by His very own power, so to say. And He not only did these things Himself, but even granted to others the power to do the same, and greater; and the latter used to do them by the mere invocation of the name of Christ. And not merely bodily miracles were worked through Christ, but spiritual ones as well; and these are much greater: namely, by Christ and at the invocation of His name the Holy Spirit is received, and so hearts are inflamed by the affection of divine charity; and minds suddenly are instructed in the knowledge of things divine; and the tongues of the unlettered are rendered skilled for setting divine truth forth to men. But works of this sort are express indications of the divinity of Christ; they are things no pure man was able to do. Hence, the Apostle says that the salvation of men "which, having begun to be declared by the Lord, was confirmed unto us by them that heard Him, God also bearing them witness by signs, and wonders, and divers miracles, and distributions of the Holy Ghost" (Heb. 2:3–4).

[12]   Granted, of course, that God's Incarnation was necessary for the entire human race, it was not, for all that, necessary that God be incarnate from the beginning of the world,

13. See above, ch. 55, ¶9.

as the ninth objection[14] ran. Now first: by the incarnate God a remedy against sin had to be brought to men, as was shown above.[15] But no one receives a suitable remedy against sin unless first he acknowledges his failure, so that man in his lowliness, not relying on himself, may put his hope in God, by whom alone sin can be healed, as was said above.[16] Man's presumption was possible, of course, both in regard to knowledge and in regard to virtue. He had, then, to be left to himself for a while to discover that he was not equal to his own salvation: not equal by natural knowledge, for before the time of the written law man transgressed the law of nature; nor equal by his own virtue, for, when he was given knowledge of sin through the Law, he still sinned out of weakness. Thus necessarily, man, presuming neither on his knowledge nor on his virtue, could at last be given efficacious help against sin by Christ's Incarnation; namely, the grace of Christ by which he was not only to be instructed in doubtful matters lest he be deficient in knowledge, but also to be strengthened against the assaults of temptation lest he be deficient through frailty. And so it happened that there were three states of the human race: the first, before the Law; the second, under the Law; the third, under grace.

Then, again, by the incarnate God precepts and perfect testimonies were to be given to men. Now, the condition of human nature requires that it be not led immediately to the perfect, but that it be led by the hand through the imperfect so as to arrive at perfection. We see this in the instruction of children. They are first instructed minimally, for they cannot grasp perfect things in the beginning. In the same way, also, if to some multitude things unheard of were proposed as great, the multitude would not grasp them immediately unless it became accustomed to these things by something less great. Thus, then, was it suitable that from the beginning the human race be instructed in the matter of its salvation by some light and lesser testimonies through the Patriarchs, and the Law, and the Prophets; and that at last, at the consummate time, the perfect teaching of Christ be set forth on earth. Thus, the Apostle says: "When the fullness of the time was come

---

14. See above, ch. 53, ¶10.   15. See above, ch. 54.
16. See above, ch. 54, and SCG, III, ch. 157.

God sent His Son" into the world. And we read in the same place: "The law was our pedagogue in Christ. But we are no longer under a pedagogue" (Gal. 4:4; 3:24–25).

One must also consider this: as the coming of a great king must be preceded by a number of envoys to prepare his subjects to receive him more reverently, so many things had to precede the coming of God to the earth: to prepare men for the reception of the incarnate God. Indeed, this did take place when, because of the promises and testimonies that had gone before, the minds of men were disposed the more readily to believe Him who had had envoys before Him, and the more eagerly to receive Him because of the previous promises.

[13] One may also grant that the coming of the incarnate God was extremely necessary for human salvation; nevertheless, it was not necessary for human salvation that He converse with men even unto the end of the world, as the tenth argument[17] was proposing. For this would have worked against the reverence which men ought to show to the incarnate God, so long as, seeing Him clothed in flesh similar to other men, they esteemed Him nothing beyond other men. But He, after the wondrous things which He did upon the earth, withdrew His presence from men, and they began to revere Him the more. For this reason He did not even give His disciples the fullness of the Holy Spirit so long as He conversed with them, as though by His absence their souls were more prepared for spiritual gifts. Hence, He Himself said to them: "If I go not the Paraclete will not come to you; but if I go I will send Him to you" (John 16:7).

[14] It was not right for God to take flesh incapable of suffering and death, as the eleventh argument[18] was proposing, but, rather, capable of suffering and death. First, indeed, because it was necessary for men to know the beneficence of the Incarnation so as to be thereby inflamed in the divine love. But to manifest the truth of the Incarnation He had to assume flesh like that of other men; namely, capable of suffering and death. For, if He had taken flesh incapable of suffering and death, it would have seemed to men who did not know

17. See above, ch. 53, ¶11.   18. See above, ch. 53, ¶12.

such flesh that it was a phantom and not the reality of flesh.

Second, because it was necessary that God assume flesh to satisfy for the sin of the human race. It happens, of course, that one does satisfy for another (as was shown in Book III[19]) in such wise, however, that the penalty for sin due to the second, and not due to the first, the first voluntarily assumes. But the penalty consequent on the sin of the human race is death and the other capacities for suffering of the present life, as was said above.[20] Hence, the Apostle says: "By one man sin entered this world and by sin death" (Rom. 5:12). Therefore, God had to assume without sin flesh capable of suffering and death, so that by suffering and dying He would satisfy for us and take away sin. And this is what the Apostle says, that "God sent His own Son in the likeness of sinful flesh" (Rom. 8:3), that is, having flesh like that of sinners, namely, capable of suffering and death; and the Apostle adds "that of sin He might condemn sin in the flesh,"[21] that is, in order that by the penalty which He sustained in the flesh for our sin He might take sin away from us.

Third, because by having flesh capable of suffering and death He gave us examples of virtue more effectively by overcoming bravely the sufferings of the flesh, and making virtuous use of them.

Fourth, because we are by this the more strengthened in the hope of immortality: that He from a state of flesh capable of suffering and death was changed into a state of flesh incapable of suffering and death; and this we can hope for ourselves, we who bear a flesh capable of suffering and death. But if from the beginning He had assumed flesh incapable of suffering and death, no occasion to hope for immortality would be given those who experience in themselves mortality and corruptibility. This, also, was required by His mission as mediator: that, while He had in common with us flesh capable of suffering and death, but in common with God power and glory, He should take away from us what He had in common with us—namely, suffering and death—in order to lead us to

---

19. SCG, III, ch. 158.   20. See above, ch. 50.
21. This is St. Thomas rather than Douay. He is paraphrasing to make his own exegesis of a text "famous for its intrinsic difficulty"; see F. Prat, S.J., The Theology of St. Paul, II, 163–166.

that which was common to Him and to God. For He was the mediator for uniting us to God.

[15] In like fashion, also, it was not expedient that the incarnate God live in this world a life of riches, and one excelling in honors or dignities, as the twelfth argument[22] was concluding. First, to be sure, because He had come to draw the minds of men, devoted to earthly things, away from earthly things and to lift them up to things divine. Hence, that His example might lead men to a contempt of riches and the other things 'which the worldly desire, He had to lead a needy and private life in this world. Second, because, if He had abounded in wealth and been established in some great dignity, what He did divinely would have been attributed more to secular power than to the virtue of the divinity. Hence, the most efficacious argument for His divinity has been this: Without the support of the secular power He has changed the whole world for the better.

[16] Accordingly, the solution is open to what was said in the thirteenth objection.[23]

[17] It is not, of course, far from true to say that the incarnate Son of God bore His death in obedience to a command of His Father, according to the Apostle's teaching (Phil. 2:8). For God's commandment to men deals with the works of virtue; and the more perfectly one carries out an act of virtue, the more is he obedient to God. Among the other virtues, charity is the outstanding one to which all the other are referred. Christ, then, when He fulfilled the act of charity most perfectly was most obedient to God. For there is no act of charity more perfect than the one by which a man bears even death for another; as our Lord Himself says: "Greater love than this no man hath that a man lay down his life for his friends" (John 15:13). Therefore, one finds that Christ bearing death for the salvation of men and for the glory of God the Father was extremely obedient to God and carried out a perfect act of charity. Nor is this repugnant to His divinity, as the fourteenth argument[24] ran. For the union in person took place in such wise that what was proper to each

22. See above, ch. 53, ¶13.   23. See above, ch. 53, ¶14.
24. See above, ch. 53, ¶15.

of the natures remained, namely to the divine and to the human, as was explained above.[25] Therefore, even when Christ suffered death and other things proper to humanity, the divinity remained incapable of suffering, although by the unity of person we say that God suffered and died. And somewhat of an instance of this appears in us because, although the flesh dies, the soul remains immortal.

[18] This, too, should be understood: Although the will of God is not for the death of men, as the fifteenth argument[26] set down, the will of God is for virtue by which a man bears death bravely, and in charity exposes himself to the dangers of death. Thus, the will of God *was* for the death of Christ, in that Christ undertook that death in charity and bore it bravely.

[19] Hence, clearly, it was neither impiety nor cruelty that God the Father willed Christ to die, as the sixteenth argument[27] was concluding, for He did not coerce one who was unwilling, but was pleased with that will in whose charity Christ undertook His death. And God even wrought this charity in the soul of Christ.

[20] In the same way, too, there is no awkwardness in saying that Christ willed the death on the cross as a demonstration of humility. To be sure, the humility does not touch God, as the seventeenth argument[28] was proposing. Truly, the virtue of humility consists in this, that one keep himself within his own limits; he does not stretch himself to what is above him, but he subjects himself to his superior. Hence, clearly, God can have no proportionate humility, for He has no superior; He Himself exists above all things. But, if a man at times subjects himself in humility to an equal or inferior, this is because the one who is his equal or inferior simply is held by the man as his superior in a certain respect. Therefore, although the virtue of humility was not fitting to Christ in His divine nature, it was fitting to Him in His human nature, and His humility was rendered the more praiseworthy by His divinity. For the dignity of the person contributes to the praise humility deserves; for example, when out of some necessity

---

25. See above, ch. 41.
27. See above, ch. 53, ¶17.

26. See above, ch. 53, ¶16.
28. See above, ch. 53, ¶18.

a great man has to suffer something lowly. But there can be no dignity of man so great as this: that he be God. Hence, the humility of the God-man was praiseworthy in the extreme when He bore those abject things which He was called on to suffer for the salvation of men. For men were by reason of pride lovers of worldly glory. Therefore, to change the spirits of men over from love of worldly glory to love of divine glory He willed to bear death—not just any sort of death, but a death abject in the extreme. For there are some who, although they do not fear death, abhor an abject death. And even to the contempt of such a death did our Lord inspire men by the example of His death.

[21] One grants also that men instructed by the divine lessons were able to be informed about humility, as the eighteenth argument[29] was proposing. For all that, deeds are more provocative of action than words; and deeds move the more effectively, the more certain is the opinion of the goodness of him who performs such deeds. Hence, although many examples of humility of other men are discoverable, it was most expeditious to arouse men to humility by the example of the God-man. He clearly could not make a mistake, and His humility is the more wondrous as His majesty is the more sublime.

[22] This, too, is clear from what has been said: Christ had to suffer death not only to give an example of holding death in contempt out of love of the truth, but also to wash away the sins of others. This indeed took place when He who was without sin willed to suffer the penalty due to sin that He might take on Himself the penalty due to others, and make satisfaction for others. And although the grace of God suffices by itself for the remission of sins, as the nineteenth argument[30] was proposing, nonetheless in the remission of sin something is required on the part of him whose sin is remitted: namely, that he satisfy the one offended. And since other men were unable to do this for themselves, Christ did this for all by suffering a voluntary death out of charity.

[23] Be it granted, also, that in the punishment of sins he

29. See above, ch. 53, ¶19.
30. See above, ch. 53, ¶20.

who sinned ought to be punished, as the twentieth argument[31] was proposing; for all that, in the matter of satisfaction one can bear another's penalty. For, when penalty is inflicted for sin, we weigh his iniquity who is punished; in satisfaction, however, when to placate the one offended, some other voluntarily assumes the penalty, we consider the charity and benevolence of him who makes satisfaction, and this most especially appears when one assumes the penalty of another. And, therefore, God does receive from one satisfaction for another, as was shown in Book III.[32]

[24] But to satisfy for the whole human race (this was shown previously[33]) was beyond the power of any mere man; neither was an angel equal to this, as the twenty-first argument[34] was proceeding. For, granted an angel in some natural properties has a power beyond man's, nonetheless in the sharing of beatitude (and by the satisfaction man was to be restored to this) the angel is man's equal. And again, there would be no full restoration of man's dignity if man were rendered obnoxious to the angel satisfying for man.

[25] One should, of course, know that the death of Christ had its satisfying power from His charity in which He bore death voluntarily, and not from the iniquity of His killers who sinned in killing Him; because sin is not wiped out by sin, as the twenty-second argument[35] proposed.

[26] And although the death of Christ was satisfactory for sin, it was unnecessary for Him to die just as many times as men sinned, as the twenty-third argument[36] was concluding. The death of Christ was sufficient for the expiation of all sins; and this by reason of the extraordinary charity in which He bore death, as well as by reason of the dignity of the satisfying person who was God and man. But even in human affairs it is clear that by as much as the person is higher, by so much is the penalty he bears reckoned for more, whether reckoned by the humility and charity of the one suffering or by the fault of the one incurring the penalty.

[27] Of course, for the satisfaction of the sin of the entire

31. See above, ch. 53, ¶21.
32. SCG, III, ch. 158.
33. See above, ch. 54.
34. See above, ch. 53, ¶22.
35. See above, ch. 53, ¶23.
36. See above, ch. 53, ¶24.

human race the death of Christ was sufficient. For, although He died only in His human nature, as the twenty-fourth argument[37] was proposing, the dignity of the person suffering—and this is the Person of the Son of God—renders His death precious. For, as was said above,[38] just as it is a greater crime to commit an injury to a person who stands out more in dignity, so it is more virtuous and proceeds from greater charity that the greater person submit Himself voluntarily to suffering for others.

[28] But, although Christ has by His death satisfied sufficiently for original sin, there is nothing awkward in this: that the penalties consequent on original sin still remain in all, even in those who are given a share in Christ's redemption, as the twenty-fifth argument[39] was proceeding. For it was both fitting and useful to have the penalty remain even when the fault was taken away. First, indeed, to achieve conformity of the faithful to Christ as members to the head; hence, just as Christ first bore many sufferings, and thus arrived at the glory of immortality, it also was becoming to His faithful first to undergo sufferings and so to arrive at immortality, bearing in themselves, so to say, the marks of the passion of Christ, in order to achieve a likeness to His glory. So the Apostle says: "Heirs, indeed of God, and joint-heirs with Christ: yet so, if we suffer with Him, that we may be also glorified with Him" (Rom. 8:17). Second, because, if men coming to Jesus were forthwith to achieve immortality and impassibility, many men would approach Christ more for these bodily benefits than for spiritual goods. And this is against the intention of Christ who came into the world to change men from love of bodily things to love of spiritual things. Third, because, if those who come to Christ were forthwith rendered incapable of suffering and death, this would somehow compel men to accept faith in Christ. And thus the merit of faith would be diminished.

[29] Granted, of course, that Christ has sufficiently satisfied for the sins of the human race by His death, as the twenty-sixth argument[40] proposed, every single one, for all that, must

37. See above, ch. 53, ¶25.
38. See above, ¶17, and *SCG*, III, ch. 158.
39. See above, ch. 53, ¶26.   40. See above, ch. 53, ¶27.

seek the remedies of his own salvation. For the death of Christ is, so to say, a kind of universal cause of salvation, as the sin of the first man was a kind of universal cause of damnation. But a universal cause must be applied specially to each one, that he may receive the effect of the universal cause. The effect, then, of the sin of the first parent comes to each one in the origin of the flesh, but the effect of the death of Christ comes to each one in a spiritual regeneration in which the man is somehow conjoined with Christ and incorporated into Him. And for this reason each must seek to be regenerated through Christ, and must himself undertake to do those things in which the power of Christ's death operates.

[30] From this it is clear that the flow of salvation from Christ to men is not through a natural propagation, but through the zeal of good will in which a man cleaves to Christ. Hence, that which each accomplishes by Christ is a personal good. Wherefore, it is not passed on to descendants, as is the sin of the first parent which is produced with the propagation of the nature. Accordingly, although the parents are cleansed of original sin by Christ, there is nothing awkward about the birth of their children in original sin, requiring the sacraments of salvation, as the twenty-seventh argument[41] was concluding.

[31] Thus, then, from what has been set down it is to some extent clear that what the Catholic faith preaches about the Incarnation contains nothing impossible and nothing inharmonious.

Chapter 56.

ON THE NECESSITY OF THE SACRAMENTS

[1] Since, however (as has already been said[1]), the death of Christ is, so to say, the universal cause of human salvation, and since a universal cause must be applied singly to each of its effects, it was necessary to show men some remedies through

41. But there is no twenty-seventh objection in ch. 53 to answer! If one rereads ch. 51, ¶12 and ch. 52, ¶16, he may agree that St. Thomas probably took out the twenty-seventh objection and possibly forgot to take out the answer. See Ed. Leon. tom. XIV, p. xxv b.   1. See above, ch. 55, ¶29.

which the benefit of Christ's death could somehow be conjoined to them. It is of this sort, of course, that the sacraments of the Church are said to be.

[2] Now, remedies of this kind had to be handed on with some visible signs.

[3] First, indeed, because just as He does for all other things, so also for man, God provides according to his condition.[2] Now, man's condition is such that he is brought to grasp the spiritual and intelligible naturally through the senses. Therefore, spiritual remedies had to be given to men under sensible signs.

[4] Second, because instruments must be proportioned to their first cause. But the first and universal cause of human salvation is the incarnate Word, as is clear from the foregoing.[3] Therefore, harmoniously the remedies by which the power of the universal cause reaches men had a likeness to that cause; that is, the divine power operates in them under visible signs.

[5] Third, because man fell into sin by clinging unduly to visible things. Therefore, that one might not believe visible things evil of their nature, and that for this reason those clinging to them had sinned, it was fitting that through the visible things themselves the remedies of salvation be applied to men. Consequently, it would appear that visible things are good of their nature—as created by God—but they become damaging to men so far as one clings to them in a disordered way, and saving so far as one uses them in an ordered way.

[6] Thus, of course, one excludes the error of certain heretics who want every visible thing of this kind removed from the sacraments of the Church. Nor need one marvel at this, for the very same men maintain that whatever is visible is evil in its nature, and is produced by an evil author. And this we rejected in Book II.[4]

[7] Nor is it unsuitable that by things visible and bodily a spiritual salvation is served. For visible things of this kind are the instruments, so to say, of a God who was made flesh and suffered. Now, an instrument does not operate by the power

2. SCG, III, ch. 111 and 119.   3. See above, ch. 55, ¶29–30.
4. See above, SCG, II, ch. 41 and 44; III, ch. 7.

of its nature, but by the power of its principal agent who puts it into operation. Thus, also, then, do visible things of this kind work out a spiritual salvation—not by a property of their own nature, but by Christ's institution, and from the latter they receive their instrumental power.

Chapter 57.

THE DISTINCTION OF THE SACRAMENTS
OF THE OLD AND THE NEW LAW

[1]   Next, this must be considered. Since the sacraments of this visible kind got their efficacy from the passion of Christ and in some way represent it, they must be such as to be in harmony with the salvation wrought by Christ. Now, this salvation was promised, indeed, before Christ's Incarnation and death but not displayed; it was the incarnate and suffering Word who brought about this kind of salvation. Therefore, the sacraments which preceded Christ's Incarnation had to be such as signified and somehow promised salvation. But the sacraments which follow the suffering of Christ ought to be such as deliver this salvation to men, not merely such as point to it by signs.

[2]   Of course, in this way one avoids the opinion of the Jews, who believe that the sacraments of the Law must be observed forever precisely because they were established by God, since God has no regrets and is not changed. But without change or regret one who disposes things may dispose things differently in harmony with a difference of times; thus, the father of a family gives one set of orders to a small child and another to one already grown. Thus, God also harmoniously gave one set of sacraments and commandments before the Incarnation to point to the future, and another set after the Incarnation to deliver things present and bring to mind things past.

[3]   But more unreasonable still is the error of the Nazarenes and the Ebionites,[1] who used to say that the sacraments of the Law should be observed simultaneously with those of the Gospel. An error of this kind involves a sort of contrariety. For,

1. St. Augustine, De haeresibus, 9–10 (PL, 42, col. 27).

while they observe the evangelical sacraments, they are professing that the Incarnation and the other mysteries of Christ have already been perfected; but, when they also observe the sacraments of the Law, they are professing that those mysteries are in the future.

Chapter 58.

ON THE NUMBER OF THE SACRAMENTS OF THE NEW LAW

[1] However, since the spiritual remedies of salvation (as was said[1]) have been given to men under sensible signs, it was suitable also to distinguish the remedies provided for the spiritual life after the likeness of bodily life.

[2] Now, in bodily life we find a twofold order: for some propagate and order the bodily life in others; and some are propagated and ordered in the bodily life.

[3] Now, in a bodily and natural life three things are necessary of themselves, and a fourth incidentally. For first, by generation or birth a thing must receive life; second, by growth it must arrive at its due size and strength; third, both for the preservation of life acquired by generation and for growth nourishment is necessary. And these are of themselves necessities for natural life, because without these bodily life cannot be perfected; wherefore, one assigns to the vegetative soul which is the principle of life the three natural powers: that of generation, that of growth, and that of nourishment. But, since there can be an impediment to natural life from which the living thing grows weak, a fourth thing is incidentally necessary; this is the healing of the sick living thing.

[4] Thus, then, in the spiritual life, also, the first thing is spiritual generation: by baptism; the second is spiritual growth leading to perfect strength: by the sacrament of confirmation; the third is spiritual nourishment: by the sacrament of the Eucharist. A fourth remains, which is the spiritual healing; it takes place either in the soul alone through the sacrament of penance; or from the soul flows to the body when this is timely,

1. See above, ch. 56.

through extreme unction. These, therefore, bear on those who are propagated and preserved in the spiritual life.

[5] Now, those who propagate and order in the bodily life are marked by two things: namely, natural origin, and this refers to parents; and the political regime by which the peaceful life of man is conserved, and this refers to kings and princes.

[6] It is, then, also like this in the spiritual life. For some propagate and conserve the spiritual life in a spiritual ministry only, and this belongs to the sacrament of orders; and some belong to the bodily and spiritual life simultaneously, which takes place in the sacrament of matrimony where a man and woman come together to beget offspring and to rear them in divine worship.

Chapter 59.

ON BAPTISM

[1] In this way, then, one can discern in the individual sacraments the proper effect of each one and the becoming matter. Now, first: Regarding the spiritual generation which takes place in baptism, one must consider that the generation of a living thing is a kind of change from non-living to life. But man in his origin was deprived of spiritual life by original sin, as was shown above;[1] and still every single sin whatever which is added draws him away from life. Baptism, therefore, which is spiritual generation, had to have the power to take away both original sin and all the actual, committed sins.

[2] Now, because the sensible sign of a sacrament must be harmonious with the representation of its spiritual effect, and since washing away filth in bodily things is done more easily and more commonly by water, baptism is, therefore, suitably conferred in water made holy by the Word of God.

[3] And since the generation of one is the corruption of another, and since what is generated loses both its previous form and the properties consequent on that form; necessarily through baptism, which is a spiritual generation, not only are

1. See above, ch. 50 and 52.

sins taken away—these are contrary to a spiritual life—but also every guilt of sins. For this reason, too, baptism not only washes away the fault, but also absolves from all guilt. Hence, no satisfaction for their sins is enjoined on the baptized.

[4] Again, when by generation a thing acquires a form, it acquires at the same time the operation consequent on the form and the place in harmony with it. For fire, as soon as generated, tends upward as to its proper place. Accordingly, since baptism is a spiritual generation, the baptized are forthwith suited for spiritual actions—the reception of the other sacraments, for example, and other things of the sort—and forthwith there is due to them the place harmonious to the spiritual life, which is eternal beatitude. Hence, we say² that "Baptism opens the gate of heaven."

[5] One should also consider that one thing has but one generation. Hence, since baptism is a spiritual generation, a man is to be baptized once only.

[6] Clearly, also, the infection which entered the world through Adam makes a man guilty but once. Hence, baptism, which is chiefly ordered against this infection, should not be repeated. There is also this common consideration: that, as long as a thing is once consecrated, it must not be consecrated again, so long as it endures, lest the consecration appear inefficacious. And so, since baptism is a kind of consecration of the one baptized, baptism must not be repeated. This excludes the error of the Donatists or Rebaptizers.³

Chapter 60.

ON CONFIRMATION

[1] The perfection of spiritual strength consists properly in a man's daring to confess the faith of Christ in the presence of anyone at all, and in a man's being not withdrawn therefrom either by confusion or by terror, for strength drives out inordinate terror. Therefore, the sacrament by which spiritual strength is conferred on the one born again makes him in some

2. Bede, *In Lucae Evangelium expositio*, I, 3 (*PL*, 92, col. 358B).
3. Cf. St. Augustine, *De haeresibus*, 69 (*PL*, 42, col. 43).

sense a front-line fighter for the faith of Christ. And because
fighters under a prince carry his insignia, they who receive
the sacrament of confirmation are signed with the sign of
Christ; this is the sign of the cross by which He fought and
conquered. This sign they receive on the forehead as a sign
that without a blush they publicly confess the faith of Christ.

[2] This signing takes place with a mixture of oil and balm
which is called chrism, and not without reason. For by the oil
one designates the power of the Holy Spirit, from whom
Christ, too, is called "anointed" (Ps. 44:8; Luke 4:18); and
consequently from Christ they are called "Christians" (Acts
9:26), so to say, as fighting under Him. And by the balm,
through its fragrance, good repute is indicated. For the public
confession of faith in Christ this good repute must be had by
those who dwell among men of this world, brought forth, so
to say, from the hidden recesses of the Church onto the field
of battle.

[3] Suitably, too, this sacrament is conferred only by bishops, who are in some sense the leaders of the Christian army.
For even in secular military forces it is the prerogative of the
army leader to select some men to be enrolled; so, also, those
who receive this sacrament seem to be enrolled somehow in
the spiritual military forces. Hence, also, a hand is laid upon
them to designate the derivation of manliness from Christ.

Chapter 61.

ON THE EUCHARIST

[1] Now, bodily life needs material nourishment, not only
for increase in quantity, but to maintain the nature of the
body as well, lest it be dissolved by continuous resolutions and
lose its power; in the same way it was necessary to have spiritual nourishment for the spiritual life that the reborn may
both be conserved in virtues and grow in them.

[2] Spiritual effects were fittingly given under the likeness
of things visible (as was said[1]); therefore, spiritual nourishment of this kind is given to us under the appearances of the

1. See above, ch. 56.

things which men rather commonly use for bodily nourishment. Bread and wine are of this sort. Accordingly, this sacrament is given under the appearances of bread and wine.

[3] But consider this: He who begets is joined to the begotten in one way, and nourishment is joined to the nourished in another way in bodily things. For the one who begets need not be conjoined to the begotten in substance, but in likeness and in power only. But nutriment must be conjoined to the one nourished in substance. Wherefore, that the spiritual effects may answer the bodily signs, the mystery of the incarnate Word is joined to us in one way in baptism which is a spiritual rebirth, and in another way in this sacrament of the Eucharist which is a spiritual nourishment. In baptism the Word incarnate is contained in His power only, but we hold that in the sacrament of the Eucharist He is contained in His substance.

[4] And since the fulfillment of our salvation took place through the passion and death of Christ, in which His blood was separated from His flesh, we are given the sacrament of His body separately under the appearance of bread, and of His blood under the appearance of wine; and so we have in this sacrament both memory and the representation of our Lord's passion. And in this our Lord's words are fulfilled: "My flesh is meat indeed, and my blood is drink indeed" (John 6:56).

Chapter 62.

ON THE ERROR OF THE INFIDELS ABOUT
THE SACRAMENT OF THE EUCHARIST

[1] Of course, just as when Christ spoke these words, some of the disciples were troubled and said: "This saying is hard, and who can bear it?" (John 6:61), so, also, against the teaching of the Church some heretics[1] have arisen to deny this

---

1. In a corresponding passage in *Summa Theologiae*, III, 75, 1, St. Thomas calls Berengarius the heresiarch of this group. The pertinent texts are cited in the Ottawa edition at that place. For the effects of the heresy, see Hughes, *A History of the Catholic Church*, II, 294–300. For further information on Berengarius, see Gilson, *History of Christian Philosophy*, p. 615.

truth. They say that the body and blood of Christ are not really present in this sacrament, but by way of sign only; thus, one understands Christ's saying when He indicated the bread: "This is My body" (Matt. 26:26) as though He were saying: "This is a sign or figure of My body." And in this way the Apostle spoke: "And the rock was Christ" (I Cor. 10:4), that is, "a figure of Christ"; and to such an understanding they refer whatever is said in the Scriptures in a similar way.

[2]   Of course, the occasion of this opinion is taken from our Lord's words. Speaking of eating His flesh and drinking His blood, to quiet the scandal which had arisen among the disciples He said—as though explaining Himself: "The words that I have spoken to you are spirit and life" (John 6:64); as though His words were to be understood not literally, but in a spiritual sense.

[3]   They are also induced to their dissent by the many difficulties which seem to follow this teaching of the Church; by reason of these "this saying" of Christ and the Church appears hard to them.

[4]   In the first place,[2] there seems to be a difficulty in the way in which the true body of Christ begins to be on the altar. For a thing begins to be where it was not before in two ways: either by local motion, or by the conversion of another into itself. This is clear in the case of fire, which begins to be in some place either because it is newly lighted there or because it is newly carried there. Manifestly, of course, the true body of Christ was not always on the altar; for the Church confesses that Christ in His body ascended into heaven.

[5]   But it seems impossible to say that here something is newly converted into the body of Christ. For nothing seems converted into the pre-existent, since what is converted into something begins to be by this sort of conversion. But, manifestly, the body of Christ pre-existed, let us say, as conceived in the virginal womb. Therefore, it does not seem possible that on the altar it begins to be anew by the conversion of another into itself.

[6]   In a similar fashion, it cannot be there by a change of

2. See below, ch. 63.

place, since whatever is moved locally begins to be in one place in such wise that it ceases to be in another in which it was before. Therefore, one will have to say that when Christ begins to be on this altar whereon the sacrament is enacted He ceases to be in heaven where He arrived after His ascension. Furthermore, no local motion has two places simultaneously as its term. But, clearly, this sacrament is celebrated simultaneously on different altars. Therefore, it is not possible that the body of Christ begins to be thereon by local motion.

[7] The second difficulty[3] comes from the place. For parts are not contained in separated places if a thing remains a whole. But, manifestly, in this sacrament the bread and wine are apart from one another in separate places. Therefore, if the flesh of Christ is under the appearance of bread and the blood under the appearance of wine, it seems to follow that Christ does not remain whole; but whenever this sacrament is performed His blood is separated from His body.

[8] Furthermore, it seems impossible that a larger body be inclosed in the place of a smaller one. Clearly, of course, the true body of Christ is greater in quantity than the bread which is offered on the altar. It seems, then, impossible that the true body of Christ be whole and entire there where the bread is seen. Of course, if it is not the whole there, but one of its parts, then the first awkwardness recurs: Whenever this sacrament is performed the body of Christ is scattered into parts.

[9] It is further impossible that one body should exist in many places. But, manifestly, this sacrament is celebrated in many places. Therefore, it seems impossible that the body of Christ is truthfully contained in this sacrament—unless one says, perhaps, that the body is contained in one of its particles here, and in another there. And on this it follows, once again, that by the celebration of this sacrament the body of Christ is divided into parts; for all that, at the same time, the quantity of the body of Christ does not seem to suffice for the division of as many particles from the body as there are places where this sacrament is performed.

[10] The third difficulty[4] lies in the things which we perceive by our senses in this sacrament. For, clearly, in this sacra-

ment we sense, even after the consecration, all the accidents of bread and wine: color, taste, odor, figure, quantity, and weight; and concerning these we cannot be deceived, for "the sense is never deceived about the proper sensibles."[5]

[11]   But accidents of this kind cannot be in the body of Christ as in a subject; in like fashion, neither can they be in the surrounding air; for, since many of them are natural accidents, they call for a subject of a determined nature, which is not like the nature of the human body or of the air.

[12]   Nor can they subsist in themselves, since "the being of an accident is by inherence."[6]

[13]   Also, since accidents are forms, they cannot be individuated except through a subject. Wherefore, with the subject removed they would be universal forms. Therefore, this remains: Accidents of this kind are in their determined subjects; namely, in the substance of bread and wine. Therefore, the substance of bread and wine is there, and the substance of the body of Christ is not, since it seems impossible that the two bodies be there simultaneously.

[14]   The fourth difficulty[7] arises from the actions and passions which appear in the bread and wine after the consecration just as they did before it. For the wine, if taken in large quantity, would make one warm and would make one drunk; the bread, of course, would strengthen and would nourish. They seem, also, if kept long and carelessly, to rot or to be eaten by mice; they can even be burned, and reduced to ashes and smoke. But none of this agrees with the body of Christ, since the faith preaches that it is incapable of suffering. Therefore, it seems impossible that the body of Christ be contained substantially in this sacrament.

[15]   A fifth difficulty[8] seems to arise especially from the breaking of the bread; indeed, this breaking appears sensibly and cannot be without a subject. It even seems absurd to say that the subject of that breaking is the body of Christ. Therefore, the body of Christ seems not to be there, but only the substance of the bread and wine.

5. Aristotle, *De anima*, III, 6 (430b 29).
6. Aristotle, *Metaphysics*, V, 7 (1017a 19).
7. See below, ch. 66.   8. See below, ch. 67.

[16] These, then, and points of this kind are the reason why the teaching of Christ and the Church concerning this sacrament appears hard.

Chapter 63.

SOLUTION OF THE DIFFICULTIES SET DOWN: FIRST, ABOUT THE CONVERSION OF THE BREAD INTO THE BODY OF CHRIST

[1] Although, of course, the divine power operates with a greater sublimity and secrecy in this sacrament than a man's inquiry can search out, nonetheless, lest the teaching of the Church regarding this sacrament appear impossible to unbelievers, one must make the endeavor to exclude every impossibility.

[2] The first consideration we meet, then, is that of the way in which the true body of Christ begins to be under this sacrament.[1]

[3] It is impossible, of course, that this take place by a local motion of the body of Christ. One reason is that it would follow that He ceases to be in heaven whenever this sacrament is performed. Another reason is that this sacrament could not be performed at the same time except in one place, since a local motion is not ended except at one term. Another reason, also, is that local motion cannot be instantaneous, but requires time. Consecration, however, is perfected in the ultimate instant of the pronouncement of the words.

[4] Therefore, one concludes by saying that the true body of Christ begins to be in this sacrament by the fact that the substance of the bread is converted into the substance of the body of Christ, and the substance of the wine into the substance of His blood.

[5] But thus appears the falsity of the opinion: not only of those who say that the substance of the bread exists simultaneously with the substance of Christ in this sacrament, but also of those who hold that the substance of the bread is reduced to nothing or is resolved into prime matter. For on each

1. See above, ch. 62, ¶4–6.

of these positions it follows that the body of Christ does not begin to be in this sacrament except by local motion. And this is impossible, as we have shown.

Furthermore, if the substance of the bread is simultaneous in this sacrament with the true body of Christ, Christ should rather have said: "My body is here" than: "This is My body." For by "here" one points to the substance which is seen, and this is indeed the substance of the bread, if it remains in the sacrament with the body of Christ.

Similarly, also, it seems impossible that the substance of the bread returns to nothingness. For much of the bodily nature first created would have already returned into nothingness from the repetition of this mystery. Neither is it becoming that in a sacrament of salvation something be reduced to nothing by the divine power. Nor is it even possible that the substance of the bread is resolved into prime matter, since prime matter cannot be without form—except, perhaps, that one is to understand by "prime matter" the primary bodily elements. To be sure, if the substance of the bread were resolved into these, this very thing would necessarily be perceived by the senses, since the bodily elements are sensible. There would also be local transmutation in the place and bodily alteration of contraries. And these cannot be instantaneous.

[6]   Nonetheless, it must be recognized that the aforesaid conversion of the bread into the body of Christ is of another mode than any natural conversion whatever. For in any natural conversion a subject persists in which different forms succeed themselves: these are accidental—white, for example, is converted into black; or they are substantial—air, for example, is converted into fire; wherefore these are named *formal conversions*. But in the conversion under discussion a subject passes over into a subject, and the accidents persist; hence, this conversion is named *substantial*. Indeed, how these accidents persist, and why, must be closely examined later.[2]

[7]   But now we must consider how a subject is converted into a subject. And this, to be sure, nature cannot do. For every operation of nature presupposes matter which individuates the substance; wherefore, nature cannot bring it about

2. See below, ch. 65.

that this substance become that substance, that this finger, for example, become that finger. But matter is subject to the divine power, since the latter brings it into being. Hence, by divine power it can come about that this individual substance be converted into that pre-existing substance. Now, just as the power of a natural agent whose operation extends to the change of a form only—and the existence of the subject is supposed—changes this whole into that whole in a variation of the species and the form—this air, let us say, into that generated fire—so the divine power, which does not presuppose matter, but produces matter, converts *this* matter into *that* matter, and, in consequence, this individual into that individual; for the principle of individuation is matter, just as form is the principle of species.

[8] In this way, of course, it is clear that in the aforesaid conversion of bread into the body of Christ there is not a common subject persisting after the conversion, since a transmutation takes place in the first subject, and this is the principle of the individuation. It is necessary, for all that, that something persist to make true the words: "This is My body"; the very words, in fact, which are significative and effective of this conversion. And the substance of the bread does not persist; neither does any prior matter (as was shown). Therefore, one necessarily says that what persists is other than the substance of the bread. Of this sort, of course, is the accident of the bread. Therefore, the accidents of the bread do persist even after the conversion mentioned.

[9] Among accidents, however, there is a certain order to be considered. For, among all the accidents, that inhering more closely to the substance is the quantity which tends to measure. Then the qualities are received in the substance with the quantity as medium—color, for example, with the surface as medium; hence, even by the division of the quantity they are incidentally divided. But, in addition, the qualities are the principles of actions and passions, as well as of certain relations—father and son, let us say, or master and servant, and others of this kind. Of course, some relations follow immediately on the quantities—greater and less, for instance, or doubled and halved, and similar relations. Therefore, one

ought to hold that the accidents of the bread persist after the conversion mentioned in such wise that only the quantity which tends to measure subsists without a subject, and on it the qualities are based as on a subject, and so in consequence are the accidents, passions, and relations. Therefore, in this conversion what takes place is the contrary of what usually takes place in natural mutations, for in these the substance persists as the subject of the mutation, whereas the accidents are varied; but here, conversely, the accident persists, the substance passes.

[10]   Of course, a conversion of this kind cannot properly be called *motion* as that is considered by the natural philosopher, since that requires a subject, but it is a kind of *substantial succession;* so there is in creation a succession of being and non-being, as was said in Book II.[3]

[11]   This, then, is one reason why the accident of the bread must remain: that something be discoverable which persists in the conversion under discussion.

[12]   But it is necessary for another reason. For, if the substance of the bread were converted into the body of Christ and the accidents were to pass on, it would not follow from such a conversion that the body of Christ in His substance would be where first there was bread, for no relationship between the body of Christ and the aforesaid place would be left. But since, after the conversion, the quantity of the bread which tends to measure does remain, and through this the bread acquired this place, the substance of the bread changed into the body of Christ becomes the body of Christ under the bread's quantity tending to measure; in consequence, the body of Christ in some way acquires the place of the bread, with the measurements of the bread, nonetheless, mediating.

[13]   Other reasons can also be given: respecting the essentials of faith, which deals with the invisible; respecting also its merit, which is so much the greater in connection with this sacrament, since it deals with the more invisible, for the body of Christ is hidden under the accidents of the bread; respecting, also, the more appropriate and worthy use of this sacrament, for it would be horrible for the receivers, and an

3. SCG, II, ch. 18–19.

abomination to those looking on, if the body of Christ were received by the faithful in its own appearance. Hence, it is under the appearance of bread and wine, which men use rather commonly for meat and drink, that the body of Christ is set forth to be eaten and His blood to be drunk.

Chapter 64.

SOLUTION OF THE OBJECTIONS MADE REGARDING PLACE

[1] Now, after we have considered these points about the mode of conversion, the way to solve the other arguments is opened up to us somewhat.[1] For it has now been said[2] that the place in which the sacrament is is ascribed to the body of Christ by reason of the measurements of the bread remaining after the conversion of the substance of the bread into the body of Christ. And in accord with this, that which is of Christ must be in the place mentioned so far as the essentials of the conversion mentioned require it.

[2] Consideration, then, must be given this: There is something in this sacrament by force of the conversion and something by natural accompaniment. Now, by force of the conversion there is in the sacrament that in which the conversion is directly terminated: so, under the appearances of bread there is the body of Christ into which the substance of the bread is converted, as is clear from the words of the consecration when one says: "This is My body"; in like manner under the appearance of wine there is the blood of Christ when one says: "This is the chalice of My blood," and so forth. But by natural accompaniment all the other things are there in which the conversion is not terminated, but which are, nonetheless, really conjoined to that in which the conversion is terminated. For it is clear that the conversion of the bread is not terminated in the divinity of Christ, nor in His soul; nonetheless, under the appearance of bread the soul of Christ is there, and His divinity by reason of the union of each of these to the body of Christ.

1. See above, ch. 62, ¶7–9.   2. See above, ch. 63, ¶12.

[3] However, if in the three-day period of the death of Christ this sacrament had been celebrated, the soul of Christ would not have been under the appearance of bread, because it was not really united to His body; in the same way, there would not have been blood under the appearance of bread, nor body under the appearance of wine, by reason of the separation of each of these in death. But now, since the body of Christ in His nature is not without blood, His body and blood are contained under each appearance: under the appearance of bread the body is contained by force of conversion, the blood by natural accompaniment; under the appearance of wine the converse is true.

[4] The same points give a solution to the objection about the inequality of the body of Christ to the place of the bread. For the substance of the bread is directly converted into the substance of the body of Christ, but the dimensions of the body of Christ are in the sacrament by natural accompaniment, and not from force of conversion, since the dimensions of the bread remain. In this way, then, the body of Christ is not related to this place with its own dimensions as medium, so that the place need be equated to those dimensions, but His body is here with the persisting dimensions of the bread as medium, and to these the place is equated.

[5] Therein, also, the solution is open to what was objected to about the plurality of places. For the body of Christ in His own dimensions exists in one place only, but through the mediation of the dimensions of the bread passing into it its places are as many as there are places in which this sort of conversion is celebrated. For it is not divided into parts, but is entire in every single one; every consecrated bread is converted into the entire body of Christ.

Chapter 65.

SOLUTION OF THE OBJECTIONS REGARDING ACCIDENTS

[1] Thus, then, with the difficulty solved arising from place, one ought to look into the one which seems to arise from the accidents which remain.[1] For it cannot be denied that the

1. See above, ch. 62, ¶10–13.

accidents of bread and wine remain, since the senses infallibly point this out.

[2] Neither the body of Christ nor His blood is affected by these accidents,[2] because without changing Him this could not be; nor has He the capacity for such accidents. Much the same can be said of the substance of the air. Hence, one concludes that they are without a subject. Nevertheless, they are without a subject in the manner mentioned:[3] namely, that only the quantity tending to measure subsists without a subject, and this supplies a subject to the other accidents.

[3] Neither is it impossible that by the divine power an accident can subsist without a subject. For one ought to make the same judgment about the creation of things and about their conservation in being. The divine power, of course, can produce the effects of any second causes whatever without the second causes themselves; so it was able to form a man without seed, and to cure a fever without the operation of nature. And this happens by reason of the infinity of His power, and because He grants to all second causes their power to act. Wherefore, also, He can conserve the effects of second causes in being without the second causes. And in this way in this sacrament He conserves an accident in being, even after the removal of the substance which was conserving it. And this, indeed, can especially be said of the quantities tending to measure; these even the Platonists[4] held to subsist of themselves, for this reason: They are separated in the understanding.[5] But it is clear that God can do more in operation than the intellect can in apprehension.

[4] Of course, the quantity tending to measure has among the remaining accidents this property: that it is in itself individuated. And the reason is this: Position, which is "the order of parts in the whole," is essentially included in this quantity, for quantity is "that which has position."[6] But wherever a diversity of parts of the same species is understood, individuation is necessarily understood, for things which are

2. *Ibid.*   3. See above, ch. 63, ¶6–7.
4. See Aristotle, *Metaphysics*, III, 4 (esp. 1001a 25, 1001b 2).
5. Aristotle, *Physics*, II, 2 (193b 36).
6. Aristotle, *Categories*, 6 (4b 21).

of the same species are not multiplied except in the individual; accordingly many whitenesses cannot be apprehended except as they are in different subjects, but many lines can be apprehended, even if they are considered in themselves. For diversity of site which is in the line of itself is sufficient for the plurality of lines. And because only the quantity tending to measure has in its essentials a possible source of the multiplication of individuals in the same species, the first root of this kind of multiplication seems to be from measurement, because even in the genus of substance the multiplication is made according to the division of matter. And this could not even be understood save by the consideration of matter under measurements, for with the quantity gone all substance is indivisible, as is clear from the Philosopher in *Physics* I.[7]

[5]   It is, of course, manifest that in the other genera of accidents, individuals are multiplied in the same species on the part of the subject. And thus one is left to conclude: Since we hold that in this sacrament the measurements subsist of themselves and that the other accidents are founded on these as on a subject, we need not say that accidents of this kind are not individuated; for there persists in the measurements themselves the root of individuation.

Chapter 66.

SOLUTION OF THE OBJECTIONS REGARDING
ACTION AND PASSION

[1]   After the consideration of these points, one should consider those belonging to the fourth difficulty.[1] And concerning these there is, indeed, something which can be dealt with easily; something else, however, offers a greater difficulty.

[2]   The fact that in this sacrament the same actions appear which previously appeared in the substance of the bread and wine (they change the senses in the same way, let us say; they even in the same way alter the surrounding air, or anything else, by odor or color) now seems fitting enough from what

7. Aristotle, *Physics*, I, 2 (185b 2).   1. See above, ch. 62, ¶14.

has been set down. For we said[2] that in this sacrament the accidents of the bread and wine persist. And among these are the sensible qualities which are the principles of actions of this sort.

[3] Again, concerning some passions (those, for instance, which take place in alterations of accidents of this kind), the difficulty which occurs is not so great, if the premises be granted. For, since it was premised[3] that the other accidents are based on the measurements as on a subject, the alteration of the other accidents can be considered in the same way with respect to this subject as they would be if the substance were there; for example, if the wine had been warmed and became cold, or if it should change its flavor, or something of this kind.

[4] But a very great difficulty appears regarding the generation and corruption which seems to take place in this sacrament. For if one were to use this sacramental food in large quantity he could be sustained, and by the wine even made drunk, as the Apostle has it: "One indeed is hungry and another is drunk" (I Cor. 11:21). And these things could not take place unless, from this sacrament, flesh and blood were generated, for nourishment is converted into the substance of the one nourished. Some may, of course, say that a man is not nourished by this sacramental food, but only invigorated and refreshed, as when one is invigorated by the fragrance of wine. But this invigoration can happen for an hour; it does not, of course, suffice to sustain a man if he remains long without food. But a trial would readily show that a man can be sustained for a long time by the sacramental food.

[5] It also seems a wonder why they should deny that a man can be nourished by this sacramental food, refusing to this sacrament the possible conversion into flesh and blood, when it appears to the senses that by putrefaction or combustion it is turned into another substance; namely, dust and ashes.

[6] And this, indeed, seems nonetheless difficult, since it does not seem possible to make a substance out of accidents; nor is it right to believe that the substance of Christ's body —which is not capable of suffering—be converted into another substance.

2. See above, ch. 65, and ch. 63, ¶6–7.   3. *Ibid.*

[7]   However, if one wishes to say that as the bread is miraculously converted into the body of Christ, so the accidents are converted miraculously into substance: first, indeed, this does not seem suitable for a miracle, the putrefaction of this sacrament, or its dissolution by combustion; and then that putrefaction and combustion are found taking place in this sacrament in the usual order of nature, which is not usually the case in things done miraculously.

[8]   To remove this hesitation a certain famous position was invented, which is held by many.[4] They hold thus: When this sacrament happens to be converted into flesh or blood by nutrition, or into ashes by combustion or putrefaction, the accidents are not converted into substance; nor is the substance of the body of Christ converted; but by a divine miracle the substance of the bread which was there previously returns, and from it are generated the things into which we find the sacrament converted.

[9]   But this, to be sure, simply cannot stand. For we have shown above[5] that the substance of the bread is converted into the substance of the body of Christ. But that which is converted into another cannot return unless, conversely, that other be reconverted into it. If, therefore, the substance of the bread returns, it follows that the substance of the body of Christ is reconverted into bread. And this is absurd. What is more, if the substance of the bread returns, it must return either while the appearances of bread persist or when the appearances of bread are already destroyed. In fact, while the appearances of bread persist, the substance of the bread cannot return, because, as long as the appearances remain, thereunder remains the substance of the body of Christ; it would follow, therefore, that simultaneously present there would be both the substance of the bread and the substance of the body of Christ. In like manner, also, if the appearances of the bread are corrupted, the substance of the bread cannot return—for this reason: The substance of the bread is not without its own appearances; and for this reason, as well: When the appear-

4. See St. Thomas Aquinas, Summa Theologiae, III, 77, 5, and the Ottawa edition notes for the names of "the many."
5. See above, ch. 63.

ances of the bread are destroyed, another substance has already been generated, and it was for the generation of this second substance that (so they were holding) the substance of the bread should return.

[10] Therefore, it seems better to say that in the consecration itself, just as the substance of the bread is miraculously converted into the body of Christ, so this is miraculously conferred on the accidents: that they subsist which is proper to substance, and, as a consequence, are able to do and to suffer the things which the substance could do and suffer if the substance were present. And so, without a new miracle, they are able to inebriate and to nourish, to be burned and to rot, in the same way and order they would if the substance of the bread and wine were present.

Chapter 67.

SOLUTION OF THE OBJECTIONS REGARDING FRACTION

[1] It remains to speculate on the points which belong to the fifth difficulty.[1] It is manifest, of course, from the aforesaid[2] that we can set down as subject of the breaking the dimensions subsisting of themselves. For all that, when dimensions of this kind are broken, the substance of the body of Christ is not broken, because the whole body of Christ remains under every portion.

[2] Now, to be sure, although this appears difficult, it has an explanation in accord with the things premised. For we said above[3] that the body of Christ is in this sacrament in His substance by force of the sacrament, but the dimensions of the body of Christ are there by their natural accompaniment to the substance; the situation here is contrary to the one in which a body is naturally in a place, for the natural body is in place with those dimensions mediating by which it is measured in the place.

[3] But something substantial is related to that in which it is in one way, and something quantified is related in another

1. See above, ch. 62, ¶15.   2. See above, ch. 66, ¶1–3.
3. See above, ch. 64, ¶2, 4.

way. For the quantified whole is in some whole so that the
whole is not in the part, but the part is in the part as the
whole is in the whole. Hence, too, a natural body is thus in
the whole place a whole which is not whole in every part of
the place, but the parts of the body are fitted to the parts of
the place. This is because it is in the place by the mediating
dimensions. Of course, if a substantial thing is whole in some
whole, it is also whole in every part thereof. So, the whole
nature and species of water is in every part of water, and the
whole soul is in every part of the body.

[4]   Since, then, the body of Christ is in the sacrament by
reason of His substance into which the substance of the bread
—the dimensions thereof remaining—has been converted, as the
whole species of bread was in every part of its dimensions,
so the entire body of Christ is in every part of the same dimensions. Therefore, that breaking or division does not touch
on the body of Christ so as to be in it as in a subject, but the
subject thereof is the persisting dimensions of the bread or
wine; so also we called[4] those dimensions the subject of the
other accidents therein persisting.

Chapter 68.

SOLUTION OF THE AUTHORITY INTRODUCED

[1]   With these difficulties removed, then, it is clear that
what ecclesiastical tradition holds about the sacrament of the
altar contains nothing impossible for God, who can do all
things.[1]

[2]   Neither is there anything contrary to the teaching of the
Church[2] in the word which our Lord spoke to His disciples,
who seemed scandalized by His teaching: "The words that I
have spoken to you are spirit and life" (John 6:64).[3] For by
these words He did not give them to understand this: in this
sacrament His true flesh was not being given to the faithful to

---

4. See above, ch. 63 and 65.   1. See above, ch. 63, ¶1.
2. See above, ch. 62, ¶2.
3. For interpretations of this text which differ and for some notes on
   its history, see F. Prat, S.J., *Jesus Christ* (Milwaukee, 1950), I,
   368–380.

eat, but that it is not given to be eaten in an ordinary manner, with the result that, like earthly foods it might be received as macerated in its own appearances. He gave them to understand that it is received in a certain spiritual fashion, apart from the manner of earthly carnal foods.

Chapter 69.

ON THE KIND OF BREAD AND WINE THAT ARE TO BE USED IN THIS SACRAMENT

[1] Now, because, as was said above,[1] this sacrament is accomplished with bread and wine, those conditions necessarily must be observed to accomplish this sacrament therefrom which belong to the essentials of bread and wine. But one calls wine only that liquid which is pressed from grapes, and one calls bread, properly speaking, only that which is made from grain wheat. But other so-called breads, for lack of wheat bread and to supplement it, have come into use; in a like way, other liquids have come into use with wine. Hence, neither from some other bread nor from some other wine could this sacrament be accomplished, especially not if the mixture of foreign matter with bread or wine be so considerable that the species is lost.

[2] However, if things happen to this sort of bread and wine which do not touch the essentials of bread and wine, manifestly one may pass these things over, and truly accomplish the sacrament. Wherefore, since to be leavened or unleavened is not essential to bread—rather, whichever of the two is the case, the species of bread is preserved—the sacrament can be accomplished from either of the two breads. This is the reason why different churches have different customs in this matter, but each of the two can be in harmony with the significance of the sacrament. For, as Gregory puts it in his *Register:* "The Roman Church offers unleavened bread because our Lord took on flesh without any mixture. But the rest of the Churches offer leavened bread, since the Word of God was clothed with

1. See above, ch. 61.

flesh, and is true God and true man, just as the leaven is mixed with the paste."[2]

[3]   Nonetheless, there is greater harmony with the purity of the mystical body, that is, the Church, of which there is also a figure in this sacrament,[3] in the use of unleavened bread; as the Apostle has it: "Christ our pasch is sacrificed. Therefore let us feast . . . with the unleavened bread of sincerity and truth" (I Cor. 5:7–8).

[4]   Thus does one exclude the error of certain Greeks, who deny that this sacrament can be celebrated with unleavened bread. And this is even clearly destroyed by the Gospel's authority, for we read in Matthew (26:17), in Mark (14:12), and in Luke (22:7) that on the first day of the unleavened bread our Lord ate the pasch with His disciples, and at that time instituted this sacrament. Now, since it was not permitted by the Law that from the first day of the unleavened bread anything leavened be found in the homes of the Jews (which is clear from Exodus 12:15), and since our Lord as long as He was in the world kept the Law, clearly He converted unleavened bread into His body and gave it to His disciples to receive. It is stupid, then, to attack in the use of the Latin Churches what our Lord observed in the very institution of this sacrament.[4]

[5]   For all that, one must acknowledge that some say He anticipated the day of the unleavened bread with His passion so near, and, then, used leavened bread. Indeed, to support this they rely on two things. First, there is what John (13:1) says, that "before the festival day of the pasch" our Lord celebrated the feast with His disciples, and at this feast consecrated His body, as the Apostle tells us (I Cor. 11:23). Hence, it seems that Christ celebrated the feast before the day of the unleavened bread, and so, in the consecration of His body, used leavened bread. Also, they want to confirm this by what is found in John (18:28): that on the Friday on which Christ was crucified the Jews did not enter the pretorium of Pilate,

2. On this author, see the references in the Ottawa Summa Theologiae, III, 74, 4.
3. See H. de Lubac, S.J., The Splendor of the Church (New York, 1956), pp. 87–113, for a development and history of this point.
4. For a somewhat milder view, see Summa Theologiae, III, 74, 4.

"that they might not be defiled but might eat the pasch." But the pasch is called the unleavened bread. Therefore, they conclude that the feast had been celebrated before the unleavened bread.

[6] Now, to this one answers that, as the Lord commands in Exodus 12,[5] "the feast of the unleavened bread was celebrated for seven days, and of these the first day was especially holy and solemn among the others, and it was the fifteenth day of the month." But, since among the Jews the solemnities used to begin on the preceding evening, they therefore on the evening of the fourteenth day began to eat the unleavened bread and they ate it for seven days following. And, therefore, we read in the same chapter (Exod. 12:18–19): "The first month, the fourteenth day of the month in the evening you shall eat unleavened bread until the one and twentieth day of the month in the evening. Seven days there shall not be found any leaven in your houses." And on the same fourteenth day in the evening they used to sacrifice the paschal lamb. Therefore, the first day of the unleavened bread is the way the three Evangelists—Matthew, Mark, and Luke—name the fourteenth day of the month, because in the evening they used to eat the unleavened bread, and then "they sacrificed the pasch," that is, "the paschal lamb"; and this, according to John, was "before the festival day of the pasch," that is, the day before the fifteenth day of the month which was the most solemn day of all, and on this day the Jews wanted to eat the pasch, that is, "the unleavened paschal bread," not, of course, the paschal lamb.[6] And thus, since no discord exists among the Evangelists, it is plain that Christ consecrated His body from unleavened bread at the feast. Hence it becomes clear that the Church of the Latins reasonably uses unleavened bread in this sacrament.

5. There is considerable condensation here.
6. On this point one may consult F. Prat, S.J., *Jesus Christ*, II, pp. 488–499.

Chapter 70.

ON THE SACRAMENT OF PENANCE, AND, FIRST, THAT MEN AFTER RECEIVING SACRAMENTAL GRACE ARE ABLE TO SIN

[1] Now, although grace is bestowed upon men by the aforesaid sacraments, they are not, for all that, rendered incapable of sin.

[2] For gratuitous gifts are received in the soul as habitual dispositions; it is not always, then, that a man acts according to those gifts. Nothing stops him who has a habit from acting in accord with the habit or against it; thus, a grammarian can in accord with grammar speak rightly, or even against grammar speak awkwardly. It is also like this with the habits of the moral virtues, for one who has the habit of justice can also act against justice. This is the case because the use of habits in us depends on the will, but the will is related to each of two opposites. Manifestly, then, he who receives gratuitous gifts can sin by acting against grace.

[3] What is more, there can be no impeccability in a man unless there is immutability of will. But immutability of will does not become man except so far as he attains his ultimate end. For what renders the will immutable is its complete fulfillment, so that it has no way to turn away from that on which it is made firm. But the fulfillment of will is not proportioned to a man except as attaining his ultimate end, for, as long as something remains to be desired, the will has not been fulfilled. Thus, then, impeccability is not proper for a man before he arrives at the ultimate end. And this, to be sure, is not given man in the grace which is bestowed in the sacraments, because the sacraments are for man's assistance along the road to the end. Therefore, no one is rendered impeccable from the grace received in the sacraments.

[4] Furthermore, every sin comes about from a kind of ignorance. Thus, the Philosopher says that "every evil man is ignorant";[1] and we read in Proverbs (14:22): "They err that

1. Aristotle, *Nicomachean Ethics*, III, 1 (1110b 28).

work evil." Therefore, then, a man can be secure from sin in the will, only when his intellect is secure from ignorance and from error. But, manifestly, a man is not rendered immune from every ignorance and error by the grace received in the sacraments; for such is a man whose intellect is beholding that truth which is the certitude of all truths; and this very beholding is the ultimate end of man, as was shown in Book III.[2] It is not, then, by the grace of the sacraments that man is rendered impeccable.

[5] Again, to that change in a man which accords with malice and virtue much is contributed by that change which accords with the soul's passions. For by a reason curbing and ordering the soul's passions a man becomes virtuous or is preserved in virtue, but by a reason following the passions a man becomes vicious. So long, then, as a man can be altered in the soul's passions, he can also be altered in vice and virtue. But alteration in the soul's passions is not taken away by the grace conferred in the sacraments; it persists in a man as long as the soul is united to the body, which is capable of passion. Manifestly, then, the sacramental grace does not render a man impeccable.

[6] There is more. It seems superfluous to warn those not to sin who cannot sin. But in the evangelical and apostolic teaching the faithful are so admonished, although they have already received the grace of the Holy Spirit through the sacraments, for we read in Hebrews (12:15): "Looking diligently, lest any man be wanting to the grace of God; lest any root of bitterness springing up do hinder"; and in Ephesians (4:30): "Grieve not the Holy Spirit of God whereby you are sealed"; and again: "He that thinketh himself to stand, let him take heed lest he fall" (I Cor. 10:12). Even the Apostle himself says of himself: "I chastise my body and bring it into subjection, lest perhaps when I have preached to others, I myself should become a castaway" (I Cor. 9:27). Therefore, men are not rendered impeccable by the grace received in the sacraments.

[7] This excludes the error of certain heretics[3] who say that

2. *SCG*, III, ch. 25 and 27.
3. St. Augustine, *De haeresibus*, 82 (*PL*, 42, col. 45); see St. Jerome, *Adversus Jovinianum*, II, 1–2 (*PL*, 23, col. 295–297).

man, after he has received the grace of the Spirit, is unable
to sin, and that, if he sins, he never had the grace of the Holy
Spirit.

[8]   They take, however, as a prop for their error the saying
of I Corinthians (13:8): "Charity never falleth away." And I
John (3:6, 9) says: "Whosoever abideth in Him sinneth not;
and whosoever sinneth hath not seen Him nor known Him."
And later on, more expressly: "Whosoever is born of God committeth not sin; for His seed abideth in him, and he cannot
sin because he is born of God."

[9]   But for establishing their proposition these texts are not
effective. For one does not say: "charity never falleth away"
on the ground that he who has charity does not sometimes
lose it, since the Apocalypse (2:4) says: "I have somewhat
against thee because thou hast left thy first charity." But "charity never falleth away" was said because, when all other gifts
of the Holy Spirit (which essentially contain some imperfection—the spirit of prophecy, for example, and this kind of
thing) "shall be made void . . . when that which is perfect
is come" (I Cor. 13:8, 10), then in that state of perfection
charity shall abide.

[10]   But the remarks taken from the Epistle of John are
said for this reason: The gifts of the Holy Spirit by which a
man is adopted or born again as a son of God have of themselves power enough to be able to preserve a man without sin,
and a man cannot sin who lives by those gifts. He can, for
all that, act against them, and sin by departing from them.
For "whosoever is born of God . . . cannot sin" was said just
as though one should say that "the hot cannot cool." What
is hot, nevertheless, can be made cool, and then it will make
cool. Or it was said as though one should say that "the just
man does no unjust things"; namely, in so far as he is just.

Chapter 71.

THAT A MAN SINNING AFTER THE GRACE OF THE SACRAMENTS CAN BE CONVERTED BY GRACE

[1] However, from what has been said it further appears that a man falling into sin after receiving sacramental grace can once more be restored to grace.

[2] For, as we showed,[1] so long as we live here the will is mutable in the matter of vice and virtue. Therefore, as one can sin after grace is received, so also from sin, it seems, one can return to virtue.

[3] Manifestly, again, good is more powerful than evil: for "evil acts only in the power of the good," as was shown above in Book III.[2] If, then, the will of man is turned away from the state of grace by sin, much more can grace call him back from sin.

[4] Immobility of will, furthermore, is not proper to anyone so long as he is on the way. But, so long as man lives here, he is on the way which tends towards the ultimate end. He does not, then, have a will unmovable in evil, so that he is not able to return to the good by divine grace.

[5] There is more. Manifestly, a man who committed sins before he received grace in the sacraments is delivered from those sins by the grace of the sacraments, for the Apostle says: "Neither fornicators nor idolaters, nor adulterers," and so forth, "shall possess the kingdom of God. And such some of you were; but you are washed, but you are sanctified, but you are justified in the name of our Lord Jesus Christ and the Spirit of our God" (I Cor. 6:9–11). Manifestly, also, the grace bestowed in the sacrament does not diminish, but increases, nature's good. Yet this belongs to the good of nature, that it can be led back from sin into the state of justice, for the capacity for good is a kind of good. If, then, sin takes place after grace is received, man can still be led back to the state of justice.

[6] If those, moreover, who sin after baptism cannot return

---

1. See above, ch. 70. 2. SCG, III, ch. 8–9.

to grace, their hope of salvation is entirely lost. But despair is the way to sinning freely, for the Apostle speaks of some who "despairing have given themselves up to lasciviousness, unto the working of all uncleanness, unto covetousness" (Eph. 4:19). This is, then, a very dangerous position which leads men to so great a cesspool of vices.

[7] There is more. We showed above[3] that the grace received in the sacraments does not make a man unable to sin. Therefore, if one who sins after receiving grace in the sacraments could not return to the state of justice, it would be dangerous to receive the sacraments. And this is obviously unsuitable. Therefore, to those who sin after receiving the sacraments the return to justice is not denied.

[8] This also is confirmed by the authority of sacred Scripture, for we read in John: "My little children, these things I write to you, that you may not sin. But if any man sin, we have an advocate with the Father, Jesus Christ, the just. And He is the propitiation for our sins" (I John 2:1–2). And these very words were clearly being set forth to the faithful already reborn. Paul also writes about the Corinthian fornicator: "To him who is such a one, this rebuke is sufficient which is given by many: so that on the contrary you should rather forgive him and comfort him." And later he says: "I am glad: not because you were made sorrowful, but because you were made sorrowful unto penance" (II Cor. 2:6–7; 7:9). We also read in Jeremias (3:1): "Thou hast prostituted thyself to many lovers; nevertheless, return to Me, saith the Lord"; and in his Lamentations (5:21): "Convert us, O Lord, and we shall be converted: renew our days, as from the beginning." And from all these one sees that if the faithful fall after receiving grace, there is open to them a second time a way back to salvation.

[9] In this way, of course, one excludes the error of the Novatians, who used to deny forgiveness to those who sinned after baptism.[4]

[10] Now, they used to set down as the occasion of their error the saying in Hebrews (6:4–6): "It is impossible for those who were once illuminated, have tasted also the heavenly

3. See above, ch. 71.
4. St. Augustine, De haeresibus, 38 (PL, 42, col. 32).

gift, and were made partakers of the Holy Ghost, have more-over tasted the good word of God, and the powers of the world to come, and are fallen away: to be renewed again to penance." [11] But the sense in which the Apostle said this is apparent from what is immediately added: "Crucifying again to themselves the Son of God and making Him a mockery." Therefore, the reason why those who have fallen after receiving grace cannot be renewed again to penance is that the Son of God must not be crucified again. One, therefore, denies to them that renewal again to penance in which a man is crucified along with Christ. And this indeed is in baptism, for we read: "All we who are baptized in Christ Jesus are baptized in His death" (Rom. 6:3). Therefore, as Christ must not be crucified once again, so he who sins after baptism must not be baptized again. Nonetheless, he can be converted to grace once again by penance. Hence, the Apostle did not say it was impossible that those once fallen should again be recalled or converted to penance, but impossible that they be "renewed"—which one usually attributes to baptism—as in Titus (3:5): "According to His mercy, He saved us, by the laver of regeneration and renovation of the Holy Ghost."

Chapter 72.

ON THE NECESSITY OF PENANCE AND OF ITS PARTS

[1] From this, then, it is evident that if a man sins after baptism he cannot have the remedy against his sin in baptism. And since the abundance of the divine mercy and the effectiveness of Christ's grace do not suffer him to be dismissed without a remedy, there was established another sacramental remedy by which sins are washed away. And this is the sacrament of penance, which is spiritual healing of a sort. For just as those who receive a natural life by generation can, if they incur some disease which is contrary to the perfection of life, be cured of their disease: not, indeed, so as to be born a second time, but healed by a kind of alteration; so baptism, which is a spiritual regeneration, is not given a second time against sins committed after baptism, but they are healed by penance which is a kind of spiritual alteration.

[2]   Let this, however, be considered: bodily healing is at times wholly from within, as when one is cured by the power of nature alone. But there are times when one is cured from within and from without simultaneously; for example, when the operation of nature is helped by the external benefit of medicine. But it never happens that one is cured entirely from without, for he still has within himself the principles of life, and from these the healing is somehow caused within him. But spiritual healing, it happens, cannot be brought about entirely from within, for we showed in Book III[1] that man cannot be delivered from fault except by the help of grace. In like fashion, also, neither can his spiritual cure be entirely from an external thing; for the soundness of his mind would not be restored unless ordered movements of will were caused in man. Therefore, the spiritual health in the sacrament of penance must proceed both from something internal and from something external.

[3]   This comes about in this way. For a man to be perfectly cured of a bodily disease, he necessarily must be freed from all the inconveniences which the disease involves. Thus, then, even the spiritual cure of penance would not be perfected unless a man were relieved of all the damages into which he has been led by sin. Now, the first damage which man sustains from sin is the disordering of the mind; in that man is turned away from the incommutable good—namely, God—and is turned toward sin. But the second damage is that he incurs the guilt of punishment, for, as was shown in Book III,[2] God the most just ruler requires a punishment for every fault. The third damage is a certain weakening of the natural good, in that man by sinning is rendered more prone toward sinning and more reluctant toward doing well.

[4]   Therefore, the first thing required in penance is the ordering of the mind; namely, that the mind be turned toward God, and turned away from sin, grieving at its commission, and proposing not to commit it; and this belongs essentially to *contrition.*

[5]   But this reordering of the mind cannot be without grace, for our mind cannot duly be turned toward God without char-

ity, but one cannot have charity without grace, as is clear from what was said in Book III.[3] Thus, then, by contrition the offense to God is removed and one is also freed from that guilt of eternal punishment which cannot be simultaneously with grace and charity; for there is no eternal punishment except by separation from God, and by grace and charity man is united with Him. Therefore, this reordering of the mind, which consists of contrition, proceeds from within, that is, from the free will with the help of divine grace.

[6] Since, however, it was established above[4] that the merit of Christ suffering for the human race works for the expiation of all sins, if a man is to be healed of sin his mind must necessarily cleave not only to God, but also to the mediator of God and men, Jesus Christ, in whom rests the remission of all sins. For spiritual health consists in the turning of the mind to God, and, to be sure, we cannot achieve this health except through the physician of our souls, Jesus Christ, "who shall save His people from their sins" (Matt. 1:21). Indeed, His merit is sufficient to take away all sins altogether, for it is He "who taketh away the sins of the world" as John (1:29) says. Nonetheless, not all achieve perfectly the effect of remission; each achieves it in the measure in which he is conjoined with Christ suffering for sins.

[7] Our conjunction, then, with Christ in baptism is not in accord with our operation (from within, so to say), because nothing generates itself in being, but it is from Christ, who "regenerated us unto a lively hope" (I Peter 1:3); therefore, the remission of sins in baptism is made in accord with the power of Christ conjoining us perfectly and entirely with Himself, so as not only to take away every impurity of sin, but also to free us entirely from every guilt of punishment; except incidentally, perhaps, in the case of those who do not get the effect of the sacrament because they approach with a false attitude.

[8] In the later spiritual healing we are conjoined to Christ in accord with our own operation informed by divine grace. Hence, we do not always entirely, nor do we all equally, achieve the effect of remission by this conjunction. For there

3. SCG, III, ch. 151.　　　　4. See above, ch. 55.

can be a turning of the mind toward God, and to the merit of Christ, and to the hatred of sin which is so vehement that a man perfectly achieves the remission of sin, not only with regard to wiping out the fault, but even with regard to remission of the entire punishment. But this does not always happen. Hence, after the fault is taken away by contrition and the guilt of eternal punishment is relieved (as was said), there sometimes persists an obligation to some punishment to maintain the justice of God which requires that fault be ordered by punishment.

[9] Since, however, to undergo punishment for a fault calls for a kind of judgment, the penitent who has committed himself to Christ for healing must look to Christ's judgment for fixing the punishment; and this, indeed, Christ does through His ministers, just as He does in the other sacraments. But no one can judge of faults which he does not know. It was necessary, then, that *confession* be instituted, the second part of this sacrament, so to say, in order to make the fault of the penitent known to the minister of Christ.

[10] The minister, therefore, to whom confession is made must have judiciary power representing Christ, "who was appointed to be judge of the living and the dead" (Acts 10:42). For judiciary power two things are required: namely, the authority to know about the fault, and the power to absolve or condemn. And these two are called the "two keys of the Church," namely, the knowledge to discern and the power to bind and loose which our Lord committed to Peter as Matthew (16:19) has it: "I will give to thee the keys of the kingdom of heaven." He is not understood to have committed these to Peter so that he alone might have them, but so that they might through him be passed on to others; otherwise, sufficient provision for the salvation of the faithful would not have been made.

[11] Of course, keys of this kind have their effectiveness from the suffering of Christ by which, we know, Christ opened for us the door of the kingdom of heaven. Accordingly, just as without baptism, in which the suffering of Christ works, there cannot be salvation for men—whether the baptism be really received, or desired to the purpose "when necessity, but

not contempt, excludes the sacrament"[5]—so for those sinning after baptism there can be no salvation unless they submit themselves to the keys of the Church, whether it be by actually confessing and undergoing the judgment of the ministers of the Church, or at least having this as a purpose to be fulfilled at the opportune time; because, as Peter says: "There is no other name given to men whereby we must be saved except by the name of our Lord Jesus Christ" (Acts 4:10–12).

[12] In this way one avoids the error of some who held that a man can achieve forgiveness of sins without confession and without the purpose of confessing,[6] and that the prelates of the Church can dispense one from the obligation of confessing. For the prelates of the Church are unable "to make vain the keys of the Church" in which their entire power consists, and they cannot bring it about that one achieve the remission of his sins apart from a sacrament which has power from the passion of Christ. This belongs only to Christ, who established the sacraments and is their author. Thus, then, as there can be no dispensation from the prelates of the Church allowing one to be saved without baptism, neither can there be one allowing a man to achieve the remission of his sins without confession and absolution.

[13] Nonetheless, there is this consideration. Baptism has some effectiveness for the remission of sins even before it is actually received, while one has the purpose of receiving it. We grant that afterwards—when it is actually received—it bestows a fuller effect both in the achievement of grace and in the remission of fault. Sometimes, too, grace is bestowed in the very reception of baptism and a fault is remitted for which previously there was no remission. And thus the keys of the Church have effectiveness in one before he actually submits himself to them, provided that he has the purpose of submitting himself to them; nevertheless, he achieves fuller grace and forgiveness when he actually submits himself to the keys by confessing and receiving absolution; and nothing prevents our

5. St. Augustine, *De baptismo contra Donatistas*, IV, 22 (PL, 43, col. 173).
6. See Peter Lombard, *Libri IV Sententiarum*, d. XVII, cap. 1 (ed. Quaracchi, ii, p. 845).

thinking that sometimes a grace is conferred by the power of the keys on one who has confessed, in the course of the absolution itself, and that by this grace his fault is dismissed.

[14] Therefore, since even in the very confession and absolution a fuller effect of grace and remission is bestowed on him who—by reason of his good purpose—had previously obtained both, manifestly the minister of the Church, absolving by the power of the keys, dismisses something of the temporal punishment for which the penitent remains in debt after contrition. He does, however, oblige the penitent to the balance by his command. And this fulfillment of the obligation is called *satisfaction*, which is the third part of penance. By this a man is entirely freed from the guilt of punishment when he pays the penalty which he owed; further, the weakness of the natural good is cured when a man abstains from bad things and accustoms himself to good ones: by subjecting his spirit to God in prayer, or by taming his flesh by fasting to make it subject to the spirit, and in external things by uniting himself by giving alms to the neighbors from whom his fault had separated him.

[15] Thus, clearly, then, the minister of the Church exercises a certain judgment in the use of the keys. But judgment is not granted to one unless it be judgment on those who are his subjects. Hence, it is manifest that it is not any priest at all who can absolve any man at all from sin—as some falsify it; he can absolve only one over whom he has received power.

Chapter 73.

ON THE SACRAMENT OF EXTREME UNCTION

[1] Now, the body is the instrument of the soul, and an instrument is for the use of the principal agent: therefore, the disposition of the instrument necessarily must be such as becomes the principal agent. Hence, the body is disposed in harmony with the soul. Therefore, from the infirmity of the soul which is sin infirmity sometimes flows into the body, when the divine judgment so disposes. To be sure, this bodily infirmity is at times useful for the soundness of the soul: so far as a man bears bodily infirmity humbly and patiently, and so

far as it is reckoned as satisfying punishment for him. At times, also, it tends to hinder spiritual health: so far as bodily infirmity hinders the virtues. Therefore, it was suitable to employ some spiritual medicine against sin, in accord with the fact that bodily infirmity flows out of sin; indeed, this spiritual medicine cures the bodily infirmity at times, namely, when this is helpful to salvation. And for this a sacrament was established—extreme unction, about which James (5:14–15) says: "Is any man sick among you? Let him bring in the priests of the Church, and let them pray over him, anointing him with oil in the name of the Lord. And the prayer of faith shall heal the sick man."

[2] Nor is the power of this sacrament prejudiced if at times the sick on whom it is conferred are not wholly cured of this bodily infirmity, for the restoration of bodily health—even in those who receive the sacrament worthily—sometimes is not useful for salvation. And they do not, for all that, receive it in vain, although bodily health may not follow on it. For, since this sacrament is set against bodily infirmity so far as this follows on sin, this sacrament manifestly was established against the other consequences of sin, which are proneness to evil and difficulty in good, and it is set so much the more as the soul's infirmities of this sort are closer neighbors to sin than bodily infirmity is. Indeed, spiritual infirmities of this sort are to be cured by penance, in that the works of virtue which the penitent performs when he makes satisfaction withdraw him from evils and incline him to good. But, since man, whether due to negligence, or to the changing occupations of life, or even to the shortness of time, or to something else of the sort, does not perfectly heal within himself the weaknesses mentioned, a healthful provision for him is made by this sacrament: it completes the healing aforesaid, and it delivers him from the guilt of temporal punishment; as a result, nothing remains in him when the soul leaves the body which can obstruct the soul in the perception of glory. And therefore James adds: "And the Lord shall raise him up." Perhaps, also, a man has neither awareness nor memory of all the sins which he has committed, so that they may be washed away individually by penance. There are also those daily sins without which

one does not lead this present life. And from these a man ought to be cleansed at his departure by this sacrament, so that nothing be found in him which would clash with the perception of glory. And therefore James adds: "If he be in sins, they shall be forgiven him."

[3]   Hence, it is clear that this sacrament is the last, that it somehow tends to consummate the entire spiritual healing, and that in it a man is, as it were, prepared for the perception of glory. For this reason also it is named *extreme unction*.

[4]   From this it is apparent that this sacrament is not to be given to anyone at all who is sick, but only to those who seem in their weakness to be approaching the end. Nevertheless, if they get well, the sacrament can be conferred on them again if they return to a similar situation. For the anointing in this sacrament involves no consecration, as does the anointing in confirmation, or the washing in baptism, and certain other anointings which are never repeated—simply because the consecration always remains, so long as the thing consecrated endures, because of the effectiveness of the divine power which consecrates. But the anointing of this sacrament is ordered toward healing, and healing medicine ought to be repeated as often as the weakness is repeated.

[5]   We grant that some are in a state close to death even without infirmity—this is clear in the case of those condemned to death—and they nevertheless would need the spiritual effects of this sacrament, but it is not to be given unless such a one is sick, since it is given under the appearance of bodily medicine, which is fitting only for one who has been weakened in the body. For in the sacraments the character of the sign must be maintained. Therefore, just as baptism requires that washing be used on a body, so this sacrament requires that medicine be applied for bodily weakness. Hence, also, oil is the special matter of this sacrament, because it has effectiveness for bodily healing by alleviating pain; just as water which cleans the body is the matter of the sacrament in which spiritual cleansing takes place.

[6]   Therein one also sees that, just as bodily medicine must be applied at the source of the infirmity, so this anointing is used on those parts of the body from which the weakness of

sin proceeds: such are the organs of the senses, and the hands and feet by which the works of sin are carried on, and—in accord with the custom of some—the loins in which the libidinous force is strong.

[7] But, since sins are forgiven by this sacrament, and no sin, of course, is forgiven except by grace, manifestly grace is conferred in this sacrament.

[8] Now, when things bestow enlightening grace on the mind, their use is proper only to priests, for their order tends to enlighten, as Dionysius says.[1] Neither does this sacrament require a bishop, since this sacrament does not confer a state of excellence, as is the case with those whose minister is a bishop.

[9] Nonetheless, since this sacrament has a perfect cure as its effect, and an abundance of grace is required in it, it becomes this sacrament to have many priests present, and to have the prayer of the whole Church help in the effect. Hence, James says: "Let him bring in the priests of the Church . . . and the prayer of faith shall save the sick man." If, nonetheless, only one priest is present, it is understood that he fulfills this sacrament in the power of the entire Church whose minister he is, and which, in person, he represents.

[10] Of course, the effect of this sacrament is obstructed by pretense in the receiver, just as can be the case with the other sacraments.

Chapter 74.

ON THE SACRAMENT OF ORDERS

[1] It is, of course, clear from what has been said that in all the sacraments dealt with[1] a spiritual grace is conferred in a mystery of visible things. But every action ought to be proportioned to its agent. Therefore, the sacraments mentioned must be dispensed by visible men who have spiritual power. For angels are not competent to dispense the sacraments; this belongs to men clothed in visible flesh. Hence, the Apostle

1. Pseudo-Dionysius, *De ecclesiastica hierarchia*, 5 (PG, 3, col. 506).
1. See above, ch. 56, 59–61, 72–73.

says: "Every high priest taken from among men is ordained for men in the things that appertain to God" (Heb. 5:1).

[2]   This argument can be derived in another way. The institution and the power of the sacraments has its beginning in Christ. For the Apostle says of Him: "Christ loved the Church and delivered Himself up for it: that He might sanctify it, cleansing it by the laver of water in the word of life" (Eph. 5:25–26). It is also clear that Christ gave the sacrament of His body and blood at the Last Supper, and ordered it to be frequented; and these are the principal sacraments. Therefore, since Christ was about to withdraw His bodily presence from the Church, it was necessary that Christ should establish other ministers in His place who would dispense the sacraments to the faithful; in the Apostle's words: "Let a man so account of us as ministers of Christ and dispensers of the mysteries of God" (I Cor. 4:1). And so He committed the consecration of His body and blood to the disciples, saying: "Do this in commemoration of Me" (Luke 22:19); the same received the power of forgiving sins, in the words of John (20:23): "Whose sins you shall forgive, they are forgiven them"; the same also were given the duty of teaching and baptizing, when He said: "Going, therefore, teach ye all nations, baptizing them" (Matt. 28:19). But a minister is compared to his lord as an instrument to its principal agent, for, as an instrument is moved by the agent for making something, so the minister is moved by his lord's command to accomplish something. Of course, the instrument must be proportionate to the agent. Hence, the ministers of Christ must be in conformity with Him. But Christ, as the Lord, by His very own authority and power wrought our salvation, in that He was God and man: so far as He was man, in order to suffer for our redemption; and, so far as He was God, to make His suffering salutary for us. Therefore, the ministers of Christ must not only be men, but must participate somehow in His divinity through some spiritual power, for an instrument shares in the power of its principal agent. Now, it is this power that the Apostle calls "the power which the Lord hath given me unto edification and not unto destruction" (II Cor. 13:10).

[3]   One must not say, of course, that power of this sort was

given by Christ to His disciples in such a way as not to flow on through them to others; it was given "for building up the Church," in the Apostle's phrase. So long, then, must this power be perpetuated as it is necessary to build up the Church. But this is necessary from the death of the disciples of Christ to the very end of the world. Therefore, the spiritual power was given to the disciples of Christ so as to pass on from them to others. Hence, also, our Lord used to address His disciples in the person of other believers. Thus, we have in Mark (13:37): "What I say to you, I say to all"; and in Matthew (28:20) our Lord said to the disciples: "Behold, I am with you all days even to the consummation of the world."

[4] This spiritual power from Christ, then, flows into the ministers of the Church; the spiritual effects on us, of course, derived from Christ, are fulfilled under certain sensible signs, as is clear from the foregoing;[2] therefore, this spiritual power also had to be passed on to men under certain sensible signs. But fixed forms of words and determined acts are of this sort: the imposition of hands, for example, the anointing, and the offering of the book or the chalice, or of something of this sort which belongs to the execution of the spiritual power. But, whenever something spiritual is transferred under a bodily sign, we call it a sacrament. Clearly, then, in conferring the spiritual power, a certain sacrament is enacted which is called the sacrament of orders.

[5] Now, this belongs to the divine liberality: that, if the power for some operation is conferred on one, there be conferred also those things without which this operation cannot suitably be exercised. But the administration of the sacraments to which the spiritual power is ordered is not suitably done unless one be helped to it by divine grace. Accordingly, grace is bestowed in this sacrament as it is in the other sacraments.

[6] Now, the power of orders is established for the dispensation of the sacraments. But among the sacraments that which is most noble and tends most to complete the others is the sacrament of the Eucharist, as is clear from what has been said. Therefore, the power of orders must be weighed

2. See above, ch. 56.

chiefly by reference to this sacrament, for "everything is denominated from its end."[3]

[7] It seems, of course, to be the same power which grants a perfection, and which prepares matter for the reception of that perfection. Just so, fire has the power both to pass its form on to another, and to dispose that other for the reception of the form. Since, then, the power of orders is extended to performing the sacrament of the body of Christ and handing it on to believers, the same power must extend itself to this: making the believers ready for this sacrament and in harmony with its reception. But a believer is made ready for the reception of this sacrament and in harmony with it by his freedom from sin; otherwise, he cannot be united spiritually with that Christ to whom he is sacramentally conjoined by the reception of this sacrament. Therefore, the power of orders must extend itself to the remission of sins by the dispensation of those sacraments which are ordered to the remission of sins; baptism and penance are of this kind, as is clear from what has been said.[4] Hence, as was said,[5] our Lord's disciples, to whom He committed the consecration of His body, were also given the power to forgive sins. This, indeed, is the power we understand by the "keys" about which our Lord said to Peter: "I will give to thee the keys of the kingdom of heaven" (Matt. 16:19). For to every man heaven is closed or is opened by this: he is subject to sin, or he is cleansed from sin; hence, too, the use of these keys is called "to bind and to loose," namely, from sins. It was of these, indeed, keys that we spoke above.[6]

Chapter 75.

ON THE DISTINCTION OF ORDERS

[1] Let us now take this into consideration: The power ordered to some principal effect by nature has under it inferior powers which serve it. This is especially clear in the arts, for the art which introduces into a thing its artificial form is served by the art which prepares the material; in turn, the one which introduces the form serves the art to which the

---

3. Aristotle, De anima, II, 4 (415b 21).   4. See above, ch. 59 and 62.
5. See above, ¶1–2.   6. See above, ch. 72, ¶10–15.

end of the artificial thing belongs; the one in turn ordered to a further end serves the one ordered to the ultimate end. Just so, the art of the wood-cutter serves that of the ship-builder, and the latter that of navigation, and this in turn the art of economy, or of warfare, or something of this sort, since the navigator's art can be ordered to different ends. Since, then, the power of orders is principally ordered to consecrating the body of Christ and dispensing it to the faithful, and to cleansing the faithful from their sins, there must be some principal order whose power extends principally to this; this is the order of the priesthood; and there must be other orders which serve this one by preparing the material, and these are the ministerial orders. Now, since the priestly power, as was said,[1] is extended to two things—namely, the consecration of the body of Christ and making the faithful ready for the Eucharist by absolution from their sins—the lesser orders must serve the priestly power either in both of these things, or else in one or the other. And, manifestly, an order is superior among the inferior orders by just as much as it serves the superior order in many things or in some worthier one.

[2] Therefore, the lowest orders serve the priestly order merely in the preparation of the people: doorkeepers, by actually keeping unbelievers out of the gathering of believers; readers, by instructing catechumens in the rudiments of the faith—hence, the Old Testament Scripture is assigned them for reading; exorcists, however, by cleansing those who are already instructed, but to some extent are obstructed by the devil from the reception of the sacraments.

[3] The superior orders serve the priestly order both in the preparation of the people and in the consummation of the sacrament. Acolytes have supervision over vessels which are not sacred and in which the material of the sacrament is prepared; hence, the cruets are handed to them during their ordination. Subdeacons, however, have supervision over sacred vessels and the disposal of material not yet consecrated. But deacons, beyond this, have supervision over consecrated material in that they dispense the blood of Christ to the faithful. Accordingly, these three orders—the priesthood, the diaconate,

1. See above, ch. 74.

and the subdiaconate—are called sacred orders because they receive a ministry over something sacred. The superior orders serve also in the preparation of the people. Hence, deacons are entrusted with the Gospel teaching to present it to the people, and subdeacons with the apostolic teaching; acolytes are entrusted with the performance in each of the two cases with what belongs to the solemnity of the teaching, namely, that they carry the lights and administer tasks of this kind.

Chapter 76.

ON THE EPISCOPAL POWER AND THAT
THEREIN ONE IS THE HIGHEST

[1]   Now, the bestowal of all of these orders accompanies some sacrament, as was said,[1] and the sacraments of the Church require some ministers for their dispensing; there must, therefore, be a superior power in the Church with a higher ministry which dispenses the sacrament of orders. And this is the episcopal power, which, although it does not exceed the power of the priest in the consecration of the body of Christ, does exceed the priestly power in what touches the faithful. For the priestly power itself flows from the episcopal power, and anything particularly difficult to be performed for the faithful is reserved to the bishops; by their authority, even priests are empowered to do that which is committed to them to be done. Hence, even in the tasks which priests perform they employ things consecrated by bishops; thus, in the Eucharistic consecration they use a chalice, an altar, and a pall consecrated by the bishop. Clearly, then, the chief direction of the faithful belongs to the dignity of the bishops.

[2]   But this, too, is clear: Although people are set apart according to differing dioceses and states, yet, as the Church is one, so must the Christian people be one. Therefore, as for the specific congregation of one Church one bishop is called for who is the head of that Church; so for the entire Christian people there must be one who is head of the entire Church.

[3]   Then, too, the unity of the Church requires that all the

---

1. See above, ch. 74.

faithful agree as to the faith. But about matters of faith it happens that questions arise. A diversity of pronouncements, of course, would divide the Church, if it were not preserved in unity by the pronouncement of one. Therefore, the unity of the Church demands that there be one who is at the head of the entire Church. But, manifestly, in its necessities Christ has not failed the Church which He loved and for which He shed His blood, since even of the synagogue the Lord says: "What is there that I ought to do more to My vineyard that I have not done to it?" (Isa. 5:4). Therefore, one must not doubt that by Christ's ordering there is one who is at the head of the entire Church.

[4] No one should doubt, furthermore, that the government of the Church has been established in the best way, since He has disposed it by whom "kings reign, and lawmakers decree just things" (Prov. 8:15). But the best government of a multitude is rule by one, and this is clear from the purpose of government, which is peace; for peace and the unity of his subjects are the purpose of the one who rules, and one is a better constituted cause of unity than many. Clearly, then, the government of the Church has been so disposed that one is at the head of the entire Church.

[5] The militant Church, moreover, derives from the triumphant Church by exemplarity; hence, John in the Apocalypse (21:2) saw "Jerusalem coming down out of heaven"; and Moses was told to make everything "according to the pattern that was shewn thee in the mount" (Exod. 25:40; 26:30). But in the triumphant Church one presides, the one who presides over the entire universe—namely, God—for we read in the Apocalypse (21:3): "They shall be His people and God Himself with them shall be their God." Therefore, in the militant Church, also, there is one who presides over things universally.

[6] Hence it is that we read in Osee (1:11): "The children of Juda and the children of Israel shall be gathered together; and they shall appoint themselves one head." And our Lord says: "There shall be one fold and one shepherd" (John 10:16).

[7] But let one say that the one head and one shepherd is

Christ, who is one spouse of one Church; his answer does not suffice. For, clearly, Christ Himself perfects all the sacraments of the Church: it is He who baptizes; it is He who forgives sins; it is He, the true priest, who offered Himself on the altar of the cross, and by whose power His body is daily consecrated on the altar—nevertheless, because He was not going to be with all the faithful in bodily presence, He chose ministers to dispense the things just mentioned to the faithful, as was said above.[2] By the same reasoning, then, when He was going to withdraw His bodily presence from the Church, He had to commit it to one who would in His place have the care of the universal Church. Hence it is that He said to Peter before His ascension: "Feed My sheep" (John 21:17); and before His passion: "Thou being once converted confirm thy brethren" (Luke 22:32); and to him alone did He promise: "I will give to thee the keys of the kingdom of heaven" (Matt. 16:19), in order to show that the power of the keys was to flow through him to others to preserve the unity of the Church.

[8]   But it cannot be said that, although He gave Peter this dignity, it does not flow on to others. For, clearly, Christ established the Church so that it was to endure to the end of the world; in the words of Isaias (9:7): "He shall sit upon the throne of David and upon His kingdom to establish and strengthen it with judgment and with justice from henceforth and forever." It is clear that He so established therein those who were then in the ministry that their power was to be passed on to others even to the end of time; especially so, since He Himself says: "Behold I am with you all days even to the consummation of the world" (Matt. 28:20).

[9]   By this, of course, we exclude the presumptuous error of some who attempt to withdraw themselves from the obedience and the rule of Peter by not recognizing in his successor, the Roman Pontiff, the pastor of the universal Church.

2. See above, ch. 74.

Chapter 77.

THAT THE SACRAMENTS CAN BE DISPENSED
BY EVIL MINISTERS

[1] From what we have premised it is clear that the ministers of the Church, when they receive their orders, receive a certain power for dispensing the sacraments.

[2] But what is acquired by a thing through consecration persists in that thing forever; hence, nothing consecrated is consecrated a second time. Therefore, the power of their orders persists in the ministers of the Church perpetually. Therefore, it is not taken away by sin. Therefore, even sinners and evil men, provided they have orders, are able to confer the sacraments of the Church.

[3] Then, too, nothing has power over that which exceeds its capacities unless the power be received from some other source. This is clear in natural as well as in civil matters: Water cannot heat unless it receives the power of heating from fire, nor can a bailiff coerce citizens unless he receives power from a king. But the things accomplished in sacraments exceed human capacity, as the foregoing made clear.[1] Therefore, no man can dispense the sacraments, no matter how good he is, unless he receives the power to dispense them. Now, goodness is in man the opposite of malice and sin. Therefore, one who has received the power to dispense the sacraments is not blocked by sin from dispensing them.

[4] A man, furthermore, is called good or bad in accord with virtue or vice, which are habits of a sort. Habit differs from power in this way: By a power we are able to do something, but by a habit we are not rendered able or unable to make something, but ready or unready in doing well or badly what we are able to do. Habit, therefore, neither gives us an ability nor removes one; rather, by habit we acquire this: to do something well or badly. Therefore, a man's being good or bad does not make him able or unable to dispense the sacraments, but suitable or unsuitable for dispensing them well.

1. See above, ch. 74.

[5] Moreover, that which acts by the power of another likens the thing modified not to itself, but to the principal agent. For a house is not made like the instrument which a builder uses; it is made like his art. The ministers of the Church do not perform the sacraments in their own power, but in the power of Christ, of whom John (1:33) says: "He it is that baptizeth." Hence, also, ministers are said to act as instruments, for a minister is an "animate tool."[2] Therefore, the malice of the ministers does not block the faithful from achieving in the sacraments the salvation which is from Christ.

[6] There is more. The goodness or malice of another man cannot be judged by man; this is God's alone, who scans the secrets of the heart. If, then, the malice of the minister could block the effect of the sacrament, a man could not have a sure confidence about his salvation, and his conscience would not remain free from sin. It seems awkward, also, that one put the hope of his salvation in the goodness of a mere man, for Jeremias (17:5) says: "Cursed be the man that trusteth in man." But, if a man were not to hope for the achievement of his salvation through the sacraments—except through those conferred by a good minister—he would appear to put the hope of his salvation to some extent in a man. That we may, therefore, put the hope of our salvation in Christ, who is God and man, we must confess that the sacraments are for salvation by the power of Christ, whether they are good ministers or bad ministers who confer them.

[7] This is apparent as well from the fact that our Lord teaches us to obey even bad prelates, whose works we must not imitate. For He says: "The Scribes and the Pharisees have sitten on the chair of Moses. All things, therefore, whatsoever they say to you, observe and do. But according to their works, do ye not" (Matt. 23:2–3). But there is much more reason to obey people who have received a ministry from Christ than there was to obey "the chair of Moses." Therefore, one must obey even bad ministers. And this would not be the case unless the power of their orders persisted in them—which is the reason one obeys them. Even bad men, therefore, have the power of dispensing the sacraments.

2. Aristotle, *Politics*, I, 4 (1253b 29).

[8] In this way one excludes the error of some who say that all good men have the power of dispensing the sacraments and no bad men have it.

Chapter 78.

ON THE SACRAMENT OF MATRIMONY

[1] Now, we grant that by the sacraments men are restored to grace; nonetheless, they are not immediately restored to immortality. We have given the reason for this.[1] But things which are corruptible cannot be perpetuated except by generation. Since, then, the people of the faithful had to be perpetuated unto the end of the world, this had to be done by generation, by which, also, the human species is perpetuated.

[2] But let us consider this: When something is ordered to different ends there must be differing principles directing it to the end, for the end is proportioned to the agent. Human generation, of course, is ordered to many things; namely, to the perpetuity of the species and to the perpetuity of some political good—the perpetuity of a people in some state for example. It is also ordered to the perpetuity of the Church, which consists in the collection of the faithful. Accordingly, generation of this kind must be subject to a diversity of directions. Therefore, so far as it is ordered to the good of nature, which is the perpetuity of the species, it is directed to the end by nature inclining to this end; thus, one calls it a duty of nature. But, so far as generation is ordered to a political good, it is subject to the ordering of civil law. Then, so far as it is ordered to the good of the Church, it must be subject to the government of the Church. But things which are dispensed to the people by the ministers of the Church are called sacraments. Matrimony, then, in that it consists in the union of a husband and wife purposing to generate and educate offspring for the worship of God, is a sacrament of the Church; hence, also, a certain blessing on those marrying is given by the ministers of the Church.

[3] And as in the other sacraments by the thing done out-

---

1. See above, ch. 55.

wardly a sign is made of a spiritual thing, so, too, in this sacrament by the union of husband and wife a sign of the union of Christ and the Church is made; in the Apostle's words: "This is a great sacrament; but I speak in Christ and in the church" (Eph. 5:32).

[4] And because the sacraments effect that of which they are made signs, one must believe that in this sacrament a grace is conferred on those marrying, and that by this grace they are included in the union of Christ and the Church, which is most especially necessary to them, that in this way in fleshly and earthly things they may purpose not to be disunited from Christ and the Church.

[5] Since, then, the union of husband and wife gives a sign of the union of Christ and the Church, that which makes the sign must correspond to that whose sign it is. Now, the union of Christ and the Church is a union of one to one to be held forever. For there is one Church, as the Canticle (6:8) says: "One is My dove, My perfect one." And Christ will never be separated from His Church, for He Himself says: "Behold I am with you all days even to the consummation of the world" (Matt. 28:20); and, further: "we shall be always with the Lord" (I Thess. 4:16), as the Apostle says. Necessarily, then, matrimony as a sacrament of the Church is a union of one man to one woman to be held indivisibly, and this is included in the faithfulness by which the man and wife are bound to one another.

[6] Thus, then, there are three goods of matrimony as a sacrament of the Church: namely, offspring to be accepted and educated for the worship of God; fidelity by which one man is bound to one wife; and the sacrament—and, in accord with this—there is indivisibility in the marriage union, in so far as it is a sacrament of the union of Christ and the Church.

[7] Now, all the other things one ought to consider in matrimony we have dealt with in Book III.[2]

2. SCG, III, ch. 122–126.

Chapter 79.

THAT THROUGH CHRIST THE RESURRECTION OF BODIES IS TO COME

[1] Now, we have shown above[1] that we have been freed by Christ from what we incurred by the sin of the first man; and, when the first man sinned, not only was the sin itself passed on to us, but also death, which is the punishment of sin, in the Apostle's words: "By one man sin entered into this world and by sin death" (Rom. 5:12). Therefore, it necessarily is by Christ that we are freed from each of these; namely, from the fault and from death. Accordingly, the Apostle says in the same place: "If by one man's offence death reigned through one; much more they who receive abundance . . . of the gift and of justice shall reign in life through one, Jesus Christ" (Rom. 5:17).

[2] Therefore, in order to make each of these clear to us in Himself, He chose both to die and to rise. He chose to die, indeed, to cleanse us from sin; hence, the Apostle says: "As it is appointed unto men once to die, so also Christ was offered once to exhaust the sins of many" (Heb. 9:27–28). But He chose to rise to free us from death; hence, the Apostle says: "Christ is risen from the dead, the firstfruits of them that sleep. For by a man came death and by a man the resurrection of the dead" (I Cor. 15:20–21).

[3] It is, then, the effect of the death of Christ in regard to the remission of sin which we achieve in the sacraments, for, it has already been said,[2] the sacraments work in the power of the passion of Christ.

[4] But the effect of the resurrection of Christ in regard to our liberation from death we shall achieve at the end of the world, when we shall all rise by the power of Christ. Hence, the Apostle says: "If Christ be preached that He arose again from the dead, how do some among you say that there is no resurrection of the dead? If there be no resurrection of the dead, then Christ is not risen again. And if Christ be not

1. See above, ch. 50 and 54.   2. See above, ch. 56, and ch. 57, ¶1.

risen again then is our preaching vain and our faith is vain"
(I Cor. 15:12–14). It is, then, a necessary tenet of faith to
believe that there will be a resurrection of the dead.

[5]   There are, however, some who are perverse in their understanding of this and they do not believe in the future
resurrection of bodies, but attempt to ascribe what we read
about the resurrection in the Scriptures to a spiritual resurrection in which some arise from the death of sin by grace.

[6]   But this error is rejected by the Apostle himself; he says:
"But shun profane and vain babblings: for they grow much
towards ungodliness. And their speech spreadeth like a can-
ker: of whom are Hymenaeus and Philebus: who have erred
from the truth of the faith, saying that the resurrection is past
already" (II Tim. 2:16–18). And this was not understandable
except of a spiritual resurrection. It is, therefore, contrary to
the truth of the faith to accept a spiritual resurrection and
deny a bodily one.

[7]   There is more. It is clear from what the Apostle says to
the Corinthians that the words cited are to be understood of
a bodily resurrection. For, after a bit, he adds: "It is sown a
natural body, it shall rise a spiritual body," wherein, manifestly, the body's resurrection is touched on; and a little later
he adds: "This corruptible must put on incorruption; and this
mortal must put on immortality" (I Cor. 15:44, 53). But the
corruptible and the mortal mean the body. Therefore, it is
the body that will rise.

[8]   Moreover, our Lord promises both resurrections, for He
says: "Amen, Amen, I say unto you that the hour cometh and
now is when the dead shall hear the voice of the Son of God
and they that hear shall live." And this seems to pertain to
the spiritual resurrection of souls, which even then was beginning to be completed, when some were cleaving to Christ in
faith. But, later, it is the bodily resurrection He expresses, saying: "The hour cometh, wherein all that are in the graves shall
hear the voice of the Son of God" (John 5:25, 28). For,
clearly, souls are not in the graves, but bodies. Therefore, this
predicts the bodily resurrection.

[9]   The bodily resurrection was also expressly foretold by
Job. For he says: "I know that my Redeemer liveth, and in

the last day I shall rise out of the earth, and shall be clothed again with my skin, and in my flesh I shall see my God" (Job 19:25–26).

[10] Moreover, to establish that there will be a resurrection of the flesh there is an evident supporting argument which is based on the points made earlier. For we showed in Book II[3] that the souls of men are immortal. They persist, then, after their bodies, released from their bodies. It is also clear from what was said in Book II[4] that the soul is naturally united to the body, for in its essence it is the form of the body. It is, then, contrary to the nature of the soul to be without the body. But nothing which is contrary to nature can be perpetual.[5] Perpetually, then, the soul will not be without the body. Since, then, it persists perpetually, it must once again be united to the body; and this is to rise again. Therefore, the immortality of souls seems to demand a future resurrection of bodies.

[11] Furthermore, there was shown in Book III[6] the natural desire of man to tend to happiness. But ultimate happiness is the perfection of the happy one. Therefore, anyone to whom some perfection is wanting does not yet have perfect happiness, because his desire is not entirely at rest, for every imperfect thing naturally desires to achieve its perfection. But the soul separated from the body is in a way imperfect, as is every part existing outside of its whole, for the soul is naturally a part of human nature. Therefore, man cannot achieve his ultimate happiness unless the soul be once again united to the body, especially since it was shown[7] that in this life man cannot arrive at his ultimate happiness.

[12] Moreover, as was shown in Book III,[8] by divine providence sinners deserve punishment, and those who do well a reward. But in this life men, composed of soul and body, sin or act rightly. Therefore, in both the soul and the body men deserve reward or punishment. But that in this life they cannot achieve the reward of ultimate happiness is clear from the points made in Book III.[9] And time after time sins are not

---

3. SCG, II, ch. 79. 4. SCG, II, ch. 68 and 83.
5. See Aristotle, *De caelo et mundo*, I, 2 (269b 9).
6. SCG, III, ch. 2 and 25. 7. SCG, III, ch. 48.
8. SCG, III, ch. 140. 9. SCG, III, ch. 48.

punished in this life; rather, in fact, as we read in Job (21:7) here "the wicked live, are advanced, and are strengthened with riches." Necessarily, then, we must assert a repeated union of the soul with the body, so that man can be rewarded and punished in the body as well as in the soul.

Chapter 80.

OBJECTIONS AGAINST THE RESURRECTION

[1] There are, of course, some things which seem to be opposed to faith in the resurrection.[1] Thus: in no natural thing does one find that which has been corrupted returning to being with numerical identity; neither does it seem possible to go back again from privation of a thing to possessing it. Accordingly, since things which are corrupted cannot be repeated with an identity in number, nature intends that the thing which is corrupted be preserved with an identity in species by generation. Since, then, man is corrupted by death, and the very body of man resolved even into the primary elements, it does not seem possible for a man with identity in number to be restored to life.

[2] Again, numerical identity is impossible to a thing if one of its essential principles cannot be numerically identical, for, if an essential principle is varied, that essence of the thing is varied by which the thing, as it is, is also one. But what is returned altogether to nothingness cannot be taken up again with numerical identity; this will be the creation of a new thing rather than the restoration of an identical thing. But there seem to be several of the essential principles of man returning to nothingness by his death. And first, to be sure, his very corporeity and the form of the compound, since the body is manifestly dissolved. Then, too, a part of the sensitive soul, and the nutritive, which cannot be without bodily organs, seem lost. Further, of course, there seems to return to nothingness the humanity itself—which is said to be the form of the whole—once the soul is separated from the body. It seems,

1. These seven objections are answered in ch. 81.

then, impossible that man should rise again being identical in number.

[3] Furthermore, what is not continuous seems not to be numerically identical. And this is manifest not only in sizes and motions, but even in qualities and forms, for if, after healing, a man becomes sick and is healed again, the health which returns will not be the same in number. Now, clearly, man's being is taken away by death, since corruption is a change from being to non-being. It is, then, impossible that man's being be repeated with numerical identity. Then, neither will the man be the same in number, for things which are the same in number are the same in being.

[4] If, furthermore, a man's identical body is restored to life, by equal reasoning whatever was in the man's body ought to be returned to the same man. But on this something extremely unseemly follows—not only by reason of the beard and the nails and the hair which are openly removed by daily trimming, but also by reason of other parts of the body which are covertly resolved by the action of the natural heat—and if these all are restored to the man rising again, an unseemly enormity will rise with him. It seems, then, that man will not rise after death.

[5] There is more. It happens, occasionally, that some men feed on human flesh, and they are nourished on this nutriment only, and those so nourished generate sons. Therefore, the same flesh is found in many men. But it is not possible that it should rise in many. And the resurrection does not seem otherwise to be universal and entire if there is not restored to every man what he has had here.

[6] Again, that which is common to all those existing in a species seems to be natural to that species. But the resurrection of man is not natural, for there is not a natural power of man which suffices to do this. Therefore, not all men will rise in common.

[7] Furthermore, if by Christ we are freed from fault and from death, which is the effect of sin, it seems that those alone ought to be freed who had a share in the mysteries of Christ by which they would be freed from sin. But this is not true of all men. Therefore, not all men will rise, it seems.

Chapter 81.

SOLUTION OF THE OBJECTIONS MENTIONED

[1]   Now, toward a solution of these difficulties this consideration is required: God, as was said above,[1] when He established human nature, granted the human body something over and above that which was its due in its natural principles: a kind of incorruptibility, namely, by which it was suitably adapted to its form, with the result that, as the life of the soul is perpetual, so the body could live perpetually by the soul.

[2]   And this sort of incorruptibility, although not, of course, natural in its active principle, was somehow natural in its order to the end; namely, as matter would be ordered to its natural form, which is the end of the matter.

[3]   When the soul, then, outside the order of its nature, was turned away from God, that disposition was lost which had been divinely bestowed on the soul's body to make it proportionally responsive to the soul; and death followed. Death, therefore, is something added as an accident, so to say, to man through sin, if one considers the establishment of human nature.

[4]   But this accident was taken away by Christ, who by the merit of His passion our "death by dying did destroy."[2] From this, then, it follows that by the divine power which gave the body incorruption the body may once again be restored from death to life.

[5]   In this way, then, one must answer the first argument,[3] that the power of nature fails the divine power, as the power of an instrument fails the principal agent. Granted, then, that the operation of nature cannot bring it about that a corrupted body be restored to life, the divine power can bring it about. The reason nature is unable to do this is that nature always operates by a form. But what has a form, already is.

---

1. See above, ch. 52.
2. This appears to be from the Preface of the Mass of Easter Sunday; see II Tim. 1:10.   3. See above, ch. 80, ¶1.

When it was corrupted, of course, it lost the form which was able to be the principle of the action. Hence, by nature's operation, what was corrupted cannot be restored with a numerical identity. But the divine power which produced things in being operates by nature in such wise that it can without nature produce nature's effect, as was previously shown.[4] Hence, since the divine power remains the same even when things are corrupted, it can restore the corrupted to integrity.

[6] What is stated in the second objection,[5] however, cannot be an obstacle to man's ability to rise with numerical identity. For none of man's essential principles yields entirely to nothingness in death, for the rational soul which is man's form remains after death, as was shown above;[6] the matter, also, which was subject to such a form remains in the same dimensions which made it able to be the individual matter. Therefore, by conjunction to a soul numerically the same the man will be restored to matter numerically the same.

[7] Corporeity, however, can be taken in two ways. In one way, it can be taken as the substantial form of a body as it is located in the genus of substance. Thus, the corporeity of any body is nothing else but its substantial form; in accord with this it is fixed in genus and species, and to this the bodily thing owes its having three dimensions. For there are not different substantial forms in one and the same thing, by one of which it is placed in the supreme genus—substance, say; by another in its proximate genus—body or animal, say; and by another in its species—say man or horse. Since, if the first form were to make the being substance, the following forms would be accruing to that which already is actually a definite something (*hoc aliquid*), and subsisting in nature; thus, the later forms would not make a definite something, but would be in the subject which is a definite something as accidental forms. Therefore, corporeity, as the substantial form in man, cannot be other than the rational soul, which requires in its own matter the possession of three dimensions, for the soul is the act of a body. Another way of taking corporeity is as an accidental form; in accord with this one says a body is in the genus of quantity. And corporeity thus is nothing other than the three

4. *SCG*, III, ch. 99.   5. See above, ch. 80, ¶2.   6. *SCG*, II, ch. 79.

dimensions which constitute the character of body. Therefore, although this corporeity yields to nothingness when the human body is corrupted, it cannot, for all that, be an obstacle to the body's rising with numerical identity; the reason is that corporeity taken in the first way does not yield to nothingness, but remains the same.

[8] In the same fashion, also, the form of a compound can be taken in two ways. In one way it is so taken that by form of a compound one understands the substantial form of the compound body. And thus, since there is not in man any other substantial form than the rational soul, as was shown,[7] one will not be able to say that the form of the compound, as it is the substantial form, yields to nothingness when man dies. Taken in a second way, a form of the compound is called that certain quality which is composed and balanced from the mixture of the simple qualities, and stands to the substantial form of the compound body as the simple quality stands to the substantial form of the simple body. Hence, although the form of the compounding when thus stated yields to nothingness, this is not prejudicial to the unity of the body arising.

[9] Thus, also, must one speak of the nutritive part and the sensitive part. For, if by sensitive part and nutritive part one understands those very capacities which are the natural properties of the soul, or, better, of the composite, then, when the body is corrupted, they are corrupted; nonetheless, this is no obstacle to the unity of the one arising. But, if by the parts mentioned the very substance of the sensitive and nutritive soul is understood, each of those parts is identified with the rational soul. For there are not three souls in man, but only one, as was shown in Book II.[8]

[10] But, in speaking of humanity, one should not understand it as a kind of form coming forth from the union of the form to the matter, as though it were really other than each of the two, because, since by the form the matter is made this actual something, as De anima II says,[9] that third form following would be not substantial, but accidental. Of course, some say that the form of the part is the same as the form

7. See above, ¶7, and SCG, II, ch. 57–62.   8. SCG, II, ch. 58.
9. Aristotle, De anima, II, 1 (412a 9).

of the whole: it is called form of the part in that it makes the matter actual being, but it is called form of the whole in that it completes the species essentially. In this way, humanity is not really other than the rational soul. Hence, clearly, when the body is corrupted it does not yield to nothingness. But humanity is the essence of man. The essence of a thing, of course, is what the definition signifies; and the definition of a natural thing does not signify the form alone, but the form and the matter. Therefore, necessarily, humanity signifies something composite of matter and form, just as "man" does. Differently, nevertheless; for "humanity" signifies the essential principles of the species, both formal and material, prescinding from the individual principles. Humanity is used so far as one is a man; one is not a man by reason of having the individual principles, but only by having the essential principles of the species. Humanity, therefore, signifies only the essential principles of the species. Hence, it is signified in the way in which a part is signified. "Man" truly signifies the essential principles of the species, but does not exclude the individuating principles from its signification, for he is called man who has humanity, and this does not shut out the ability to have other things. For this reason, man is signified as a whole is, for it signifies the essential principles actually, but the individuating principles potentially. "Socrates," however, signifies each set of principles actually, just as the genus contains the difference in potency, but the species contains it actually. Hence, it is clear that man returns numerically the same both by reason of the permanence of the rational soul and by reason of the unity of matter.

[11] However, what is said in the third argument[10]—that being is not one because it is not continuous—rests on a false foundation. For, clearly, the being of matter and form is one; matter has no actual being except by form. Nonetheless, in this respect the rational soul differs from other forms. For there is no being of other forms except in their concrete union with matter, since they exceed matter neither in being nor in operation. But the rational soul plainly exceeds matter in its operation, for it has an operation in which no bodily organ takes part; namely, the act of understanding. Hence, its being,

10. See above, ch. 80, ¶3.

also, is not merely in its concrete union with matter. Its being, therefore, which is that of the composite, remains in the soul even when the body is dissolved; when the body is restored in the resurrection, it is returned to the same being which persisted in the soul.

[12] The fourth objection,[11] also, fails to remove the unity of the one who rises. For what is no obstacle to a man's numerical unity while he continues to live manifestly cannot be an obstacle to the unity of one who rises. But in the body of man, so long as he is alive, it is not with respect to matter that he has the same parts, but with respect to his species. In respect to matter, of course, the parts are in flux, but this is not an obstacle to his being numerically one from the beginning of his life to the end of it. An example of this can be taken from fire: While it continues to burn, it is called numerically one because its species persists, yet wood is consumed and new wood is applied. It is also like this in the human body, for the form and species of its single parts remain continuously through a whole life; the matter of the parts is not only resolved by the action of the natural heat, but is replenished anew by nourishment. Man is not, therefore, numerically different according to his different ages, although not everything which is in him materially in one state is also there in another. In this way, then, this is not a requirement of man's arising with numerical identity: that he should assume again whatever has been in him during the whole time of his life; but he need assume from that matter only what suffices to complete the quantity due, and that especially must be resumed which was more perfectly consistent with the form and species of humanity. But, if something was wanting to the fulfillment of the quantity due, either because one was overtaken by death before nature could bring him to the quantity due or because mutilation perhaps deprived him of some member, the divine power will supply this from another source. This, however, will be no obstacle to the unity of the body of the one rising, for even the work of nature adds to what a boy has from some other source to bring him to his perfect quantity. And this

addition does not make him numerically other, for the man is the same in number whether he is boy or adult.

[13] From this it is clear, also, that there is no obstacle to faith in the resurrection—even in the fact that some men eat human flesh, as the fifth objection[12] was maintaining. For it is not necessary, as has just been shown, that whatever has been in man materially rise in him; further, if something is lacking, it can be supplied by the power of God. Therefore, the flesh consumed will rise in him in whom it was first perfected by the rational soul. But in the second man, if he ate not only human flesh, but other food as well, only that will rise in him which came to him materially from the other food, and which will be necessary to restore the quantity due his body. But, if he ate human flesh only, what rises in him will be that which he drew from those who generated him, and what is wanting will be supplied by the Creator's omnipotence. But let it be that the parents, too, have eaten only human flesh, and that as a result their seed—which is the superfluity of nourishment—has been generated from the flesh of others; the seed, indeed, will rise in him who was generated from the seed, and in its place there will be supplied in him whose flesh was eaten something from another source. For in the resurrection this situation will obtain: If something was materially present in many men, it will rise in him to whose perfection it belonged more intimately. Accordingly, if something was in one man as the radical seed from which he was generated, and in another as the superfluity of nourishment, it will rise in him who was generated therefrom as from seed. If something was in one as pertinent to the perfection of the individual, but in another as assigned to the perfection of the species, it will rise in him to whom it belonged as perfection of the individual. Accordingly, seed will arise in the begotten, not in his generator; the rib of Adam will arise in Eve, not in Adam in whom it was present as in a principle of nature. But, if something was in both in the same degree of perfection, it will rise in him in whom it was the first time.

[14] Now, however, what is said in the sixth objection[13] can be answered from what has been said. Resurrection is natural

---

if one considers its purpose, for it is natural that the soul be united to the body. But the principle of resurrection is not natural. It is caused by the divine power alone.

[15]   Nor must one deny that there will be a resurrection of all, although not all cleave to Christ by faith, and are not imbued with His mysteries.[14] For the Son of God assumed human nature to restore it. Therefore, what is a defect of nature will be restored in all, and so all will return from death to life. But the failure of the person will not be restored except in those who have adhered to Christ; either by their own act, believing in Him; or at least through the sacrament of faith.

Chapter 82.

THAT MEN WILL RISE IMMORTAL

[1]   From this it is clear, also, that in the resurrection to come men will not so rise that they are to die again.

[2]   For the necessity of dying is a deficiency brought upon human nature by sin. But Christ, by the merit of His passion, repaired the deficiencies of nature which sin had brought upon nature. For, as the Apostle says: "Not as the offence, so also the gift. For if by the offence many died, much more the grace of God, and the gift, by the grace of one man, Jesus Christ, has abounded unto many" (Rom. 5:15). From this one gathers that the merit of Christ is more effective for removing death than the sin of Adam for introducing it. Therefore, those who will rise by the merit of Christ, freed from death, will suffer death no more.

[3]   Furthermore, that which is to last forever has not been destroyed. Therefore, if the men who rise will still die again so that death lasts forever, in the death of Christ death has by no means been destroyed. But it is destroyed: right now in its cause, as the Lord had foretold in Osee (13:14): "O death, I will be thy death"; at the end it will be actually destroyed, according to the word: "The enemy death shall be destroyed last" (I Cor. 15:26). One must, then, hold with the faith of the Church that those who rise will not die again.

14. See above, ch. 80, ¶7.

[4] An effect, moreover, is likened to its cause. But the resurrection of Christ is the cause of the future resurrection, as was said.[1] But Christ so rose from the dead as to die no longer, in the Apostle's words: "Christ rising again from the dead dieth now no more" (Rom. 6:9). Therefore, men will so rise as to die no longer.

[5] Moreover, if the men who rise are to die a second time, they will either rise again from that second death or they will not. If they do not rise, they will remain forever as separated souls—and this is awkward, as was said above.[2] In fact, to avoid this awkwardness, they were held to rise the first time; in other words, if after the second death they are not going to rise, there will be no argument for their rising after the first death. On the other hand, if after the second death they do rise again, they will either rise to die again or they will not. If they are not to die again, the same reasoning will have to hold for the first resurrection. But, if they are to die again, the alternation of death and life in the same subject goes on to infinity—and this seems awkward, for the intention of God ought to have a determinate term. But the successive alternation of life and death is a kind of changing back and forth, so to say, and this cannot be an end, for it is essentially contrary to motion that it be an end; every motion tends toward another.

[6] There is more. In action, the intention of an inferior nature bears on perpetuity. For every action of an inferior nature is ordered to generation, and its very end is safeguarding the perpetual being of the species; wherefore, nature does not intend this individual as ultimate end, but the conservation in him of the species. And nature has this end, in that it acts by the power of God who is the first root of perpetuity. Hence, even the end of generation is held by the Philosopher[3] to be this: that the generated share in the divine being by perpetuity. All the more, then, does the action of God Himself tend to something perpetual. But the resurrection is not ordered to the perpetuity of the species, for this could be safeguarded by generation. It must, then, be ordered to the perpetuity of

---

1. See above, ch. 79. 2. *Ibid.*
3. Aristotle, *De generatione et corruptione*, II, 10 (336b 31–337a 1).

the individual: but not in the soul alone, for the soul already had perpetuity before the resurrection; therefore, in the composite. Man rising, therefore, will live forever.

[7]   Again, the soul and body appear to be related in a different order in the first generation of man and in his resurrection. Now, in the first generation the creation of the soul follows the generation of the body, for, when the bodily matter is prepared by the power of the separated seed, God infuses the soul by an act of creation. But in the resurrection the body is adapted to the pre-existing soul. Of course, that first life which man acquires by generation follows the condition of the corruptible body in this: man is deprived of that life by death. Then, the life which man acquires by resurrection will be perpetual according to the condition of the incorruptible soul.

[8]   Again, if life and death succeed one another to infinity in the same subject, the alternation of life and death will in species be a kind of circular motion. But every circular motion in generable and corruptible things is caused by the first circular motion of the incorruptible bodies. For the first circular motion is found in local motion, and in its likeness is transferred to other motions. The alternation of death and life, therefore, will be caused by a celestial body. And this cannot be, because the restoration of a dead body to life is beyond the capacities of an action of nature. Therefore, that there is such alternation of life and death cannot be asserted, and, consequently, that the bodies which rise may die.

[9]   Furthermore, whenever things succeed one another in the same subject they have a fixed measure of their duration in time. Everything of this kind is subject to the celestial motion on which time follows. But the separated soul is not subject to the celestial, for it exceeds the whole of bodily nature. Therefore, an alternation of its separation from the body and union to it is not subject to celestial motion. Therefore, there is no circular motion in the alternation of death and life such as that which follows if those who rise are to die again. They will rise, then, never again to die.

[10]   Hence, we read in Isaias (25:8): "The Lord shall cast

death down headlong forever"; and in the Apocalypse (21:4):
"Death shall be no more."

[11] Thus, of course, one avoids the error of certain ancient
Gentiles, who used to hold that "the same periods and events
of time are repeated; as if, for example, the philosopher Plato
having taught at the school in Athens which is called the Academy, so numberless ages before, at long but certain intervals,
this same Plato and the same school, and the same disciples
existed, and so also are to be repeated during the endless cycles
yet to come"; so Augustine describes the position in the *City
of God*.[4] To this position, so he himself tells us in the same
place, some like to refer the words of Ecclesiastes (1:9-10):
"What is it that hath been? The same thing that shall be.
What is it that hath been done? The same thing that shall
be done. Nothing under the sun is new, neither is any man
able to say: Behold this is new: for it hath already gone before
in the ages that were before us." This is not, indeed, to be
understood as though things numerically the same are repeated through various generations, but things similar in species. So Augustine explains in the same place. And Aristotle,
at the end of *De generatione*, taught the same thing, speaking
against the group mentioned.[5]

Chapter 83.

THAT AMONG THE RISEN THERE WILL BE
NO USE OF FOOD OR SEXUAL LOVE

[1] From what has been set down it follows that among
those who rise there will be no use of sexual activity or of food.

[2] For, when the corruptible life is taken away, those things
must be taken away which serve the corruptible life. But,
clearly, the use of food serves the corruptible life, for we take

---

4. St. Augustine, *De civitate Dei*, XII, 13, 2 (*PL*, 41, col. 361). The
translation quoted is that of M. Dodds in *The Basic Writings of
St. Augustine* (New York, 1948), II, 192. The "ancient Gentiles"
were the Stoics.
5. Aristotle, *De generatione et corruptione*, II, 11 (338b 14). In the
passage Aristotle seems to have in mind followers of Empedocles;
St. Augustine, the Stoics. The cyclical motion is common to them.

food to avoid the corruption which can follow on the consumption of natural moisture. At present, moreover, the use of food is necessary for growth; after the resurrection there will be no growth in men, since all will rise in their due quantity, as has been made clear.[1] In the same way, the intimate union of man and woman serves the corruptible life, for it is ordered to that generation by which what cannot be perpetually preserved in the individual is preserved in the species. Now, it was shown[2] that the life of those who rise will be incorruptible. Therefore, among those who rise there will be use neither for food nor for sexual activity.

[3]   Again, the life of those who rise will not be less ordered than the present life, but better ordered. For man will reach that life only through God's action, but he leads this life with nature co-operating. In this life the use of food is ordered to an end, for one takes food to convert it into the body by digestion. If, then, there is to be food at that time, it will be for the purpose of converting it into the body. Therefore, since nothing will be resolved from the body, because it will be an incorruptible body, we will have to say that everything converted into the body from nourishment must be devoted to its growth. However, man will rise in his due quantity, as was said above.[3] Therefore, he will achieve a size beyond moderation, for an immoderate size is that which exceeds the quantity due.

[4]   The man who rises, furthermore, will live forever. Therefore, either he will use food always, or not always but during a fixed time. But let him use food always: since the food will be converted into a body in which no dissolution takes place, it necessarily will cause an increase in some dimension and we will have to say that the body of the man who rises will be increased to infinity. And this cannot be, because increase is a natural motion and the intention of a natural moving power is never infinity, but is always something fixed. For, as the De anima says, "in everything established by nature there is a term of size and increase."[4] If the man who rises will not always use food, but will always live, one must grant a time

---

1. See above, ch. 81.   2. See above, ch. 82, ¶5–7.
3. See above, ch. 81.   4. Aristotle, De anima, II, 4 (416a 17).

in which he does not use food. Accordingly, this must be done from the beginning. Therefore, the man who rises will not use food.

[5] But if he will not use food, it follows that neither will he have sexual union for which the separation of the seed is required. Of course, the seed will not be separable from the body of the one who rises, nor from his substance. There is this reason: It is contrary to the seed in its essentials, for it would be seed as corrupted and as withdrawing from nature, and so it could not be the principle of a natural *action*, which the Philosopher makes clear in his *De generatione animalium*.[5] And there is this reason as well: Out of the substance of those existing incorruptible bodies nothing will be able to be resolved. Finally, the seed cannot be the superfluity of nutriment if those who rise do not use food, as was shown.[6] Therefore, among those who rise there will be no sexual union.

[6] Again, sexual union is ordered to generation. If, then, after the resurrection there is to be sexual union, it follows—unless it is to be in vain—that there will be human generation then just as there is now. Therefore, there will be many men after the resurrection who were not before the resurrection. In vain, then, does the resurrection effect this great difference: that all who have the same nature receive life at the same time.

[7] And again, if after the resurrection there is to be human generation, those who are generated will either be once again corrupted or they will be incorruptible and immortal. But, if they are to be incorruptible and immortal, the awkward consequences are many. First, indeed, one will have to hold that those men are born without original sin, since the necessity of dying is a punishment that follows on original sin. This is contrary to the Apostle's word: "By one man came sin to all and by sin death" (Rom. 5:12). Next, it follows that not all would require the redemption which is from Christ, and so Christ will not be the head of all men. And this is contrary to the Apostle's teaching: "As in Adam all die so also in Christ all will live again" (I Cor. 15:22). There would also be this awkward result: Men whose generation is the same would

5. Aristotle, *De generatione animalium*, I, 18 (725a 1–4).
6. See above, ¶3–4.

not have the same term of generation, for by generation from seed they achieve a corruptible life now, but then they would achieve an immortal one. Allow, on the other hand, that the men who will then be born will be corruptible and will die: if they do not rise again, it will follow that their souls will remain forever separated from their bodies. And this is awkward, since they are of the same species as the souls of the men who do rise. But if they, too, are to rise, their resurrection has to be waited for, by the others, that all who share the same nature may simultaneously receive that benefit of resurrection which is proper to the restoration of that nature (as is clear from what has been said[7]). And, what is more, there does not seem to be a reason for waiting for the simultaneous resurrection of some, if one does not wait for the resurrection of all.

[8]   Again, if the men who rise will use sexual union and generate, this will always take place or it will not always take place. If it always takes place, the multiplication of men will go on to infinity. The intention of the generating nature after the resurrection cannot be for any other end than the multiplication of men; it will not be for the conservation of the species by generation, since men are going to live incorruptibly. It will follow, therefore, that the intention of the generating nature is infinity; and this is impossible. But, if they do not generate always, but only for a fixed time, they will not generate after that time. For this reason one should attribute to them right from the start no use of sexual union and no generation.

[9]   Now, let one say that in those who rise there will be eating and sexual union, not for the preservation and growth of the body, nor for the preservation of the species and multiplication of men, but simply for the pleasure which there is in these acts, so that no pleasure will be lacking in man's final reward: in many ways, indeed, is it clear that such is an awkward position.

[10]   The first reason is this: The life of those who rise will be better ordered than our life, as was said above.[8] But in the present life it is a disordered and vicious thing to use food and

7. See above, ch. 81.   8. See above, ¶3.

sexual union for mere pleasure and not for the necessity of sustaining life and begetting offspring. And this is reasonable, for the pleasures which are in the activities mentioned are not the ends of those activities. It is, rather, the converse, for nature ordered the pleasure of those acts for this reason: lest the animals, in view of the labor, desist from those acts necessary to nature, which is what would happen if they were not stimulated by pleasure. Therefore, the order is reversed and inharmonious if those operations are carried out merely for pleasure. By no means, therefore, will such a thing be found among those who rise; their life is held to be one of perfect order.

[11] The life of the risen, moreover, is ordered to the preservation of perfect beatitude. But the beatitude and felicity of man do not consist in bodily pleasures, and such are the pleasures of eating and of sexual union as was shown in Book III.[9] One should not, therefore, hold that there are pleasures of this kind in the life of those who rise.

[12] Furthermore, the acts of the virtues are ordered to beatitude as to an end. If, then, in the state of beatitude to come there be the pleasures of eating and sexual love, as constituents, so to say, of this beatitude, it would follow that in the intention of those who perform virtuous acts the pleasures mentioned are somehow or other present. And this excludes temperance by essence, for it is contrary to the essence of temperance that one abstain now from pleasures to become able to enjoy them the more later on. This would, therefore, render all chastity wanton, and all abstinence gluttonous. But allow that the pleasures mentioned are to be, and are, nonetheless, not to be as constituents, so to say, of beatitude, so that they are in the intentions of those who act virtuously: even this cannot be. For whatever is, is for another or for itself. But the pleasures mentioned are not for another; they are not for the actions ordered to the end of nature, as was already shown.[10] It follows, then, that they are for themselves. But everything like this is either beatitude or a part of beatitude. Therefore, if the pleasures mentioned are to be in the life of those who rise, it must be that they belong to its beatitude.

9. SCG, III, ch. 27.   10. See above, ¶2.

And this cannot be, as was shown.[11] There is, then, no way for pleasures of this kind to be in the future life.

[13] There is more. It seems ridiculous to search for bodily pleasures which the brute animals share with us there where the loftiest pleasures which we share with the angels are expected—the pleasures in the vision of God which will be common to us and the angels, as was shown in Book III.[12] Unless, perhaps, someone wants to say that the beatitude of the angels is imperfect because the angels lack the pleasures of the brutes—which is completely absurd. Pertinent to this is our Lord's saying in Matthew (22:30), that "in the resurrection they shall neither marry nor be married, but shall be as the angels of God."

[14] By this, of course, one avoids the error of the Jews and of the Saracens, who hold that in the resurrection men will have use for food and sexual pleasure as they do now. And even certain Christian heretics have followed them; they hold that there will be on earth for a thousand years an earthly kingdom of Christ, and in that space of time "they assert that those who rise again shall enjoy the leisure of immoderate carnal banquets, furnished with an amount of meat and drink such as not only to shock the feeling of the temperate, but even to surpass the measure of credulity itself, such assertions can be believed only by the carnal. Those who do believe them are called by the spiritual Chiliasts, a Greek word, which we may literally reproduce by the name Millenarians"; so Augustine says in the *City of God*.[13]

[15] Some points, however, seem to favor this opinion. First, indeed, there is this: Before his sin Adam had an immortal life; nevertheless, eating and sexual love were in his power while in that state, for before his sin he was told: "Increase and multiply" and "Of every tree of paradise thou shalt eat" (Gen. 1:28; 2:16).

[16] Again, one reads of Christ Himself that He ate and

11. See above, ¶11–12.   12. SCG, III, ch. 48–63.
13. St. Augustine, *De civitate Dei*, XX, 7, 1 (*PL*, 41, col. 667). The translation, with the addition "a Greek word" is taken from M. Dodds, *The Basic Writings of St. Augustine* (New York, 1948), II, 518.

drank after His resurrection. For Luke (24:43) says that "when He had eaten before them, taking the remains, He gave to them." And in Acts (10:40–41) Peter says: "Him," namely, Jesus, "God raised up the third day, and gave Him to be made manifest, not to all the people but to witnesses preordained by God, even to us, who did eat and drink with Him after He arose again from the dead."

[17] There are also some authorities which seem to promise men the use of food in the state of which we speak. For Isaias (25:6, 8) says: "The Lord of hosts shall make unto all people in this mountain a feast of fat things full of marrow, of wine purified from the lees." And we are to understand this of the state of those who rise, as is clear from the addition: "He shall cast death down for ever: And the Lord God shall wipe away tears from every face." Isaias (65:13, 17) also says: "Behold my servants shall eat, and you shall be hungry; behold, my servants shall drink, and you shall be thirsty." And that this refers to the future life is clear from the addition: "Behold, I create new heavens and a new earth," and so forth. Our Lord also says: "I will not drink from henceforth of this fruit of the vine until that day when I shall drink it with you new in the kingdom of My Father" (Matt. 26:29); and He says in Luke (22:29–30): "I dispose to you as My Father hath disposed to Me, a kingdom; that you may eat and drink at My table in My kingdom." And we read in the Apocalypse (22:4) that "on both sides of the river" which will be in the City of the Blessed, there will be "the tree of life bearing twelve fruits." It also says: "I saw . . . the souls of them that were beheaded for the testimony of Jesus . . . and they lived and reigned with Christ a thousand years" (Apoc. 20:4–5). From all of which the opinion of the heretics mentioned seems to be confirmed.

[18] But the solution of these points is not difficult. The first objection, about Adam,[14] is not effective. For Adam did have a certain personal perfection, but human nature was not yet perfected when the human race was not yet multiplied. Adam, therefore, was established in the kind of perfection which suited the first source of the entire human race. Ac-

14. See above, ¶15.

cordingly, he had to generate for the multiplication of the human race, and consequently had to take food. But the perfection of those who rise will be at a time when human nature is arriving at the fullness of its perfection and the number of the elect is already complete. Accordingly, generation will have no place, and neither will the use of food. For this reason the immortality and incorruption of those who rise will be of one kind; those which were in Adam were of another. For those who rise will be immortal and incorruptible in such wise that they cannot die; nor can any dissolution take place within their bodies. Adam, however, was immortal thus: he could not die if he did not sin; and he could die if he did sin. And the preservation of his immortality could take place not by the exclusion of dissolution within the body; rather, it could be helped by preventing loss of the natural moisture through the assumption of food, lest his body arrive at corruption.

[19] With regard to Christ, however, we ought to say that He ate[15] after the resurrection not out of necessity, but to establish the truth of His resurrection. Hence, that food of His was not changed into flesh, but returned to the prior material state. But there will be no such reason for eating in the general resurrection.

[20] Now, as for the authorities which appear to promise the use of food after the resurrection: one must understand them spiritually. For divine Scripture proposes intelligible things to us in the likeness of sensible things, "so that the soul from what it knows may learn to love the things it knows not."[16] And in this fashion the pleasure of contemplation of wisdom and the assumption of the intelligible truth into our intellect is customarily indicated in sacred Scripture as the use of food; the saying of Proverbs (9:2, 4–5), for example, about wisdom: "She hath mingled her wine and set forth her table . . . And to the unwise she said: Come, eat my bread and drink the wine I have mingled for you"; and Ecclesiasticus (15:3): "With the bread of life and understanding, she shall feed him, and give him the water of wholesome wisdom to drink." And

---

15. See above, ¶16.
16. St. Gregory, *Homiliae in evangelia*, I, hom. 11, i (*PL*, 76, col. 1114).

of the same wisdom we read in Proverbs (3:18): "She is a tree of life to them that lay hold on her: and he that shall retain her is blessed." Therefore, the authorities mentioned above[17] do not require us to say that those who rise will make use of food.

[21] Of course, the words of our Lord in Matthew (26:29) can be understood in another sense. Thus, they can refer to the fact that He ate with His disciples after His resurrection and actually drank new wine, that is, "newly" namely not out of necessity, but as proof of His resurrection. He then says "in the kingdom of My Father" because in the resurrection of Christ there is a demonstrable beginning of the kingdom of immortality.

[22] Now, the saying of the Apocalypse (22:2) about "the thousand years" and the "first resurrection of the martyrs" must be understood of that first resurrection of souls from their sins, of which the Apostle says: "Arise from the dead and Christ shall enlighten thee" (Eph. 5:14). And by the thousand years one understands the whole time of the Church in which the martyrs as well as the other saints reign with Christ, both in the present Church which is called the kingdom of God, and also—as far as souls are concerned—in the heavenly country: for "the thousand" means perfection, since it is the cube whose root is ten, which also usually signifies perfection.[18]

[23] Thus, then, it becomes clear that those who rise will not spend their time eating and drinking and in acts of sexual union.

[24] From this one can see, finally, that all the business of the active life—it seems ordered to the use of food, to sexual activity, to the other necessities of the corruptible life—will come to a halt. Therefore, only the occupation of the contemplative life will persist in the resurrection. This is the reason one reads in Luke (10:42) of Mary's contemplation that she "hath chosen the best part which shall not be taken away from

17. See above, ¶17.
18. St. Thomas is following the interpretation of St. Augustine, for which see *De civitate Dei*, XX, 6–8, the passage cited above, ¶14, n. 13, and M. Dodds, *op. cit.*, pp. 515–520.

her." Hence, too, we read in Job (7:9–10): "He that shall go down to hell shall not come up. Nor shall he return any more into his house, neither shall his place know him any more." In these words Job is denying the kind of resurrection some have asserted who said that after the resurrection a man will return to the kind of business he has now: to building houses, for example, and carrying on other duties of this kind.

Chapter 84.

THAT THE BODIES OF THOSE WHO RISE WILL BE THE SAME IN NATURE

[1]   For some, of course, the points mentioned have been an occasion of error about the conditions of those who rise. For there were some who held that, since a body composed of contraries seems necessarily subject to corruption, those who rise do not have bodies composed of contraries in this way.

[2]   Some among these held that our bodies do not rise in a bodily nature, but are changed into spirit. They were moved by what the Apostle says: "It is sown a natural body; it shall rise a spiritual body" (I Cor. 15:44).[1] But others were moved by the same words[2] to say that our bodies in the resurrection would be subtile bodies, similar to the air and the winds. For air is called a "spir-ation", so that airy things may be called "spir-itual."[3] But others said that in the resurrection the souls will assume bodies: not earthly ones, to be sure, but heavenly. Their occasion is this word of the Apostle speaking of the resurrection: "There are bodies celestial and bodies terrestrial." And all this seems supported by what the Apostle says in the same place: "Flesh and blood cannot possess the kingdom of God" (I Cor. 15:40, 50). It thus appears that the bodies of those who rise will not have flesh and blood and, consequently, no other humors.

[3]   But the error of these opinions is quite evident. For our

1. See Origen, Peri Archon, III, 6 (PG, 11, col. 339).
2. See St. Gregory, Magna Moralia, XIV, 56 (PL, 75, col. 1077D).
3. St. Thomas says spiritus and spiritualia.

resurrection will conform to the resurrection of Christ, as the Apostle has it: "He will reform the body of our lowness, made like to the body of His glory" (Phil. 3:21). After His resurrection, of course, Christ had a body one could touch, constituted of flesh and bones, because after His resurrection—so we read in Luke (24:39)—He said to the disciples: "Handle and see; for a spirit hath not flesh and bones as you see me to have." Therefore, when other men rise, they will have bodies one can handle, composed of flesh and bones.

[4] The soul is, furthermore, united to the body as form to matter. Of course, every form has its determined matter, for there must be proportion between act and potency. Since, therefore, the soul is the same in species, it appears that its matter must be the same in species. Therefore, the body will be the same in species after the resurrection as before. And so it has to consist of flesh and bones and other parts of this kind.

[5] Again, in the definition of a natural thing which signifies the essence of the species, one includes the matter; necessarily, then, whenever the matter is varied in species, the species of the natural thing is varied. But man is a natural thing. If, therefore, after the resurrection he is not to have a body consisting of flesh and bones and parts of this kind as he has now, he who rises will not belong to the same species, but will be called man only equivocally.

[6] There is, moreover, a greater differentiation between the soul of a man and a body of some other species than there is between one human body and that of another man. But no soul can be united in turn to the body of a second man, as was shown in Book II.[4] Much less, then, will it be able in the resurrection to be united to a body of another species.

[7] There is more. For a man to rise with numerical identity there must also be numerical identity in his essential parts. Therefore, if the body of the man who rises is not to be composed of the flesh and bones which now compose it, the man who rises will not be numerically the same man.

[8] But all these false opinions are most clearly rejected by

4. SCG, II, ch. 83, ¶34-37.

the words of Job (19:26–27) who says: "Once again I shall be clothed with my skin, and in my flesh I shall see my God. Whom I myself shall see and not another."

[9]   Of course, each of the opinions mentioned has its own awkward consequence.

[10]   For to hold that a body changes into a spirit is altogether impossible. Things do not change into one another unless they have matter in common. But spiritual things and bodily things can have no communication by matter, because spiritual substances are entirely immaterial, as was shown in Book II.[5] Therefore, it is impossible that the human body is changed into a spiritual substance.

[11]   Again, if the human body is changed into a spiritual substance, it will be changed either into the same spiritual substance which the soul is or into some other. But, if it is into the soul itself, then after the resurrection there would be in a man only his soul, just as there was before the resurrection. Therefore, the condition of man would not be altered by the resurrection. But, if the body is to be changed into another spiritual substance, it will follow that from two spiritual substances some unit in nature is effected. And this is entirely impossible, for every spiritual substance subsists of itself.

[12]   In like fashion, it is impossible that the body of man who rises be like air and kindred to winds.

[13]   For the body of man and of any animal must have a determined figure both in the whole and in the parts. But a body which has a determinate figure must be terminable of itself, for figure is that which is comprised by a term or terms. Air, however, is not terminable in itself, but is terminated only by the term of something else. It is, therefore, not possible that the body of man when he rises be like the air or the winds.

[14]   There is more. The body of man when he rises must have the capacity to touch, for without touch there is no animal. But that which rises must be animal if it is to be man. But an aerial body can have no capacity for touch, just

5. SCG, II, ch. 50.

as no simple body can, for the body in which the touch sensation takes place must be midway between the tangible qualities so as to be in potency to them, as the Philosopher proves in *De anima*.[6] It is impossible, then, that the body of man who rises be like the air or the winds.

[15] From this it is also apparent that it will not be able to be a celestial body.

[16] For the body of man or of any animal must be receptive to tangible qualities, as was just said. But so to be is impossible for a celestial body which is not hot or cold, nor wet or dry, nor anything else of the sort, whether actually or potentially, as the Philosopher proves in *De caelo*.[7] Therefore, the body of the man who rises will not be a celestial body.

[17] Celestial bodies, moreover, are incorruptible and cannot be changed from their natural disposition. But the figure due to them naturally is the spherical, as the Philosopher proves.[8] It is not possible, then, for them to receive the figure which is naturally due to the human body. It is, then, impossible that the bodies of the risen be in nature those of celestial bodies.

Chapter 85.

THAT THE BODIES OF THE RISEN WILL HAVE ANOTHER DISPOSITION

[1] Although the bodies of the risen are to be the same in species as our bodies are now, they will have a different disposition.

[2] First, to be sure, in this respect: All the bodies of those who rise, both the good and the evil, will be incorruptible.

[3] And the reason for this is threefold.

[4] One reason is taken from the very purpose of the resurrection. For both the good and the evil will rise for this: that in their very own bodies they may receive their reward or their punishment for the deeds they performed while they

6. See Aristotle, *De anima*, II, 11 (esp. 423a 14–16).
7. See Aristotle, *De caelo et mundo*, I, 3 (270a 25–35).
8. See Aristotle, *De caelo et mundo*, II, 4 (286b 10).

lived in the body. But the reward of the good, felicity, that is, will be everlasting; in like fashion, too, everlasting punishment is due to mortal sin. Each of these points was established in Book III.[1] Necessarily, then, in each case an incorruptible body must be assumed.

[5] The second reason is taken from the formal cause of those who rise which is the soul. We said above[2] that, lest the soul remain forever separated from the body after the resurrection, the soul will once again assume the body. Since, then, this reception of the body is provided for the perfection of the soul, it is suitable that the disposition of the body be proportioned to that of the soul. But the soul is incorruptible. Hence, the body restored to the soul will be incorruptible.

[6] The third reason can be found in the active cause of the resurrection. For God, who will restore the already corrupted bodies to life, will be able to grant this so much more firmly by preserving forever the life regained in them. And by way of example of this, when He chose He preserved even corruptible bodies from corruption unharmed, as He did the bodies of the three youths in the fiery furnace (see Daniel 3:93–94).

[7] Thus, then, must one understand the incorruptibility of the state to come: that this body, corruptible now, will be made incorruptible by the divine power, so that the soul will have perfect dominion over the body in the course of vivifying the body; nor will this communication of life be subject to any obstacle at all. Hence, also, the Apostle says: "This corruptible must put on incorruption, and this mortal must put on immortality" (I Cor. 15:53).

[8] Therefore, man when he rises will be immortal, not for this reason: he has assumed another body which is incorruptible (as the opinions mentioned[3] held); but for this reason: This same body which now is corruptible will become incorruptible.

[9] One must, therefore, understand the Apostle's saying—"Flesh and blood cannot possess the kingdom of God" (I Cor. 15:50)—in this way: that the corruption of flesh and blood

1. SCG, III, ch. 62 and 144.
2. See above, ch. 79, ¶10–12, and ch. 82, ¶7.   3. See above, ch. 83.

will be taken away in the state of the resurrection, while the substance of flesh and blood nevertheless persists. Hence, he adds: "neither shall corruption possess incorruption."

Chapter 86.

ON THE QUALITY OF GLORIFIED BODIES

[1] Grant, of course, that in the resurrection the merit of Christ does remove the deficiency of nature commonly from all men—from both the good and the evil; nonetheless, a difference will persist between the good and the evil in respect to what is suitable to each group personally. Now, it is an essential of nature that the human soul is the form of the body which vivifies the body and preserves it in being, but by its personal acts the soul merits to be elevated to the glory of the divine vision or to be excluded from the order of that glory by reason of its sin. The body, then, will be commonly disposed in all men in harmony with the soul, with this result: The incorruptible form bestows an incorruptible being on the body in spite of its composition from contraries, because in respect to corruption the matter of the human body will be entirely subject to the human soul. But the glory and power of the soul elevated to the divine vision will add something more ample to the body united to itself. For this body will be entirely subject to the soul—the divine power will achieve this —not only in regard to its being, but also in regard to action, passion, movements, and bodily qualities.

[2] Therefore, just as the soul which enjoys the divine vision will be filled with a kind of spiritual lightsomeness, so by a certain overflow from the soul to the body, the body will in its own way put on the lightsomeness of glory. Hence, the Apostle says: "It is sown in dishonor. It shall rise in glory" (I Cor. 15:43); for our body is dark now, but then it will be lightsome; as Matthew (13:43) has it: "The just shall shine as the sun in the kingdom of their Father."

[3] Moreover, the soul which will enjoy the divine vision, united to its ultimate end, will in all matters experience the fulfillment of desire. And since it is out of the soul's desire that the body is moved, the consequence will be the body's

utter obedience to the spirit's slightest wish. Hence, the bodies of the blessed when they rise are going to have agility. This is what the Apostle says in the same place: "It is sown in weakness, it shall rise in power." For weakness is what we experience in a body found wanting in the strength to satisfy the desire of the soul in the movements and actions which the soul commands, and this weakness will be entirely taken away then, when power is overflowing into the body from a soul united to God. For this reason, also, Wisdom (3:7) says that the just "shall run to and fro like sparks among the reeds"; this is not said because there is motion in them by reason of necessity—since they who have God want nothing—but as an indication of their power.

[4]   Of course, just as the soul which enjoys God will have its desire fulfilled in the achievement of every good, so also will its desire be filled in the removal of every evil, for with the highest good no evil has a place. Therefore, the body perfected by the soul will be, proportionally to the soul, immune from every evil, both in regard to act and in regard to potency. This will be actually so, indeed, because there will not be in them any corruption, any deformity, any deficiency. It will be potentially so, however, because they will not be able to suffer anything which is harmful to them. For this reason they will be incapable of suffering. Nonetheless, this incapability of suffering will not cut them off from the modification essential to sense knowledge, for they will use their senses for pleasure in the measure in which this is not incompatible with their state of incorruption. It is, then, to show their incapacity for suffering that the Apostle says: "It is sown in corruption, it shall rise in incorruption" (I Cor. 15:42).

[5]   Furthermore, the soul which is enjoying God will cleave to Him most perfectly, and will in its own fashion share in His goodness to the highest degree; and thus will the body be perfectly within the soul's dominion, and will share in what is the soul's very own characteristics so far as possible, in the perspicuity of sense knowledge, in the ordering of bodily appetite, and in the all-round perfection of nature; for a thing is the more perfect in nature, the more its matter is dominated by its form. And for this reason the Apostle says: "It is sown

a natural[1] body, it shall rise a spiritual body" (I Cor. 15:44). The body of the risen will be spiritual, indeed, but not because it is a spirit—as some have badly understood the point—whether in the sense of a spiritual substance, or in the sense of air or wind;[2] it will be spiritual because it will be entirely subject to the spirit. Just so, the Apostle calls it now an "animal body," not because it is a soul, but because it is subject to animal passions and requires nourishment.

[6] This, then, is clear from the points now made: Just as the soul of man will be elevated to the glory of heavenly spirits to see God in His essence, as was shown in Book III,[3] so also will his body be raised up to the characteristics of heavenly bodies: it will be lightsome, incapable of suffering, without difficulty and labor in movement, and most perfectly perfected by its form. For this reason the Apostle speaks of the bodies of the risen as heavenly, referring not to their nature, but to their glory. Hence, after he had said that "there are bodies celestial and bodies terrestrial," he added: "one is the glory of the celestial, and another of the terrestrial" (I Cor. 15:40). Just as, of course, the glory to which the human soul is exalted exceeds the natural power of the heavenly spirits, as was shown in Book III,[4] so does the glory of the risen bodies exceed the natural perfection of the heavenly bodies so as to have a greater lightsomeness, a more stable incapacity for suffering, an easier agility, and a more perfect worthiness of nature.

Chapter 87.

ON THE PLACE OF THE GLORIFIED BODIES

[1] Now, because place must be in proportion to that which is in place, there is this consequence: Since the bodies of the risen will achieve the characteristics of heavenly bodies, they, too, will have a place in the heavens, or, rather, "above all

---

1. "Natural," here in Douay-Rheims, is a rendering of *animale*. Hence, St. Thomas refers just below to "soul" (*anima*) and to "animal passions" (*animalibus passionibus*), which are modifications of sensory appetitive and cognitive powers.   2. See above, ch. 84, ¶2.
3. SCG, III, ch. 57.   4. SCG, III, ch. 53.

the heavens,"[1] so as to be at once with Christ, whose power will lead them to this glory. The Apostle says of Him: "He ascended above all the heavens that He might fill all things" (Eph. 4:10).

[2]   It seems frivolity, of course, to make an argument against this divine promise out of the natural position of the elements, alleging the impossibility of elevating the body of man, since it is earthly and by its nature holds the lowest place, to a place above the lighter elements. For, manifestly, by the power of the soul the body which it perfects need not follow the inclinations of the elements. For even now, by its power, so long as we live the soul holds the body together lest it be dissolved by the contrariety of the elements; and also by the power of the soul to move the body is raised high; and it will be raised the more fully, as the motive power will have the greater strength. But, manifestly, it will be then a soul of perfect power when it will be united to God by vision. Therefore, it ought not be looked on as difficult if the body be then preserved by the power of the soul immune from every corruption and be lifted up above every body whatever.

[3]   Neither does this divine promise meet an impossibility in the assertion that celestial bodies are unbreakable so the glorious bodies may not be elevated above them. For the divine power will bring it about that the glorious bodies can be simultaneously where the other bodies are; an indication of this was given in the body of Christ when He came to the disciples, "the doors being shut" (John 20:26).

Chapter 88.

ON THE SEX AND AGE OF THE RISEN

[1]   One ought, nevertheless, not hold that among the bodies of the risen the feminine sex will be absent, as some have thought. For, since the resurrection is to restore the deficiencies of nature, nothing that belongs to the perfection of na-

---

1. St. Thomas is quoting the Preface of the Mass of Pentecost: "*qui ascendens super omnes caelos sedensque ad dexteram tuam,*" as well as St. Paul.

ture will be denied to the bodies of the risen. Of course, just as other bodily members belong to the integrity of the human body, so do those which serve for generation—not only in men but also in women. Therefore, in each of the cases members of this sort will rise.

[2] Neither is this opposed by the fact that there will be no use for those members, as was shown above.[1] For, if for this reason such members are not to be in the risen, for an equal reason there would be no members which serve nutrition in the risen, because neither will there be use of food after the resurrection. Thus, then, a large portion of the members would be wanting in the body of the risen. They will, therefore, have all the members of this sort, even though there be no use for them, to re-establish the integrity of the natural body. Hence, they will not be in vain.

[3] In like fashion, also, the frailty of the feminine sex is not in opposition to the perfection of the risen. For this frailty is not due to a shortcoming of nature, but to an intention of nature. And this very distinction of nature among human beings will point out the perfection of nature and the divine wisdom as well, which disposes all things in a certain order.

[4] Nor is this position forced on us by the words of the Apostle: "Until we all meet into the unity of faith, and of knowledge of the Son of God, unto a perfect man, unto the measure of the age of the fulness of Christ" (Eph. 4:13). For he did not say this because everyone in that meeting when the risen shall go forth "to meet Christ into the air" (I Thess. 4:16) will have the male sex. He said it to point out the perfection of the Church and its power. For the whole Church when meeting Christ will be like a perfect man, as is clear from the words which precede and follow.[2]

[5] But all must rise in the age of Christ, which is that of youth, by reason of the perfection of nature which is found in that age alone. For the age of boyhood has not yet achieved the perfection of nature through increase; and by decrease old age has already withdrawn from that perfection.

1. See above, ch. 83.
2. See I Thess. 4:12–17; F. Prat, S.J., *The Theology of St. Paul,* II, 364–369.

Chapter 89.

ON THE QUALITY OF THE RISEN BODIES
AMONG THE DAMNED

[1] From these points one can, of course, reasonably consider what sort of condition there will be in the risen bodies of those to be damned.

[2] For those bodies, too, must be proportioned to the souls of those to be damned. Of course, the souls of the wicked have a good nature, indeed, since it is created by God, but they will have a disordered will which will be failing its very own end. Their bodies, then, so far as nature is concerned, will be restored to integrity; because, as one can see, they will rise in the perfection of age, without any members diminished, without any deficiency or corruption which the error or the weakness of nature has introduced. Hence, the Apostle says: "The dead shall rise again incorruptible" (I Cor. 15:52); and clearly this ought to be understood of all, both the good and the evil, according to what precedes and follows in his text.

[3] But because in its will their soul will be turned away from God, and deprived of its own end, their bodies will not be spiritual, that is to say, entirely subject to the spirit; rather, by its affection their soul will be carnal.

[4] Nor will their bodies have agility obeying the soul, so to say, with no difficulty; rather, they will be burdensome and heavy, and in some way hard for the soul to carry, just as their very souls are turned away from God by disobedience.

[5] They will also remain capable of suffering, as they now are, or even more so; in such wise, nonetheless, that they will indeed suffer affliction from sensible things; and, for all that, no corruption; just as their souls also will be wracked, frustrated entirely in their natural desire for beatitude.

[6] Their bodies also will be dense and darksome, just as their souls will be foreign to the light of divine knowledge. And this is what the Apostle says: "We shall all indeed rise again but we shall not all be changed" (I Cor. 15:51). For

the good alone shall be changed for glory; it will be without glory that the bodies of the wicked shall rise.

[7] There is a chance, of course, that someone may see an impossibility in the fact that the bodies of the wicked are capable of suffering and, for all that, are not corruptible, because "every passion when intensified takes something away from substance."[1] For we see that a body, if it remains in a fire a long time, is finally consumed; and sorrow, if it be too intense, separates the soul from the body. But this entire process takes place on the basis of the transmutability of matter from form to form. But after the resurrection the human body will not be transmutable from form to form, in the case of the good or of the wicked; for in each class the body will be entirely perfected by the soul so far as its natural being is concerned. Thus, it will no longer be possible to remove this form from such a body, nor to introduce another form, when the divine power is subjecting the body entirely to the soul. Hence, also, that potency for every form which is in prime matter will be somehow bound by the power of the soul, lest it be able to be reduced to the act of another form. But, in regard to some conditions, the bodies of the damned will not be entirely subject to the soul; therefore, they will be sensibly afflicted by the contrariety of the sensibles. For they will be afflicted by bodily fire, so far as the quality of fire by its own excellence is the contrary of the equal balance and harmony that is connatural to the sensibility although it is unable to dissolve it. Nevertheless, such an affliction will not be able to separate the soul from the body, since the body necessarily must persist under the same form.

[8] Now, just as the bodies of the blessed, by reason of the newness of their glory, will be lifted above the heavenly bodies, so also the lowest place, one of darkness and punishment, will in proportion be set aside for the bodies of the damned. Hence the Psalmist says: "Let death come upon them and let them go down alive into hell" (Ps. 54:16). And the Apocalypse (20:9–10) says that "the devil who reduced them was cast into the pool of fire and brimstone where both

1. Aristotle, *Topics*, VI, 6 (145a 5).

the beast and the false prophet shall be tormented day and night for ever."

Chapter 90.

HOW INCORPOREAL SUBSTANCES MAY SUFFER FROM BODILY FIRE

[1] But a doubt can arise as to the manner in which the devil, who has no body, and the souls of the damned before the resurrection, can suffer from the bodily fire by which the bodies of the damned will suffer in hell. As our Lord says: "Depart from Me you cursed into everlasting fire which was prepared for the devil and his angels" (Matt. 25:41).

[2] One must not, then, judge the matter thus: that non-bodily substances can suffer from bodily fire so that their nature is corrupted by fire, or altered, or in any other way at all transmuted, as our corruptible bodies do now suffer by fire; because non-bodily substances have no bodily matter so as to be able to be changed by bodily things, and they are not even receptive to sensible forms except intelligibly—such reception, of course, is not proper to punishment, but tends, instead, to perfect and to please.

[3] Neither can it be said that they suffer affliction from bodily fire by reason of any contrariety, as the bodies will suffer after the resurrection, because the non-bodily substances do not have organs of sense and do not use sense powers.

[4] Therefore, the non-bodily substances suffer from bodily fire in the manner of a certain bondage. For spirits are able to be bound by bodies: this can be by way of form, as the soul is bound to the human body to give it life; or it can be without being the form of a something, as the necromancers by the power of devils bind spirits by images or that sort of thing. Therefore, much more can the divine power bind the spirits to be damned by bodily fire. And this is to them the greater affliction: they know they are in bondage to the lowliest things as a punishment.

[5] It is also becoming that the damned spirits should be

punished by bodily penalties. For the sin of every rational creature grows out of this: It is not subject to God in obedience. Punishment, of course, should answer to fault proportionally, with this result: that in its punishment the will suffer an affliction which is the contrary of that for whose love it sinned. Therefore, a befitting punishment to a sinning rational nature is this: to be subject somehow to the bondage of things which are its own inferiors, namely, bodily things.

[6] Again, the sin committed against God deserves not only the punishment of loss, but the punishment of sense, as we showed in Book III,[1] for the punishment of sense answers to the fault in regard to the soul's disordered turning toward a changeable good, as the punishment of loss answers to the fault in regard to its turning away from the unchangeable good. But the rational creature, and especially the human soul, sins by its disordered turning to bodily things. Therefore, its becoming punishment is affliction by bodily things.

[7] If, furthermore, an afflicting punishment be due to sin, the one we call "the pain of sense," such punishment ought to come from that which can bring on affliction. But nothing brings on affliction except so far as it is the contrary of the will. But it is not contrary to the natural will of a rational nature that it be united to a spiritual substance. Say, rather, this is a pleasure to it, and belongs to its perfection, for it is a union of like to like and of intelligible to intellect, since every spiritual substance is intelligible in itself. But it is contrary to the natural will of a spiritual substance to be in subjection to a body from which in the order of its own nature it ought to be free. It is, then, fitting to punish a spiritual substance with bodily things.

[8] In consequence, this, too, is clear: Grant that one understands the bodily aspects of the rewards of the blessed mentioned in Scripture spiritually, as was said[2] about the promise of food and drink; nonetheless, when Scripture threatens certain bodily punishments to sinners, these are to be understood in a bodily fashion and taken in their own meaning. For there is nothing suitable about rewarding a superior nature by the use of an inferior one—the reward, rather, is in the union to

---

1. SCG, III, ch. 145.   2. See above, ch. 83.

the superior—but a superior nature is suitably punished by being turned over to its inferiors.

[9] For all that, there is no reason why even some of the things we read in Scripture about the punishments of the damned expressed in bodily terms should not be understood in spiritual terms, and, as it were, figuratively. Such is the saying of Isaias (66:24): "Their worm shall not die": by worm can be understood that remorse of conscience by which the impious will also be tortured, for a bodily worm cannot eat away a spiritual substance, nor even the bodies of the damned, which will be incorruptible. Then, too, the "weeping" and "gnashing of teeth" (Matt. 8:12) cannot be understood of spiritual substances except metaphorically, although there is no reason not to accept them in a bodily sense in the bodies of the damned after the resurrection. For all that, this is not to understand weeping as a loss of tears, for from those bodies there can be no loss, but there can be only the sorrow of the heart and the irritation of the eyes and the head which usually accompany weeping.

Chapter 91.

THAT IMMEDIATELY AFTER THEIR SEPARATION FROM THE BODY THE SOULS WILL RECEIVE PUNISHMENT OR REWARD

[1] From these points, of course, we can gather that immediately after death the souls of men receive either punishment or reward according to their merits.

[2] For the separated souls are susceptible to punishment, not only to spiritual, but even to bodily, punishment, as has been shown.[1] That they are susceptible to glory is manifest from the points treated in Book III.[2] For the separation of the soul from the body makes it capable of the divine vision, and it was unable to arrive at this so long as it was united to the corruptible body. Now, in the vision of God consists man's ultimate beatitude, which is the "reward of virtue."[3]

1. See above, ch. 90.   2. SCG, III, ch. 51.
3. See Aristotle, Nicomachean Ethics, I, 9 (1099b 17).

But there would be no reason why punishment should differ from reward, in each of which the soul can share. Therefore, immediately after its separation from the body the man's soul receives its reward or punishment "according as he hath done" in the body (see II Cor. 5:10).

[3] In that life, too, there is the state of being paid or docked; hence, the comparison to "warfare" and "the days of the hireling," as is clear in Job (7:1): "The life of man upon earth is a warfare, and his days are like the days of a hireling." But, after the state of warfare and the labor of the hireling, the reward or punishment is straightway due those who have fought well or badly; hence, we read in Leviticus (19:13): "The wages of him that hath been hired by thee shalt not abide with thee until the morning"; and in Joel (3:4): "I will very soon return you a recompense upon your own head." Immediately after death, therefore, the souls receive either reward or punishment.

[4] There is, moreover, in the order of fault and merit a harmony with the order of punishment and reward. But merit and fault are fitted to the body only through the soul, since there is essentially no merit or demerit except so far as a thing is voluntary. Therefore, both reward and punishment flow suitably from the soul to the body, but it does not belong to the soul by reason of the body. There is, therefore, no reason in the infliction of punishment or bestowal of reward why the souls should wait for the resumption of their bodies; rather, it seems more fitting that, since the souls had priority in the fault or merit, they have priority also in being punished or rewarded.

[5] Then, too, the same providence of God owes rational creatures their reward or punishment which bestows on the natural things the perfections due them. But it happens this way in natural things: Everything immediately receives the perfection for which it has capacity unless there is an obstacle on the part of the one receiving or of the one giving the perfection. Therefore, since the souls immediately after they are separated from the body have a capacity for glory or punishment, they will straightway receive one or the other, and neither the reward of the good nor the punishment of the evil is put off until the souls take up their bodies again.

[6]   Nonetheless, one must weigh the fact that in the case of the good there can be an obstacle to keep the souls from receiving their ultimate reward, which consists in the vision of God, right after their release from the body. To that vision no rational creature can be elevated unless it be thoroughly and entirely purified, since that vision exceeds the whole of the creature's natural powers. Hence, Wisdom (7:25) says of wisdom that "no defiled thing cometh into her"; and Isaias (35:8) says of "the holy way, the unclean shall not pass over it." But by sin the soul is unclean in its disordered union to inferior things. To be sure, the soul is purified from this uncleanness in this life by penance[4] and the other sacraments,[5] as was said above, but it does at times happen that such purification is not entirely perfected in this life; one remains a debtor for the punishment, whether by reason of some negligence, or business, or even because a man is overtaken by death. Nevertheless, he is not entirely cut off from his reward, because such things can happen without mortal sin, which alone takes away the charity to which the reward of eternal life is due. And this is clear from what was said in Book III.[6] They must, then, be purged after this life before they achieve the final reward. This purgation, of course, is made by punishments, just as in this life their purgation would have been completed by punishments which satisfy the debt; otherwise, the negligent would be better off than the solicitous, if the punishment which they do not complete for their sins here need not be undergone in the future. Therefore, if the souls of the good have something capable of purgation in this world, they are held back from the achievement of their reward while they undergo cleansing punishments. And this is the reason we hold that there is a purgatory.

[7]   This position, of course, is supported by the Apostle's saying: "If any man's work burn, he shall suffer loss; but he himself shall be saved yet so as by fire" (I Cor. 3:15). There is also support in the universal custom of the Church which prays for the dead; such prayers would be useless, indeed, if one holds there is no purgatory after death. For the Church

4. See above, ch. 62, esp. ¶8.
5. The point is made in several places; see, for example, ch. 56, 59–61, 70, and 72–74.   6. SCG, III, ch. 143.

does not pray for those who are already at the goal of good or of evil, but for those who have not yet arrived at the goal.

[8] Now, the attainment immediately after death of the punishment or of the reward if there be no obstacle is established by Scriptural authorities. For Job (21:3) says of the wicked: "They spend their days in wealth, and in a moment they go down to hell"; and Luke (16:22): "And the rich man died and he was buried in hell." Hell, of course, is the place where souls are punished. The same point is clear about the good, for, as Luke (23:43) has it, our Lord hanging on the cross said to the thief: "This day thou shalt be with Me in paradise." By paradise one understands the reward which is promised to the good, as in the Apocalypse (2:7): "To him that overcometh I will give to eat of the tree of life which is in the paradise of My God."

[9] However, some do say that by "paradise" one understands not the ultimate reward which will be in heaven, as in Matthew (5:12): "Be glad and rejoice for your reward is very great in heaven," but an equal reward upon earth. For "paradise" seems to be an earthly place, from what Genesis (2:8) says: "The Lord God had planted a paradise of pleasure wherein He placed man whom He had formed." But let a man consider rightly the words of sacred Scripture and he will find that the final recompense promised to the saints in heaven is given immediately after this life. For the Apostle, after he had spoken of the final glory, said: "That which is at present momentary and light of our tribulation worketh for us above measure exceedingly an eternal weight of glory, while we look not at the things which are seen but at the things which are not seen. For the things which are seen are temporal; but the things which are not seen are eternal" (II Cor. 4:17–18). Clearly, he is speaking of the final glory which is in heaven, and to show when and how this glory is had he adds: "For we know, if our earthly house of this habitation be dissolved, that we have a building of God, a house not made with hands, eternal in heaven" (II Cor. 5:1). By this he manifestly gives us to understand that when the body is dissolved the soul is led to an eternal and heavenly mansion which is nothing but the enjoyment of divinity as the angels enjoy it in heaven.

[10] But someone may choose to contradict and to assert that the Apostle did not say that immediately on the dissolution of the body we are to have an eternal home in heaven in fact, but merely in hope, and at long last we are to have it in fact. Clearly, however, this is contrary to the Apostle's intention, for, even while we live here, we are to have the heavenly mansion according to divine predestination; and we already have it in hope, as Romans (8:24) says: "For we are saved by hope." Vainly, then, he added: "if our earthly house of this habitation be dissolved," for it would have been enough to say: "We know that we have a building of God," and so forth. The point is again and more expressly clear in the addition: "Knowing that while we are in the body we are absent from the Lord. For we walk by faith and not by sight. But we are confident and have a good will to be absent rather from the body, and to be present to the Lord" (II Cor. 5:6–8). But we should be willing in vain "to be absent from the body," meaning "separated," unless we were to be straightway present to the Lord. But we are not present except when we behold by sight, for as long as we walk by faith and not by sight "we are absent from the Lord," as he says there. Straightway, therefore, when the holy soul is separated from the body, it sees God by sight. And this is the ultimate beatitude, as was shown in Book III.[7] The same truth is also made manifest by the words of the same Apostle: "Having a desire to be dissolved and to be with Christ" (Phil. 1:23). Now, Christ is in heaven. Therefore, the Apostle was hoping that immediately after the dissolution of his body he would arrive in heaven.

[11] In this way one avoids the error of some of the Greeks, who deny purgatory and say that before the resurrection souls neither ascend into heaven nor descend into hell.

Chapter 92.

THAT THE SOULS OF THE SAINTS HAVE AFTER
DEATH AN UNCHANGEABLE WILL IN THE GOOD

[1] From these points this is clear: souls immediately after their separation from the body become unchangeable in will,

7. SCG, III, ch. 51.

with the result that the will of man cannot further be changed, neither from good to evil, nor from evil to good.

[2] As long as the soul can be changed from good to evil or evil to good, it is in a state of struggle and warfare,[1] for it must with solicitude resist evil[2] lest it be conquered by evil, or it must try to be freed from it. Immediately after the soul is separated from the body it will not be in a state of warfare or struggle, but in a state of receiving reward or punishment, because it "hath lawfully or unlawfully striven" (II Tim. 2:5). For it was shown that reward or punishment follows immediately.[3] No longer, then, is the soul able to be changed in its willing, whether from good to evil, or from evil to good.

[3] Then, too, in Book III[4] it was shown that beatitude which consists in the vision of God is everlasting; and in like fashion we showed in the same Book[5] that mortal sin deserves eternal punishment. But a soul cannot be blessed if its will is not going to be right—and it ceases to be right by being turned away from the end—but it cannot simultaneously be turned away from the end and enjoying the end. Necessarily, then, the rectitude of the will in the blessed soul is everlasting; as a result, it cannot be changed from good to evil.

[4] The rational creature, furthermore, naturally desires to be happy; hence, it cannot wish not to be happy. For all that, its will can be deflected from Him in whom its true beatitude consists; this is the perversity of will. And this takes place because that in which there is the true beatitude is not grasped essentially as beatitude, but something else is, and toward this the disordered will is deflected as though to an end. For example, take the man who puts his end in bodily pleasures; he thinks they are the greatest good, and this is essential to his beatitude. But those who are already happy grasp that in which there truly is beatitude essentially as beatitude and as ultimate end; otherwise, there would be therein no quiet of the appetite and, in consequence, they would not

---

1. See above, ch. 91, ¶3.
2. For consideration of the virtue of solicitude in a similar figure, see Charles J. O'Neil, *Imprudence in St. Thomas Aquinas* (Milwaukee, 1955), pp. 89ff.   3. See above, ch. 91, ¶1–5 and 10.
4. *SCG*, III, ch. 61.   5. *SCG*, III, ch. 144.

be happy. Therefore, all those who are happy cannot turn their wills away from Him in whom the true happiness is. Therefore, they can have no perversity of will.

[5] Then, too, when what one has suffices him, he seeks nothing beyond it. But whoever is happy has what suffices him in the true beatitude; otherwise, his desire would not be fulfilled. Therefore, whoever is happy seeks nothing which does not belong to that in which true beatitude consists. But no one has a perverse will unless he wills something repugnant to Him in whom true beatitude consists. Therefore, there is no one of the blessed whose will can be changed to evil.

[6] There is more. Sin cannot take place in the will without some sort of ignorance in the intellect, for we will nothing but the good whether true or apparent. For this reason Proverbs (14:22) says: "They err who work evil"; and in the *Ethics* the Philosopher says "every evil man is ignorant."[6] But the soul which is truly happy cannot be in ignorance at all, since in God it sees everything which belongs to its perfection. Therefore, there is no way for it to have a bad will, especially since that vision of God is always actual, as was shown in Book III.[7]

[7] Our intellect, again, can be in error about some conclusion before a resolution into the first principles is made; once the resolution into the principles is made, one has knowledge of the conclusions in which there can be no falsity. "But what the principle of demonstration is in speculative matters, so the end is in matters of appetite."[8] Therefore, as long as we do not achieve the ultimate end our will can be perverted, but not after it arrives at the enjoyment of the ultimate end which is desirable in itself, just as the first principles of demonstration are known in themselves.

[8] The good, furthermore, is precisely as good the lovable. Therefore, that which is grasped as the best is the most lovable. But a happy rational substance that sees God grasps Him as the best. Therefore, it loves Him the most. But this is an essential of love: the wills of those who love each other are

6. Aristotle, *Nicomachean Ethics*, III, 1 (1110b 28).
7. *SCG*, III, ch. 62.
8. See Aristotle, *Nicomachean Ethics*, VII, 8 (1151a 15–17).

in conformity.⁹ Therefore, the wills of the blessed are most in conformity with God, and this makes rightness of will, since the divine will is the first rule of all wills. Therefore, the wills of those who see God cannot be rendered perverse.

[9] Once more: So long as a thing is by nature changeable to another it does not have its ultimate end. Therefore, if the blessed soul can still be changed from good to evil, it is not yet in its ultimate end. And this is against the essentials of beatitude. It is clear, then, that the souls which immediately after death are beatified become immutable in their wills.

Chapter 93.

THAT AFTER DEATH THE SOULS OF THE WICKED HAVE A WILL UNCHANGEABLE IN EVIL

[1] In the same way, also, the souls which immediately after death are made miserable in punishment become unchangeable in their wills.

[2] For we showed in Book III¹ that mortal sin deserves everlasting punishment. But there would be no everlasting punishment of the souls of the damned if they were able to change their will for a better will; it would be unjust, indeed, if from the moment of their having a good will their punishment would be everlasting. Therefore, the will of the damned soul cannot be changed to good.

[3] There is more. The very disorder of the will is a kind of punishment and one of extreme affliction. The reason: So far as one has a disordered will he is displeased by whatever is done rightly, and the damned souls will be displeased because God's will is fulfilled in all those who by sinning have sided against Him. Therefore, their disordered will shall never be taken away from them.

[4] The change of a will, furthermore, from sin to good takes place only by the grace of God, as what was said in Book III makes clear.² But, just as the souls of the good are admitted to a perfect sharing in the divine goodness, so the souls of

9. *Ibid.*, IX, 4 (1166a 2–5).
1. *SCG*, III, ch. 144, and above, ch. 92, ¶3.   2. *SCG*, III, ch. 157.

the damned are entirely excluded from grace. Therefore, they will not be able to change their will for the better.

[5] Then again: Just as the good when living in the flesh make God the end of all their works and desires, so also the wicked do with some improper end which turns them away from God. But the separated souls of the good will cleave unchangeably to the good they have set before themselves in this life; namely, to God. Therefore, the souls of the wicked will cleave unchangeably to the end which they themselves have chosen. Therefore, as the will of the good will not be able to become evil, so the will of the evil will not be able to become good.

Chapter 94.

ON THE IMMUTABILITY OF WILL IN
SOULS DETAINED IN PURGATORY

[1] There are some souls, however, which do not attain beatitude immediately after separation, and for all that are not damned, such are those who carry with them something subject to purging, as was said;[1] therefore, one ought to show that not even souls of this kind after separation from the body are able to be changed in their wills. Now, the blessed and the damned souls have an unchangeable will by reason of the end to which they adhered, as what was said makes clear;[2] but the souls which carry with them something subject to purging do not differ in end from the blessed souls, for they depart in charity by which we cleave to God as to an end. Those very souls, then, will have an unchangeable will.

1. See above, ch. 91.
2. See above, ch. 91–93, esp. ch. 92, ¶7 and below, ch. 95, esp. ¶2 and 7.

Chapter 95.

ON THE IMMUTABILITY OF WILLS COMMONLY IN ALL SOULS AFTER THEIR SEPARATION FROM THE BODY

[1] That the unchangeable character of will follows from the end in all the separated souls can be made clear this way.

[2] "For the end," as was said,[1] "acts in matters of appetite as the first principles of demonstration do in speculative matters." Of course, principles of this kind are known naturally, and, should there be an error about principles like these, it would come from the corruption of nature. Hence, a man could not change from a true acceptance of these principles to a false one—or conversely—except by a change in his nature, for he who errs in the principles cannot be called back by something more certain, as a man *is* called back from his error about a conclusion. In the same way, one could not be led away from his acceptance of the principles by something more evident. Thus, then, it is with regard to the end, for every man has by nature a desire of the ultimate end.

[3] To be sure, it follows universally on rational nature to desire beatitude, but the desire of this thing or that thing under the aspect of beatitude and ultimate end arises from some special disposition of nature; hence, the Philosopher says that "as a man is, so also the end appears to him."[2] Therefore, if that disposition in which something is desired as ultimate end cannot be removed from the man, neither will his will be able to be changed in respect to desire of that end.

[4] Dispositions like these, of course, can be removed from us so long as the soul is united to the body. For, that we desire a thing as the ultimate end sometimes happens from our being so disposed by a passion which quickly passes; hence, too, this desire of the end is easy to remove, as appears among the continent. Sometimes, however, we are disposed to the desire of a good end or a bad one by a habit, and that disposi-

1. See ch. 92, ¶ 7 and note 8.
2. Aristotle, *Nicomachean Ethics*, III, 5 (1114b 1).

tion is not easily taken away; hence, such a desire for an end persists rather strongly, as is clear among the temperate. For all that, an habitual disposition can be removed in this life.

[5] Thus, therefore, it is manifest that so long as the disposition persists in which a thing is desired as ultimate end, the desire of that end is not changeable, because the desire of the ultimate end is an extreme; hence, one cannot be called from desire of the ultimate end by something more desirable. The soul is, of course, in a mutable state so long as it is united to the body, but it will not be after it has been separated from the body. A disposition of the soul is changed incidentally with some change in the body, for, since it is at the service of the soul for its very own operations, the body was given to the soul by nature with this in view: that the soul existing within the body be perfected, be, as it were, moved toward its perfection. When it shall, then, be separated from the body it will not be in a state of motion toward the end, but in a state of rest in the end acquired. The soul's will, therefore, will be immovable regarding a desire for the ultimate end.

[6] Now, on the ultimate end the entire goodness or wickedness of the will depends, for whatever goods one wills in an order toward a good end he wills well; whatever evil he wills in an order toward an evil end he wills badly. Therefore, there is not in the separated soul a will changeable from good to evil, although it is changeable from this object of will to that so long as the order to the same ultimate end is preserved.

[7] It is now apparent that such immutability is not in conflict with the power of free will whose act it is to choose, for choice is of the things for the end; choice is not of the ultimate end. Therefore, just as there is now no conflict with free will in the fact that with an immutable will we desire beatitude and fly from misery in general, so there will be no contrariety to free will in the fact that the will is unchangeably fixed upon some definite thing as upon an ultimate end. The reason: Just as there now inheres in us unchangeably that common nature by which we desire beatitude in general, so then there will persist in us unchangeably that special disposition by which this thing or that is desired as ultimate end.

[8] On the other hand, the separate substances—namely, angels—are in the nature in which they are created closer neighbors to their ultimate perfection than human souls are, for they do not need to acquire knowledge from the senses nor to arrive at conclusions by reasoning from principles as souls do; rather, they are able by infused species to arrive straightway at the contemplation of truth. And therefore, just at the moment they adhered to the end which was due, or that which was not, they persisted unchangeably therein.

[9] For all that, one should not think that the souls, after they take up their bodies again in the resurrection, lose the immutability of will; rather, they persevere therein, because, as was said above,[3] the bodies in the resurrection will be disposed as the soul requires, but the souls will not be changed by means of the bodies.

Chapter 96.

ON THE LAST JUDGMENT

[1] From the foregoing it is clear, then, that there is a two-fold retribution for what a man does in life: one for the soul—and this he receives as soon as the soul has been separated from the body; but there will be another retribution when the bodies are assumed again—and some will receive bodies which are incapable of suffering and glorious; but others, bodies capable of suffering and ignoble. The first retribution is made to men singly and one by one, in that men die separately and one by one. But the second retribution will be made to all and at the same time in that all will rise at the same time. Every retribution, of course, wherein different decisions are rendered according to differing merits demands a judgment. Necessarily, therefore, the judgment is twofold: There is one, regarding the soul, in which separately and one by one punishment or reward is determined; there is another common one, however, regarding the soul and body—in it there will be determined for all at the same time what they have earned.

3. See above, ch. 85.

[2] And since by His humanity in which He suffered and rose again Christ earned for us both resurrection and eternal life, it is to Him that universal judgment belongs, in which those who rise are rewarded or punished. For this reason we read of Him in John (5:27): "He hath given Him power to do judgment, because He is the Son of man."

[3] A judgment, of course, ought to be proportional to the matters judged. And because the last judgment will be about the reward or punishment of visible bodies, it is suitable that it be carried on visibly. Hence, also, Christ will carry out that judgment in the form of humanity which all may be able to see, both the good and the wicked. The sight of His divinity, however, makes men blessed, as was shown in Book III.[1] Accordingly, this will be visible only to the good. The judgment of the soul, of course, since it is about invisible things, is carried on invisibly.

[4] Granted, of course, that Christ has the authoritative act of judging in that last judgment, nonetheless at the same time those will judge with Him—sitting with the judge, as it were—who adhered to Him more than others. These are the Apostles, of whom it was said: "You, who have followed Me, shall sit on twelve seats judging the twelve tribes of Israel" (Matt. 19:28); and this promise is extended also to those who follow in the footprints of the Apostles.

Chapter 97.

ON THE STATE OF THE WORLD AFTER THE JUDGMENT

[1] When, therefore, the last judgment is completed, human nature will be entirely established in its goal. However, since everything bodily is somehow for the sake of man (as was shown in Book III[1]), at that time, also, the entire bodily creation will be changed—and suitably—to be in harmony with the state of the men who then will be. And because men will then be incorruptible, the state of generation and corruption will then be taken away from the whole bodily creation. And

1. SCG, III, ch. 25, 51, and 63.   1. SCG, III, ch. 81.

this is what the Apostle says: that "the creature also itself shall be delivered from the servitude of corruption, into the liberty of the glory of the children of God" (Rom. 8:21).

[2] Now, generation and corruption in inferior bodies are caused by the movement of the heavens. Therefore, that generation and corruption may come to a stop in the inferior bodies, the movement of the heavens must also come to a stop. And on this account the Apocalypse (10:6) says "that time shall be no longer."

[3] It ought not, of course, seem impossible that the movement of the heavens come to a stop. For the movement of the heavens is not natural in the way the movement of heavy and light bodies is—that is, they are inclined to movement by an interior active principle—but it is called natural in that the heavenly body has an aptitude for such movement; the principle of that motion, however, is an intellect, as was shown in Book III.[2] The heaven is moved, therefore, as are things moved by a will. But a will moves for a purpose. Of course, the purpose of the motion of the heavens cannot be the very movement itself, for motion, since it always tends toward another, does not have the character of an ultimate end. Neither can one say that the end of the heavenly motion is this: the reducing of the heavenly body from potency to act in place where. This potency can never be entirely reduced to act, for, while the heavenly body is actually in one place where, it is in potency to another such, just as is the case of prime matter with respect to forms. Therefore, just as nature in generation does not have as end the reduction of matter from potency to act, but something consequent on this reduction—namely, that perpetuity in things by which they approach a divine likeness—so the end of heavenly motion is not the being reduced from potency to act, but something consequent on this reduction: namely, to be made like to God in the act of causing. But all things generable and corruptible caused by the motion of the heaven are somehow ordered to man as to an end, as was shown in Book III.[3] Therefore, the motion of the heaven is especially on account of the generation of men; in this it does most to accomplish a divine likeness in the act of caus-

2. *SCG,* III, ch. 23.   3. *SCG,* III, ch. 81.

ing, since man's form—namely, the rational soul—is immediately created by God, as was shown in Book II.[4] But the
multiplication of souls to infinity cannot be an end, for infinity is contrary to the notion of end. Nothing awkward, then,
ensues if we hold that, when a fixed number of men is filled
out, the motion of the heavens ceases.

[4] Nonetheless, when the motion of the heavens and generation and corruption in the elements have come to a stop,
their substance will continue to be by reason of the change-
lessness of the divine goodness, "for He created all things that
they might be" (Wis. 1:14). Hence, the being of things which
have an aptitude for perpetuity will remain in perpetuity. Both wholly and in part, of course, the heavenly bodies
have the nature to be everlasting. The elements, however, have
it wholly, but not in part, for in part they are corruptible.
Man, of course, has it in part, but not wholly: for the rational
soul is incorruptible; the composite, corruptible. These, then,
which in any way at all have an aptitude for being everlasting
will abide in their substance in that last state of the world,
and God in His power will supply what is wanting in their
own weakness.

[5] But the other animals, the plants, and the mixed bodies,
those entirely corruptible both wholly and in part, will not
remain at all in that state of incorruption. In this way, then,
must the saying of the Apostle be understood: "The fashion
of this world passeth away" (I Cor. 7:31), that this appearance of the world which now is will cease to be, but the
substance will remain. Thus, also, is understood what Job
(14:12) says: "Man, when he is fallen asleep, shall not rise
again: till the heavens be broken," that is, until that disposition of the heaven ceases to be, that in which it is moved and
causes motion in others.

[6] But, since among the other elements fire is the most
active, and tends to consume the corruptible, the consumption of the things which ought not remain in the future state
will most suitably take place by fire. Hence, one holds in accord with the faith that at the last the world will be purified
by fire, not from corruptible bodies alone, but from that in-

4. SCG, II, ch. 87.

fection which the place incurred by serving as the dwelling of sinners. And this is what is said in II Peter (3:7): "The heavens and the earth which are now, by the same word are kept in store, reserved unto fire against the day of judgment," so that we may understand by "heavens" not the very firmament in which the stars are, whether fixed or wandering, but those heavens of air which are close to the earth.

[7] Since, then, the bodily creation will at the last be disposed in harmony with the state of man—since men, of course, will not only be freed from corruption[5] but also clothed with glory, as what has been said makes clear[6]—necessarily even the bodily creation will achieve a kind of resplendence in its own way.

[8] AND, HENCE, THE SAYING OF THE APOCALYPSE (21:1): "I SAW A NEW HEAVEN AND A NEW EARTH." AND ISAIAS (65:17–18): "BEHOLD I CREATE NEW HEAVENS, AND A NEW EARTH: AND THE FORMER THINGS SHALL NOT BE IN REMEMBRANCE AND THEY SHALL NOT COME UPON THE HEART. BUT YOU SHALL BE GLAD AND REJOICE FOREVER." AMEN.

5. See above, ch. 85.   6. See above, ch. 86.

INDEX OF PROPER NAMES